Bill Hartack

Bill Hartack

The Bittersweet Life of a Hall of Fame Jockey

BILL CHRISTINE

McFarland & Company, Inc., Publishers
Jefferson, North Carolina

Library of Congress Cataloguing-in-Publication Data

Names: Christine, Bill, author.
Title: Bill Hartack : the bittersweet life of a hall of fame jockey / Bill Christine.
Description: Jefferson, North Carolina : McFarland & Company, Inc.,
Publishers, 2016. | Includes bibliographical references and index.
Identifiers: LCCN 2016042286 | ISBN 9781476663623 (softcover : acid free paper) ♾
Subjects: LCSH: Hartack, Bill, 1932–2007. | Jockeys—United States—Biography.
Classification: LCC SF336.H36 C47 2016 | DDC 798.40092 [B]—dc23
LC record available at https://lccn.loc.gov/2016042286

British Library cataloguing data are available

ISBN (print) 978-1-4766-6362-3
ISBN (ebook) 978-1-4766-2545-4

Front cover: Bill Hartack, circa 1957 (Nancy Lang collection)

Printed in the United States of America

McFarland & Company, Inc., Publishers
Box 611, Jefferson, North Carolina 28640
www.mcfarlandpub.com

For Pat,
my one and only muse.

Table of Contents

Preface

Oscar Fraley was supposed to write this book.

Bill Hartack was supposed to write this book.

John Ball was supposed to write this book.

Fraley was a popular sports columnist for the old UPI wire service. They called his column "Fearless Fraley." In 1964, in the auxiliary press box at the old Sportsman's Park in St. Louis, I sat next to Fraley for the Cardinals–New York Yankees World Series. Oscar was already rich; he and Eliot Ness had written *The Untouchables* several years before. Oscar spent considerable parts of every game making passes at the ballpark organist, who played in a booth within earshot. I read his columns later—every one filthy with insight.

As the story goes, Hartack asked Fraley to write his life story. They got halfway through when Hartack lost interest in the project, and the manuscript disappeared.

Hartack then decided to write the book himself. With help from Whitney Tower—but not that much help—he had written a three-part series about his life and career for *Sports Illustrated* in 1967. By the 1980s, Hartack was said to be well along with his autobiography. He gave Maryjean Wall of the *Lexington Herald-Leader* an interview, but he kept cutting her off by saying, "I can't answer that question. It's going to be in my book." Unfortunately, the book was a victim of Hurricane Katrina in 2005. Hartack's apartment in New Orleans was wiped out by the floods Katrina brought, and the manuscript and most of the rest of his possessions were never recovered.

Nancy Lang is the widow of Chick Lang, the agent with whom Hartack had some of his biggest years in the 1950s. She apparently squirreled away every newspaper and magazine article that ran during the Hartack–Chick Lang years. Chick and Nancy had been friends with John Ball since the days when Ball worked for the Jockeys' Guild and Chick was a guild consultant. After Chick died in 2010, Nancy called Ball, told him about her archive and suggested that he write a book about Hartack. I, too, knew Ball through the guild, from my days of covering horse racing for the *Los Angeles Times*. Among Ball's many duties was coordinating interviews in the Churchill Downs jockeys' room after the Kentucky Derby.

Ball called one day, told me about Nancy Lang's idea, and asked what I thought about the possibility of a book about the enigmatic Hartack. It hadn't occurred to me that no one had written Hartack's story: the hardscrabble, tragic early years; his serendipitous entry into race riding; the success and riches on the track; his chip-on-the-shoulder approach to life; and the bittersweet years after he rode his last horse.

Ball and I talked for more than an hour, after which he said, "We got the wrong guy. Maybe you should be the one who writes this book."

Hartack was well off everybody's radar. Even today, when jockeys who win the Derby are given diamond rings by the Bill Hartack Foundation, some of them only have vague notions of his accomplishments.

I had started coming around the race track toward the end of Hartack's riding career, and while I knew him during his years as a racing official, we never had any deep conversations. Hartack wasn't doing any significant conversing with anyone in those days. This was what made Ball's invitation so inviting: What made Bill Hartack tick? How did he forge such a fantastic oeuvre in spite of himself?

Ball offered to pack up the Nancy Lang trove, which she had boxed and mailed from Maryland to him in Pittsburgh, and forward it to me in Los Angeles. I'll never know why the U.S. Post Office goes in the red. The box that Ball sent me was big enough to hold a twenty-five-inch TV set.

That was only a start. I needed so much more. I found both of Hartack's sisters, one in West Virginia and the other in Las Vegas, and they were pleased to help. That was important, because Hartack, in the limited interviews he allowed, was loath to talk about his early years.

Tad Dowd, a friend of Hartack's, was a big help. It was Tad and a few other Hartack cronies, including LeRoy Neiman, who started the charitable Bill Hartack Foundation soon after his death in 2007. I already knew Tad well—he was a California race-track junkie, and hard to miss during all those years I covered the sport. We had talked over time about Hartack long before the book idea surfaced.

But I had never heard Gary Condra's name. He was one of Hartack's best friends. How good of a friend? When Hartack died, Condra took responsibility and made sure there was a proper resting place, which, as it turned out, wasn't easy. He lived in Florida, Hartack's remains were in the boonies of Texas (almost to Mexico), and the cemetery was in the boonies of Missouri. The website for the cemetery in Iberia, Missouri, has two listings:

All interments: 1,334
Famous interments: 1

Condra, like Dowd, took me beyond the race track, talking about a life that Hartack eschewed discussing. "Anybody who liked Bill should thank Gary Condra," said Wayne Harris, a retired jockey who hunted with Hartack all over the United States. "What he did about burying 'Tack was a wonderful thing."

I got lucky in delving into Hartack's Hong Kong years, which were the last he spent in the saddle. The Hong Kong Jockey Club, thanks to Bill Nader, an old friend from New York, inundated me with data. Horsemen who overlapped with Hartack in Hong Kong not only were available but also had good memories.

Nobody ever said that a biographer's lot was a bed of roses, and, in a way, I had been warned, albeit fifty years ago. It was then that Jack Olsen interviewed Hartack for a magazine article and said, "His full biography will have to be written by a war correspondent."

1

Catching Up with Arcaro

The Saturday before the 1969 Kentucky Derby, Bill Hartack came into the jockeys' room at Churchill Downs; he sat down on a wooden white bench in front of his locker as Chuck Corolla, his valet, helped him take off his black leather boots.[1] Minutes before, Hartack had ridden Majestic Prince to a facile win in something called the Stepping Stone Purse, a cut-rate prep race for the Big Race. With Hartack in the saddle, Majestic Prince had won all six of his races in California, five of them by gaping margin. He had intimidated almost everyone in Kentucky. The Stepping Stone drew only two other horses. There was also expected to be a small field for the ninety-fifth running of the Derby, which would be a special day no matter who won. President Nixon was scheduled to attend. Other presidents had been to the Derby, but none while they were in office.[2]

"That horse couldn't have set himself up any better,"[3] said Corolla as he finished removing Hartack's size-four boots. During a seventeen-year career as a jockey at mostly small tracks around the Midwest, Corolla had never been aboard a horse good enough to run in a Derby. By contrast, Hartack, in the wake of the retired Eddie Arcaro, had become Mr. Derby. He won four Derbys in eight years, and now, with the undefeated Majestic Prince, he had a chance to win the race for a fifth time and tie Arcaro's record.[4]

In the seven-furlong Stepping Stone, Majestic Prince finished six lengths ahead of the second-place horse, and he beat the third-place horse by twenty-one lengths. His time was only a fifth of a second slower than the track record.

Majestic Prince's trainer was Johnny Longden, only three years removed from the saddle, after riding a record 6,032 winners.[5] Unlike Hartack, Longden rode only one Derby winner, Count Fleet in 1943, but they went all the way, also winning the Preakness and the Belmont Stakes and sweeping the Triple Crown. Of Hartack's four Derby winners, only Northern Dancer, in 1964, gave him a chance at the Triple Crown, but they were beaten in the Belmont.[6]

When Hartack first came around a race track, at age eighteen at Charles Town, West Virginia, in 1951, it would have been impossible to project how accomplished and famous he would become. He had no goals, not even to ride in a race, and arrived at this minor-league track virtually out of desperation. His mother had died, after an automobile accident, when he was barely eight. The family home burned down a few months later, leaving them indigent and reliant on neighbors and friends. Hartack's father, a struggling coalminer, had been embittered even before these tragedies. When Hartack finished high school with honors, the father dashed his thoughts about following him into the Pennsylvania mines; he was too young to work in a steel mill, and the U.S. Navy said he was too small. Hartack went off to Charles Town after a jockeys' agent, a friend of his father's, said that he was the right size for a jockey.[7]

By the time Hartack won his fifth Derby with Majestic Prince, he was close to the four-thousand mark in career wins. But he had also tired of reciting his life story, and there were parts of the story that he didn't want to tell at all. Once, between races in the jockeys' room at Randall Park near Cleveland, Corolla asked him about his family. Hartack cut him off, and Corolla never mentioned the subject again.

During Derby week in 1969, Hartack and Corolla spent most of their idle time in the jockeys' room reminiscing about the early days in Ohio, when Hartack was just starting out and Corolla, five years older, was trying to eke out a living as a journeyman rider.

"Remember that new car and how you wanted to show it off?" Corolla said.

"1953?" Hartack asked.

"Somewhere in there," Corolla said. "You still had the bug (apprentice standing), or had just lost it."

"If I bought a new car, I had to have won a few races," Hartack said. "Where the hell were we?"

"Randall," Corolla replied. Randall Park closed in the late 1950s, ultimately becoming a shopping mall.

"I guess I had the Cadillac," Hartack said.

"No, it wasn't the Caddy," Corolla said. "It was before the Caddy."

"They made us park it in the regular lot and walk all that way to the jocks' room," Hartack said. "Those bastards couldn't take a joke."

"You were pretty good with that gravel in the jocks' lot," Corolla told him. "You could take a handful and hit the front porch of the racing secretary's office. They had to clean it off all the time. But then one day somebody saw you and reported it. They claimed I was with you. Which I guess I was. We were banned from the jocks' lot. We had to park way out there."

"Bastards," Hartack said.

After riding, Corolla took every race-track job there was. In 1962, he was an exercise rider for Ridan, third-place finisher as the favorite in the Derby. Hartack won that Derby with Decidedly, after he had lost the mount on Ridan. By 1969, Corolla was working in the jockeys' room at Churchill Downs. He asked the other valets if he could take care of Hartack, because of their long friendship. The other valets agreed, even though they were giving Corolla the Derby favorite. Valets work largely from jockeys' tips, and a rider winning the Derby will usually duke his valet handsomely. Hartack was considered one of the big tippers among the jockeys.

Midway through Derby week in 1969, Jim Bolus, working for the *Louisville Courier-Journal*, hoped to get an interview with Hartack, but he knew the fiery jockey despised the press. Hartack's snubs of reporters after his Derby victories were the stuff that feuds were made of.

However, Bolus knew Corolla. He asked him to intercede and see if Hartack was willing to be interviewed.

"I wouldn't do it for anybody but you, Jim," Corolla said. "You know how Bill is about these things. Very sensitive. But for you I'll at least ask. No promises, though."

Hartack was reluctant. "You know this guy much?" he asked.

"For a long time," Corolla said. "I wouldn't ask you, Bill, if he wasn't a good guy."

Later Hartack met Bolus outside the jockeys' room before the races.

"They ask me why I give radio and TV interviews, but shut out newspaper reporters," Hartack said. "When I'm on radio or TV, what I say goes out just the way I say it. The newspaper guys screw it up all the time. They twist what I say. They misunderstand. They interpret. It doesn't come out any way at all the way it's supposed to. Happens all the time. So what we're doing here—will it come out exactly the way I say it? Can you guarantee that?"

"No, I can't," Bolus said. "I've got editors. They can take stuff out, without telling me. Somebody else writes the headlines. I've got no influence on that."

"If that's the case, my answer is no," Hartack said. "No interview."

He went into the jockeys' room, leaving Bolus with an empty notepad. Of the many books Bolus went on to write about the Kentucky Derby, none contained much about Hartack. Even though he was arguably the best rider in the history of the race—five wins out of twelve tries, whereas it took Arcaro twenty-one Derbys to get his five-pack—Hartack's truculence made him a difficult subject.[8]

The day after Hartack met Bolus, he saw Jack Mann, who was covering the Derby for the *Washington Star*. Mann knew horse racing, which helped with Hartack, who didn't feel it was his job to educate would-be turf writers.

"I've got a bone to pick with you," Hartack said to Mann. Hartack was then embroiled in a lengthy income-tax beef with the Internal Revenue Service, which had placed a lien on Hartack's stylish home in Miami Springs, Florida. More than three-quarters of a million dollars was involved. The story broke in October 1968, and Mann, aware that Hartack was riding in a major race in Toronto, put in a call to the Canadian hotel where he believed the jockey was staying. Hartack wasn't registered, so Mann asked the front desk if George Stidham, his business agent and friend, was in the hotel (he was).

Stidham picked up the phone and said that Hartack was sleeping. Mann left word, but Hartack never called back. Mann, up against a deadline, filed his story without any Hartack quotes.[9]

Now, the first time since that story ran, the writer and jockey were face to face at Churchill Downs.

"You stuck it to me," Hartack said. "You said I was in a hotel under an assumed name, and that was wrong."

Mann tried to defend himself, but Hartack cut him off: "I don't care what the hotel said, you should have talked to me before you wrote that. I didn't say it was a lie. I don't know anything about your motivation. I'm just not talking to you anymore."

Liz Tippett, a wealthy horsewoman from Virginia, also attended the 1969 Derby. She raced a bicoastal stable, and Hartack sometimes rode her horses.

"How does it feel to be here as the hero?" Tippett good-naturedly asked.

Hartack ignored the remark.

"I do not appreciate being asked [by Tippett's California trainer, Charlie Whittingham] to ride your filly out there when she is short [not prepared to run a distance]," Hartack said. "Then, not being asked to ride her back the next time, when she might be ready. Frankly, I'd rather not ride her at all."

Taken aback, Tippett tried to apologize.

"That's your business," Hartack said. "All I know is that it happened, and it shouldn't have."[10]

The Derby was never fun for Hartack. Going to Kentucky was a business trip. He paid attention to his work and rode his horses. He also paid attention to his superstitions, though he didn't have many. Tad Dowd, an old friend, had the habit of wearing a black derby and a red jacket to the Derby. He wore the hat when Hartack won the Derby with Decidedly in 1962, and again with Northern Dancer in 1964.

The morning of the 1969 race, Hartack saw the bareheaded Dowd at the track.

"Where's that lucky derby?" Hartack asked.

"It's pretty well beat up," Dowd replied. "I left it home."

"You have to have a derby," Hartack said. He reached in his pocket and gave Dowd a couple of twenty-dollar bills. A half-hour later, Dowd and Michael Stidham, George Stidham's 11-year-old son, were going from store to store in downtown Louisville, looking for a derby. In the fourth store, they found one.

After 1969, Dowd's Derby derby was forgotten, until he was leaving for the race in 1984. He and Hartack had a ritual of talking on the phone the week before every Derby, exchanging views about the race. This time, Laffit Pincay Jr. was riding in his eleventh Derby. A Hall of Fame jockey, Pincay had finished second three times but had never won the race. Dowd loved Pincay. In the meantime, Hartack, who had retired from riding in 1980 after six years in the saddle in Hong Kong, had become a racing official and was working at Hollywood Park.

"Bill," Dowd said, "you know that old derby of mine? The lucky derby from 1969? Would you have any objections if I wore it this time? I know it's your Derby hat, but it might bring Laffit some luck. Lord knows, he needs it."

"Absolutely," Hartack said. "Wear the hat."[11]

Pincay and Swale won by almost three lengths,[12] and Tad Dowd threw his magic derby into the air.[13] Hartack was there as well, doing color commentary of the race for ABC television. He was a good fit for that job, meshing nicely with Howard Cosell, Jim McKay and Jack Whitaker, although he held the position for only a few years.[14]

It was ironic that Hartack became part of the media, if only temporarily. As a jockey, he dreaded the post–Derby interviews, which in those days were done on the fly, with reporters given free access to the jockeys' room as soon as the horses crossed the finish line.[15]

Hartack and Jim McKay were partners on several ABC TV telecasts of Triple Crown races. This ABC publicity photo ran in *Blood-Horse* magazine on April 20, 1985.

Rather than answer questions, Hartack would either sit in silence or use the opportunity to harangue the press. Jockeys are independent contractors, so even a track with the heft of Churchill Downs was powerless to get Hartack to cooperate. He would talk privately to Joe Hirsch, his friend who wrote a column for the *Daily Racing Form*, but few others.[16]

A couple of times, through Hirsch's intervention, Hartack agreed to write a post-race analysis of the Derby for the *Daily Racing Form*. But the second year, his byline read, "By Willie Hartack." Somebody on the copy desk had slipped up. All his life, Hartack lectured the press that his name wasn't Willie.[17] Calling him "Willie" was one sure way to tick him off, although some writers continued to use Willie, just to get his goat.[18] After the "Willie Hartack" byline, he did no more writing for the *Daily Racing Form*.

The day before the 1969 Derby, Hartack showered after the races and dressed in front of his locker. He wasn't much for chit-chat with other riders. He was a life-long loner, and the other riders knew to keep their distance.

Hartack had no plans for the evening. "Do you know of a place," he asked Chuck Corolla, "where we can go and hide?"

"Yeah," Corolla said. "My brother-in-law's place, O'Shea's on Poplar Center Road."

"Just you and me, right?" Hartack asked.

"That'll be it," Corolla said.

Corolla sent word ahead that they were coming, and the regulars at the bar left them alone. Hartack sat at the bar with his valet and had a few glasses of white wine, keeping largely to himself.[19]

Hartack didn't talk to anybody. Jimmy Breslin, known for invading the minds of his subjects, couldn't get to the bottom of Hartack; Breslin once wrote four thousand words about Hartack for *True* magazine but was unable to plumb his psyche. Sammy Boulmetis frequently rode against Hartack. "I can't figure him out," Boulmetis said. "One day he seems nice to you. Next day, he won't even talk to you." Eddie Arcaro said almost the same thing: "I tried to be nice to him, but ... I don't know."[20]

Hartack was the middle child of his family. He had a sister one year older, and another seven years younger. He encouraged his younger sister to go to college and paid her way for the two years that she attended. Over the years, however, he and his sisters grew distant. The older one moved away to Cleveland and got married. The younger married a jockey, after her brother told her to stay away from the race track.[21] Hartack once showed a friend twenty letters he had received from his sisters; he hadn't opened any of them. He died alone, suffering a heart attack on a hunting trip. He never married or had children. An old friend came forward and buried him in the middle of the country, among strangers.[22]

Johnny Longden, the trainer of Majestic Prince, was also the son of a coalminer. His family immigrated to Canada from England (a late train to Southhampton prevented them from sailing on the *Titanic*). Longden was much like Hartack as a rider. He rode with abandon and battled himself when he didn't win. Longden said that he might have won more races if he had had the equanimity of a Bill Shoemaker, who broke his record for career wins.[23] Away from the track, however, Longden and Hartack were opposites—Longden was a hail-fellow-well-met, everybody's favorite. He lived to be ninety-six, and every year Santa Anita threw a party on his birthday, which was also Valentine's Day.[24]

By 1969, Hartack's career was on a downward arc. At thirty-six, he had been riding for seventeen years, and he hadn't led the country in either wins or purses since 1960. He won only 66 races in 1967, and 105 in 1968.[25] He had worn out his welcome with numerous major stables, including the vaunted Calumet Farm. Weight was becoming an issue, which would be a factor in his moving to Hong Kong to ride in the 1970s.[26] His agents, the indispensable front men who helped find live horses and booked his mounts, came and went. Chick Lang, the agent with whom Hartack had enjoyed the greatest success, wearied of apologizing for his boorish behavior, and so, in quick succession, did many others.[27]

From 1965, the year after his fourth Derby win with Northern Dancer, until 1969 and Majestic Prince, Hartack rode in only three out of a possible twelve Triple Crown races, never finishing better than sixth place.[28] As early as 1963, *Sports Illustrated* cataloged Hartack's decline with a story that was headlined "Whatever Happened to Bill Hartack?" Hartack was quoted as saying, "I go out there to do everything in my power to win. And then I'm disliked for my attitude. Evidently the way I operate is distasteful to certain people. It insults them, and the funny part about it is that insulting anybody is the last thing on my mind. I don't believe in being insulting to anyone, but I do believe in telling the truth, and if it's taken as an insult, well then I can't help it."[29]

When Majestic Prince was ready for the first race of his career at the end of 1968, Hartack wasn't Longden's first choice to ride. The trainer wanted Shoemaker, but he was *hors de combat* with a broken thighbone, suffered when a horse fell on him at Santa Anita early in the year. Longden, his veterinarian nursing a splint bone that Majestic Prince had popped in his right foreleg, finally had the colt pegged to make his debut at Bay Meadows, near San Francisco, on Thanksgiving Day. Santa Anita didn't open until the day after Christmas, and Longden was anxious to get started, so that Majestic Prince would have enough seasoning to run a mile and a quarter in the Kentucky Derby the following May.[30]

If not for a jockeys' agent named Pete Wilson, Hartack wouldn't have gotten the mount on Majestic Prince. With Shoemaker on the shelf, Longden wanted Hartack for the Bay Meadows race, but finding him was something else entirely. At the time Hartack was hunting for elk in Montana with two other jockeys, Jerry Lambert and Wayne Harris.[31] Longden was pestered by agents representing other riders, but he felt Hartack was still among the best and was willing to wait until entry day before making a commitment.[32]

Along came Alan C. "Pete" Wilson. His San Francisco family came from money, but, said another agent, "Pete chose to live like a race-track bum." Wilson never learned how to drive a car, was afraid to ride in one, and traveled around the backstretch on a bicycle. From their army days, he was a friend of the actor David Janssen, who got him work as an extra in a few films. Wilson didn't represent Hartack, but he liked him, liked Longden and kept working on Montana phone numbers until one led to Hartack.[33]

It was Lambert who had rekindled Hartack's interest in hunting, something Hartack would pursue for the rest of his life. "I gave Bill his first shotgun," Lambert later said. "At least it was his first shotgun since he had been hunting as a kid, back in Pennsylvania."

The three jockeys were hunting for elk in southern Montana, about halfway between Butte and Bozeman. But Hartack's heart didn't seem to be in it.

"What's wrong?" Lambert asked. "You don't seem to be enjoying this."

"What I really want is a bear," Hartack said.

"A bear?" Lambert said. "We ain't seen no bear. We're lookin' for elk."

"Yeah, I know, but I'd like to have a bear," Hartack told him.[34]

Meanwhile, Pete Wilson was working hard to find the right phone number. He called

Hartack, an avid fisherman and hunter, went after a lot of animals, including caribou on Curt Gowdy's *American Sportsman* TV show (Gary Condra collection).

Tucker Slender. A former jockey, Slender was working on the starting gate, as an assistant starter, at the California tracks. But Slender was no help. Finally, Wilson reached Pat McDowell, who was Lambert's agent, and got the number.

"'Tack, that colt of Johnny's is tight as a drum," Wilson told Hartack. "If you want to win another Derby, get your ass to San Francisco."[35]

It was a holiday week, and most of the flights were booked. But there were airports in both Butte and Bozeman that might have a flight open to Los Angeles, and then up to San Francisco. They found out that the best chance for a flight was out of Butte, eighty miles away. Lambert drove Hartack there.

"Hell," Lambert said, "everybody was trying to get on that horse. I was even trying to ride him."[36]

Frank McMahon, the wealthy Canadian oilman, had relied on Longden's eye for a horse and in 1967 paid a record $250,000 for Majestic Prince at a yearling auction in Kentucky.[37] The race on Thanksgiving in 1969 was only for a few thousand dollars, against maidens (i.e., winless horses). Some, like Majestic Prince, were making their first starts.

Although Majestic Prince was a top-heavy 1-to-2 favorite,[38] the race drew eleven other horses, and Longden knew what that meant: they were all eligible for problematic trips; inexperienced 2-year-olds are not to be trusted. The distance was only six furlongs, which left little room and time for a horse, even a good one, to compensate if there was early trouble. Longden was nervous. He had prepared his colt as well as he could in the mornings, and the splint injury seemed to be behind them, but racing luck is as fickle as a firefly. Longden had told McMahon that a win in the Derby could be in the cards, but now the sawed-off trainer had a bad feeling in the pit of his stomach. He hoped that he hadn't gone overboard.[39]

If Hartack ever went into a race with trepidation, he never let on. When Longden gave him a leg up on Majestic Prince, helping him to board the horse in the Bay Meadows paddock, Hartack thought that this was just another race he could win. He took the winners for granted. "It's the losers that hurt," he said.[40] His lifetime winning percentage was .198—4,272 wins out of 21,535 mounts. Racing isn't like baseball; .198 is an outstanding average for a jockey. Shoemaker's career win rate was .219, and Arcaro's was .198, the same as Hartack's.[41]

Until Majestic Prince's debut race, Hartack had never been on the handsome colt's back. But the buzz was all over California about the potential champion Longden had. Only troglodytes hadn't picked up the vibes.[42] Majestic Prince drew the No. 4 post. He was expected to show speed, and if he broke well, favorable early position would be a certainty. Longden had been working him fast in the mornings, to build up his speed.

As if on cue, Majestic Prince outsprinted the others leaving the gate. He was never headed, winning by almost three lengths. Hartack hit him only once, with his left hand, when it looked as though another horse might challenge them at the eighth pole.[43]

Hartack let Longden do the talking after the race. Years later, when asked about Majestic Prince, Hartack said, "He was the epitome of a race horse as far as I was concerned. He was extremely easy to ride, he was an ideal horse. He had plenty of size [sixteen hands, at four inches to the hand, and Longden once weighed him at 1,100 pounds]. Size is something Northern Dancer didn't have. Majestic Prince was easy to communicate with, he didn't require a lot of manhandling or anything. He kind of fit into your hands just as easy as a glove. When you wanted to use him, you could use him. If you didn't want to use him, you didn't have to take a tremendous hold on him to slow him up. He was a pretty maneuverable horse."[44]

After the win at Bay Meadows, Majestic Prince won five races at Santa Anita over the next three months. Only the first of those was close, when the colt won by a nose on a sloppy track on December 26.[45] Hartack was unconcerned, but Longden fretted about Majestic Prince's painful mouth, caused by a sensitivity to the bit. After one of the races, Longden said, "The horse will run better when Bill can handle him better. His tender mouth was caused by some caps on his teeth. They were supposed to have been shed naturally, but for some reason they haven't been.... It's a tricky business of give-and-take between horse and rider."[46]

Although Longden didn't feed into the rumors, there was still speculation that Shoemaker, now on the mend, might eventually take over the mount.[47] Hartack hadn't done anything wrong. Longden, loyal to the core, never wavered and once said of Hartack, "His riding and his ethics are beyond reproach. He's as smart as they come. But where he can get along with horses, he can't seem to with people."[48] Fortunately, Hartack got along with Longden, which was the trainer's only concern.

If there was any doubt about Longden's admiration for Hartack as a horseman, one morning at Santa Anita, a couple of weeks before the Santa Anita Derby, was all the evidence required to put an end to lingering questions. Johnny Bucalo, Majestic Prince's regular exercise rider, was aboard the horse for a workout in company with another of Longden's horses, who was ridden by Hartack. The track was a muddy mess, and Majestic Prince's time was much slower than what Longden expected. In fact, the lesser horse, the one ridden by Hartack, beat Majestic Prince to the finish line by a couple of lengths. Longden, a stop-watch in his hand, clocked the workout from a seat high up in Santa Anita's near-empty grandstand. As Bucalo and Hartack pulled up their mounts, Longden, in high dudgeon, raced down the steps to get to Bucalo and chew him out for misjudging the workout. The 4-foot-11 Longden, his short legs churning, was so hurried that he stumbled a couple of times and almost fell down the stairs. Once he got trackside, he started to unload on Bucalo when Hartack jumped in.

"Johnny," Hartack said, "you can't believe how bad that track is. My horse was laboring something terrible, and so was Bucalo's horse. Both horses did the best they could."

Longden cut off his tongue-lashing. He accepted what Hartack said.

"I didn't know Hartack that well," Bucalo later said. "But he went to bat for me, and it really helped."

As it turned out, Bucalo would lose the job as exercise rider for Longden anyway. Bucalo didn't feel that he was getting a fair share of Majestic Prince's stakes purses—typically, an exercise rider might expect 1 percent—and he mentioned it to Longden. The next day, Longden told Bucalo that he was through, and the sixty-two-year-old trainer said that he would start galloping Majestic Prince himself. Longden added that he had been giving the 1 percent to his son Eric, who was one of his assistants. "He needs the money more than you do," he told Bucalo.

Bucalo laughed as he recalled the story: "Here I talk myself off the future Kentucky Derby winner, only a few weeks before the race. It wasn't exactly a brilliant career move on my part."[49]

The 1969 Santa Anita Derby, on March 29, took place five weeks before the Kentucky Derby. Before Hartack came out of the jockeys' room for the race, Majestic Prince scared the bejesus out of Longden and his other handlers when he got loose in his saddling stall and almost shook off his bridle.[50] Longden settled him down, and the rest of the day went according to plan. Hartack's whip was excess baggage. He sat chilly, in third place, through the first six furlongs of the nine-furlong race. Then, on the far turn, Majestic Prince responded to Hartack's urging. They had the lead at the head of the stretch and won by eight lengths, the biggest margin in the thirty-two runnings of the race. Afterward, Hartack hinted that he had left something in the tank for Kentucky.[51]

Although the Kentucky Derby drew only eight horses, it made for good theater. Top Knight, the best the East Coast had to offer, was in the field. For a while, so was Shoemaker, with the formidable Arts and Letters, but the hard-luck jockey was badly injured when a filly flipped in the Hollywood Park paddock three days before the Derby. Pinned between a hedge and a concrete wall, Shoemaker suffered multiple injuries, including a pelvis that was cracked in five places.[52] So he missed the chance to ride Majestic Prince because of one spill, and then he missed out again, with the horse that might have beaten Majestic Prince, because of another accident. As Shoemaker's replacement, the veteran Braulio Baeza would ride Arts and Letters for the first time. The outcome in the Derby was so close that some thought that Shoemaker being off, and Baeza on, could have been the difference between victory and defeat.[53]

President Nixon joined the crowd of 100,000, as advertised, and leading up to the race it was difficult to tell which horse he and his wife Pat were pulling for. Always the politician, the day before the race, Nixon said his favorite was Fleet Allied, because they were both

California-breds. But maybe none of his aides told him that only three California-breds had ever won the Derby, and Fleet Allied hardly looked like he would be the fourth, having lost seven straight races. Pat Nixon wore a yellow outfit that looked much like the colors of Kentucky's Claiborne Farm, whose Dike had won three straight starts in New York. As it happened, the Nixons' third-floor clubhouse box was not far from where Longden and McMahon were sitting. Frank and Betty McMahon brought their young daughters, one of whom was wearing an "I Like Bill Hartack" badge. Early in the day the president looked over at the McMahons and said, "I'll be cheering for your horse." The Nixons thus had three of the eight horses covered, one way or the other.[54]

Majestic Prince drew the outside post. Hartack didn't like that, but in a small field No. 8 was no drawback.[55] Churchill Downs is a one-mile oval, which means that for the mile-and-a-quarter race, the horses run past the stands twice, the first time out of a chute that leads on to the main track, and the second time for the stretch run. If the worrywart Longden was uneasy, it was more about his horse's five-furlong workout two days before the race. The colt was clocked in 58 1/5 seconds, more than a tad fast. The line for the naysayers formed to the right. Over and over again it was said that an undefeated horse hadn't won the Derby in forty-seven years.[56]

The Churchill Downs paddock was teeming, the horses separated only by wire netting from many fans who had overextended themselves with mint juleps. Inside the enclosure, there was barely enough room for the horses.

There was not much conversation between Hartack and Longden. Frank McMahon, said to be ill with the flu, stayed upstairs in his box.[57] Fortunately, Hartack knew the horse inside-out by now.

"Arts and Letters is the one to beat," Longden said. He had seen Arts and Letters win his final Derby prep by fifteen lengths.

"We got the best horse," Hartack said. "He looks good."

"You don't need the lead," Longden told him. "Just make sure the others don't get away from you."

Hartack nodded and said nothing. The clamor in the paddock was so loud that Longden might not have been able to hear him anyway.[58]

The horses left the paddock, went through a tunnel and pranced as they came on to the track. The record crowd joined together in singing "My Old Kentucky Home," the Stephen Foster song that was the Derby anthem.[59]

Longden, leaving the paddock, rejoined the McMahons in their box. "By God, John, he looks fit and ready," Frank McMahon said.

"As ready as he'll ever be," the fidgety Longden replied.[60]

Majestic Prince swerved to the right when his stall opened. There were no horses outside him; otherwise Hartack might have had to snatch him away. He just let the big colt regain his stride. Nothing had happened to disrupt the plan. Hartack spotted him in the middle of the pack. The horse in front, Ocean Roar, had four lengths on Majestic Prince, but Ocean Roar had been running at Beulah Park, a minor-league outpost in Ohio, and didn't figure to last.

When Ocean Roar dropped back after a half-mile, Top Knight took over the lead, with Majestic Prince in close pursuit. If Majestic Prince had lost any ground by coming wide on the first turn, he had made up that deficit by now. Baeza was saving ground with Arts and Letters along the rail. Dike, known for late runs, was taking his time.

Nearing the quarter pole, the gateway for the stretch run, Baeza moved Arts and Letters off the fence, and they shot between Top Knight and Majestic Prince to take the lead. Hartack could have panicked, but he hadn't asked his horse to run yet, and the 1,234.5-foot stretch was the second longest in U.S. racing. A natural lefthander, Hartack had room to use his whip from that side.[61]

At the top of the stretch, Majestic Prince inched ahead of Arts and Letters. There were still three-sixteenths of a mile left—time, Baeza thought, to regain the lead. "I tried to get by him repeatedly," Baeza said, "but the winner just wouldn't be beaten."[62]

Most of the crowd couldn't tell whose nose was going to be on the wire. Dike was coming, but he had too much to do. "Majestic Prince is holding on," Chic Anderson, the track announcer, said, but there were still a few strides left. "Majestic Prince, holding on by a head.... Majestic Prince wins it by a head!"[63]

The official margin was a short neck; Dike was only a half-length from the first two.[64] Hartack allowed Majestic Prince to gallop out past the finish line; then he eventually did a U-turn and headed back toward the winner's circle in the Churchill Downs infield.

Hartack looked around for those he knew. They took the photos, and as soon as he dismounted he gently tapped Chuck Corolla, his valet, on top of the head. He hugged George

1969: Derby win No. 5. While Hartack and Majestic Prince posed in the winner's circle, two of his friends—Gary Condra [standing far left] and Tad Dowd [crouched, black hat]—tried to talk Churchill Downs ushers into letting them join the festivities. They succeeded (Gary Condra collection).

Stidham, his business agent. Then he spotted Gary Condra, his friend from Florida. Almost four decades later, Condra would take responsibility for Hartack's burial, transporting the body from rural Texas to Condra's family plot in a cemetery in central Missouri.

"What the hell are you doing here?" Hartack shouted to Condra. Security was typically tight, as well as heavy-handed, at Churchill Downs, and Condra had no credentials. (The trainer LeRoy Jolley, after winning the Derby with the filly Genuine Risk in 1980, would have to talk his way into the winner's circle.)

Hartack had been with Condra and other friends in the days leading up to the Derby, but he was surprised to see Condra gain access to the roped-off winner's circle. Condra and Tad Dowd, wearing his famous derby, had raced across the track and into the infield as soon as Majestic Prince had won. They were stopped on the infield side of the running strip. Although this was Derby day, Dowd looked silly wearing one. While Dowd tried to explain his presence, Condra took him by the arm and said, "Hey! That guy's with me!" The confused guard let them both pass.[65]

Jim Bolus, who had the standing assignment from his newspaper to interview the winning jockey, stood in the background, observing the jubilant scene. This was the Jim Bolus who had been left in the lurch by Hartack a few days before.

For national TV, Hartack took viewers through the race with the broadcaster Jack Whitaker. Then Hartack said, "If he hadn't been a real fighter, we would have never made it."

Hartack left Whitaker and headed for the jockeys' room, with Bolus trailing him closely. It was a long walk—out of the infield, across the track, through a tunnel, through the paddock, and up an escalator that led to the jockeys' room door. Bolus kept his distance and resisted asking any questions as they walked along. But as they went through the door, Bolus finally said, "Are you excited?"

"I'm not excited," Hartack replied. "You guys are excited. I'm not."

Granted, Hartack had done this four times before, but now he had tied Arcaro's record of five Derby wins. Bolus was hoping for something better. Everybody was.

A radio reporter with a microphone rushed up and asked an odd question: "What's next as far as your career is concerned?"

"I don't know," Hartack said. That wasn't much of an answer, but it was truthful, and it certainly justified a lame question.[66]

A valet—not Corolla, but Bob Powell—helped Hartack take off his boots. Hartack then began to take off his riding silks and the rest of his outfit. A ring of reporters surrounded him as he got down to his underwear. Ignoring their questions, he got up, dropped his shorts and padded toward the showers in a pair of flip-flops.

They waited for him to finish. Deadlines were ticking away. He returned in a few minutes with a yellow towel around his waist and a green towel around his neck.

"Who won?" somebody asked, trying to break the ice.

Hartack didn't bite. "Who knows?" he said.

More silence as Hartack began to put on his street clothes.

Pulling a T-shirt over his head, he announced, "I think the press has been unfair to me. I refuse to be interviewed."

Manny Ycaza, whose Top Knight had finished fifth, stood at the next locker, tying his necktie. He smiled and shook his head.

A reporter asked Hartack a question.

"Call me at my hotel tomorrow," Hartack said. "If I can fit you in for an interview, I will." He didn't sound serious.

Jack Mann, of the *Washington Star*, bravely asked a question.

"No interviews," Hartack said again. "Especially you." He went on to say, "I've put up with newspapermen. Now they've got to put up with me. If you start treating jockeys like men, then maybe we'll start treating you like men."

Fully dressed, Hartack headed for the door. As the group of newsmen disbanded, one of them said, *sotto voce*, "Thank you, Mr. President."[67]

Hartack took a right turn at the door and went into the jockeys' lounge, where he gave an interview to Russ Harris, the veteran turf writer from Miami. Harris was on Hartack's short list of favorites—a very short list.[68]

Hartack's attitude was frequently compared to that of Ted Williams, the slugger for the Boston Red Sox who feuded with the press and once spit at his hometown fans. When Williams referred to the press as "the knights of the keyboard," nobody missed his pejorative tone.[69]

Joe Nichols of the *New York Times* said that the difficulty with Hartack was caused by his "intentness," but his tough early life, the death of his mother, and the corporal punishment from his father were all things that stuck in his craw.[70]

The day after the 1969 Kentucky Derby, Arthur Daley, the Pulitzer Prize–winning columnist for the *New York Times*, wrote a column that was called "Persecution Complexes." In it, Daley pointed out that Betty McMahon, whose husband owned Majestic Prince, had said, "Sometimes [Hartack] doesn't even speak to us." At the end of the column, Daley said, "Winsome Willie may behave great for television. But off-camera, he is able to lapse into being his disagreeable self."[71]

The night of the Derby, there was a party honoring Hartack at a restaurant in a Louisville shopping center. Among the guests, at the far end of the head table, was Eddie Sapir, a New Orleans judge and a friend of Hartack's. At the time, Sapir was traveling with his girlfriend. Molly was a beautiful girl, and Hartack eyeballed her all evening, something not lost on Sapir.

Toward the end of the night, Hartack sent George Stidham, his business manager, over to ask Sapir about Molly. But Sapir stopped Stidham in his tracks. "Look," he said. "He might have won the fucking Derby, but he's not winning Molly."[72]

In 1973, Hartack, in his next-to-last Derby, rode Warbucks to a last-place finish (he would also finish far back in 1974 with Sir Tristram, a 25–1 shot). The story in 1973 was the great Secretariat. On the first turn, Secretariat and Warbucks came close to bumping. Ron Turcotte, riding Secretariat, yelled something at Hartack, and Hartack shouted something back. Watching from the press box high atop Churchill Downs, I witnessed the byplay through my binoculars.

In the jockeys' room, before I could get to Turcotte, I saw Hartack. I was working for a Pittsburgh paper, and Hartack had grown up in Pennsylvania, and I figured that might help me get on his good side.

"I just got one question," I said. "What did Turcotte say, and what did you say?"

Hartack smiled a thin smile. "I would like to answer you," he said. "But you know how it is."

He walked off, and I wasn't about to follow him into the shower. All I would get there was wet.

2

The Triple Frown

They run the Preakness two weeks after the Kentucky Derby, at Pimlico in Baltimore, and the Belmont Stakes three weeks after that, at Belmont Park in New York. This grueling schedule of races—different towns, different tracks, different distances—is what makes the Triple Crown sweep so difficult. Twelve horses have done it, but from 1978, when Affirmed won all three races, until 2015, when American Pharoah swept it, there was a thirty-seven-year gap, the longest in Triple Crown history. When Bill Hartack and Majestic Prince won the 1969 Derby and jumped into the fray, there hadn't been a sweep in twenty-one years.[1]

As the Majestic Prince entourage arrived in Baltimore for the Preakness, Chick Lang was named general manager of Pimlico. What goes around, comes around. There was Hartack, in the limelight again, and hosting the next mountain to climb was Lang, who had been Hartack's agent, booking his mounts, during the glory years. But early in 1960, after more than six years together, there was a no-holds-barred breakup.[2] "He's the leading rider in the country right now, but he's dissatisfied all the time," Lang said. "He abuses everyone in the sport, from grooms and exercise boys to trainers.... It's his world, and the rest of us are just supposed to let him run it."

Hartack didn't go down without taking a few swings of his own. "[Lang and I] haven't agreed about who I should ride for the last two years," he said at the time. "I can't accept defeat. If I ever get to that point, I'll quit. When I'm paying the bills, it's my right to decide which horses I ride."[3]

From 1953 through 1957, Hartack had averaged 355 wins a year, more than anybody in racing. In 1958 and 1959, he averaged 250 wins.[4] Lang was getting the standard 20 percent of the purse commissions that Hartack earned, his share running to $50,000 a year or more. He joined Pimlico in the racing office soon after the split; he was promoted to the top job nine years later. It was Lang who was responsible for the Preakness rising from its place as the least visible of the Triple Crown races to become an event that regularly drew more than a hundred thousand fans, just like the Derby. "We've got one thing the Derby will never have," he said. "The winner of the Kentucky Derby."[5]

As the 1969 Preakness approached, there were no signs of the renewal of the Hartack-Lang feud. Through the years, Hartack would sometimes finish the season at Oaklawn Park, in Arkansas, and head up to Baltimore for the opening of Pimlico. He once called Lang and asked him to line up an agent in Maryland.[6] But in 1967, with the help of Whitney Tower, Hartack wrote a three-part, eighty-thousand-word series for *Sports Illustrated* that recounted his life and career; he never mentioned Lang once.[7] When Hartack had made the cover of *Time* magazine in 1958, Lang was an important part of the story.[8]

When they were together, Hartack won his first of three Preaknesses, with Fabius in

1956. That day they beat Needles, the Derby winner. Fabius, a son of Citation, the 1948 Triple Crown champion, ran for Calumet Farm and was trained by Jimmy Jones.[9]

"They got on me again yesterday," Hartack told Jones at his Pimlico barn, a few days before Fabius' victory.

"I heard some of that," Jones said. They were talking about the fans booing Hartack after he lost a race.

"It's the two-dollar guys that yell the loudest," Hartack complained. "The guys who have the least to win, and risk the least if they lose."

"What can you do?" Jones asked. "I saw 'em give [Eddie] Arcaro a rough time, too, and look how many races he's won."

Hartack was frequently featured on the front cover of national magazines as well as racing periodicals, as seen here on *Turf and Sport Digest* in 1956 (Jim Raftery).

"Don't these guys realize that I have to win, too?" Hartack demanded. "If I don't win, I get almost nothing for getting on a horse. They should know that I have to produce in order to earn a living. Sometimes you can't do enough for some people. Look at Ted Williams. They booed him so much in Boston, that one day he spit at 'em, and then they fined him. That was the biggest injustice I ever heard of. He's one of the greatest, and he always did his best. When they booed him, it burned me up. They should have fined the fans, not him."

"Look at it this way," Jones said. "They hardly ever boo a bum."[10]

By 1969, Jones and Hartack were no longer close, and his days of riding regularly for Calumet Farm were well behind him. They had a falling out in 1958, when Hartack broke his leg shortly before he was to ride Calumet's Tim Tam in the Derby. Milo Valenzuela took over and won both the Derby and the Preakness, but he finished second with Tim Tam in the Belmont. Hartack had resumed riding by the time of the third race and thought Jones should have given him the mount again.[11]

Two horses from the 1969 Derby—Arts and Letters, who was barely beaten, and Top Knight, whose dull race brought no excuses—moved on to Pimlico to tackle Majestic Prince again. A couple of days before the Preakness, trainer Johnny Longden worked Majestic Prince for a half-mile, and his clocking of forty-five seconds flat was thought to be the fastest a horse had ever drilled before the race.[12]

"This horse is sitting on ready," said Clem Florio, a veteran Maryland clocker who, it was rumored, went to bed with a stopwatch under his pillow.[13]

Five new shooters were also in the field, none of them given much of a chance. There was so much betting on Majestic Prince that if he won, a bettor would collect only sixty cents on the dollar.[14]

Braulio Baeza, who had been the injured Bill Shoemaker's replacement in the Derby, retained the mount on Arts and Letters. He and Hartack were a contrast in riding styles. Baeza was the classic sit-still rider. When he left the paddock on the horse, his posture was so perfect, he looked like a statue. Conversely, Hartack was unsettled on the horse. He bounced around a lot. "He reminds me," said the Hall of Fame trainer Charlie Whittingham, "of a cowhand roping a calf." Hartack answered these jibes by saying that "if race-riding is a beauty contest, I'll quit tomorrow."[15]

Even Baeza, however, was bouncing around shortly after the start of the Preakness. Top Knight, Arts and Letters, Majestic Prince and Al Hattab were all squeezed, and Arts and Letters, who took the worst of it, almost went down. Baeza had to check his horse in order to avoid disaster.

After that near-calamity, Hartack was able to gain clear position going down the backstretch. He stayed close to one of the long shots, the only horse ahead of him, and eased Majestic Prince to the front as they neared the quarter pole. Then he went to work. He hit the colt six times, all lefthanded, from the top of the stretch to the wire. Arts and Letters, who had to circle four horses for his run in the center of the track, came flying, and inside the sixteenth pole, he looked like the winner this time.[16]

"Arts and Letters is driving.... It's going to be a horse race," said the announcer, Chic Anderson once again. "As Majestic Prince holds on.... Arts and Letters is trying.... Arts and Letters on the outside, Majestic Prince on the inside.... They're coming to the wire.... This is still close.... Majestic Prince is holding on to that lead.... Just like the Derby, he wins by a head."[17]

The race might have been over, but the "official" sign on the tote board was yet to be turned on. After Hartack and Baeza let their horses gallop out, they returned to the finish line. Baeza dismounted and went to a phone that was a direct line to the three stewards upstairs. He claimed foul against Majestic Prince and Hartack for the disturbance early in the race.

"Judge, they almost knocked me down," Baeza told Fred Colwill, the Maryland state steward. "The six-horse [Majestic Prince] came out, and made me crowd the gray [Al Hattab]. I took back and lost stride bad. I got going again, but I lose four or five lengths."

Colwill asked Baeza to hand the phone to Hartack.

"I didn't come out that much," Hartack said. "The other horse [Top Knight], the one inside me, came out into me. That's what started it. I would have been straight except for that other horse."

Hartack and Baeza stood on the track, only a few feet apart, while Colwill and his two associates reran footage of the incident several times. They watched it in real time and then slowed it down. They watched what is called the "pan" (panorama) shot, taken from the stands' side of the track, and they watched the head-on angle. The grooms of the two horses led them by their lead shanks in small circles in front of the crowd. No one could leave because there was a winner's circle photo to be taken—if the stewards could ever determine the winner.[18]

It took twenty-six minutes. The national telecast was scheduled to go off the air, but they stayed on until the "official" sign went up. Somebody on the telecast said, "They're not exactly treating this like the fourth race at Cahokia Downs."[19]

While the decision was still up in the air, Longden came down to the track and stood next to Hartack.

"The longer they take, the worse off we are," Longden said grimly.

"I'm not so sure," Hartack said. "If they take me down, they should have their heads examined. We ran the best horse."

"Yeah, but sometimes that ain't got nothin' to do with it," Longden told him.[20]

There was a lot at stake. First place was worth $129,500; second paid only $30,000. In those days—Chick Lang really liked to hit Churchill Downs and the Derby where they lived—winning the Preakness paid more than first place in the Derby. Hartack's share was 10 percent of what the horse earned. And of course, most important, a win by Majestic Prince would keep alive his chances for the Triple Crown.[21]

Finally, the stewards decided to leave the result alone. Majestic Prince had won the Preakness and was eligible to become the ninth Triple Crown winner in another three weeks.

The stewards, unlike Hartack, didn't agree that Top Knight had started the ruckus. Colwill said, "Hartack steered as straight a course as possible. Al Hattab had far more to do with the trouble to Arts and Letters than Majestic Prince. If Baeza had tried to drive between them, it could have been real trouble. I agree, but he sensed this and took back. It wasn't Hartack's fault, but it certainly didn't help Baeza much, either."

When the public-address announcement was made that Majestic Prince had won, Longden clapped his hands. But the stolid Hartack showed no reaction. He just walked in the direction of the infield, where the winner's circle presentation would be made.[22]

In the jockeys' room, Baeza was outspoken. "I don't know if it was deliberate or not," he said. "But it made quite a difference. My horse ran a winning race. Hartack stopped me going into the first turn."

Reporters searched for Hartack. He appeared wearing only a blue towel around his midriff and flip-flops for the shower. "What happened?" he was asked. He just kept walking and stepped into the shower. A few with later deadlines waited for him to finish, but finally they gave up, too.

The morning after the Preakness, all turf writers found at Majestic Prince's barn was the horse and Mike Bao, Longden's stable foreman. The big question was whether Frank McMahon, Majestic Prince's wealthy owner, and Longden were going to shoot for the Triple Crown. Not many horses skip the Belmont after winning the first two legs, but Longden had parried the question the day before. Majestic Prince seemed to be getting out through the stretch. That could have been due to Hartack's aggressive lefthanded whipping, or the colt might have been telling his trainer that he was hurting.

"Nobody's here," Bao said.

"Where's Johnny?" someone asked.

"Back at the hotel, probably."

"When's he due?"

"I don't know. Maybe not at all. They're getting a plane ready to take the horse back to California."

It was three weeks before the Belmont Stakes, but if Majestic Prince was to run, it didn't make sense that they would send him cross-country twice.

"If your horse runs in the Belmont, can he beat Dike?" somebody asked. Dike, third in the Derby, had skipped the Preakness and would be a fresh horse in Majestic Prince's path if there was a bid for the Triple Crown.

A vein on the right side of Bao's neck looked like it was going to pop. While Longden kept himself low-key during the Triple Crown campaign, Bao had become the barn's cheerleader. He took exception to the suggestion that Majestic Prince could be beaten in the Belmont.

"What do you mean?" Bao sputtered. "You damn newsmen are all alike with your stupid questions. He beat Dike in the Derby, didn't he? He beat every horse he ever ran against." Bao held up both hands. He counted off all the fingers on one hand, and all but the thumb on the other. "He's run nine times, and he's won nine races," he said. "What more can you ask of a horse? He's done it all, and all you guys do is put the knock on him. You ask me questions like that, and I can see why Hartack hates newspapermen."[23]

While Bao tended to Majestic Prince, McMahon and Longden, at a hotel near the track, were discussing whether they would go for the Belmont. Longden didn't tell McMahon about the plane he had ordered. That proved to be a mistake. There were newspapermen at the barn who knew about the plane; yet McMahon didn't.

Somebody put in a call to Leslie Combs, who had bred Majestic Prince and was going to stand him at stud, at his Spendthrift Farm in Kentucky, when the horse was retired.

"He's raced a lot, and he's worked hard between his races," Combs said. "He won't run in the Belmont if I have anything to do with it."

That was another mistake. Now both Longden and Combs had crossed McMahon. Hartack didn't say anything.

On May 26, 1969, *Sports Illustrated* carried the headline "The Prince Ducks the Big One." McMahon felt like he was being painted into a corner. After all, he was the guy who signed everybody's checks.

"What kind of a champion can he be if he doesn't win at a mile and a half?" a trainer asked.

Longden had ordered a cargo plane from American Airlines, scheduled to leave Friendship International Airport three days after the Preakness. McMahon returned to his home in Palm Beach, Florida. He started by stewing; then the stew grew into a seething. He had left Baltimore agreeing with Longden that they didn't need the Belmont, there would be other races, but when McMahon learned that the plane had been ordered before they spoke, he had second thoughts. On top of that, Combs, albeit McMahon's friend in the business, acted as though he were managing the horse.

"Leslie, you're the breeder," McMahon said when he called Combs, "and you're my friend. But I own the horse, 100 percent, and you shouldn't have anything to do with the decision."

Then McMahon called Longden, who was still in Baltimore. "Johnny, I want to ship this horse to Belmont Park," McMahon said. "I know what was said, but I own him, and that's the way I want it to be."

"If you want the press to train the horse, that's OK with me," Longden said.

"The press is not training the horse," McMahon said. "You are. Do you think you can win the Belmont?"

"Yes," Longden said.

"OK, that's what I want you to do," McMahon said. "Do your best to win the Belmont."

When they hung up, McMahon still had the feeling that Majestic Prince could wind up on the plane to California. He knew that if Longden got the horse back to the West Coast, there'd be no returning for the Belmont. McMahon called the stable gate at Pimlico, identified himself and gave an order that the horse not be permitted off the grounds. Then he called American Airlines. "Whatever you do," he told them, "don't let that horse on that plane."[24]

Longden had already won a Triple Crown, as a jockey, with Count Fleet in 1943. But he felt the horse had bobbled in the stretch of the Belmont. He had tried to pull up the colt, but Count Fleet wouldn't let him. Count Fleet fractured a small bone in his left foreleg and was subsequently retired.

Longden didn't want to put Hartack in a similar position in a Belmont with Majestic Prince. Hartack had already earned $53,920 from riding the horse—10 percent of the purses, plus three $5,000 bonuses that McMahon had paid for winning the Santa Anita and Kentucky Derbys and the Preakness. Longden had banked $73,380; his commission on purses was 15 percent, and he got the same bonuses as Hartack.[25]

Hartack called Longden and asked what was going on. If Majestic Prince wasn't going to run in the Belmont, Hartack wanted to make himself available to ride another horse.

"The man changed his mind," Longden said. "We're going to the Belmont."

"The horse didn't feel completely right coming back the other day," Hartack commented.

"I was surprised the guy wants to run in New York," Longden said. "I checked him out. He's got a tendon."

"Tendons only get worse," Hartack said.

"What do they say about tendons?" Longden joked. "The only cure for one is another trainer?" Despite the attempt at humor, he was concerned; Longden had looked forward to having Majestic Prince for another year, to run as a 4-year-old.

"What are you going to do?" Hartack asked.

"I got a couple of weeks to talk [McMahon] out of it," Longden said. "He could still run good, I guess. He could even win. It won't be a very big field. Do me a favor. Come out some morning and gallop him."

After the gallop, the problematic tendon wasn't any better. Longden called McMahon and told him about the tendon for the first time.

"But we've come so far," McMahon said. And that was the end of it.

The week of the Belmont, Longden told Hartack that he didn't think there was any danger of Majestic Prince breaking down.

"I won't ride him if there's any chance of that," Hartack said. "I'll scratch his ass at the gate if I have to."

Longden knew that Hartack wasn't just talking. He jumped off horses in the post parade all the time. But scratching a horse at the eleventh hour with the Triple Crown on the line? That would make Longden and McMahon both look like fools.

The Greek Circle incident at Hialeah had been a *cause célèbre* that everybody remembered. The horse belonged to Fred Hooper, a hands-on owner who had won the Kentucky Derby in 1945 with Hoop Jr., the first horse he ever owned.

"My horse isn't right," Hartack had yelled to the official starter. "He can't coordinate himself. He's almost falling down. I'm getting off."

The track veterinarian, George Barksdale, was called. "He's fine," Barksdale had said. "Take him to the gate. He'll run fine."

There was more than $135,000 already bet on Greek Circle. The money would have to be refunded if he were scratched.

Disregarding the money at stake, Hartack got off the horse. Barksdale called the stewards, and they scratched him.

The six-foot-five Hooper, in high dudgeon, had thundered down from the stands. He towered over the five-foot-four Hartack.

"The horse is sore," Hartack had said, before walking off.

In response, Hooper found his trainer and said, "This guy has gotten too good and too smart. He'll never ride another horse for me."[26]

Before Frank McMahon and his wife Betty left Florida for New York, they had discussed how many tickets they would need for the Belmont Stakes. She said that their list for the race was up to sixty people, and most of them would probably also be attending a post-race party at Toots Shor's in Manhattan.

McMahon mentioned the possibility that Majestic Prince might not run. He told Betty how the trainer was opposed to running. "But right now," McMahon said, "he's running. At least as far as I'm concerned."

Arts and Letters, who would try again to beat Majestic Prince, ran one more time before the Belmont, winning the Metropolitan Mile over the Belmont track in a blazing minute and thirty-four seconds. Then, during the week of the Belmont, Arts and Letters worked five furlongs in a scalding fifty-seven and three-fifths seconds. The same day, Majestic Prince was clocked in fifty-nine seconds. One morning, Longden and McMahon excused themselves from reporters and could be heard shouting at one another in the back of the barn.[27]

Hartack did the Dick Cavett TV show a few days before the race. The other guests were actors—Lillian Gish, Lynn Redgrave and Richard Boone. Without any prompting from Cavett, Hartack trashed a few sportswriters. A reporter, hoping to get an interview, waited for Hartack after the show. "My life is my private concern," Hartack said, getting in a limousine that would take him back to his hotel.[28]

The day before the Belmont, Joe Namath, who had become a good friend of Hartack's, singlehandedly upstaged the race. Namath, who had led the New York Jets to an incredible Super Bowl upset of the Baltimore Colts several months before, had recently opened a bar with two partners on the East Side. They called their establishment Bachelors III, in honor of themselves. It had a sports motif, and on one of the walls was a big photo of Hartack, right next to a picture of Mickey Mantle of the New York Yankees.[29]

The characters hanging around Bachelors III unnerved Pete Rozelle, commissioner of the National Football League, and he ordered Namath to sell out his interest. At a teary press conference the morning before the Belmont, Namath announced that he was keeping the bar and quitting the Jets and pro football. He would renege on this statement several weeks later, instead quitting the bar and rejoining the Jets. But for a while, Namath was on the front pages, and the Belmont Stakes was a lesser story.[30]

Namath had met Hartack through Joe Hirsch, a columnist for the *Daily Racing Form*. Hirsch, introduced to Namath by Sonny Werblin, who owned both a racing stable and the Jets, shared an apartment with the quarterback for several years. Hirsch wrote a flattering cover story about Hartack for *Sports Illustrated* in 1957 and became one of Hartack's rare confidants among the press corps. There is an old photo of Hirsch, working at his typewriter in the Pimlico press box, and Hartack, in mufti, reading something while patiently waiting for his friend to finish his column.[31]

Namath and Hartack, with their girlfriends, were sometimes seen as a foursome around New York. They might turn up at the Pussycat or the Copacabana. One night, at Dudes 'N Dolls, a club where Goldie Hawn got her start, Namath and Hartack were the judges for a dance contest.

After an especially galling Jets defeat, on a day when Namath had played poorly, he found solace with Hartack and a couple of other friends at an out-of-the-way bar in the East Forties. Late in the evening, a drunk at the other end of the bar spotted them and came down, demanding of Namath, "You know how much money I lost on you today?"

Namath tried to ignore him. But the belligerent tosspot wouldn't let up. Hartack got off his stool, reached over and gave the drunk a left hook to the jaw that left him flat on his back . Prostate on the floor was someone who outweighed the 112-pound Hartack by about fifty pounds.

The night before the Belmont, Namath had recovered from his retirement press conference, and by 1 a.m. he came into Bachelors III with Suzie Storm, his girlfriend.[32] Hartack was not with them and had reportedly gone home. Friends of his, when asked about that night, said he was back at his hotel by then. A jockey at Belmont Park said that Hartack spent the night at Joe Hirsch's apartment. Friends of Hartack also reported that he wasn't drinking much (he was known for separating the parties from the ponies during his career). Tad Dowd, a friend of Hartack's, said that he accompanied Hartack from Manhattan to Belmont Park on the morning of the race. Dowd said that he was in either Hartack's car or a trailing car. If Hartack was the worse for wear, Dowd said that it didn't show.[33]

This information is relevant because in conducting research for this book, I was told a fantastic story by the late Biff Lowry, something that was told to Lowry by Johnny Longden after Longden had retired from training. Lowry, son of a *Los Angeles Times* racing writer, was working for the satellite betting locations in California and taking Longden from site to site to entertain the fans. One day, en route to Palm Springs, Longden told Lowry that when he saw Hartack on the morning of the 1969 Belmont, he decided that he wasn't fit to ride that afternoon. In Longden's judgment, Hartack had partied too much the night before. Longden, Lowry said, went to the stewards and asked that Hartack be taken off Majestic Prince. And who did the trainer have in mind as a replacement? Longden himself, apparently. Somewhat far-fetched, since Longden hadn't ridden in a race in three years, but even at sixty-two he still exercised Majestic Prince on a regular basis.[34]

Was it possible that this was another way for Longden to get the stewards to help him do what McMahon wouldn't let him do—not run Majestic Prince? A horse can be scratched from a stake without reason—no permission from the stewards is required—but a late scratch of a horse one win away from the Triple Crown would have caused a seismic reaction. Saying Hartack was ill would at least soften the outburst. But that would have been wishful thinking, for Hartack would not have played the game and cooperated with the ruse. He hadn't played the game in 1958, when Tim Tam's trainer, Jimmy Jones, had asked Hartack to say that he wasn't fit enough to ride in the Belmont Stakes. Jones had won the Kentucky Derby and the Preakness with Milo Valenzuela, and he didn't want to switch jockeys for the windup of the Triple Crown. (Valenzuela got his chance when Hartack was sidelined with a broken leg.)[35]

The night before the 1969 Belmont, Longden stopped by the hospitality room at the Gotham Hotel, where many members of the press were still gathered. "He told us all to save our money, not to bet his horse," Dave Johnson said. "He said there was something wrong with his horse, that he wasn't at the top of his game." Johnson later became the track announcer in New York and also worked for many years as a racing telecaster for the networks.[36]

Tommy Trotter, racing secretary at Belmont Park in 1969, said that he had never heard the story Lowry claimed Longden had told him. Nor had Sam Kanchuger, the publicity director for the track. "The only way you could document that story would be to talk to the stewards," Trotter said. "All three of them are dead."

Trotter worked for a few years as a steward with Hartack at Arlington Park in suburban Chicago, and he said Hartack never mentioned the story. "But Hartack," Trotter added, "never brought up much of anything."[37]

Ron Turcotte, who would win the Kentucky Derby with Riva Ridge in 1972 and then in 1973 sweep the Triple Crown with Secretariat, was told Lowry's hand-me-down story from Longden and doubted every word of it. Turcotte was one of the few fellow jockeys given the time of day by Hartack, and he said that it was his understanding that Hartack spent the night before the Belmont at Joe Hirsch's apartment in Manhattan. According to Turcotte, on Belmont day, Hartack appeared to be clear headed and well rested. "I think Longden was playing his hangover card," Turcotte said. "At that point, he was doing everything he could to get Frank McMahon to scratch the horse."[38]

Longden reportedly finished his story to Lowry by saying that the stewards insisted he make do with Hartack.[39] Only six horses were entered, the smallest Belmont field in twelve years. Half of them appeared to be running for second money. It looked like a three-horse race—Majestic Prince, Arts and Letters, and Dike.

Hartack rode two horses with good chances on the Belmont undercard. One of them ran last; the other finished sixth. When Hartack left the jockeys' room and entered the paddock for the Belmont, many of the fans who ringed the circle greeted him with Bronx cheers. Steely-eyed, Hartack acted as though he didn't hear them. With his whip at his side, he walked purposefully in the direction of Longden, who stood beside Majestic Prince in the No. 3 saddling stall.[40]

Longden hadn't planned to give Hartack any instructions. Hartack had ridden Majestic Prince in all nine of his races. His rides in Louisville and Baltimore were impeccable.

"If I was riding, I'd be tempted to put this horse on the lead," Longden said to Hartack. "Because there's no pace to speak of. But that's me."

Hartack said nothing. If Longden was trying to draw him out, he had failed.

"Do what you want," Longden told him. "Play it the way it comes up."[41]

Because Belmont Park is a mile-and-a-half oval, the same as the distance of the race, and the horses start at the finish line and go around once, it is the most vexing of the Triple Crown races to ride. Jockeys in the United States seldom ride in races that are this long. And jockeys who don't ride regularly at Belmont are not accustomed to the track's sweeping turns. Jockeys unfamiliar with Belmont sometimes move prematurely with their horses at the start of the far turn, which is still a thousand yards from the finish line.[42] Hartack, however, knew the lay of the land. He had won with Celtic Ash in 1960, the first Belmont he ever rode in. He had ridden in two Belmonts since then, both with Kentucky Derby winners, as Decidedly finished fourth in 1962 and Northern Dancer ran third in 1964.[43]

The record crowd of sixty-six thousand made Majestic Prince a slight favorite over Arts and Letters. When the gates opened, no one wanted to push the issue. Dike went to the lead by default. Hartack snatched up Majestic Prince, and after a half-mile they were ahead of only one horse.[44]

"Frank, he's too far back," Longden said to McMahon. "We're gonna be second."

McMahon winced. "I don't think we can win with an express train."[45]

The opening half-mile was run in the slowest time for a Belmont in twenty years. After the long run down the backstretch, Baeza inched Arts and Letters ahead of Dike just before they reached the far turn. Meanwhile, Majestic Prince continued to lag. On the turn for home, Arts and Letters extended his lead on Dike, and far outside them, as close to the grandstand as he was the inner rail, came Majestic Prince. Baeza couldn't believe how easy Arts and Letters' five-and-a-half-length win was.

Surprisingly, there were no catcalls when Hartack returned to the unsaddling area with his mount. There was an ovation for Arts and Letters, a New York horse who had thwarted a would-be Triple Crown champion, fair and square.[46] Arts and Letters would go on to other wins, beating older horses, and he was voted Horse of the Year.[47] However, in a poll of racing authorities by *Blood-Horse* magazine in 1999, Majestic Prince was ranked the forty-sixth best of all-time; Arts and Letters came in sixty-seventh.[48]

After the race, Hartack was mute. He declined to go on TV and explain the race, and he ignored questions in the jockeys' room. Johnny Rotz, who finished fourth with the long shot Distray, tried to get Hartack off the hook. "I don't think any kind of tactics would have let the second horse beat the first horse today," Rotz said.[49]

Others were not as generous. "How such an experienced veteran, riding such a speed horse as Majestic Prince, could be suckered by such an unbelievably slow pace, is something to wonder about," one magazine account of the race declared. "Reporters wondered whether Hartack was trying to prove something."[50]

Years later, Hartack finally opened up about what happened. His comments made it sound like he had babied the horse: "I had the same opinion as Longden [about not running]. You don't have to read the papers to decide who was right and who was wrong. The horse never raced after that. Now who could possibly have been right, and who could possibly have been wrong? It's not even debatable. Here's a horse who, if he had missed that race and been given some time off—the rest of the year, in fact—there's no doubt in my mind that he would have come back and been the champion horse the following year."[51]

A day after the race, Majestic Prince looked like he had been through the wringer. He was seen sleeping on his side in his stall, something he had never done before. Most horses sleep standing up.[52]

Win or lose, Frank McMahon had booked Toots Shor's, one of the most famous saloons in the United States, for a party on the night of the Belmont. Longden and Hartack both attended. Longden's son Eric, who worked at the barn, also came. "Don't get mad and say something nasty," his father told Eric as they left Belmont Park and made the twenty-five-mile trip into Manhattan.[53]

The horse owner Liz Tippett had brought Jane Russell to the races (Hartack's guest was Hugh Hefner), and both Tippett and Russell went to the party, such as it was. Black crepe would have been an appropriate touch. It was a dull and poorly attended affair. A small band tried to enliven the evening, but there's nothing like a Triple Crown letdown to poop a party. Hartack came in, took a back table and sat by himself.

Jane Russell was introduced to the McMahons. Betty McMahon, who as Betty Betz once wrote a syndicated advice column for teenagers, told Tippett that Hartack "rode our horse poorly."

On the CBS telecast, Eddie Arcaro, winner of six Belmonts (and five Derbys, the same number as Hartack), was especially harsh about Hartack's ride. Part of this rancor might have been due to the fact that Arcaro and Hartack didn't get along, an animosity that dated back to Arcaro's riding days. "I've never seen anyone trapped by such a slow pace in a Belmont as Hartack was," Arcaro said. "I think it cost him his chance for the Triple Crown."

At Shor's, a lithe brunette sat down at Hartack's table. "I'm sorry you lost the Triple Crown," she said.

"You can't lose something you didn't have," he snapped. "The horse didn't have it."

Liz Tippett was within earshot when Hartack made this comment.[54] She used to like Hartack when he rode for her; she even showed up at the barns one morning wearing only a fur coat and a smile and flashed him.[55] Tippett, once married to Jock Whitney, did a Scarlett O'Hara screen test for *Gone With the Wind*, mainly because Whitney was bankrolling half the film. She also flew her own helicopter and kept her dead dogs in a freezer in the basement.[56] Five weeks before the Belmont, she'd had a run-in with Hartack at the Kentucky Derby.

Walking away from the simmering Hartack, Tippett said to someone, "I can't stand this. He says that, and he blew the race."

An acquaintance of the brunette walked past the table, and she repeated what Hartack had said: "The horse didn't have it."

Hartack heard her and glared. "You should have said that when you sat down here."[57]

3

"Get Out of the House!"

Ten-year-old Dolly Hartack heard the words as though they came in a dream: "Get out of the house!"

Dolly was caught in the cobwebs of a deep sleep. The frantic male voice was coming from the only bedroom, in the back of the small house, where her father slept. This balmy September night in 1941, he was sleeping with the family housekeeper, who would stay over from time to time. William Hartack Sr.'s wife, Nancy Hartack, only twenty-eight, had died the previous Christmas, from massive injuries suffered in an automobile accident twelve days before. Hartack Sr. was left with three children—Dolly, who was nine at the time of her mother's death; William Jr., then eight years old; and Maxine, barely a year old.

Dolly slept on the living-room couch, while Maxine slept in a crib in a corner of the bedroom. When she started coughing that fateful night, she woke her father, who smelled the smoke. Young William, the future jockey, slept on a cot in an alcove between the kitchen and the living room. Dolly, now awake, also smelled the smoke. Through the haze, she saw an outline of her brother as he carried, in a case, the saxophone that their father played.[1]

The father was a sinewy, thirty-three-year-old Czechoslovakian immigrant who spent long hours working in the western Pennsylvania coal mines. For many years, Cambria County averaged at least 16 million tons of raw coal a year.[2] Before the fire, Hartack Sr. had gone to bed worn out from his work, but now he was storming into the living room with the night-gowned, barefooted housekeeper, eight years his junior, trailing him. He picked up a small bookcase of encyclopedias and flung it out the front door. The books scattered in all directions.

Dolly was outside by now. The five of them—the three children, the father and the housekeeper—stood there in the crisp night and watched almost everything they owned burn away. On the dewy ground were the saxophone, the strewn encyclopedias and a white Zenith radio.

The Hartacks couldn't afford a phone. The fire department was in Ebensburg, several miles away. "Bright yellow and orange flames," said Dolly as she remembered the fire. (Her real name is Evelyn, but she came to be known as "Dolly" early on, in part because her mother dressed her up like Shirley Temple, the movie star. Dolly was once voted "the cutest baby in Cambria County." The next year, her brother Bill won the same award. Even after so many years, Dolly still refers to her only brother as "Sonny." He was Willie to some—mostly his enemies as the years rolled by—and Bill to the majority. Only his oldest sister called him "Sonny.")

The fire moved quickly, leaving little of the uninsured house. Neighbors called it the "dollhouse" because it was so small. There was no running water inside; the Hartacks got

William Hartack, Sr., with his children "Dolly," Maxine and Bill, photographed in front of the family home that was destroyed by fire in 1941 (Evelyn "Dolly" Hartack Ferguson collection).

their water from a well near the house. Since the fireplace in the living room had not been lit, the Hartack children grew up believing the housekeeper had caused the fire. She was the only smoker in the house, and she liked to smoke in bed.

The fire occurred while the family was still reeling from the death of Nancy Hartack. The children never got over the loss of their mother. Dolly Hartack claimed that her mother could do no wrong. Maxine was too young to remember the accident or her mother, but by the time she was old enough to realize the consequences, Dolly had ingrained in her how wonderful her mother was, and how great her loss had been.

"She was such a great mother," Dolly said. "She kept the family together. I can remember her cleaning all the time. Everything had to be clean. We didn't have a lot, but it had to be clean. She waxed and waxed until everything was spotless."

For a long time, young Bill Hartack couldn't stomach Christmas. While his classmates looked forward to the holiday, anticipating the gifts that came with it, he humbugged the day.

For several years after Nancy's death, the family ignored the commercial trappings of Christmas, including Christmas trees. Finally, because of Maxine, her father began buying trees again, and they gradually eased back into the Christmas traditions.

"Black Friday" was how Dolly described the day of the auto accident. She meant December 13, 1940. Her father, who had just been paid, was driving through the center of Ebensburg, accompanied by Nancy and thirteen-month-old Maxine, who was sitting in her mother's lap. They were on their way to Johnstown to do some Christmas shopping. The car was a new beige Dodge sedan. To buy it, Hartack Sr. had scrimped, worked a lot of overtime hours, and borrowed.

There was a major intersection in Ebensburg that had four stop signs but no stop-and-go light. The traffic light would be installed the following year. It was said that had there been a light, the accident might have been avoided. The Hartack car had made its stop, but before Hartack Sr. could shift gears and move through the intersection, a trailer truck slammed into the Dodge from behind. The Hartack car was knocked into a deep gully, and the father and mother were crushed inside. Baby Maxine was thrown from her mother's arms upon impact, her head cracking the windshield. Her right arm was badly mangled.

Dolly was a fourth grader in Mylo Park Elementary School. The accident happened toward the end of the school day. Her brother Bill was in the third grade. They had talked about coming home, expecting that their parents would have already returned from Johnstown, and imagining what Christmas gifts had been hidden in the hall closet.

Dolly's class was interrupted by the sound of sirens. A police car. An ambulance. A fire truck. She wondered what was happening in her quiet little town.

Several minutes after the commotion outside, the principal came into Dolly's classroom and asked her teacher to excuse the girl for the rest of the day. Outside, in the hall, the principal told Dolly what had happened.

A friend of the family gave Dolly and her brother Bill a ride to the hospital. The attendants let the children see their sister, who had been given a sedative, and their father, but they said doctors were still with their mother and they would have to wait to see her.

TO WISH YOU EVERY JOY THAT CHRISTMAS
AND THE NEW YEAR CAN BRING

William Hartack, Sr., his wife Nancy and their three children—from left to right, Maxine, Bill and "Dolly,"—posed for a Christmas card in 1940. Nancy Hartack was injured in an automobile accident shortly before the holiday and died on Christmas day. The cards were never sent (Evelyn "Dolly" Hartack Ferguson collection).

Their father had suffered multiple injuries and also was in shock. "Keep the family together," he told Dolly in a whisper. He had already been informed that his wife's chances of survival were slim.

A doctor came into the room to talk to the father. They spoke in whispers, out of earshot of the two older children.

"Your daughter's arm is severely damaged," the doctor said. "She has lost a lot of blood. I would suggest that we amputate."

The doctor had a clipboard with several papers attached. He asked Hartack Sr. to sign them.

"I won't do it," the injured father said. "I won't let you take my little girl's arm. Just do the best you can."

Maxine had several surgeries, the last one eleven years after the accident, when she was in the seventh grade. She now has limited use of two of her fingers, but she has full use of the rest of the arm.

Olive Smith, who lived two farms over from the Hartacks, volunteered to look after Dolly and Bill while their parents and sister were in the hospital. Olive, who had no children, was related to one of the early settlers of Cambria County. The borough of Ebensburg was the county seat. Olive owned some valuable property in town, land that the five-and-dime store sat on. She lived with her sisters—Mabel helped her keep house, and Viola was a first-grade teacher in the school that Bill and Dolly Hartack attended. Initially, Olive Smith's house was not on the bus route that took the children to school. She called the school to explain the situation, and the route was changed. In Ebensburg, there wasn't much that Olive Smith asked for that she didn't get.

A few months after the auto accident, William Hartack Sr. was released from the hospital. Shortly after that, Maxine was allowed to go home—to Olive Smith's house, that is.

Nancy Hartack had been the bulwark of the family. "Everything seemed to go to pot after my mother passed away," said Dolly, who married a man named Ferguson, moved to Southern California, divorced her husband after twenty-nine years, and then moved to Las Vegas with a new love. "I think that Sonny's [Bill's] problems in dealing with people began when our mother died. He was always on the shy side. But he got in a lot of fights. He was much smaller than the other kids, and they teased him. They called him 'Runt,' they called him 'Termite.' He hated it. After a while, he started fighting back."

Hartack's father asked his oldest child, Dolly, to watch out for her brother and keep him from fighting. "How can I?" she asked. "I have to watch out for Maxine. She's all I have the time for."

Nancy had been musically inclined, like her saxophone-playing husband. She played the accordion, and, together with a clarinet player and a drummer, they formed a four-piece band that would play for any occasion—graduations, birthday parties, holidays. A radio station in Johnstown heard about the combo and invited them to come play. The song they chose to perform was "Boo Hoo," the Guy Lombardo standard.

The Hartacks' son was a trap drummer. He was too small to play sports, and his father, a martinet, wouldn't have allowed him to participate anyway. Hartack Sr. had no use for sports. But young Bill was allowed to go to football games because he played the drums in the school band.[3]

"I hated the drums," Hartack later admitted. He liked music (he once dated Connie

Francis, the pop singer) but not the drums. Long after he had started riding, he gave them one more chance. It was a disaster. He said he had forgotten everything he ever learned. But he taught himself the guitar. His unrealized ambition was to play the guitar on national television.[4]

His father was working a swing shift, different hours depending on the week, and from twelve to sixteen hours a day. He needed the extra pay to keep the family going. All three children wore hand-me-downs.[5]

"I worked from when the sun came up to when the sun came down," Hartack Sr. said. "I got paid for the amount of coal I loaded. I set a record for soft coal that lasted until they brought in the machines. I'd come to work with only some water in my lunch pail, not even a piece of bread, but I couldn't let anybody dig more coal than me. Once, another fella dug more than me during a week. I was so mad when I went home, I couldn't sleep nights. I couldn't wait to get back and dig more coal than that guy. It had me crazy. You couldn't talk to me until I beat out that other guy again."[6]

He wouldn't whip his daughters, but young Bill felt his father's leather belt as well as a wooden stick that stood in a corner of the kitchen. Hartack said years later that the hardships of breaking in around the track were not that tough compared to the home life he had left behind.[7]

"I had a terrible temper," Hartack's father said. "In the mines, I would argue with anybody. When I got older, I mellowed." Later, the jockey's mean-spirited ways reminded his father of himself. But Hartack Sr. thought his son's sour disposition would vanish with age, which never happened. Hartack was just as snarly in his seventies as he had been in his twenties.[8] He was hard on almost everybody, and most of all the press.

Working as a minor racing official at Hollywood Park long after he had ridden his last horse, Hartack was playing cards in the jockeys' room late one day (probably in violation of an unwritten fraternization rule). Someone called from the press box and asked Harold Wolk, the room's custodian, to ask Fernando Toro, the veteran rider, a question. I was interviewing Toro at his locker at the time. Overhearing the phone conversation from the card table, Hartack asked, "Who wants to know?"

"The press," Wolk answered.

"Tell 'em to go fuck themselves," Hartack said.[9]

* * *

Hartack's grandfather, on his father's side, was Steve Shutak, which was the original family name. It was Nancy, the jockey's mother, who tried to Americanize the name by changing it to Hartack. Shutak, an immigrant from Czechoslovakia, had accumulated wealth overseas, though he lost much of it due to political unrest in his homeland. In the United States, Shutak virtually started over, but he worked hard in the coal mines and may have accrued some money during mysterious, periodic trips to New York, which he never explained to the family. Eventually, Shutak owned the biggest farm in Cambria County, Pennsylvania. After the fire that wiped out his son's place in 1941, Shutak sold Hartack Sr. fifty acres of land in neighboring West Virginia, near Charles Town, where he took two or three years to build his family a new house. During that time, the Hartacks lived with one of Hartack Sr.'s sisters and her husband.

After Dolly graduated from high school, she moved to Cleveland to take a job. In the early 1950s, her father married again. "He didn't want a wife, he wanted a babysitter for Maxine," Dolly said. The marriage was annulled in less than a year.[10] Meantime, Bill Hartack's riding career flourished from the start, and he told Maxine that he would pay for her to attend college at the University of Miami. Maxine wasn't even thinking about going to college—her brother *ordered* her to go. Planning to study interior design, she flew from Pennsylvania to Miami—the first time she had ever been on a plane—and was surprised not to see her brother at the Florida airport. Instead, Hartack sent one of his girlfriends, an Eastern Airlines stewardess, who assisted Maxine in registering for classes.

There was a restaurant just off campus called the Merry-Go-Round. Maxine could eat there anytime, merely by signing her famous brother's name. After two years, she knew virtually everyone who worked at the restaurant.

Maxine couldn't understand why her brother hardly ever saw her. She can remember only three times when they got together during her two years in college. In 1960, Hartack was riding in the Kentucky Derby, and instead of inviting Maxine to Louisville for the race, he offered her the use of the sprawling ranch-style house he had bought and remodeled in Miami Springs. Maxine and Hartack's housekeeper sat in front of a TV set, watching her brother win the second of what would be a record-tying five Derbys.

Hartack told Maxine that he didn't want her hanging around the race track, because he thought there were too many lowlifes there. But one weekend a jockey named Joe French, who had ridden with Hartack at the Charles Town track, came to Miami and asked Maxine out to dinner. He was ten years older than Maxine, and her brother didn't approve, but not long afterward they were married and Maxine quit college and moved to West Virginia, where her new husband was still riding. "He was very nice looking," Maxine said. "All the girls were after him." They lived for a time in what was called a tenant house, behind the home that Hartack bought for his father. The marriage, which produced two children, lasted until the early 2000s, at which time Maxine divorced and remarried.

Bill Hartack got along with his father, who sometimes went out of town to watch his son ride. The father enjoyed the company of women, and he loved to dance. Hartack Sr. was proud of the many big races that his son won. In 2008, after both father and son were dead, a street bordering the County Day School near Charles Town was renamed Hartack Lane, in honor of all the races Bill Hartack had won at the West Virginia track. "Having that street named after him wouldn't have meant a thing to my brother," Maxine said. "He just wasn't that way, he didn't get emotional about anything. But my dad would have been thrilled."[11]

By 1963, Bill Hartack had been riding for ten-plus years and had won more than three thousand races. He had already been enshrined in the Racing Hall of Fame in Saratoga Springs, New York. During the summers, he would ride at Arlington Park in suburban Chicago, but when important races were run elsewhere, he was in demand and always on call for a top mount. Such a race, the Christiana Stakes, was scheduled for June 22, 1963, at picturesque Delaware Park just outside Wilmington. On the evening of June 21, Hartack flew in to ride the precocious colt Chieftain, the probable favorite.[12] Chieftain was owned by Raymond Guest, who was a second cousin of Winston Churchill. In a few years, Guest would be named the U.S. ambassador to Ireland.[13]

The week of the race, Hartack had called his father and invited him to Delaware Park. His father was juggling a couple of girlfriends at the time. One of them, Frances Clara

Brant, had moved in with him nine months earlier. Brant was forty-seven, eight years younger than Hartack Sr., who had promised Brant that he would marry her.

Delaware Park was an easy drive, about 150 miles, from where Hartack Sr. lived. When he mentioned the trip, Brant wanted to go along. Later he called his son and said that he wouldn't be there for the race.[14]

On Friday, the day before the race, William Hartack Sr. and Frances Brant were sitting in his living room, having a couple of drinks. It was the middle of the afternoon. They argued about not going to Delaware Park, and perhaps other things, and a struggle ensued between them.

Hartack Sr. had long collected guns—he enjoyed showing his son how they worked—and among them was a small-caliber handgun. As he and Brant fought, they both got their hands on the gun and the chambers were emptied—six .22-caliber shots were fired. One struck Hartack in the chest, near his heart. He stumbled out the front door of his house, careening in the direction of his pickup truck.

On the floor inside the house, Brant struggled to reach the phone. She had been shot in one arm and cut in the other as the fight escalated. She clutched the phone and told the operator there was an emergency. The call was put through to the Emergency Communications Center in Charles Town, the equivalent of a 911 call.

"There's been a shooting," a hysterical, crying Brant yelled into the phone. Then she gave the location and dropped the receiver.

Meanwhile, Hartack reached his truck, bleeding badly. He turned on the engine and instinctively groped for his thick, horn-rimmed glasses. They were back in the house, knocked off during the struggle. He was nearsighted and never drove without them, but in his condition it wouldn't have made any difference.

He steered the small truck toward the dirt road that led from the house to Route 51, which was the way to the nearest hospital. He didn't get far. The truck crashed into one of the telephone poles that lined both sides of the road. After the collision, he opened the driver's-side door and fell out. He began walking blindly, fell again, and this time he didn't get up. The crash had demobilized phones in the area, including the one Brant had used inside the house. Attempts by the emergency operator to call her back were in vain. When the state police arrived, less than a half-hour later, they found Hartack dead at the scene. There was another car in front of the house, later identified as Frances Brant's.[15]

Besides Brant, inside the house was a barking dog. The dog, a boxer, was called "Nero." He had been a surprise gift from Bill Hartack to his father, who had gone over to Federal Express unsure of what would be waiting for him. The elder Hartack loved the dog; even as a child, he had not had one.[16]

The injured Brant was rushed to Charles Town General Hospital, where she was patched up and kept overnight. After her release, she was arraigned, and bail was set at $10,000. The original charge was murder.[17]

The day Bill Hartack's father died, attempts to reach him were unsuccessful. Hartack was en route from Chicago, and no one knew where he was staying in Wilmington. He went to the track on the day of the race not knowing his father was dead. At Delaware Park, Frank Whiteley stopped by the barn where Chieftain was stabled, and a groom told him that the colt had been coughing since early afternoon. Whiteley poked his head inside

Chieftain's stall and heard the horse cough once or twice. A veterinarian was called, and he recommended that Whiteley not run the horse.

"A damn shame," Whiteley said. "The owner [Raymond Guest] has come to see him run, all the way from Virginia."

Whiteley put in a call to the stewards and said that he was scratching Chieftain, telling them that the horse had a cough. Because it was a stakes race, he didn't need a reason for the scratch.[18]

Whiteley then made a second call, this time to the jockeys' room, where Bill Hartack had been studying the *Daily Racing Form* past performances, so as to gain insight on the running patterns of the other horses in the race. "We got you here for nothing," Whitleley told Hartack. "The horse is coughing away, and there's no sense taking a chance. He's got a lot of other races ahead of him."

Hartack hung up, reached for his street clothes, and asked his valet to phone the airlines and get him a flight from Philadelphia back to Chicago. Before Hartack finished dressing, however, he was called to the phone in the jockeys' room a second time.

"What is it this time?" he asked peevishly. He was not happy that he had come all the way to Delaware and now wouldn't be able to ride the horse who looked like a sure winner.

"Mr. Hartack, this is Corporal Holman of the state police, back in West Virginia. We've got some bad news, I'm afraid. Your father's been shot. At his place. By the time we got there, there was nothing we could do for him."

"What you're saying is that he's dead, right?"

"Yes, sir, I'm afraid so."

"What the hell happened?"

"We're trying to sort it out, sir. There's a woman involved. Do you know a Frances Brant?"

"Yeah, I think so."

"Well, she's in the hospital. She was shot, too."

"Who did this?"

"We're not sure. Like I say, we don't have much to go on. It was just the two of them at the house. But it was your father's handgun, and our best guess is that they probably shot one another."[19]

Maxine Hartack French, then married to Joe French, the jockey who rode at the Charles Town track, was no longer living in the small place behind her father's house where she and her husband had started out. Maxine and Joe had since moved into an apartment in Charles Town, a few miles from the track.

Joe French answered Corporal G.G. Holman's call. Maxine was only listening out of one ear, but she could tell that her husband was upset.

"It's your dad," Joe said after he had hung up. "He's been shot and killed."

Maxine started crying, and Joe tried to settle her down. At the time she was more than seven months' pregnant with her daughter, who would be named Christina.

"They said they already called your brother," Joe told his wife.

Maxine was able to reach Dolly in Manhattan Beach, California, where she lived with her husband. Dolly knew about her father being with Frances Brant, and she also knew her father was seeing another woman at the same time. Her first thought was that the other woman was the shooter.

"No, it's Frances Brant," Maxine said.

Hartack and his father, who owned a large collection of handguns, c. 1958. One of the guns was later used in the 1963 killing of the senior Hartack by his girlfriend (Nancy Lang collection).

The sisters seldom spoke anymore, and their brother didn't speak to them, either. The sisters didn't even speak when their brother died in 2007.[20]

When their father died, Dolly was thirty-three, Bill was thirty and Maxine was twenty-three. They all came to Charles Town for the funeral. Services were held at the St. James Catholic Church, and the burial took place at the Catholic cemetery in Harpers Ferry, West Virginia. Besides his children, William Hartack Sr.'s survivors included five sisters, three brothers and three grandchildren. In the early 1980s, Maxine asked her brother if they could move their mother's remains to Harpers Ferry, since there was room next to their father's grave. Hartack spent $10,000 to move his mother.[21]

Frances Brant pleaded not guilty to the reduced charge of involuntary manslaughter. She had left a pony, her riding horse, at the Hartack farm. Maxine knew whose horse it was. After a couple of weeks, she called Brant, who had posted bail. "You better come get your horse," Maxine said. "This is the only call I'm going to make."

On August 8, less than two months after her father's death, Maxine gave birth to a daughter.

In early fall, Frances Brant's trial began. The prosecutor for Jefferson County was John C. Skinner Sr. Skinner's son, who was a law student at West Virginia University, had gone to high school with Maxine.

In the court room, Maxine sat in the first row, directly behind Frances Brant and her attorney. She was so close she could have reached out and touched them. Maxine stared at Brant throughout the proceedings. She had also gone over to her father's home and torn to shreds the clothes Brant had left in the closet.[22]

The first morning of the trial didn't go well for the defendant. As it turned out, that would be the only morning. After lunch, Brant's attorney told the judge that his client wanted to change her plea to guilty of manslaughter. The judge huddled with the attorneys in his chambers, came out a little later and sent the jury home. On October 15, Frances Clara Brant was given a one- to five-year sentence in the state penitentiary.[23]

4

Goggles Optional

At the time of their father's murder, in June 1963, Bill Hartack's sisters had not seen their brother for a long time. Maxine Hartack, seven years younger than her brother, had married the jockey Joe French, ten years her senior, and Bill didn't approve. Hartack had promised Maxine that he would pay her way through college, and he was disappointed when she dropped out of the University of Miami after two years. Bill Hartack had been a good student. His high school principal once remarked that he had only seen a few students who could surpass Hartack's need to achieve. Hartack couldn't afford college, but it would have been a feather in his cap had Maxine earned her degree.[1] Evelyn, his other sister (also known as Dolly), was a year older than Bill. She said there were no jobs to speak of in Pennsylvania, so she moved away, took work in Cleveland, married a metallurgist and relocated to California.[2]

"I once wrote to Bill, asking him what I had done for him to shut me out," Maxine said. "I told him I could not think of one thing that would make him treat me like that. He never answered. People told me he probably never got the letter. But when he died [in 2007], the letter was found among his possessions. It had been opened. So it just sat there, for many, many years, and he chose not to answer it."

In late June 1963, the three siblings were together for a couple of days in Charles Town, West Virginia, near where their father, fatally shot by the woman he had been living with, was being buried. It was the first time they had been together since Bill became a jockey, and the last time the three of them would be in one another's presence.[3]

Dolly Hartack Ferguson had come from Manhattan Beach, California, where she lived because of her husband's work. She lived forty miles from the Santa Anita track, where her brother sometimes rode. The day their father was buried, she and Bill—whom she still called "Sonny"—exchanged phone numbers. He never called.[4]

For two days, Maxine tried to get Bill to sit down and discuss family business. There was a large farm that their father had left behind, as well as other estate issues that were up in the air. But Bill parried most of Maxine's questions. The funeral was scheduled for the third day, and Bill would be leaving town on the fourth. An angry, frustrated Maxine went to her brother's motel room and pounded on the locked door. He knew who was outside, but he refused to answer. Maxine then went to the front desk, telling the motel manager that she had an emergency, and he went to Hartack's room with the key. When Hartack finally appeared, Maxine said, "Look, Bill, I know you don't like me anymore, and I don't know why. But we need to talk about some things. We need to talk alone. You've got no right to avoid this, and make things difficult for me." They agreed to meet, just the two of them, at a restaurant later in the day.[5]

Hartack had come to Charles Town with a small entourage, which included George Stidham, who had ridden against him in West Virginia during his salad days and had become his business manager years later. It wasn't discernible at the time, but 1963 was the start of a downward swing that would lead to the end of Hartack's career in the United States eleven years later. In 1963, the final two of Hartack's five Kentucky Derby wins were still ahead of him, but 1962 was the last year in which he would win two hundred or more races.[6]

After Hartack and Maxine sat down at a restaurant following their father's funeral, Maxine never saw him or spoke to him again. She watched on television as Hartack won the 1964 Derby with Northern Dancer and the 1969 Derby with Majestic Prince.

The year after the funeral, Hartack was riding at Santa Anita. His sister Dolly called him, and he invited her to the track. Between races, outside the jockeys' room, they spoke briefly.

After Bill went inside to prepare for an upcoming race, a few fans came up to Dolly. "He was so polite to you!" one of them said. "He's usually not like that. He's usually not very friendly."

"I'm his sister," Dolly told them.

Dolly said that it was difficult that day to speak to Bill alone, to exchange some intimate family thoughts. She referred to George Stidham and a few others. "They stuck to him like glue," she said.

Dolly gave him her phone number for the second time, but he never called. In the forty or so years that followed, up until his death, she never heard from him again.[7]

* * *

Bill Hartack graduated from Blacklick Township High School in June 1950. There were thirty-four in the class, only eleven of them boys. For the class photo, eight girls were seated in the front row, with Hartack, the only boy, seated on the far left, his hands folded in his lap. This was the boy they teased by calling him "Termite." He was easily the smallest student in his row.[8]

He didn't like to study and was enough of a pest that teachers sent him to the principal's office several times, but he still finished in the upper third of the class. His solid marks were remarkable, for he was practically working full-time at the family farm. Sometimes he wouldn't finish his chores until 10 o'clock at night. In the subjects that he resisted, such as English and history, he barely got by, but in mathematics, biology, physics and general science he did quite well.[9]

Hartack didn't turn eighteen until December 9, when he would have been old enough to work at the Johnstown plant of Bethlehem Steel. And that's where he might have wound up if Andy Bruno hadn't entered his life.[10]

Bruno, well connected to the United Mine Workers of America, held a federal post in Washington, D.C., thanks to his association with John Torquato Sr. Torquato, since the end of World War II, singlehandedly ran the Democratic political machine in Cambria County, where Bill Hartack's grandfather once had a large farm. Torquato's stranglehold ended in the late 1970s, when he was convicted on thirty-one counts of extortion and conspiracy in connection with forcing state contractors to pay kickbacks.[11]

By 1950, Bruno might have been ahead of the political pundits when he surmised that

Harry Truman's presidential term, which ran through 1952, was going to be his last.[12] Actually, Truman flirted with running again, but when he was routed in the early New Hampshire primary, that cleared the way for Dwight Eisenhower and the Republicans.[13]

Bruno was right—with the Democrats no longer in power, he lost his job in D.C., but he had already been sniffing around Charles Town Race Track for work. For one thing, Bruno liked the races; he would show up at Charles Town on a regular basis, usually at least twice a week. By many accounts, it was an expensive pastime. Bruno was terrible as a handicapper and lost many more bets than he won. But he got to know some of the jockeys' agents at the track and thought that might not be a bad way to go.

"One thing about a jocks agent," Bruno once said, "is that there's no overhead. All you need is a pencil and a condition book." A condition book is a periodic publication out of a track's racing secretary's office that lists, several days in advance, the day-by-day schedule of races and what type of horses might be eligible for each event. Even in the 1950s, there were some jockeys' agents, who hobnobbed with the trainers in securing the riders' mounts, earning 20 percent of what their jockeys raked in.

Eventually, Andy Bruno indeed became a jockeys' agent. He began patrolling the backstretch at Charles Town, trying to sign up a rider or two.

One day over the Thanksgiving weekend, Bruno was talking with Arnold Smorto, a Cambria County attorney who worked with the mine workers' union, and another union official, Mike De Gretto. "There's a kid around Balsano [north of Johnstown, Pennsylvania] who's the right size for a jockey," Smorto said. "His old man's in the mines. The father gave the kid a horse, an old mare, a few years ago. He's been riding that mare up and down those hills ever since."

"What's his name?" Bruno asked.

"Hartack," Smorto told him. "They're both William Hartack. Junior and senior."

"Hartack," Bruno said. "That's a funny name."

"It's not their real name," Smorto said. "The mother, who got killed in a car smashup, changed it from Hartuk to Hartack. The father's from Czechoslovakia, came here with his parents when he was two years old. If the kid's anything like the old man, you might be all right. The old man knows nothing but hard work. He's very proud. He wears his pride on his sleeve."

"Remember hard tack?"[14] Bruno asked. "They make hard tack anymore?"[15]

"I think they do," Smorto said, "only they call it a different name now. But that's this kid's name. Hardtack without the 'd.' William Hartack."

Bruno wrote William Hartack Sr. a letter. He told him that he was a jockeys' agent at Charles Town, that Smorto and De Gretto were his friends, and that they thought young Bill might make a rider if he got the chance.

At the time, the senior Hartack was trying to keep his son from following him into the coal mines. When he told his son about Bruno's letter, Hartack said that it had never entered his mind that he could become a jockey, even though he was the right size.[16]

Balsano didn't have a bus depot; passengers had to stand by the road and flag the bus down. The bus to Charles Town made similar stops on the outskirts of small towns along the way—Claysburg, Everett, Mercersburg and Hancock. The 155-mile trip took almost four hours.

A couple of weeks before Hartack's arrival, Bruno told one of the trainers at Charles

Town, Norman "Junie" Corbin, that he had a jockey prospect coming in.[17] Corbin was a regular on the West Virginia half-mile racing circuit (so named because the tracks were, if not a half-mile, no larger in circumference than five or six furlongs). The tracks included Charles Town, Wheeling Downs and Waterford Park. Purses were small, hardly enough to sustain a racing stable, and in order to make a living Corbin and other trainers needed to bet on the races. Without cashing a bet now and again, many of them would have gone out of business.[18] Honesty was not always part of the equation. Jockeys' fees, for the most part, were below the standard of living. "There are some riders at those tracks," a jaded bettor said, "who would run a horse backwards if you gave them forty dollars."[19]

Once around the oval at Charles Town was six furlongs, which is three-quarters of a mile. The track was built in 1932, during the Depression, and it would have gone belly-up after its first two years of operation, but a Baltimore investor, Albert Jones Boyle, plowed $160,000 of his own money and convinced state regulators that they should keep it open. The track raced in the wintertime, when there was no competition. But operators didn't

Composite winner's circle photo, with the top half showing Howard Craig riding War Belle to victory at Ascot Park in Akron, Ohio, on July 18, 1952—three months before Hartack rode in his first race. The bottom half, featuring the winner's circle, left to right: trainer Norman "Junie" Corbin; Hartack; Alkie Darlington, another aspiring jockey; an unidentified groom; and Howard Craig (Alkie Darlington collection).

get around to fully enclosing the stands until 1960. For a time, customers were kept warm by steel drums that were filled with searing coke under the stands. Good horses seldom found their way to Charles Town. The biggest historical event came in 1969, when Barbara Jo Rubin became the first woman to ride the winner of a parimutuel race in the United States.[20]

Junie Corbin was in his early thirties. No one called him Norman, even though that was the name listed in the track programs. He was a savvy horseman who knew what made horses tick. Hartack couldn't have begun with a better teacher. The tall, hawk-nosed Corbin was a quiet man, considered fair, someone who only expected a hard day's work out of his stablehands. His exercise riders came and went, and he was regularly reeducating recruits who showed up at the barn. Corbin was also a loyal family man, married with three children. He treated some of his help like they were an extension of that family, and Hartack would say later that he became closer to Corbin than he ever did to his father.

Ironically, after setting up Hartack's arrival weeks ahead of time, Andy Bruno disappeared. "Where's Bruno?" Corbin said one day. "He's never around when you want him. I got this kid coming in for a job, and I can't find Bruno."

Corbin turned to Joe Verrone, another fledgling jockeys' agent who was starting a career that would last sixty years. Verrone looked like a jockey; he stood barely five feet tall. Patsy Cline, the country music singer, once asked him to be her agent when she was just coming out of Winchester, Virginia. Verrone knew the race track, but he didn't know music. "We'd go broke together," he told Cline.

When Hartack's bus rolled into Charles Town, Verrone was there to meet him. Hartack was carrying a small duffel bag and had no money in his pocket. Verrone didn't know it, but all that Hartack owned was in that bag.

"He was a nice-looking boy," Verrone recalled, "but he had terrible teeth in front. He needed a dentist real bad."

A few weeks later, Verrone made an appointment with Steve Bondy, a dentist in Charles Town. Bondy's office was on the ninth floor of the tallest building in town. All the way up in the elevator, Hartack moaned about how he didn't want to be there. When they got out, Hartack pushed the "down" button, got back in, and left Verrone standing at the door to Bondy's office. Much later, after he started earning money for winning races, Hartack made his own dental appointment and got his teeth fixed.

From the bus stop, Verrone took Hartack over to a rooming house in town where Charles "Pappy" Wright and L.T. McKnight were staying. Wright was Corbin's stable foreman, McKnight one of his exercise riders.[21] Corbin also employed Alkie Darlington, a 15-year-old local boy who told everybody that he was older. Darlington mucked stalls, hot-walked horses after their morning exercises, and cleaned tack before he moved up to galloping horses. Corbin, from what he had heard of Hartack, envisioned him progressing the same way within the barn.

Early the next morning, Hartack bundled up to protect himself from the winter cold, walked several blocks from the rooming house to the track and introduced himself to Corbin at the barn. Corbin told him to watch what everybody was doing and ask any questions that popped into his head. Before long, it was time to go to the races. Charles Town, years away from installing lights, was a daytime racing operation.[22]

The first race Hartack saw, on a frozen track that denied the runners any traction, there was a terrifying spill involving six horses. A horse in the lead snapped his leg and fell, and the chain reaction resulted in five other horses going down. Animals and jockeys were strewn across the track.

Hartack watched in horror from the grandstand. He shuddered at the thought of making a livelihood in such a dangerous profession. "Mr. Corbin," he said, "does this happen every day?"

Two of the horses were so badly injured that they had to be destroyed. Several jockeys were removed from the track in an ambulance; one of them suffered brain damage and had to have a steel plate inserted in his head. The rest of the day's races were canceled. One of the more fortunate jockeys was Nick Shuk, who came away with only bumps and bruises. Shuk went on to ride for thirty more years and won more than 2,600 races.

Hartack told himself on the spot that he would never become a jockey. He thought that if he stayed at the race track, it would only be as an exercise rider. That was the safe way to go. In the mornings, a jockey was just responsible for the horse he was riding, and he didn't have to worry about other horses and riders getting in the way.

At the start, Corbin paid Hartack no salary. Corbin paid for the room that Hartack shared with Wright and McKnight, bought him some clothes, and gave him a small amount of spending money. Hartack didn't complain. At the end of week, he would have $10 or $20, all of his bills were paid, and he had a roof over his head. He was pocketing more money than he had ever seen in his life.

Corbin started off Hartack with walking horses. They skipped a step—newcomers to the track usually groom the horses. But Corbin wanted Hartack to get a feel for these powerful animals. Hartack was good at taking instructions, and right away Corbin told him what he was looking for in a jockey.[23]

"One of these days, we'll let you get on a horse," Corbin said. "You've got to be on your toes. If you do nothing else, be on your toes. Some horses will try to lug in on you, some might lug out. Some horses will be greener than others, especially the younger ones. You get a green horse, you don't know what they're liable to do. When you get on a horse in the gate, it's important they stand calmly for you. Keep the starter informed. He'll usually give you some extra time if you let him know the horse isn't standing right. Horses need to change leads, by shifting weight from one side to the other, when they go into turns. You can get them to do this with a tap of the whip if they won't do it by themselves. A horse doesn't [change lead feet], you ain't got much of a chance, son."

The first time Hartack got in the saddle, the horse ran off with him. The next time, the horse went to his knees and almost threw Hartack, head-first.

"What'll I do, Junie?" he shouted. (Corbin had told the young man that he wasn't old enough to be called "Mr. Corbin.")

Corbin laughed. "You figure it out."

Hartack was so green that the first time he observed a string of Corbin's horses walking around the shedrow, he didn't realize they were the same half-dozen horses going in a continuous circle. "Boy, Junie, you sure got a lot of horses," Hartack said.

One morning, Pappy Wright—no one called him Charles—put Hartack on an ornery young horse for a swing around the shedrow.

"We'll never see him again," Wright said.

But in a couple of minutes, the horse had completed the circuit, and as he and Hartack came around the final corner, heading in Wright's direction, the animal seemed calm and actually enjoying himself. Wright was impressed. So was Corbin.

"I knew right away," Corbin said after Hartack had made the big-time. "I knew after a week. He had nerve and strong hands. Tell him something once and he'd learn it."

Hartack began to exercise horses. That's all he wanted to do. The money was good, compared to what he had grown up with, and he couldn't shake the memory of that massive spill in which horses died and jockeys were seriously injured. But Corbin kept telling him that he could be a successful jockey.

Corbin owned a few of the horses he trained, and those were the ones Hartack tried to ride first in the mornings. One of them, a filly, fell near the barn, and Hartack fell on top of her, landing on her head. The frightened horse began kicking, but she couldn't get up. Hartack yelled for help. Corbin, four barns away, came running and got the filly to her feet.

Another Corbin filly was due to go to the track for a gallop, and Wright told Hartack to get on her and see what he could do. Wright warned Hartack that the filly was difficult, but he told him to give her her head and not fight her. Hartack followed the instructions, and the filly gave him no trouble for a quarter of a mile. But when they reached the part of the track where the finish line was located, she took off like a rocket for the clubhouse turn. Hartack was tempted to try pulling her up, but that would mess up the whole exercise.

Corbin had pulled into a parking lot where there was a view of the track, and his jaw dropped when he saw this inexperienced rider on one of his stock, unable to control her. Corbin drove straight to his barn, and when Hartack, Wright and the filly returned, he was on his stable pony, waiting for them.

"You think you're smart, don't you?" Corbin said before Hartack dismounted.

"Well, sir, I must say that that was fun," Hartack said.

Corbin sloughed off the incident, and because he still thought there was some innate talent in this five-foot-four, hundred-pound beginner, he was ready to give Hartack another chance. He told another of his exercise riders, Alkie Darlington, that he would share some of his duties with Hartack.

Darlington, slightly younger than Hartack, was a local boy who lived with his parents on Third Avenue, less than a mile from the Charles Town track. He had started working during the summers for Corbin in 1948, when he was thirteen. He was underage, but nobody bothered to check. For several months in 1951, Hartack and Darlington shared a bedroom at his parents' home. In the mornings, they got up early and walked together to the track. Later, Hartack moved into a second-floor apartment with Pappy Wright, above Bill Hennessey's jewelry store.

Corbin paid Hartack $100 a month and threw in his room and board. In ten-dollar increments, he gave Hartack a meal ticket that could be used in the track kitchen, where the regulars said the food was the best in all of Charles Town. Hartack loved hotdogs, and, unlike some riders at the track, he could eat a plateful without gaining weight. One place he liked was Coney Island, where they poured firehouse chili over the sandwiches. Another place was Pete's, on West Washington Avenue. Pete's was fronted by a large plate-glass window; passersby would look in and see the hotdogs and hamburgers sizzling on the grill. The smell was so tantalizing that Hartack seldom walked by without giving in to temptation.[24]

When the Charles Town meet ended, Corbin's stable would move on to Waterford Park and Wheeling Downs in West Virginia, and Randall Park near Cleveland. At Wheeling, Corbin put his crew up at the ten-story Hotel Windsor, built in 1815. Some of the rooms looked down on the Ohio River, which was literally just across Water Street. Darlington and Hartack shared a room.[25]

In 2013, Darlington was working at Charles Town as a morning clocker and night-time entry clerk, besides hosting a weekly half-hour racing show out of Martinsburg, West Virginia. "We got along like brothers," he said. "Neither one of us was riding races yet, but when Bill went to the track, he paid attention to every race. In the mornings, when he got on a horse, he was all business. He would be focused on that horse and nothing else. He was a natural. You could see that he was going to hit it big someday."

In 1994, Alkie Darlington was doing a racing interview show for a radio station in Aiken, South Carolina. Hartack was working as a steward at the Fair Grounds in New Orleans, and Darlington, once like a brother, called him to come on the show.

"You know how it is, Alkie," Hartack said. "I don't care for the media."

"But I'm not the media," Darlington said. "This is Alkie."

There was a pause on the other end of the line.

"OK," Hartack said. "I'll do it." He gave Darlington a long, engaging interview.[26]

"Has success spoiled Hartack?" his good friend, Joe Hirsch of the *Daily Racing Form*, once asked. "Not in the sense of giving him a swelled head; Bill is breezy, but not cocky. However, he does indulge himself in the vilest of black moods during which he refuses to speak to close friends, scowls and glowers at almost everyone and is generally a trial to his intimates."[27]

It was Christmas 1951, and Hartack, just turned nineteen, was doing a high-wire act with two girlfriends around Charles Town. Hartack hated Christmas, because his mother had died on that day, but he still went over to Johnstown, and at Penn Traffic, the large department store, he bought jewelry for one girl and a winter coat for the other. But he had miscalculated, and one morning at the track he saw Joe Verrone, the jockeys' agent.

"I got this coat that I don't know what to do with," Hartack told Verrone. "I got it for somebody and it's too small."

"Take it back," Verrone said. "They'll let you exchange it."

"You know," Hartack said, "I'll bet it would be just right for Rose [Verrone's wife]. She need a coat?"

"Don't do that," Verrone said. "Just take it back."

"I got it in my room," Hartack said. "I'll give it to you tomorrow."[28]

He wasn't particularly close to his father, and the first year he was away from home, there were no letters, no phone calls exchanged between them. It was as though one was trying to see how long the other would go before touching base. But in 1956, when Hartack won 357 races, his take-home pay, before taxes and his agent's commission, was more than $200,000. He bought a 175-acre farm in the Charles Town area, called his father and said, "Pack your shirt. I'm taking you out of the mines. I just bought a farm, and you're gonna run it."[29]

In years gone by, however, they weren't so cordial. Hartack's father wasn't sure where his son had landed after he boarded that bus in Balsano during the winter of 1950. But Hartack Sr. called around and drove over to Charles Town unannounced.

"I come down to take you home," he said.

"What are you talking about?" Hartack asked.

"You might as well be home, what you're doing here."

"You don't even know that."

"I know that this isn't much of a life. Do you win any races?"

"I haven't even rode in any. I don't need to. I'm doing all right doing what I'm doing."

"Where you been, this whole year?"

"I never wrote a letter in my life, and you ain't got a phone, so what am I supposed to do?"

"We got a phone. If you'd take the time, you'd know we got a phone now."

"Well, nobody told me."

"Come on back with me."

"Dad, you can take me home if you want to. I would need you to sign my contract if I ever decided to ride, anyway. But if you took me home, the first time you turned your back, I'm just going to leave again. So the only thing we can do is work out something between us. I promise to write once in a while. I like this job. The horses are fun, and I'm getting to know what I'm doing. I don't know how long I'm going to like it, but right now everything is fine."

His father accepted this. He stayed in Charles Town for a couple of days, was introduced to Junie Corbin at the track and liked him. Corbin told Hartack Sr. that his son might have a bright future riding horses. The father went home satisfied that his son wasn't wasting his time.[30]

A year later, the winter of 1951, Corbin's stable hit hard times. Most of his horses were claimers—horses that ran in claiming races. For a prearranged fee (usually nothing much), a rival trainer could claim—or buy—them if they showed promise. As a result, Corbin was down to just a few horses, and he couldn't afford to claim anybody else's. He had no need for both Hartack and Alkie Darlington as exercise riders. Hartack heard that a stable in Florida was looking for help. He moved on to Tropical Park in Miami and started working for Virginia McKenney, who had a farm in Manassas, Virginia, and raced horses in Florida as well as West Virginia.

Hartack said that while working with the McKenney horses, through sheer volume he was able to hone skills that would serve him well once that day came when he began riding races.

"I started breaking a lot of horses out of the gate," Hartack said. "Mrs. McKenney had horses that were of every size and description. Some were heavy-headed. You had to keep yanking on them. There were horses that lugged in toward the rail, others that had a tendency to bear out. Some bucked. There were some that wheeled [stopped in their tracks and tried to turn around]. None of them were perfect. They all had at least one trait that needed to be dealt with. But it was good experience. I was dealing with traits that I'd come across hundreds of times after I started riding races."

McKenney encouraged young riders like Hartack, but she would not brook any of them striking her horses with a whip.[31] Hartack avoided the whip to satisfy the situation, but later on he became what is known in the trade as a very good whip rider. With some trainers, that was a plus, but there were others—John Nerud of Tartan Farms, for one—who thought that he punished his mounts excessively.

"There were two reasons I didn't use Hartack," Nerud said. "One, if you gave him instructions in the paddock, he didn't pay attention much. You were by and large wasting your breath. He was going to ride the horse the way he wanted to. Two, after a race, his horse came back raw, almost bleeding, on its backside."[32]

Hartack was a natural lefthander—he wrote and did almost everything from the left side—and he rarely whipped horses with his right hand. An analysis of his five Kentucky Derby wins shows that he never hit any of those horses righthanded.[33]

Phil Georgeff was a Chicago institution. According to the *Guinness Book of World Records*, he called more than ninety-six thousand races, most of them at Chicago-area tracks.

"I called thousands of Hartack races from 1959 onward," Georgeff said. "I called his three-thousandth win on a horse called Big Steve at Arlington Park in 1962. Yet I can't recall him ever hitting a horse with his right hand. He must have, but I just can't remember when. He revolutionized race-riding with a formidable left-sided whip. I think he surprised many horses, who were used to being hit righthanded, and they responded."[34]

Hartack thought it was an advantage to hit from the left side. "There are more races lost because a rider can't hit lefthanded," he once said. "The horses run to the left, and they're crowded in the direction of the rail to save ground. So when you're on the inside, and there's a horse crowding you from your outside, there's not room to hit him righthanded much of the time. If the track were run the opposite way, the way most of the tracks are in England, the righthanded rider would have the greatest advantage. I use my right hand only when a horse is trying to run out. I'm not that good with my right hand, but what I can do that way is sufficient."[35]

When the McKenney horses left Florida and returned to Charles Town after the winter of 1951–1952, Hartack was fired.

"You've been touting my horses to bettors," Virginia McKenney told him.

Hartack was crushed. "That's not so, Mrs. McKenney. I would never do that. I've never done it once."

"Well, this is what I've been hearing and what I believe," she said. "I'm going to hire somebody to replace you."[36]

Around that time, Hartack admitted that he successfully bet some of his own horses. Jockeys are prohibited from betting rival horses in races. Later in his career, Hartack didn't bet at all. Gary Condra, a good friend for the last fifty years of Hartack's life (he buried him in the Condra family plot in Missouri), was a race-track dilettante. When Condra asked Hartack to help him handicap and bet horses, he was told, "Stay away from it. You can't beat 'em over the long haul. There are too many ways to lose a race."[37]

Junie Corbin's stable was making a comeback, so Hartack, having been dismissed by the McKenney outfit, went back to the trainer who had introduced him to the game. Hartack accompanied the Corbin horses to Randall Park near Cleveland. Corbin persisted in trying to get him to ride races.

"You gallop a horse pretty good," Corbin said. "Don't you think you're ready?"

"I don't know anything about it," Hartack said. "I don't want to ride."

After Randall's season ended, they went back to Waterford Park, where Corbin suggested that Hartack go home and get his father to sign his riding contract, just in case. Just to shut up Corbin, Hartack borrowed the trainer's two-year-old Oldsmobile 98 and drove to Balsano, where his father signed a standard jockey's contract, calling for a salary of $25 a week, plus room and board.[38]

"These contracts were like slave labor," said Joe Verrone, the jockeys' agent. "Young jocks were scared to death that they might get dumped after they signed a contract, and nobody else would want them. It was a one-way street. The trainers could break the contract, but if the riders wanted to get out of it, they risked getting in trouble with the stewards." If the trainer didn't have a horse in a race, a jockey under contract would need permission to ride for another stable.[39]

Driving back from Balsano, Hartack stopped at a diner and bought a Pittsburgh newspaper. He took a stool at the counter, ordered a milkshake and scanned the sports section for the racing entries the next day at Waterford Park. He wanted to know if Corbin was running anything. And there, in small type, under the listing of horses for the first race, it read, "6 furlongs, Purse $1,200, Claiming price, $2,000. Hal's Play (W. Hartack) 108."[40]

Hartack almost knocked over his milkshake. He brought the newspaper closer to his face, to make sure it said what he thought it said.

"Jesus," Hartack said.

The waitress thought he had called for her. "Can I get you something else?" she asked.

"No," he said vacantly. "No. I gotta get going. I gotta get out of there."

Hal's Play was one of Corbin's horses, all right—a 5-year-old gelding who had trouble winning. Hartack had been on his back many times in the mornings.

For an instant, Hartack thought that Corbin was having trouble finding a rider for the horse and just listed his name before he could line up somebody else for the race. But that didn't make any sense. In those days, trainers weren't required to list a jockey at entry time. It was not uncommon to see "no boy" next to a horse's name in the entries. If Corbin hadn't secured a jockey, all he had to do was tell the entry clerk to put down "no boy."

Hartack got to Corbin's house in Charles Town around 10 p.m. He knew the trainer would be asleep, but that didn't make any difference.

Corbin came to the door in a nightshirt. Hartack didn't wait to get inside to start talking.

"You can't do this to me," he said.

"You'll be all right," Corbin told him. "Get the feel of a race under you, and see if you like it."

"You got to scratch the horse. I'm not going to ride him."

"Yes, you are. The stewards at Waterford are tough. They won't let you off. You don't want to start off by getting fined, do you?"

"I don't have any tack. This is crazy."

Corbin told him that he had bought him a saddle and a fancy set of riding boots, and he had called a valet in the Waterford jockeys' room who would take care of him.

"My father didn't sign the contract," Hartack said, lying through his teeth.

Corbin went out to the car, got Hartack's suitcase, and rooted through it. He found the contract, signed and legal.

"Come on, son," he said. "This is a kind horse. You're not going to win, but you'll thank me for the experience."

The day was a Saturday, October 11, 1952. A few minutes before 2 o'clock, Hartack left the jockeys' room. He spotted Corbin in the small Waterford paddock.

"I don't know what the hell to do," Hartack said.

"We're 65 to 1," Corbin said. "Nobody's expecting too much. Just let the horse take you where he wants to go. Stay off the rail and you won't get hurt."[41]

Waterford, later to be known as Mountaineer Park when the slot machines came to town and it became an all-purpose gambling establishment, drew big crowds on weekends. The track was an easy hour's drive from Pittsburgh, and it also was handy for Clevelanders. This day, there were more than eight thousand on hand.[42]

"I was petrified," Hartack said later. "I forgot to pull my goggles down. The dirt hit me in the face and nearly blinded me."[43]

Hal's Play was never in contention and finished eighth. The race was won by Orthopedic, with F.D. Rivera riding. George Stidham, who rode the horse that finished sixth, would become a long-time business manager for Hartack in years to come.[44]

Corbin was waiting when Hartack pulled up Hal's Play and brought him back to the unsaddling area.

"You only got beat about three lengths," Corbin said.

"It looked more like about six to me," Hartack said.[45]

The next day, Corbin ran a couple of horses with other jockeys riding, and Hartack figured he had given up on making a jockey out of him. But the day after that, Corbin named Hartack to ride War Belle, a 6-year-old mare who was 90–1. Hartack made the same mistake with the goggles, and he finished seventh as Stidham's mount won the race at 22–1.[46]

On Tuesday, October 14, Corbin named Hartack again, this time on a 5-year-old gelding, Nickleby, who actually had a chance to win. Corbin owned Nickleby. When he had bought a couple of fillies from somebody in Cleveland, the seller also wanted him to take Nickleby for an extra hundred dollars.

"He don't look like much," Corbin had said at the time.

"He's related to Man o' War," the seller said.

"I don't care if his daddy was Pegasus, he still don't look like much."

"Take him," the seller said. "For a hundred bucks, you can use him as a stable pony."

"It'll cost a hundred bucks a month just to feed him," Corbin said. But he thought both of the fillies had promise and was worried that the guy wouldn't sell them unless he also took Nickleby.

"I'll take him," Corbin finally said.

He ran Nickleby twice at the Cranwood track in Cleveland, without success. "He wasn't a bad horse," said Alkie Darlington, who rode him both times. "I was inexperienced. I was the one that got him beat."[47]

Nickleby's race with Hartack on October 14 was the seventh on an eight-race card. For Hartack, the wait in the jockeys' room was interminable.

"Loan me a pack of cigs," he said to Corbin early in the day. "I'll need 'em." Corbin was used to loaning Hartack cigarettes, but usually it was one at a time.

About an hour before post time, Hartack was sitting on a bench in the jockeys' room, studying the past performances of the other horses in the race. He had looked at the sheet so much that it seemed as though his blue eyes were burning a hole through the page. Another jockey, Sam Palumbo, walked by. He had ridden Nickleby a while back, finishing second with him.

"That horse you got can really run," Palumbo said. He was trying to be friendly, easing the tension for Hartack.

"Don't tell me that," Hartack said. "It's bad enough as it is. You tell me that, and everybody will expect too much."

Hartack looked at the previous races of Palumbo's horse. He saw how that horse liked to run close to the lead, the opposite of Nickleby's running style. Hartack figured if he followed Palumbo's horse, he would be all right. Just stay close to Palumbo and then let Nickleby loose when it was time to make a move.

Nickleby was breaking from the outside post in a twelve-horse field. The race was a mile and an eighth, which would give Hartack plenty of time to gain position.

In the paddock, Corbin tried to calm Hartack down. "Don't worry about the break," he said. "Just let this horse settle. Save some ground. This horse will pick it up."[48]

For such a cheap race—a $1,200 purse, with $708 going to the winner—there were some established jockeys riding against Hartack. George Stidham was one; Tommy Barrow was another.[49]

The horses cleared the walking ring and filed on to the track. There was hardly a titter. This was a field of cheap claiming horses that hardly inspired applause. Any of them could be bought for $2,000.[50]

Indeed, Nickleby was kin to Man o' War, one of racing's greatest horses and considered by many polls the greatest horse who ever ran. Man o' War only lost once; he was beaten by the aptly named Upset in a race at Saratoga.[51] But Man o' War's genes must have skipped before they reached Nickleby. Nickleby's dam, Marching Along, was a daughter of Man o' War. But Nickleby's sire, Big Pebble, was an obscure stallion.

Hartack sat upright on Nickleby's back as the horse was led into his stall in the starting gate by one of the assistant starters. Hartack was surprised that his mount was so mannerly, but Nickleby was a veteran campaigner, not intimidated by his cramped surroundings. Hartack, however, had only been inside a gate in the mornings, and twice for races in recent days. In this case, it was the man, not the horse, who was liable to be spooked.

Nickleby having drawn the outside post, he was the last horse to be loaded. As soon as the half-door slammed behind him, the official starter, standing on a platform just on the infield side of the inner rail, pressed a button; the panels in front of the horses promptly opened, and the field was on its way. Nickleby broke alertly, ahead of the horses immediately to his inside, and Hartack was able to ease him to the left. As they headed for the clubhouse turn, Nickleby was in good position, not far from the leaders and about five horse paths from the rail. Going down the backside, Hartack nudged him, and he moved past the horses in front of him without extending himself. From there, he was never headed. "[He] held on safely to the end," the *Daily Racing Form*'s chart footnotes read.

Nickleby beat Rout E Four, the second-place horse, by a length and a half, running a mile and an eighth in 1:54 3/5. He was so full of run that Hartack didn't have to use his whip. The fourth choice in the betting, Nickleby paid $18.40 for a $2 win bet. The favored Sweep Clean, who was ridden by Barrow, finished third, two lengths behind Nickleby.

For the third straight race, Hartack forgot to pull down his goggles. He remembered a sixteenth of a mile from home, and by then his face was caked with dirt, his eyes almost blinded.[52]

There would be 21,532 more races, and 4,271 more winner's circle photos, to come.[53]

5

Leaky Roofs

Trainers at Waterford Park were not lining up at Bill Hartack's door after he won his first race, with only his third mount, at the West Virginia track in October 1952. It was all Hartack could do to stay aboard Nickleby, his first winner. When the veteran George Stidham, another of the riders in the race, came into the jockeys' room afterward, one of his fellow riders reminded him of a promise that he had made several days before.

"Damn right," Stidham said. He dropped his whip to the floor and threw down his cap. He ripped off his colors and added them to the pile of clothes. Then he took off his boots and heaped them on top. He picked up the stack and stuffed everything into the locker that had his name taped over it.

"If I can't beat a kid who rides that bad, I shouldn't be out there," Stidham declared. "I'll say it again. He looks pretty bad on a horse. He looks like it's all he can do, just to stay on. I haven't seen him use his right hand with the whip yet."[1]

Stuffing his riding things in the locker was only a *beau geste*, and Stidham quickly reneged. He was only five years older than Hartack, and he still had some races to ride. They soon became fast friends, and by the 1960s Stidham was retired from the saddle and had become Hartack's *aide de camp*. Wherever Hartack went, Stidham was at his side, making travel arrangements, driving him to airports, and otherwise tending to the needs of one of the country's most successful riders. Stidham was also a shield for those in the prying press corps who tried to invade Hartack's private life.

Corbin wasn't surprised by Hartack's first win. He was a young man who paid attention in the mornings. Additionally, he was always asking questions. He accepted criticism willingly, using it as part of the learning process. But other West Virginia trainers were unimpressed. Hartack's lumpy riding style was a put-off. The horsemen at Waterford Park wanted to see more.[2]

The Waterford Park meeting lasted twenty-four days, and by the end Hartack had ridden in thirty-three races, a little more than one a day. He won seven of those races, which left him tied for fourth place in the standings. George Stidham was on top with twenty-two wins. Hartack won two races in the same day, with the quick return of Nickleby and another horse named Meringue, and on the final day of the meet, he rode in every race on the card. This was a departure from the early days of the meet; trainers other than Corbin were now sending horses Hartack's way.[3]

Riding in the last eleven weeks of 1952, Hartack ended up with 172 rides and 36 wins. Fifteen mounts a week is not enough to make a living, but the bright side was that Hartack won with 21 percent of the few mounts he had, a very good percentage for a jockey. Hartack's percentage for his entire career, not counting his six seasons in Hong Kong from 1974 to 1980, came to .198.

"It looked like my boss [Corbin] was going to keep riding me, and I couldn't let him down," Hartack said at the end of 1952. "I couldn't let him down. He put everything on the line for me, and he taught me everything. He instilled in me the kind of confidence that would help any young jockey who was starting to ride. He really didn't have to tell me when I made a mistake, I was smart enough to know that on my own. He would wait and beat around the bush to see if I would admit to my own mistakes. Sometimes he wouldn't even let me take credit—if that is the word—for a mistake. He'd say, 'Yeah, but you couldn't help it,' trying to make me feel good, I guess. He knew how to handle a young kid and get the best out of him. All I know is that, thanks to Junie, I did everything in my power to be good."[4]

Corbin emphasized that the shortest way around the track is to keep your horse close to the rail. He also stressed honesty—not a hot commodity at the third-rate tracks of the era. He told Hartack that if he gave his best on every horse he rode, no matter where he finished, no one would have a legitimate complaint. Hartack promised Corbin that he'd never give in to the skullduggery that was rampant around the track.[5]

"I always rode the last race on the card with the same urgency as the Kentucky Derby," Hartack said. "There is something wrong with not trying. The man who owns a cheap horse deserves the same treatment as the man with a good horse. I wouldn't be honest with myself if I tried harder on one man's horse than I did on another."[6]

When the Waterford Park season ended, Junie Corbin moved his horses to another West Virginia track, Wheeling Downs, and Hartack went along with him. Corbin put up his crew at the Windsor Hotel, which was a couple of blocks from Market Street, the avenue that went through the center of Wheeling.[7] Market had tamed somewhat by the early 1950s, but there was still residue from the days when it was the scandalous private turf of William "Big Bill" Lias, a convicted bootlegger who had the town in a vise. With Lias' illicit operation in full bloom, Market Street theoretically had something for everybody—after-hours nightclubs, tattoo parlors, brothels, gambling joints and drug hangouts. Lias also had time to run a lucrative numbers business and several racebooks, and in 1945 he had bought Wheeling Downs, in a bankruptcy sale, for $262,000. A stretch that Lias had served in the Atlanta federal prison apparently did not bother the West Virginia Racing Commission when it issued him an operator's license.

Not much of what Lias did was on the up and up, but one thing he came by honestly was his nickname. In a profile in *Life* magazine, they said he weighed 365 pounds. Lias was not offended by references to his weight. "How much does Big Bill weigh?" one of his associates once asked. "Four jockeys." His real name was Vassilios Liakakos, but he denied that he was born in Greece and fought off deportation by the federal government several times. What did stick, however, was a charge that Lias owed almost $3 million in back income tax. By 1957, the government forced him to sell the race track at auction. The winning bid was almost $2 million.[8]

When Hartack arrived at Wheeling early in 1953, he heard the stories about the track's troubled history, such as the time the Ohio River overflowed and flooded the grounds,[9] or the fires that killed dozens of horses,[10] or a foot of snow that forced cancellation of the races.[11] When Hartack was there, torrential rains made the running surface so gooey and dangerous that thirty jockeys refused to ride. After an hour's delay, management coerced seven jockeys into riding the small field that made up the first race. After the race, four additional jockeys said the track was too dangerous. But management canvassed the jockeys' room and rustled up fourteen riders who stayed until the end, riding out the rest of the card. It is unclear which side Hartack was on.[12]

Hartack, finding it difficult to line up mounts, won five races during Wheeling's twenty-one-day meeting.[13] After the Wheeling meet ended, Charles Town opened. Located in the northern part of the Shenandoah Valley, in West Virginia's panhandle, Charles Town had been in business for twenty years by the time of Hartack's inauspicious arrival. Sixty-five miles from Washington, D.C., and about the same distance from Baltimore, Charles Town would draw horsemen and their stock from Pimlico after the Preakness meet at the Baltimore track ended in mid-May. When it was the only game in town, Charles Town would draw a mix of baseball players and senators; even John F. Kennedy attended the races there once.[14]

Talking about the horses that ran at the Charles Town races, the journalist/telecaster Heywood Hale "Woody" Broun said, "These old warriors have more mileage on them than a New York City cab.... But I often think, when people speak of the 'leaky roof' circuit, that the detractors don't know what vast schemes and impossible dreams are hatched as the geriatric cavalry circles under the lights."[15]

Junie Corbin's horses, who had been laid up most of the winter, began to come around, and Hartack was positioned to ride most of the veteran trainer's winners. From Charles Town, they traveled to Randall Park, near Cleveland, where Hartack won eighty-eight races during a forty-four-day meeting. Hartack never considered, until the very end of the year, the enormity of what he was on his way to accomplishing: winning 350 races in his first full year in the saddle.[16] Bill Shoemaker, in his first full year, won 388 races, but in Shoemaker's debut year, 1949, he began riding in March and finished with 219 wins.[17] By contrast, Hartack, riding less than three months in 1952, won thirty-six times. So there was a 90 percent increase in his win output from one year to the next; Shoemaker's win total from the debut year to the first full year went up about 44 percent.[18]

Winning 350 races in one year would ordinarily have been enough to make a jockey a contender for the national title, but, unfortunately for Hartack, the 1953 yardstick was Shoemaker. At twenty-two, a year older than Hartack, Shoemaker won 485 races in 1953, a record that would stand for twenty years. Shoemaker amassed his total even though he took off two weeks in December. He rode at all the major tracks in California, and he won five stakes races at Del Mar alone.[19]None of Hartack's wins came in a major stakes race. He was still considered the biggest in a small pond and had yet to get an opportunity to ride prominent horses.[20]

When Shoemaker came along, Eddie Arcaro was still riding—and would continue until 1962—but his marquee days were gone. Arcaro led the country in purses six times, but never after 1955.[21] Three of his five Kentucky Derby wins came in the 1940s, and his fifth win was in 1952, the first year Hartack rode.[22]

Shoemaker's horses earned $1.7 million in 1953, whereas Hartack's horses earned less than $600,000. If Arcaro was passing on the baton to anyone, it was Shoemaker. One night at the Mocambo nightclub in West Hollywood, California, Arcaro and Shoemaker were in the audience, listening to a young singer named Ella Fitzgerald. During an intermission,

Charlie Morrison, co-owner of the club, brought the two jockeys up to the stage. When Arcaro was introduced as "the champ," he pointed to Shoemaker and said, "Meet the new champ."[23]

Hartack and Arcaro were never chums, but Hartack never really got close to any of his fellow riders. He reasoned that the closer he came to other jockeys, the duller his competititve edge.[24] He dropped out of the Jockeys' Guild after the organization refused to support another rider, Milo Valenzuela, who got into a beef with the Arlington Park stewards in a dispute about who should ride a stakes horse. Hartack felt that the guild had a lot of drawbacks and offered few benefits, and at one time he tried to launch a rival jockeys' group. Arcaro, once president of the Jockeys' Guild, was a lifelong supporter of the organization. The breach between Arcaro and Hartack was exacerbated because of their feelings about the guild.[25]

In 1958, when Arcaro was guild president, Hartack finished first in a race at the Atlantic City track, but the stewards ruled that he had interfered with the second-place horse, who was ridden by Jimmy Johnson, an apprentice rider. After an inquiry, Hartack's horse was disqualified and Johnson's horse declared the winner. In the jockeys' room afterward, the two riders exchanged heated words, and Hartack punched Johnson.

Hartack's version was that his horse was lugging in, and he couldn't correct him. Hartack said that he was standing over a water bucket in the jockeys' room, trying to think about the next race, when Johnson confronted him. He claimed that Johnson shook his finger at him, accusing him of trying to force him over the fence. "I called him a liar, and said I never tried to put anybody over the rail," Hartack said. "I told him not to shake his finger in my face. But he kept doing it, and we had a few more words, and then I belted him. I'm sorry I hit him. I lost my head. But I didn't hit him because my number was taken down. I hit him because he wouldn't let me alone."

The stewards suspended Hartack for fifteen days—ten for the incident on the track and five for the fistfight.[26] The *Morning Telegraph*, a racing newspaper not known for taking editorial stands, came out with a review of the controversy that was titled "Hartack Must Mature." The *Telegraph*'s star columnist, Charles Hatton, wrote, "Jockey-ship as a profession has dignity, a tradition of sportsmanship imparted to it by such great little men as Isaac Murphy, Sir Gordon Richards, Earl Sande, Eddie Arcaro, George Woolf, Johnny Longden and Charlie Elliott. Small in stature, they were big enough for success. Bill Hartack, nor any other rider, has the right to jeopardize the higher repute of jockey-ship. He will remain Willie here until such time as he matures to Bill."

Arcaro, riding in New York, was asked to comment, in his position as guild president, about the Atlantic City brouhaha. He said, "Hartack will calm down. He'll have to. There's more to this game than just winning. He must realize he's just another rider like I am. He has to live with others."[27]

During Arcaro's salad days, he was a take-no-prisoners rider, not unlike Hartack. In 1942, when Arcaro was twenty-six, another jockey, Vincent Nodarse, cut off him and his mount shortly after the start of a stakes race at Aqueduct in New York. A steaming Arcaro caught up with Nodarse going down the backstretch and tried to crowd him into the fence and knock him into the infield. The stewards, because of Arcaro's stature, were prepared to write off the incident and let him go with a slap on the wrist. But at the hearing, instead of being repentant, Arcaro blurted out, "I would have killed that Cuban SOB if I could have." The stewards suspended him for a year.

In the 1980s, a reporter caught up with a long-retired Nodarse, who was living in Miami. In his living room was a fancy ceiling fan.

"That's a very nice fan," the reporter said. "It really does the job on a hot day."

"Yes," Nodarse said. "Eddie Arcaro gave me that fan."[28]

Because Hartack seldom rode in New York, and didn't ride regularly in California until late in his career, after Arcaro had retired, they were seldom in one another's company, except at major races. One of those occasions came in 1961, almost three years after the Jimmy Johnson incident in Atlantic City. In the Florida Derby at Gulfstream Park, Hartack finished second on Crozier and Arcaro ran third on Beau Prince. After the race, while Arcaro was being interviewed by a reporter in the jockeys' room, Hartack walked past. Neither of them exchanged a word and they avoided eye contact. The reporter couldn't help but notice the coolness, and he asked Arcaro what that was all about. "You know," Arcaro said, "that guy's been snubbing me for two years, and I don't even know it."

Russ Harris, then with *Miami Herald*, was one of the few reporters who could get answers when he asked Hartack probing questions. When Harris asked him about Arcaro, Hartack said, "I didn't like what he said about what happened in Atlantic City. He should have investigated the facts before he made any public statements. I don't see how he could have anything to say, since he was at Belmont Park. All he could go on was hearsay. I always thought he was a great rider and a great guy. Now, as far as I'm concerned, he's just a great rider."[29]

Arcaro, when he was doing color commentary for network television on the Triple Crown, was quick to criticize Hartack for some of his rides. After Northern Dancer lost the 1969 Belmont Stakes, with the Triple Crown on the line, Arcaro put the blame entirely on Hartack for what Arcaro felt was a poorly judged ride.[30]

"Billy could never reach Arcaro," said Chick Lang, Hartack's long-time agent, when asked about the feud. (Lang was one of only a handful of people who could get away with calling Hartack "Billy.") "He couldn't make an impression on him. It was like trying to psych [out] Babe Ruth or Jack Dempsey—they're so big they just ignore you. Arcaro would be asked to name the best jockeys he had ridden against and he would say Shoemaker, Braulio Baeza, and maybe two or three others. But never Hartack."[31]

Winning all those races at Randall Park in 1953, Hartack began padding his bank account for the first time. He even bought himself a new Jaguar. It was an English import, with the steering on the righthand side.

Randall Park only raced five days a week, and with two of the dark days coming up, Hartack asked another jockey, Alkie Darlington, whose parents had befriended him early on in Charles Town, if he'd like to accompany him on a trip down to Pittsburgh to tend to some personal business.

"Some car," Darlington said as he got in.

"It does over a hundred [miles an hour], easy," Hartack said.

Leaving Cleveland, they were whistling down a highway in Pennsylvania when Darlington glanced at the speedometer and saw that they were up to 110 MPH.

Sixty miles outside of Pittsburgh, Hartack came out of a blind turn only to be greeted by a state policeman sitting on a motorcycle. The cop signaled for Hartack to slow down and pull over. Hartack braked quickly, throwing Darlington forward, and skidded to a stop to await his fate. The ticket, issued because he was traveling about twice the speed limit, resulted in a suspension of his Pennsylvania operator's license.

The next day, Hartack went to Charles Town's department of motor vehicles and applied for a license. Information about his violation hadn't caught up with him yet. He told the Charles Town driving officials that he was a jockey who moved around a lot, and his business depended on being able to drive. He told them that his hired driver had quit, leaving him with a car but no driver. He was well known in Charles Town even then. His license was railroaded through the system, and he drove with a West Virginia license for several years.[32]

While Hartack was piling up victories, he was also moving from agent to agent; by year's end, nine different agents had booked his mounts. It was a pattern that, with the exception of the six years he spent with Chick Lang, would hold up for his entire career.

An agent who might have lasted longer than most was Eddie Litzenberger, a former jockey whose riding career had been cut short after he suffered a broken leg in a spill at the old Jamaica track in New York. But Litzenberger took ill and had to give up Hartack's book. Some of the other agents were dismissed because Hartack felt they weren't picking the right horses for him to ride. Roughly, Hartack was winning with one out of every four mounts, which was one of the best averages around, but he thought his strike rate should be even better. At Wheeling Downs, Hartack was especially frustrated when he logged only

Hartack was an avid fisherman and hunter; he died while on a hunting trip. He and his agent, Chick Lang, left, both caught big ones in Florida in 1955 (Nancy Lang collection).

five wins. By the time the West Virginia circuit moved to Charles Town, he had hired Charlie Wells as his agent.

Wells was a hard drinker but faithful to the task. Trainers liked him. He never took a call on a horse that his jockey wouldn't honor. He virtually committed to memory the condition book, which was a periodic listing of future races, complete with eligibility requirements. He knew the book inside and out, and he helped trainers spot their horses. Wells was a consummate race tracker; with more personal discipline, he could have been a successful trainer.[33]

Before Hartack came along, Wells had been booking mounts for a couple of other jockeys, R.J. "Bobby" Martin and Oliver Cutshaw, who had been riding since 1948. Like Wells, Martin never met a brass rail he didn't like. Sam "The Genius" Lewin, the stable agent and handicapping maven, once moved Martin into his home, in the interest of keeping the jockey's nose clean. One night Martin said he was going out to get a magazine and didn't show up again until the middle of the next morning. He was a mess, but he talked Lewin into keeping his mounts and rode three winners that afternoon.[34] When Martin was ruled off by the stewards for betting on a horse other than one he was riding, Wells moved on to Cutshaw. But Cutshaw broke his leg in a spill, and Wells signed on with Hartack while Cutshaw recovered.

Hartack thrived with Wells, winning twenty-four races in nineteen days at Charles Town, but Wells had a dilemma: What to do when Cutshaw healed, since an agent was allowed only one journeyman rider at a time? Other agents were salivating at the possibility of picking up Hartack, but Wells wasn't so sure he wanted to let his new rider go. Hartack was five years younger than Cutshaw, and winning many more races.[35]

Among the agents waiting for Hartack was 27-year-old Chick Lang, who was bred for the race track. Lang's father and grandfather were also called Chick. His father, the son of a trainer, rode Reigh Count to victory in the 1928 Kentucky Derby. Lang's maternal grandfather, John Mayberry, was the trainer of Judge Himes, winner of the 1903 Derby. Chick Lang, Mayberry's grandson, tried to become a jockey, but he looked so bad on a horse that people would say, "I don't believe that boy could be the son of somebody who rode a Derby winner." Chick's ineptness in the saddle was soon rendered academic, since he quickly grew to six feet tall and weighed two hundred pounds. He dropped out of high school to take whatever jobs might be available at the track. At nineteen, he married his sweetheart Nancy Christman, who was three years younger.[36]

Wells and Lang were friends. Lang was at Sunshine Park in Tampa, Florida, without a rider to represent. He asked Wells whether he was going to choose Cutshaw or Hartack when the time came.

"I like the kid a lot," Wells said. "But I've been with Oliver for a while."

Lang wanted Hartack badly. He tried to push Wells in Cutshaw's direction but could get no commitment.[37]

Meanwhile, Cutshaw, now out of rehab, was galloping horses in the mornings to sharpen himself for the rides at night.

Finally, in Tampa, Lang got a call.

"I'm gonna flip a coin," Charlie Wells said.[38]

6

Heads It's Cutshaw, Tails It's Hartack

Charlie Wells' coin flip—with himself—went Chick Lang's way. Lang got Bill Hartack, the jockey he wanted. Lang wasn't even there for the flip; he didn't have to be. He was in Tampa, Florida, waiting for Wells' phone call to report the outcome. Wells, with no witnesses, flipped the coin and told himself that if it came up heads, he would go back to Oliver Cutshaw, whose broken leg had healed. If it had been tails, Wells would have become Hartack's agent and told Cutshaw that he was sorry. For his part, Hartack was comfortable with either man, Wells or Lang. In the end, it was heads, meaning that Cutshaw went to Wells, and Hartack to Lang. Wells did all right with Cutshaw, before he retired from riding in the late 1960s and moved on to other race-track jobs. Meanwhile, Lang landed a jockey who would enable him to make the most money of his life.[1]

It would be easy to say that the precocious Hartack would have gone on to greatness with either Wells or Lang. Maybe so, maybe not. At the time, Hartack's ambitions were not as lofty as Lang's. Lang was aiming for the moon.[2] Hartack, by contrast, was content with cranking out winners on the circuit that included Charles Town. Lang envisioned his jockey riding big-time horses for big-time stables, competing in the Kentucky Derby and other classics. While Wells was personable, he was not as gregarious as Lang, who was happy-go-lucky with a wry sense of humor.[3] Hartack was to morph quickly into a jockey with fickle mood swings, a temperament that, while tolerated by Lang, would have shoved many other agents to the brink.[4]

Lang might have been preordained, because of his bloodlines, to be a race tracker, but he found his way into an agent's job purely by accident. He was walking hots (cooling off horses after they exercised) for a Maryland trainer, Jim Arthur, when a jockey, John Tammaro, came by the barn asking a favor. Tammaro had a couple of riding calls, but he was late for an appointment and asked Lang to go to the racing secretary's office and make sure his name was placed on the entries. Lang didn't tell Tammaro, but he needed directions to the racing secretary's office. Once there, he was engulfed by a crowd of agents, jockeys, trainers and horse owners.

"Anybody got somebody open in the second and third [races]?" shouted Eddie Dennison, the racing secretary.

"Tammaro's open," Lang said.

Tammaro won with both horses, and he hired Lang as his agent.[5]

Lang's father (another Chick) was Canadian. He led North America in wins in 1921 and finished second in 1922. His agent was Jim Arthur, the same horseman who became a trainer and gave young Chick a menial job at his barn before he switched to agenting. Chick's father's contract was sold by Arthur for $25,000, believed to be a record transfer. The older Chick's 1928 Derby winner, Reigh Count, was owned by John Hertz, whose money came from taxicabs and rental cars.[6]

Young Chick Lang was two years old when his father won the Derby. He said that he watched his father battle weight all his life, living on a diet of cigarettes and coffee.[7] The father, who gave up the struggle with weight and became a trainer, died in 1947. He was forty-one, and his son was twenty-one.[8]

Nancy Christman, like her future husband, grew up in the Pimlico section of northwest Baltimore. Chick was almost three years older than Nancy, whose mother liked him. He spun enthralling race-track stories and told how the Kentucky Derby was embedded in his family tradition. At age sixteen, Nancy and Chick were married. Their honeymoon was a day of racing at Monmouth Park, near the New Jersey shore. Lang was working there at the time, booking mounts for a jockey named Bobby Bowers.

Two children, a boy and a girl, came along quickly, and while Lang's job as a jockeys' agent took him to tracks all over the mid-Atlantic region and farther off, he and Nancy agreed that the children should remain in Baltimore, where they squeezed in with Nancy's mother. When Lang was young, his father, the jockey, had moved them all around. Young Chick was frequently pulled out of school without notice. One time, the move was so quick that he didn't have to time to clear out his locker. Chick and Nancy were determined that their children would never be vagabonds.[9]

As an agent, Lang moved from jockey to jockey, looking for a Bill Hartack or somebody like him. By 1953, however, while Hartack and his bevy of agents were piling up wins by the hundreds, Lang was out of work. He began selling Lincolns and Mercurys at a Baltimore agency, and by several accounts he did well. He said it was not unlike selling a jockey to a trainer—you have to convince someone that they're getting top value, and smile, and maybe tell a funny story while you're doing it.

Early in 1954, Lang left the car business to take up booking mounts for Johnny Weir, a jockey riding at Sunshine Park near Tampa, Florida. Lang was upfront with Weir, telling him that he was eyeballing this Hartack kid in West Virginia. He promised Weir that he would give him as much notice as possible should Hartack pan out.

Then came the eventful coin flip, and Lang told Weir that he was leaving for West Virginia to take up with Hartack.[10]

While Hartack was still under contract to Junie Corbin, the terms were that he was to ride first call on Corbin's horses, but he could ride for other trainers if Corbin wasn't represented in a race. This gave Hartack and Lang the pick of virtually all the horses at Charles Town. The toughest job for Lang would be to pick the better horse if they were offered two to ride in the same race.

Lang began pushing Hartack almost immediately to move their base to the one-mile tracks in Maryland—Pimlico, Bowie and Laurel. Hartack had a fast car and custom suits; he was eating at the best restaurants and dating the prettiest women. He saw no reason to move. Not right away, that is.

"You take me to the milers," Hartack said, "and it would be like riding in a different county."

Inadvertently, Corbin helped them make the move when he ran afoul of the stewards at Charles Town. After Hartack had won a race with Spring Lark, one of Corbin's horses, the post-race urinalysis came back positive for caffeine, a mild but illegal stimulant. Spring Lark was disqualified, and his purse money was forfeited.

Corbin faced a hearing before the stewards, with a suspension looming. He told Hartack that he was worried, that he couldn't explain the dirty test.

Hartack tried to cheer him up, reminding Corbin that he had a clean record and would probably get off with a fine instead of a suspension.

The senior steward at Charles Town was Snooks Winters, who was described as the Judge Roy Bean of racing officials. Winters skirted a fine line. He bought jewelry at wholesale prices and sold it to jockeys; he even made plays for jockeys' girlfriends. He was a walking conflict of interests, ignored by track officials and state racing authorities.

The day of the hearing, Corbin suggested that Hartack appear as a character witness. Hartack said that even if he had to skip races, he would be there. Hartack ultimately rode the entire card, with word of the hearing never reaching him in the jockeys' room. The hearing was held after the last race, without Hartack. Corbin saw him later that night and asked why he hadn't come; Hartack said nobody had notified him. Corbin said that it probably wouldn't have mattered—Winters was determined to make an example of him and gave him a six-month suspension.

The next morning, at the barn, Charles "Pappy" Wright, Corbin's stable foreman, took over the training duties. Some of the horses were being sent to other trainers. Others, those that were both owned and trained by Corbin, were going to be sold. But they were mostly bottom-of-the-barrel claimers and wouldn't bring much.[11]

Hartack was incensed. Corbin was responsible for jump-starting his career and they were closer than was customary for most trainers and jockeys. After training hours, Hartack stopped in a downtown café for breakfast. Before he could order, Winters and a correspondent for the *Daily Racing Form* walked in. Hartack stood up and confronted Winters.

"What you did to Junie wasn't right," Hartack said.

"This isn't the place for this," Winters replied.

"Junie doesn't hop horses, and you know it," Hartack said.

"He did this time," Winters told him. "We got the test. Somebody has to be responsible, and it's the trainer."

"He's got a good record," Hartack pressed. "You could have let him off with a lot less."

"We have to protect the bettors," Winters said.

"Junie doesn't bet much," Hartack insisted. "All he got from that race was the purse. You think he's going to fool around for such a small pot?"

"There's nothing I can do about it," Winters said.

Winters tried to walk past Hartack and take a seat, but Hartack shifted his position, blocking his path.

"You're not much," Hartack declared. "I always heard you weren't much, and this proves it."

"Son, that kind of talk is going to get you into just as much trouble as the trainer," Winters said.[12]

Two days later, Hartack was called into the stewards' office. One of the other stewards said that Hartack should be removed from all of his mounts because of his disrespect for Winters. Hartack asked why he hadn't been told about the hearing and was informed that they weren't able to locate him. Hartack accused them of lying, which led to a reprimand.

"What did the stewards ever do for me?" Hartack asked. "You don't buy me clothes, or buy me a meal. Junie took me from nothing and turned me into something. Then they asked me to back down on his behalf."

With Corbin on the sidelines, Hartack continued to win races. Corbin called him, congratulated him, and said that he was struggling to make ends meet. He mentioned the possibility of selling Hartack's contract to another outfit. Hartack didn't like the idea of splitting up, but he was agreeable if the price would be enough to sustain Corbin during the remainder of his suspension.

Corbin had been contacted by T.J. "Tommy" Kelly, a thirtyish horseman who had recently become the stable trainer for Ada Rice, a wealthy Chicago philanthropist who owned a breeding farm and campaigned horses at tracks in Florida, Maryland, Illinois, California and elsewhere. Kelly, the son of a Baltimore bartender, was looking for a contract rider and was interested in Hartack.

The price was $15,000, to be shared by Corbin and Hartack. Hartack said he would consider the deal on one condition: that Corbin get all the money. A grateful Corbin used some of the money to buy a house on Route 9, on the outskirts of Charles Town.[13] Later, Corbin sold the contract of another of his jockeys, Alkie Darlington, for $100. "I paid for the weathervane for that house," Darlington said.[14]

The terms of the contract didn't change; Hartack could ride other horses as long as Ada Rice and her husband Dan didn't have entries in a race. As for Lang, he was busy on another front, paving the way for the two of them to invade the larger Maryland tracks. Hirsch Jacobs, the son of a Brooklyn tailor and a self-taught horseman, knew Chick Lang through Lang's father. Jacobs, who won more than 3,500 races in his career, including the $1,500 claim of Stymie that led to purses of almost $1 million, was ensconced in Maryland. Jacobs promised Lang that there would be plenty of business for Hartack if he came to Maryland.

Word got around Pimlico that Chick Lang's ship had come in.

"Hey, Chickie baby, how's it going?" one of the hired hands said to Lang as he made his way through the stable area.

"Couldn't be better, Baby Cakes, couldn't be better," Lang said as he moved on.

"Hey, Chick, everything OK?" somebody else asked.

"Mr. Squirrel," Lang said, "I'm having the time of my life."

A few steps later, somebody said, "The Chicken man. Where you been?"

"Hi, Hard Times," Lang replied. "I've been where you ain't."

At the door to the track kitchen, an oldtimer who went by Drop Cord said, "Hey, Chick, spare me a sawbuck?"

"Remember 'Gone with the Wind'?" Lang asked. "Great movie. Remember what they told Scarlett O'Hara at the end? 'Tomorrow is another day'? Well, Drop Cord, that's the way it is with me and your sawbuck."

"Whatever you say," Drop Cord said. "You're the man, Chick, you're the man."[15]

One of the first horses that Kelly got for the Rices was Pet Bully. He was a reclamation project. The colt had broken a bone in his foot when he was a 2-year-old and had made the rounds with some of the other Rice trainers in Illinois, New York, Florida and California.

Pet Bully favored his left foreleg so noticeably that he seemed to be flapping it as he made his way around the track. He was said to have "the clumsiest action of any good horse in the country."[16]

In April 1954, running for Kelly for the first time and getting Hartack, the new stable jockey, on his back, Pet Bully rebounded from a tendon injury and won a pair of races at Bowie. He broke the track record, set twenty-seven years before, for five-and-a-half furlongs. In May, Pet Bully won a handicap at Garden State Park in New Jersey. The winner's share of the purse was enough to compensate the Rices for what they had paid Corbin for Hartack's contract.[17]

In June, Pet Bully won his fourth straight under Hartack, this time at Delaware Park. As they sometimes say on the backstretch, he was a horse "that didn't have to carry his race track around with him."[18]

Tempted by the chance to run Pet Bully under a reasonably light weight, Kelly flew the horse to Los Angeles for the California, a new stake at Hollywood Park. This was Hartack's first trip to the West Coast. Imbros, the local favorite, was Pet Bully's chief challenger, and a crowd of fifty thousand turned out.

Earlier on the card, Hartack rode Postscript, a horse who was assigned 109 pounds. Hartack weighed more than that, but Postscript, carrying three extra pounds and at 9–1 odds, still won.

Unfortunately for Pet Bully, Imbros lived up to his reputation. Ridden by Johnny Longden, he tied the world record for a mile and a sixteenth as Pet Bully struggled home fifth. Kelly went trackside to discuss the race as Hartack dismounted. "I nearly got knocked off the fence," Hartack said,[19] although the *Daily Racing Form*'s chart didn't reflect that.[20]

Two days later, Hartack was back east, riding several mounts that Lang had booked at Monmouth Park in New Jersey. The resilient Pet Bully ran three more times that summer, finishing first, second and third. In September, Kelly sent Pet Bully to Chicago, the Rices' hometown, for the Washington Park Handicap, which was worth $110,000 to the winner. Pet Bully won by one length,[21] after which Kelly announced a three-race plan—the Fall Highweight Handicap, the Woodward and the Vosburgh, all in New York. Pet Bully won the first two with Hartack, but he missed the Vosburgh because of a suspension.[22] Five days before the race, Hartack won three races at Atlantic City, which gave him a meet-leading sixty-one, but in the stretch run of the stake his horse drifted badly into the path of another horse. The stewards ruled that Hartack's furious whipping with his left hand had contributed to the foul. They set him down for ten days, a suspension that was also in effect in New York. After Pet Bully's second-place finish in the Vosburgh, two reasons were proffered: his 134-pound impost and/or a questionable ride by Sammy Boulmetis, who stood in for Hartack.[23]

Two days after his suspension ended, Hartack was back to ride Pet Bully at Garden State. The assigned weight was 135 pounds, one more than the Vosburgh. Pet Bully spotted the field fifteen pounds and more, but he still won to finish the year with nine wins, two seconds and one third out of fourteen starts.[24]

Despite Hartack's contributions to Pet Bully's successes, in 1956 Dan Rice had a conversation with Jimmy Jones, the trainer for Calumet Farm. "You got a good jock," Jones said. "But he's a sprint rider. Around two turns, he's not as good. You'd do better in the [longer races] if you had somebody else." There is a suspicion that the cagey Jones was

Bill Hartack (center), with Chick Lang (left) and Tommy Kelly (ca. late 1980s). Lang booked mounts for Hartack longer than any other agent. Kelly, a member of the Racing Hall of Fame, was the trainer when Hartack began riding for his first major stable (Nancy Lang collection).

trying to land Hartack's exclusive services for Calumet. Hartack's first of five Kentucky Derby wins came the next year with Calumet's Iron Liege. The Rices would eventually win the Derby with Lucky Debonair (Frank Catrone training, Bill Shoemaker riding) in 1965, but ten years before, with Pet Bully retired, the stable was in the doldrums.

Dan Rice went to Kelly with what Jones had said, and the suggestion that they not renew Hartack's contract. Rice told Kelly that they could get Hartack on the fly most of the time anyway.

"Drop Hartack?" Kelly asked. "Look at all the races he's won for us. I think this would be a big mistake."

"Don't tell me what I can and cannot do," Rice said.

"I'm not trying to do that," Kelly protested. "I'm just saying that Hartack's a very good rider and I think you're making a mistake."

"Well, I don't like people telling me what to do," Rice said. "I can fire Hartack, and if you don't like it, I can fire you, too."

Rice ultimately made good on his threat: he fired both his trainer and his jockey.[25] Neither suffered. Kelly went on to freelancing; then he trained privately for several well-heeled owners, and he was voted into the Racing Hall of Fame in 1993.[26] When a couple of hundred Hartack mourners assembled at a Lutheran church in Miami Springs, Florida, after his death in 2007, Tommy Kelly delivered the eulogy.[27]

As for Jimmy Jones and Calumet, after Hartack's Derby win for them on Iron Liege, there was a falling out the next year. With Hartack injured, Jones used Milo Valenzuela to win the Derby and the Preakness with Tim Tam. Hartack, riding again, feuded with Jones about whether he should ride Tim Tam in the Belmont Stakes (the colt ultimately finished second with Valenzuela).[28] Hartack won four more Derbys, and Calumet just one.[29] The theory that Hartack couldn't win long races was either a gambit or a gaffe, and perhaps a little of both.

7

Shoemaker's Large Shadow

Unlike Bill Hartack, Bill Shoemaker's first agent was, in the parlance of the race track, a stayer. Shoemaker and Harry Silbert were Damon and Pythias for almost forty years, until Silbert died in 1987. Silbert, a cigar-chomping ex–New Yorker, looked like an understudy for Damon Runyon's *Guys and Dolls*. Once he and Shoemaker shifted into high gear, Silbert called California "the land of milk and honey."[1]

Chick Lang, who had been with Hartack since early in 1954, considered Silbert a friend. While agents competed vigorously for jockeys and horses, there was also a club-like camaraderie among them. Lang, an officer of a national agents' association, was one of the organizers of an annual dinner dance that the association sponsored. He was well liked by many trainers as well as other agents.[2]

For a number of years, Shoemaker was based in Southern California, while Hartack operated out of the East Coast and Florida. Hartack seldom rode in California, whereas Shoemaker traveled extensively to ride in major stakes all over the map. One day, they were both at Arlington Park in suburban Chicago, and the morning before the race, outside the racing secretary's office, Hartack spotted Lang having a long conversation with Silbert. After Silbert left, there was a confrontation.

"What are you doing, talking to that guy?" Hartack demanded.

Lang was puzzled. "What the hell are you talking about? Harry's my friend. I've known him for a long time."

"He might be your friend," Hartack said, "but he works for Shoemaker, and that's the guy I've been trying to beat out."

"Talking to a guy doesn't mean I'm trying to help him out," Lang said. "I'm just being sociable."

"We're trying to win races," Hartack insisted. "You don't talk to the guy you're trying to beat when you're trying to win races."

"When you get on a horse, that's the time to be beating the other guy," Lang said.

"Just do me a favor: stay away from him," Hartack said.

"I'm not gonna turn my back on somebody I've known for all these years," Lang protested.

Neither of them gave in. Their breakup was five years away, but this was a start.[3]

* * *

Although Shoemaker was only about a year older than Bill Hartack—he was born in 1931,[4] Hartack in 1932[5]—Shoemaker began riding in 1949, and he had finished four full seasons before Hartack completed his first full year. When Hartack notched his first win, on October 14, 1952, Shoemaker had already won more than eleven hundred races.

They were one-two in the national standings in 1953 and 1954, but statistically Shoemaker dwarfed Hartack. Shoemaker was *numero uno* in most racing circles. He was riding in one of the major racing centers, California, and was latching on to a steady run of Kentucky Derby horses.[6]

By 1955, however, Hartack began turning a corner. With the amiable Chick Lang infusing continuity, Hartack began to build off the canny stakes rides he had given Pet Bully the year before. What's more, the contract with Ada and Dan Rice and their trainer, T.J. "Tommy" Kelly, brought a steady stream of horses, most of them with good chances to win. Hartack seemed ripe to close the gap with Shoemaker. Publicly, Hartack said that he was just out to win every race he rode. He insisted that he didn't pay attention to what Shoemaker was doing, but in reality he fretted about Shoemaker's superiority.[7]

With Shoemaker, what you saw was what you got. He was a classy, congenial guy who had other jockeys rooting for him. He liked to play cards after the races in the jockeys' room, and he was also a practical joker. Harpo, the silent Marx brother, could have been his muse. He would slip an uncapped bottle of catsup in someone's coat pocket, or he might tie a person's shoelaces together. But the uptight Hartack was all business. He kept to himself in the jockeys' room and had little to say to his fellow riders. He played cards, but with such intensity that he was not fun to play with.[8]

Other riders gave Hartack a wide berth. Once before the races at Pimlico, Hartack brought his dog into the jockeys' room and gave him a sudsy bath in the showers. The drain was clogged. The other riders were loath to complain, but finally one of them, out of earshot, called the general manager's office. "What do you want me to do about it?" a track executive asked. People came to see Hartack ride, and they bet freely on his horses because he always gave them maximum effort. Pimlico didn't want to discourage him from riding there.[9]

Shoemaker was known to champion Hartack. The trainer Charlie Whittingham, one of Shoemaker's best friends and the horseman who gave him thousands of mounts (including Ferdinand, Shoemaker's 1986 Kentucky Derby winner), once said that Hartack rode horses "like a cowhand roping a calf."[10] "I don't agree," Shoemaker said. "Hartack is a great rider. He gets things done. Racetrackers say I sit too quiet on a horse, that I don't push and scrub. That's my style. Hartack has his style. I sit on a horse one way, and his seat is different. He's a rival, but I have a lot of respect for him as a competitor. So he doesn't like being called Willie. It never bothered me, but it bothered him, and that's all right."[11]

Hartack rode in 1,702 races in 1955. That was easily the most rides he would ever have in one year, and it was the most any national leader—either in wins or purses—had ever had. Nowadays it is not uncommon for jockeys to be that busy, but in the 1950s, ten-race cards were virtually unheard of—eight races was more the norm—and winter racing wasn't as widespread as it is now.

Hartack won 417 races, his career best by a wide margin. Shoemaker, with about 600 fewer mounts (traveling with Swaps and other important horses cut into his regular business in California), won 307 races. It was Eddie Arcaro, at thirty-nine, who won the money title that year. Arcaro rode half as many races as Hartack; yet his mounts totaled \$1.8 million, beating out Shoemaker by less than \$15,000. Hartack finished about \$100,000 in arrears.[12]

Sheer volume was what kept Hartack in the money race, because he rode no major stakes winners to speak of. His biggest win, with the Irish-bred, Chicago-owned Blue Choir in the United Nations Handicap at Atlantic City, didn't come until the end of September. First place was worth $74,000 to the horse's owner.[13]

All year long, he won races in bunches. On a showery April 25 at Laurel, he won with six of his seven mounts. All of the winners were short prices, 3–1 or less. The only race he didn't win was when he finished third on a 13–10 favorite.

Hartack threw in another six-bagger on November 5, when he won with all but two of his eight mounts at Laurel. With a little luck, he could have swept the card. After winning the first four races, Hartack had a good chance on a 7–2 shot in the fifth, but the best they could do was fourth place. In the sixth race, Hartack finished first, but his mount was disqualified for interference, and the horse that was moved up to first was ridden by Oliver Cutshaw. Hartack would never win six races in a day again, although there would be dozens of five-win days along the way.[14]

Ten days before that United Nations win with Blue Choir at Atlantic City, Hartack just missed a six-pack. In the middle of the card, for a piddling purse of $3,800, he was introduced to Fabius, a Calumet Farm 2-year-old who would launch him into Triple Crown prominence in 1956. Fabius was one of the first sons of Citation, Calumet's 1948 Triple Crown champion. Citation was a bust as a stallion, but Fabius was an exception. Trained by Jimmy Jones, Fabius was passed around from jockey to jockey before Hartack got his chance. Shoemaker even rode him once, and so did Arcaro, but after winning the first start of his career, at Arlington Park in June 1955, Fabius lost six in a row.

The losing streak ended with Hartack riding him to victory at Atlantic City.[15] Afterward, Jones told Hartack that Fabius was a slow-developing April foal.[16] Other jockeys, including Arcaro once again, got their chances with Fabius in the fall of 1955, but it was Hartack who rode him for his next win, in a sprint at Hialeah in January 1956. Then Fabius went on another losing streak, mainly because of strong opposition in Florida. At the forefront was Needles, the emerging Kentucky Derby favorite by dint of wins in the Flamingo at Hialeah in February and the Florida Derby at Gulfstream Park in March.[17]

Hugh Fontaine, who trained Needles, put the colt on the shelf for six weeks, until the Kentucky Derby on May 5. By contrast, Jones continued running Fabius. Hartack didn't ride either race as Fabius knocked off two small fields while running short at Keeneland. After that, the Derby Trial at Churchill Downs loomed on May 1. Today, running a horse just a few days before the grueling Kentucky Derby would be outrageous, but in the 1950s the one-mile Trial was *de rigueur.* Six of the previous eight winners of the Derby has finished either first or second in the Trial.[18]

For the 1956 Trial, Hartack was back aboard, riding Fabius for the first time since February in Florida. Calumet had another colt, Pintor Lea, pointed for the Derby, and Hartack would be given his choice of mounts. Fabius helped with the decision when he won the Trial by a length, although he was carrying only 112 pounds, fourteen pounds less than what he would be handed in a few days.[19]

The Trial was on Tuesday, and Hartack had to make up his mind between Fabius and Pintor Lea by Thursday, when post positions would be drawn for the Derby. The day after the Trial, he discussed his options with Ben Jones, who had stepped down as Calumet's trainer as his son Jimmy took over. Ben had stayed on as the farm's general manager, and he told Hartack that if it were up to him, he would take Fabius.[20]

At the time, Pintor Lea had a swollen right front knee that Jimmy Jones was watching closely. If Hartack had picked Pintor Lea to ride, and the horse wound up getting scratched, he would have been allowed to jump back to Fabius, the other half of the Calumet entry. Dick Baird, who accepted the mount on Pintor Lea, also knew that if for some late reason Fabius didn't run, he would be bumped by Hartack.

Both horses ran. Needles was the 2–1 favorite on the morning line, and the Calumet horses were lumped together at 3–1. But for Needles' long layoff, he would have been a shorter price, and, as it turned out, his odds dropped to 8–5 by post time.[21]

The day started ominously for Calumet when Hartack, scheduled to ride in the first race, didn't get to Churchill Downs in time. Jimmy Bidwell took his place and won the race.[22]

The Joneses were buoyed by the fact that Citation had won the Trial before he won his Derby. But Needles had even more history going for him: his sire, Ponder, had won the Derby in 1949, and Ponder's sire, Pensive, was the Derby winner in 1944.[23]

There was a mount in the seventeen-horse field named Ben A. Jones, named after the Calumet trainer but running for another stable. It was Ben A. Jones, Fabius and Terrang, the Shoemaker-ridden colt from California, who were the pace-setters. Fabius put them away and was in the lead as the field reached the quarter pole. Needles, ridden by Dave Erb, who had been riding for sixteen years and had never won a Derby, had only one horse beaten when the race was half over, but he got into gear in the middle of the track and was at Fabius' throat-latch with an eighth of a mile left to run. Needles' winning margin was three-quarters of a length, but visually the win was more convincing than that.[24]

Hartack offered no excuses. He objected to a question that suggested that Fabius might have "quit." "Are you kidding me?" he asked. "He gave me everything he had."[25]

The Preakness, at Pimlico in Baltimore, was two weeks off. It was a race that Chick Lang, a native Baltimorean, wanted to win more than the Derby. Jones didn't waver about running Fabius, but the closer Preakness day got, the less confidence he had that his colt could turn the tables. The Needles camp was not brimming with optimism, either. The shorter distance—the Preakness wire comes up 110 yards sooner than the Derby's—and the tighter turns at Pimlico were expected to work to Fabius' advantage.

The no-shows among the Calumet Farm people would have sent bettors scurrying to wager on Needles or the six other horses. Lucille Markey and her husband, Gene, were gallivanting, as was their wont. Gene Markey, a Hollywood screenwriter and film producer, was married to Joan Bennett, Myrna Loy and Hedy Lamarr before he married Lucille Parker Wright, the widow of Warren Wright Sr., who founded Calumet. Also missing in Baltimore was Ben Jones, who stayed in Kentucky and watched the race on television.

The crowd of 29,774 would be an embarrassment on a Preakness day now, but in the 1950s the middle jewel of the Triple Crown was considered an afterthought in many quarters. Eventually Preakness attendance grew exponentially, to the point that crowds in the neighborhood of a hundred thousand were not unusual. The significant growth in Preakness attendance can be traced to the arrival of Chick Lang in the Pimlico front office in 1960, after he broke up with Hartack.

Jimmy Jones and Calumet got a rousing start to the big day. Two of their 3-year-old fillies, Beyond and Princess Turia, dead-heated for the win at Belmont Park in the Acorn Stakes. At Garden State Park, Calumet's Trentonian won his third race of the year.

At Pimlico, Dave Erb rode Needles exactly as he had in the Derby—which is to say, not only did they dawdle in the early part of the race, but it also looked as though they were running in a different postal code. Needles was last after the opening half-mile, more than twelve lengths from the front. Eiffel Blue and Golf Ace, a pair of long shots that hadn't run in the Derby, set the pace for three-quarters of a mile, but Hartack and Fabius, in third place, had a clear shot at the lead, and it seemed as though it was only a question of when Hartack would press the button. Hartack released his tight hold on the far turn, and Fabius shot to the front. Needles also began to pass horses, setting the stage for a rematch of the two colts through the stretch.

But this time Needles couldn't close the gap, and he finished second, almost two lengths behind Fabius. Before unsaddling, Hartack leaned over to kiss Fabius on the nose. Erb said that perhaps the Derby had taken more out of Needles than anybody realized. Prior to the Preakness, his races had been more spaced out.[26]

On national television, while CBS ran a few commercials, Chris Schenkel stood outside the winner's circle with a microphone in his hand and Hartack nearby. On his way to the winner's circle, the governor of Maryland, Theodore R. McKeldin, stopped to shake Hartack's hand.

"Tell them around the country that this was your biggest win," McKeldin said.

"It wasn't," the jockey said. "It was just *one* of my biggest."

"Well, tell 'em anyway," McKeldin urged.

Back on camera, Schenkel played McKeldin's game and asked Hartack if this was his biggest win.

"I can't say that," Hartack answered. "But it was one of my biggest."

The interview over, Hartack turned to a friend and asked, "Who the hell was that?"

"The governor of Maryland," he was told.

"I don't care who the hell it was," Hartack said. "Nobody's going to tell me what to say."[27]

The Belmont Stakes, the third leg of the Triple Crown, would be run in three weeks in New York. Shooting from the hip, Jimmy Jones ran Fabius a week after the Preakness, and he won the Jersey Stakes. Then Jones wheeled his colt back on June 9, a week before the Belmont, and, despite giving twelve pounds, he was upset by Ricci Tavi, a 21–1 shot, in the Leonard Richards Stakes at Delaware Park. The day before that race, Hartack rode a horse at Delaware and was blamed for a crowding incident that led to a spill. Hartack was suspended for ten days for "careless riding," an all-inclusive penalty that knocked him out of the Belmont. Needles rebounded to win the Belmont by a neck over Career Boy while Fabius, with Paul Bailey stepping in for the sidelined Hartack, finished third.[28]

Hartack didn't suffer the inevitable lows gladly, but Calumet was happy to have him on their side for many races. "Jockeys get high hat more than anyone in the world once they get a few bucks in their jeans," said Dee Brooks, the stable agent for the farm. "But I've known Hartack for a while now, and money hasn't changed him one bit. His word is as good as gold. What's funny is that he's careless in many ways. I've gone off to his house in Florida maybe five times and found that he had gone off fishing or something else when he said he would see me. But where riding is concerned, he's all business. You can rely on him, and you never have to worry about him not being there or refusing to ride because a better horse came along. He won't change mounts, once he's given his word."[29]

Hartack didn't win any more stakes in 1956 with Fabius—they finished second in the Ohio Derby—but Bardstown filled the gap in the second half of the year. Trained by Jimmy Jones for Calumet, Bardstown and Hartack combined to win five stakes. In late October, Garden State Park ran the Garden State Stakes for 2-year-olds. With a purse of $319,210, it was advertised as the richest race in the world. Not surprisingly, a bulging field of nineteen horses ran, including the Calumet pair of Barbizon (ridden by Hartack) and Iron Liege (who went to Hedley Woodhouse after Hartack had opted for Barbizon).[30]

In a three-horse rush to the wire, Barbizon, on the outside, won by a nose over Federal Hill, who was on the rail. Amarullah, between them, finished third. The finish was so close that many in the crowd of forty thousand thought Federal Hill had won. The winner's share of the purse was $168,000, with 10 percent going to Hartack.[31] Barbizon was crowned the champion two-year-old male and became the early favorite for the Kentucky Derby. However, Barbizon's career nosedived after Garden State; he won two of fifteen races and was forgotten.[32] He didn't even run in the Derby. But Iron Liege did, and it wasn't until eight hours before the race that Hartack found out he was going to ride him.[33]

8

A Derby Windfall

The mighty Calumet Farm began 1957 with dozens of promising 3-year-olds, horses that might fly the devil's-red-and-blue silks of the Lexington, Kentucky, monolith in the winner's circle on Kentucky Derby day. There were three horses at the top of the list—Barbizon, who had been crowned the champion 2-year-old colt in 1956; Gen. Duke, whose precocity in two races in 1956 had suggested greatness; and Iron Liege, who, like Gen. Duke, was a son of Bull Lea, an aging sire who had been the cornerstone of Calumet's success as a racing and breeding giant. Before he was done, Bull Lea sired dozens of future stakes winners, including Citation, the 1948 Triple Crown champion.[1]

Bill Hartack, who had won the 1956 Preakness with Calumet's Fabius, rode Barbizon, Gen. Duke and Iron Liege as 2-year-olds. So did other jockeys; the majordomos of Calumet, the trainer Ben Jones and his son Jimmy, had to juggle so many horses in so many locales that it was impossible to commit the same rider to every horse.[2] Besides Hartack, the inimitable Eddie Arcaro was in the mix, as was Dave Erb, who had won the 1956 Kentucky Derby with Needles as Hartack and Fabius finished second.[3] Erb would come to regret his connection with Calumet, however, and even Hartack would have a blow-up with Jimmy Jones that would result in his losing Calumet's business by 1958.[4]

Hartack played close to the vest with his opinions of horses. The morning of an important race, he was asked what he thought about the horse he was riding. "I'll know more tonight," he said, meaning that those interested should see him after the race. But even after races, he treated words as though they were rare stamps.[5]

Despite Hartack's closed mouth, there was the sense, as 1957 began, that he ranked Gen. Duke as the best of the Calumet contenders, and in late March, six weeks before the Kentucky Derby, it was difficult for him not to be gushing after the chocolate-colored colt wiped out a small field in the Florida Derby at Gulfstream Park. The Joneses had no compunctions about running their horses against one another, and Iron Liege was one of the opponents who was outrun by Gen. Duke that day, as was Bold Ruler, who was considered the leading Kentucky Derby candidate among non-Calumet horses. Gen. Duke's time for the mile-and-an-eighth Florida Derby was 1:46 4/5, which tied the world record and is still the record for the Gulfstream stake.[6]

By the time of the Florida Derby, Calumet had given up on Barbizon as a Kentucky Derby hopeful. His big win in 1956, the lucrative Garden State Stakes, had come at one and one-sixteenth miles, but as he became a 3-year-old distance races were his undoing. In Florida, he ran in the Fountain of Youth Stakes, same distance as the Garden State race, and was badly beaten, finishing in the middle of a ten-horse field. Barbizon seemed to be headed backward, and Hartack quit riding him to concentrate on other Calumet horses.

"I don't think Gen. Duke is necessarily a better horse than Barbizon," Jimmy Jones said, "but he seems more likely to stand up under the rigors of training."[7] After a while, Jones proved to be right about Barbizon and wrong about Gen. Duke.

No journalist was closer to Hartack than Joe Hirsch, of the *Morning Telegraph* and the *Daily Racing Form*. Hirsch estimated—and he may actually have known, since Hartack frequently confided in him—that Hartack had earned almost $450,000, before taxes, in 1956. This was an era when jockeys were the best-paid athletes. The highest salary in baseball, $100,000, belonged to Ted Williams of the Boston Red Sox. Hartack, Arcaro and Bill Shoemaker were all making more than that. Arcaro reportedly hit the $100,000 plateau in 1950 and did as well or better through the rest of the decade.[8]

For Hartack, money was only a means of keeping score. When it was all over, he was in debt to the Internal Revenue Service, having lost his last appeal, and needed to keep working, as he did as a racing official at several tracks.[9] He downgraded his lifestyle, from extravagant to penny pinching, so that it would match his reduced earning power.[10] When Tim Tam had won the 1958 Kentucky Derby and Milo Valenzuela rode him instead of an injured Hartack, Lucille Markey of Calumet Farm wrote a check with a five-figure sum on it "because maybe it might make the young man [Hartack] feel a little better." The check didn't reach Hartack until after that year's Belmont, which had brought on the showdown with Jimmy Jones and the end of Hartack's business relationship with Calumet. Out of pique, Hartack never cashed it.[11]

Hartack was the only jockey Gen. Duke ever had. The colt's career included those two wins in 1956 and a series of races leading up to the Florida Derby during the winter of 1957. Gen. Duke was first or second in every one of them.

Gen. Duke kept running into Bold Ruler, who won seven of his ten races as a 2-year-old. They battled on January 30 at Hialeah, where Bold Ruler, despite carrying twelve more pounds, gave the Calumet runner a thrashing at seven furlongs. They met again on February 16 in the Everglades Stakes, this time running a mile and an eighth, and Gen. Duke, still packing twelve fewer pounds, overtook Bold Ruler in the final strides to eke out a narrow decision. Their next common date was March 2, the day of the Flamingo Stakes at Hialeah.[12] Bold Ruler had to run a mile and an eighth in near-world-record time to win by a neck, but Arcaro, riding Bold Ruler, sloughed off the close finish. In racing parlance, Bold Ruler was a "cheater," a horse who gets lazy once he or she is leading in a race. Arcaro said that Bold Ruler tried to pull himself up when he had a clear lead in the stretch of the Flamingo, then got serious again when Gen. Duke and Hartack pulled up alongside him. Arcaro hit Bold Ruler five times—three in a series, then two more a few strides later—to give him the message. Iron Liege, Gen. Duke's stablemate, finished third for Dave Erb, but he was no threat to the first two.[13]

Gen. Duke racked up one more win before the Florida Derby, a day when Bold Ruler finished second. On Florida Derby day, Chick Lang, Hartack's agent, walked into the track wearing a blinding madras jacket. Somebody wrote down all the colors Lang wore: blue, yellow, purple, green, red and black (and he may have missed a couple). "I don't want to antagonize any of our owners," Lang said. "It's got the colors of every stable we ride for."[14]

After the race, they allowed Lang in the winner's circle anyway. Finally, Bold Ruler got a break in the weights—he and Gen. Duke each carried 122 pounds—but in a five-horse field, Gen. Duke beat Bold Ruler fair and square by a length and a half. Arcaro, riding Bold

Ruler, said that Calumet ganged up on him: "I looked over one shoulder, and there was Gen. Duke. I looked over the other shoulder and there was Iron Liege. Gen. Duke went by me in a wink." Iron Liege did slightly better than the last time, finishing third, beaten by less than two lengths.[15]

The Kentucky Derby was run on May 4, and instead on taking on the Calumet pair again, in the Derby Trial four days before the Derby, Bold Ruler was sent to the Jamaica track in New York for the Wood Memorial on April 20. A heavy 1–2 favorite, Bold Ruler was beaten three jumps before the wire, but he surged for Arcaro and nipped Gallant Man by a nose.

After the race, Ralph Lowe, who owned Gallant Man, told his trainer, John Nerud, that he wanted to replace their jockey, Johnny Choquette, with Bill Shoemaker. But Nerud wanted to keep Choquette. He reminded Lowe that Choquette had been riding for ten years and was familiar with Gallant Man, and, despite Shoemaker's reputation, making a jockey change just before the Derby was foolhardy.

Lowe persisted. He reminded Nerud that Shoemaker had won the Derby with Swaps in 1955. Nerud, adamant, said that if Lowe wanted to replace his jockey, he might consider replacing his trainer, too.

Inadvertently, the stewards at Jamaica settled the disagreement. They suspended Choquette ten days for rough riding in the Wood, which made him ineligible for the Derby. But Lowe would later rue the day that he hired Shoemaker.[16]

The Tuesday before the Derby, six horses ran in the Derby Trial, which was a genuine Derby preview. Federal Hill, Better Bee and the Calumet duo—Gen. Duke and Iron Liege—were also slated to run in the Derby. For Gen. Duke, this would be his second race in Kentucky prior to the Derby. On April 19, eleven days before, he had faced only two other horses in a seven-furlong race at Keeneland, but he ran third and last, behind Iron Liege and One-Eyed King, who really was a horse sightless in one eye.

The morning of the Trial, Catherine Drinker Bowen, the noted biographer, was at Jimmy Jones' barn. Bowen, whose oeuvre included the lives of Oliver Wendell Holmes and Tchaikovsky, was attending her first Derby on assignment for a national magazine. Hartack, frequently testy with the media, turned into a paragon of politeness when introduced to Bowen, who asked him which horses he would have to beat in the Derby.

"I'm not worrying about the other horses," Hartack said. "I'm not thinking about them. I'm just worrying about mine. About my own horse."

Hartack never would have guessed that between the time of his conversation with Bowen on Tuesday and Derby day on Saturday, he would be riding another jockey's horse. And the horse he was worrying about on Tuesday wouldn't even run in the race—and, in fact, would never run another race anywhere.

The conversation between Bowen and Hartack turned into small talk, something Hartack usually eschewed.

"What's that bird dog doing around here?" Bowen said, pointing to a speckled, tail-pointing animal on the other side of the fence where she and Hartack were standing.

Hartack glanced at the dog and smiled. "Grasshoppers," he said. "He's not pointing at birds, he's pointing at grasshoppers."

Then Hartack excused himself. "See you," he said as he walked away. "Nice meeting you, ma'am."

For the one-mile Trial, Hartack was riding Gen. Duke, Dave Erb was aboard Iron Liege, and Willie Carstens was in charge of Federal Hill. Settling into a box seat early in the day at Churchill Downs, Catherine Drinker Bowen flipped through her program, pausing when she came to the page with the Derby Trial. She read the names of the jockeys, top to bottom, and stopped when she came to Better Bee, whose rider was John Adams. Bowen had written about the American presidency. "I'm not a bettor, and goodness knows, there's nothing I know about betting," she said to her seatmates. "But if John Adams wins that race, and I don't have at least two dollars on him, I'll never live it down."[17]

Gen. Duke and Iron Liege, coupled for betting purposes, went off at the short, short price of forty cents on the dollar. Federal Hill was the modest second choice, at 2–1, and the price was no underlay. He had run twenty-one times in his career, which was then only eleven months old, and there was one race in the small type of the *Daily Racing Form* that all but leaped off the page: In November 1956, in the Kentucky Jockey Club Stakes, he had gone to the front leaving the gate and was never overhauled in a sharp effort. That race was also at Churchill Downs, and also at a mile distance.[18]

In the two major Kentucky Derby preps in Florida (the Flamingo and the Florida Derby), Federal Hill had also been a speed factor, but their mile-and-an-eighth distances had been hemlock, and he was not a factor in either stake. Milton Riser, Federal Hill's trainer, said that he loved his horse as a miler but couldn't get excited about his chances in the Kentucky Derby. Occasionally, Federal Hill would prove Riser wrong—he had won twice beyond a mile, including a victory in New Orleans in March in the Louisiana Derby.

As expected, Carstens gunned Federal Hill to the front in the Trial, and that's where he stayed. He won by two and a half lengths; Gen. Duke was second and Iron Liege, a big disappointment, beat only one horse and finished seven lengths behind the winner.[19]

That night, Hartack was eating in a restaurant with Joe Hirsch of the *Daily Racing Form* when a racing writer from Los Angeles saw them, came over to their table and asked a question about the Trial. Hartack's eyes turned to lasers. "I didn't come here to answer questions," he said. "I came to eat. If you want to ask questions, see me around the barns tomorrow."

The writer walked away, his tail between his legs. He turned to a colleague and said, "A simple 'no comment until tomorrow' would have sufficed. I only asked one question. In the time he took to chew me out, he could have answered it."

Hartack then told Hirsch everything he wanted to know. Their trust was so great that Hirsch knew what to omit and what to use when he wrote his columns; Hartack didn't have to tell him what was on and off the record. For Hirsch, such intimacy was a double-edged sword. His unlimited access was a tremendous asset, but he could be hamstrung, his mind cluttered with information that he knew Hartack preferred to keep *sub rosa.*

Hartack informed Hirsch that Gen. Duke might have a sore ankle; the colt had taken a misstep at Keeneland. However, Hartack claimed that a horse with such a fluid stride was unlikely to bobble.[20]

Dave Erb, living in retirement near Saratoga Springs, New York, recalled the Keeneland race: "The track was officially listed as 'fast,' but nothing could have been further from the truth. It was a bad race track. It was pretty spotty, and you had to be careful. Iron Liege never really caught a hold of it."

Erb was confident that his colt would run better on Derby day, when Churchill Down usually had the track rock hard, so as to ensure fast times. Erb had been Iron Liege's rider for seven straight races, from February at Hialeah through the Derby Trial.

"When Jimmy Jones gave me the mount the first time, he said that if the horse got that far, I would be his Derby rider," Erb said. "He liked the idea that I had won the Derby the year before, with Needles. I was really looking forward to it. I thought I was going to get the chance to do something that hadn't been done too often. Up to that time, only two jockeys had ever won the Derby in two straight years, Isaac Murphy [1890–1891] and Jimmy Winkfield [1901–1902]."

Two days after the Derby Trial, Erb was sitting in the tack room at Jimmy Jones' barn at Churchill Downs. Ben Jones, Jimmy's father and the general manager of Calumet, was also there. They discussed what had happened in the Trial, and what might happen in the Derby.

"We can throw out Iron Liege's race," Jimmy Jones said.

"He was spinning his wheels, all the way around," Erb said.

"He'll get a better race track on Saturday," Jimmy said.

"Did Gen. Duke come out of the race all right?" Ben Jones asked.

"He's got a bruise on his left front," Jimmy said.

"How bad?" Ben wanted to know.

"I think we can still run him. I'm going to breeze him an eighth Saturday morning and we'll see."

Erb sat between the two men, quietly taking in the conversation. There was no mention of a jockey switch—Hartack replacing him on Iron Liege if Gen. Duke wasn't available for Hartack to ride. Erb thought his Derby mount was secure.

Later that morning, after Erb worked a horse for another trainer, he was walking between barns when Joe Hirsch caught him from behind and put his arm around him.

"Tough break, Dave," Hirsch said. "Sorry."

"What do you mean?" Erb asked.

"It looks like Gen. Duke is out," Hirsch said. "They're going to use Hartack on Iron Liege."

"What I hear is that it's not for sure," Erb said.

"I hope I'm wrong, Dave," Hirsch said.[21]

Hirsch frequently knew—he was a confidant to many trainers, including Jimmy Jones—but the rest of the press didn't. *Sports Illustrated* asked six handicappers to pick the winner. All six opted for Gen. Duke. "He's the only Derby-distance horse in the race," said Dave Feldman of the *Chicago American*. "He's a cinch for the Triple Crown," agreed Joe Tanenbaum of the *Miami News*. "He will not only win, maybe he will run the fastest Derby ever," declared Earl Ruby of the *Louisville Courier-Journal*.[22]

After Gen. Duke's two-furlong blowout on the morning of the race, Jimmy Jones called Bill Corum, president of Churchill Downs, to tell him that half of the Calumet entry wouldn't run. At the same time, Dee Brooks, Calumet's stable agent, was in the racing office, filling out a scratch slip.

It was 9 a.m., and betting was scheduled to begin in fifteen minutes. According to racing rules, Jones could have waited until forty-five minutes before the race to declare Gen. Duke, on the off chance that his injury might improve with last-minute treatment, but he didn't want the public betting on two horses when only one was going to run. The horses were coupled for betting purposes, which meant that refunds would have been made only if both horses were scratched.

After the Derby, Gen. Duke was shipped to Baltimore for a possible start in the Preakness, but that didn't work out, either. In July, about two months after the Derby, it was determined that he had fractured the foot. They tried to bring him back in 1958 as a 4-year-old, but he had become a wobbler—a horse with a neurological condition that impairs its balance. Gen. Duke had no offspring as a sire. He died late in 1958 and was buried at Calumet's cemetery, where many of the farm's other stalwarts, including the Triple Crown champions Whirlaway and Citation, were interred.[23]

Dave Erb's agent, Eddie Rice, caught up with his rider on the Churchill backstretch not long after word circulated about the Gen. Duke scratch.

"You heard?" Rice asked.

"Not from Jones," Erb said. "Joe Hirsch told me this was coming, but I really didn't believe him, because I sat with those guys for a long time on Thursday, and they didn't say boo. I really thought we had a great chance with Iron Liege. It was Hartack. He knew I was trying to get in with other Calumet horses, and that I'd be a danger to his business if I did."[24]

When Jones told Hartack about Gen. Duke's defection, and that Hartack would move over to Iron Liege, the jockey didn't want the substitute mount. "Iron Liege has been getting beat by most of the horses he'll be running against," Hartack protested. "I don't see how we can win the Derby with him. There are a lot of jocks available. Why don't you get somebody else, and I'll go to New Jersey and ride Fabius in the stake there? And you got two nice fillies running in New York. I could go there and ride."

"Let me call Mrs. Markey," Jones said, referring to the owner of Calumet Farm. Iron Liege was one of Lucille Markey's favorites. She had paid the Jockey Club the $100 it cost to rename a horse who had never raced. Iron Liege's original name was Iron Lea (his sire was Bold Lea, the dam Iron Maiden). While that name made sense, based on bloodlines, Markey never liked it. For the new name, she kept the connection with the dam but went back three generations and got the "Liege" from Plucky Liege, who was the granddam of Bull Lea.

When Jones told Markey that Hartack was reluctant to ride, she asked her trainer to request that Hartack stay and ride as a favor to her. Unlike Hartack, Markey thought Iron Liege had a chance. Hartack reluctantly accepted the mount.[25]

The scratch of Gen. Duke prompted Churchill Downs to revise the morning line. The Calumet entry, now reduced to just Iron Liege, lost the favorite's role, which fell to Bold Ruler at 2–1. By the time the horses left the gate, Bold Ruler remained the favorite; Round Table and Gallant Man, separated by only a dime in the odds, were the second and third choices; Federal Hill came next on the infield tote board at 7–1, and after Iron Liege at 8–1, the other four horses were 42–1 or more.[26]

Springtime was late in coming to Louisville in 1957. It was a bitterly cold day, raw and windy. The temperature failed to reach the fifty-degree mark. Crowds of a hundred thousand were common for the race, but this one, despite its stellar field, was seen by 58,465. The Joneses wore big overcoats that ran almost to their ankles. Hot chocolate and coffee were running neck and neck with mint juleps as the leading sellers at the concession stands. But not even the threat of chilblains could keep the politicians away. Albert "Happy" Chandler, governor of Kentucky and former commissioner of major league baseball, was there to present the trophy in the winner's circle. A few Republicans also showed up, including James Mitchell, President Eisenhower's secretary of labor.[27]

The night before the Derby, Ralph Lowe, the owner of Gallant Man, and John Nerud, trainer of the colt, played gin rummy in Lowe's suite at the Brown Hotel. Lowe had made his money in Texas oil. He was a wildcatter whose wells had come in. When he decided to invest in thoroughbred racing, the sky was the limit. He sent a representative to Europe to survey horses that the Aga Khan planned to sell. Lowe bought nine horses in a package, pending approval of his veterinarian, and all but one passed muster. The standout had a bad ankle, but Lowe didn't let the lone marginal horse put the quietus on the deal. "The hell with it," Lowe said when told about the horse with the problem. That horse was Gallant Man.

"I had the craziest dream last night," Lowe said. "I dreamed that our horse had clear sailing in the stretch of the Derby, and our jockey pulled him up too soon. Another horse came from out of the pack and nipped us at the wire."[28]

In 1956, in the Californian Stakes at Hollywood Park, Shoemaker had ridden Swaps, the 1955 Derby winner. Shoemaker had the finish line in sight and let up on his mount, at which point Porterhouse had rallied to clip them at the wire.[29]

"Well," Nerud said after Lowe related his dream, "Shoemaker's your rider. You better remind him about that dream."[30]

Jim Thomson, the official starter at Churchill Downs, stood on a ten-foot-high stand on the infield side of the track. When he pressed the button in his hand, the stall gates would open and the field would be sent on its way. Beneath him was, arguably, the deepest collection of solid horses to ever run in the race. In 1999, forty-two years later, Hirsch recalled the 1957 Derby and said, "It was the best Derby ever run. It was the best field, let me put it that way. There's never been a Derby with that depth of quality. Most every horse in the field, not just the Big Five, went on to earn a considerable amount of money."[31]

This was Jim Thomson's first Derby as starter, but he was no beginner. He was fifty-two years old, a lifetime race tracker, and had been a veteran assistant starter for several years. The field of nine, requiring only one starting gate, was expected to be duck soup for Thomson and his crew. In 1971, the Derby field grew to twenty horses—fourteen breaking from the main gate and six breaking from an auxiliary gate. Thomson would work that Derby and two more before retiring.

Federal Hill, who was expected to be the early speed in the race, drew the number-two post position, just outside the long shot Mister Jive on the rail. Just outside Federal Hill in the gate were Round Table and Gallant Man. It didn't make much difference where Gallant Man drew, since he was a deep closer and would drop back leaving the gate no matter where his post was. Bold Ruler began in the seven hole, with two long shots outside him.

The goal of most starters at the Derby is to load the complete field in two minutes or less, depending on the number of horses. That is, get the last horse into his stall inside of two minutes after the first horse has been loaded.[32]

The clunky iron starting gate can be an intimidating instrument for a green horse, but this was a seasoned group. The nine of them had run 162 times going into the Derby. Of the Big Five, Federal Hill had been the busiest, with twenty-two starts. There wasn't a horse in the field with fewer than ten starts on his record.

Hartack was undefeated on Iron Liege, winning two sprints with him at Hialeah in January. When Dave Erb took over in February, he won two of the seven races in which he rode the horse.[33]

In the paddock, Jones didn't give Hartack any instructions. "He was a headstrong guy," Jones said. "Ill-tempered. You had to be a real diplomat to get along with him. But I put up with it because he could ride. My gosh, he could ride. Best finisher I ever saw in racing. I can't recall him ever getting beat in a photo finish."[34]

In front of Gallant Man's paddock stall, while Nerud fastened the colt's girth, Ralph Lowe told Shoemaker about the strange dream he had had two nights before. "Doesn't that beat all?" Lowe asked.

"Won't happen to me," said Shoemaker, who in a matter of minutes would be eating his words.[35]

At 4:32 p.m., the gates opened, and the crowd roared.[36] Churchill Downs is a track with a one-mile circumference, which means that the horses break from a chute to the far left of the finish line. They run down the stretch, in front of the stands, the first time, and then they circle the whole track in order to complete a mile and a quarter. Thus, they go under the finish line twice.[37]

Bold Ruler and Eddie Arcaro did not get the best of the break. The horse outside them, Sham Pac, broke inwardly. Iron Liege, just inside Bold Ruler, was away sharply, and in a couple of strides he was clear of the trouble. Indian Creek, inside Iron Liege, ducked out, which left Bold Ruler sandwiched between him and Sham Pac. Arcaro said later that he was still able to gain a favorable position despite the disturbance.

Running past the stands the first time, Federal Hill, Mister Jive and Bold Ruler were vying for the lead, their riders playing cat and mouse and using snug holds to keep their mounts from prematurely expending themselves. Hartack, trying to avoid getting pinched by the other horses, had hit Iron Liege once out of the gate, then eased him back into fourth place, about five feet off the rail. Jimmy Jones' horse was exactly where he was supposed to be.[38]

Federal Hill held a short lead all the way around. But at the start of the long run down the backstretch, Hartack looked up at the horses ahead of him and sensed that Federal Hill and Bold Ruler wouldn't last.[39]

Mister Jive faded by the time the field hit the far turn. Federal Hill came over toward the rail, and for a moment Iron Liege's path was blocked. Hartack reacted by shifting his mount one path to the outside. He now had Federal Hill measured anytime he wanted, but Hartack didn't want to move to the front too soon. Gallant Man and Shoemaker, once thirteen lengths behind, were starting to make a serious run. Round Table was also making a move, but his rider, Ralph Neves, needed to be concerned about tiring horses backing up in front of him.

Nearing the quarter pole, and the head of the stretch, Iron Liege was just a stride or two away from gobbling up Federal Hill. Arcaro, on Bold Ruler, was the first jockey to go to the whip, but he was getting no response. The favorite was not going to win this Derby.[40] When the horses straightened out for the stretch run, Hartack looked to his left and saw Round Table, who had finally cleared the other horses, running hard near the rail, where Federal Hill had once been. On Hartack's outside was Gallant Man. Inside the eighth pole, only for a stride or two, Gallant Man stuck his head in front.[41]

Iron Liege was resolute. Hartack was whipping with his left hand, his natural hand, his strong hand, and his mount was digging in. Shoemaker looked to his left, past Iron Liege, and saw the sixteenth pole, which for an instant he misread as the finish line. He raised in the saddle for a stride or two. Accounts differ as to whether Gallant Man lost stride. Realizing his error, Shoemaker sat down and quickly resumed riding, and Gallant Man was back in gear.[42] Not many in the press box saw what happened, but Don Fair, the chart caller for the *Daily Racing Form*, spotted the gaffe. In Fair's chart footnotes, it read, "[Gallant Man] was going stoutly when his rider misjudged the finish line."

Eddie Arcaro, white shirt, celebrated with Bill Hartack, left, after Hartack won the 1957 Kentucky Derby with Iron Liege. Arcaro rode the favored Bold Ruler to a fourth-place finish. On the right is Arthur Daley of the *New York Times*, who frequently roasted Hartack in his columns (*Louisville Courier-Journal*).

Hartack had to be told later what happened. "I was in front of him, so how could I tell?" he asked. "I wasn't looking behind me, I was busy riding the hell out of my horse."

Hartack said that when Gallant Man reached Iron Liege's head, Iron Liege spurted, and that was the difference, as the horses were separated by only a nose at the wire.[43]

In the box seats, Nerud, standing next to Lowe, had said at the sixteenth pole, "Go down and get your roses. Get your roses and take 'em back to Texas."[44]

After Shoemaker dismounted, he was called to the trackside phone. Upstairs, Lincoln Plaut, the chief steward, waited to talk to him.

"What happened?" the steward asked.

"The horse took a bad step," Shoemaker answered.

"It looked like you quit riding," the steward said.

"I made a mistake," Shoemaker said. "I misjudged the finish line."[45]

The stewards had trouble resolving which explanation was accurate. They didn't think it could have been both. But for the moment, there was nothing that could be done. The most severe penalty had already been meted out at the finish line: Shoemaker had lost the Derby by a nostril when even the slightest error could have been a factor.[46]

Nerud and Lowe went down to the jockeys' room and asked for Shoemaker. He came out wearing only his riding pants and a white T-shirt. "What can I say? I just screwed it up," he said.

"All of those poles are painted the same color," Nerud said. "That might have helped."

The next year, Churchill Downs painted the pole at the finish line with a bull's-eye. So did many other tracks. Shoemaker had ridden at Churchill Downs before, of course, but it had been a year since he had competed at the track, and on Derby day he didn't ride in any of the early races.

Years later, Nerud was playing golf with Dave Erb at a course in Saratoga Springs, New York. The 1957 Derby had turned out horribly for them both. Erb had lost the mount at the last minute on Iron Liege, who won the race with Hartack, and Nerud's Gallant Man might have won if one of the best jockeys ever hadn't erred.

"You know," Nerud said to Erb, "it's a good thing Shoemaker owned up."

"How's that?" Erb asked.

"If he hadn't, I think I might have punched him right in the face."[47]

Bill Hartack flanked by jockey Dave Erb and trainer Jimmy Jones, before a race at the Keeneland track in 1957. Erb, who won the 1956 Derby on Needles, was supposed to ride Iron Liege in the 1957 race, but Jones replaced him at an eleventh hour with Hartack, who then won his first Derby (Keeneland/Meadors).

Erb said that he rode for Jimmy Jones only one more time. Basically, he told Jones that he could never forgive him for losing the mount on Iron Liege. The one time Erb broke that promise was as a favor to his agent (he won the race).[48]

Ralph Lowe, who would never have another Derby horse, handled the turn of events with equanimity. He asked Shoemaker to come back to Dallas with him, and together they would get over it. The Preakness, which would be run in two weeks, was still a possibility for Gallant Man, and plans needed to be made.

Two days after the Derby, Shoemaker got a telegram from the Churchill Downs stewards. It said that he was being suspended for fifteen days for careless riding. That ruling guaranteed that Shoemaker would miss the Preakness.[49]

"They didn't do that because of the mistake; they did it because he lied to them," Nerud said.[50]

"I didn't like the way they did it," Shoemaker said later. "It was an honest mistake, and they owed it to the betting public to do something. It was something that a professional rider shouldn't have done."[51]

Lowe was incensed about Shoemaker's suspension. He called Nerud and told him they weren't running in the Preakness, even with a different jockey. "If they won't let me have my jockey, they don't deserve my horse," Lowe declared.

"Suits me, anyway," Nerud said. "I always thought the Preakness was a garbage race. This horse is better with more time between his races. We'll win the Belmont."[52]

Then Lowe called an automobile dealer in Dallas and bought Shoemaker a new Chrysler.[53]

When Hartack heard about what happened, he smiled. "Shoemaker loses the Derby and he gets a brand new car," he said. "I win the race, and get a dinner with Mrs. Markey."

Shoemaker said he didn't know whether his mistake cost Gallant Man the race. As for Hartack, he said, "You'd have to ask Shoemaker. Nobody knows. There are certain horses that if you raise up on them, they relax. They lose their momentum. If Gallant Man was that type, it had to cost him something. The films show that Shoe wasn't up more than a stride or two, so it might not have hindered his horse whatsoever. I never rode Gallant Man, so I don't know what category he fell in."[54]

Through the intervention of their columnist, Joe Hirsch, the *Daily Racing Form* hired Hartack to write a post–Derby story about the race. Somebody on the copy desk made the byline read, "By Willie Hartack," the first name that Hartack abhorred.

"[My horse] deserved to win," Hartack wrote. "At the same time, I think Gen. Duke has the edge over him so far. He's already beaten Iron Liege and I prefer his overall temperament. However, I don't have a closed mind on the subject. If Iron Liege shows a marked improvement over Gen. Duke when they come up to their next race together, I'd ride him. He never gave up that last sixteenth of a mile, and he could have. He could have finished third and I think we would have all been satisfied, me and everyone else connected with him. He proved himself a little better than we thought he was. I thought I'd need Gen. Duke in order to win the Derby. I guess if they raced again, I'd still pick Gen. Duke to ride. Iron Liege ran gamer than I've ever seen him. I'm glad he made a liar out of me."[55]

With Gen. Duke not running in the Preakness, Hartack didn't need to pick a horse. Iron Liege was a slight favorite, but it was Bold Ruler, the second choice, who beat the Derby winner and Hartack by two lengths.[56] Only six horses ran in the Belmont three weeks

A young Hartack around 1957, when, at twenty-four, he became the first jockey to ride horses that earned $3 million in a single year. It was a record that would last for nine years (Nancy Lang collection).

later, and Iron Liege skipped the race. Nerud was right about Gallant Man: the extra time played in his favor. Not only did Gallant Man win easily, but he also ran the mile and a half in a smashing 2:26 3/5. The old Belmont Park record had been set fifteen years before, and Gallant Man's record would stand until Secretariat broke it in 1973.[57] At year's end, however, it was Bold Ruler who snared the Horse of the Year vote. No one could argue: he had won eleven of his sixteen races.[58]

Hartack won two more stakes with Iron Liege that year, which was his best ever. His 341 wins were 70 fewer than in 1955, but in 1957 his mounts went over the $3 million mark for the only time in his career, and he set a record with forty-three stakes wins, an achievement that lasted until Shoemaker, fourteen years later, won forty-six.

Shoemaker's record 1971 output was anchored by the Charlie Whittingham barn, which supplied him with twenty-nine stakes wins, most of them in California.[59] By contrast, Hartack in 1957 traveled hither and yon to rack up his record forty-three wins. They came at fifteen tracks in eight states, none west of Illinois. He won three stakes in January and kept right on going: four in February, six in March, one in April, five in May, six in June, one in July, four in August, five in September, six in October and two in November. Twenty-six horses won stakes for Hartack.[60]

Hartack turned twenty-five in December 1957. In Florida, where he lived in a sprawling, luxurious bachelor home near the Hialeah track, he had a "little black book" full of numbers. One of them, he hinted, was his one and only, but when asked about marriage, Hartack said, "My God! I know hundreds and hundreds of dames. I might have to give them up. That would be a helluva problem."[61] In the end, he never married.

"I could never have imagined Hartack married to anybody," Hartack's friend Larry King admitted.[62] Said Nancy Lang, the widow of Chick Lang, who was Hartack's agent for six years, "Who could have put up with him? They would have spent every day picking up the clutter he would have left lying around the house."[63]

Hartack would have to wait two years, until 1959, for his next chance at the Kentucky Derby. His absence in 1958, however, was not of his choosing.

9

The Split with Calumet

Bill Hartack's body of work stretched from the time he rode his first race in 1952 until his remarkable career ended quietly in Hong Kong in 1980. The year 1957 was the acme. He won 341 races, and while there were three years when he won more, there were no years when he won with almost 28 percent of his mounts. Thanks to such horses as Iron Liege (his first Kentucky Derby winner), Bardstown, Jewel's Reward, Decathlon and Nadir, Hartack's 1957 purse total ballooned to more than $3 million. He would never come close to that total again, and in the next thirteen years only one jockey, Braulio Baeza, would clear the $3 million mark.[1]

Hartack punctuated 1957 by winning forty-three stakes races, three more than the record-setting Eddie Arcaro five years before.[2] Typically, however, the October day in New Jersey when Hartack broke the Arcaro record was marred by controversy. The winner of the Garden State Stakes at Garden State Park was the towering (sixteen hands, more than five feet, at the withers)[3] Nadir, ridden by Hartack, while Elizabeth Arden Graham, owner of the seventh-place finisher, Jewel's Reward, stewed because Hartack didn't ride her colt.

Graham had started with $1,000 of her own money and founded what became an international women's cosmetic empire decades before.[4] Hartack had won important races in Chicago and New York with Jewel's Reward earlier in the year,[5] and Graham understood that he was going to ride her horse "all the way."[6] But the week of the Garden State Stakes, which at $277,000 was the richest in the world,[7] Chick Lang, Hartack's agent, told Ivan Parke, Graham's trainer, that Hartack had opted to ride for Claiborne Farm (owner of Nadir) in the rich race. "I thought he was going to ride for me," Graham told the *Daily Racing Form* when she heard the news. "I didn't think he'd go back on me. He's a bad boy for doing that."

It is surprising that Hartack would have been hired to ride Graham's horses in the first place. She discouraged jockeys from using the whip on her stock, and Hartack was known as one of the most aggressive whip riders in the game. His left forearm, almost twice as large as his right, was evidence of that.[8]

"Bill's commitment was to ride L'il Fella in the Garden State race," Chick Lang said on behalf of the jockey. "But that horse is hurt and can't run. After that, Bill had no commitment whatsoever to ride Jewel's Reward." Graham paid the inimitable Bill Shoemaker a $2,500 retainer to ride Jewel's Reward, but it might not have made any difference. Joe Hirsch of the *Daily Racing Form* reported after the race that Jewel's Reward ran with a crack in one of his front heels, an injury that no doubt compromised his chances. (Jewel's Reward was a favorite of Graham's, but early in 1959 Graham was visiting the horse at his barn at Santa

Anita when the playful horse bit off the tip of one of her fingers. When told about the accident, the wise-cracking Helena Rubinstein, one of Graham's not-so-friendly rivals in the cosmetic business, asked, "Tell me, how is the horse?")[9]

Graham's squabble with Hartack was mild, however, compared to the celebrated breakup he had with Calumet Farm and its trainer, Jimmy Jones, in 1958.[10] With Jones' father, who was known as Plain Ben Jones, leading the way, Calumet had already won the Kentucky Derby six times, the most recent with Iron Liege and Hartack. It would win two more,[11] but neither victory was achieved with Hartack, who abruptly severed his relationship with Calumet prior to the 1958 Belmont.[12]

The year started for Hartack in Florida, where the promising colt, Tim Tam, was part of the Calumet contingent. A stablemate had fallen on Tim Tam early in 1957, causing an injury that prevented Jimmy Jones from bringing the horse to the races until October.[13] A fourth-place finish was Tim Tam's only start as a 2-year-old, but when he turned three, Jones subjected him to a rigorous campaign. From mid-January through late March, Tim Tam ran eight times at Hialeah and Gulfstream Park, with Hartack in the saddle for all but two. Included were major wins in the Flamingo and the Florida Derby.[14]

In the Flamingo, Jewel's Reward, one of the leading 2-year-olds from 1957, outfinished Tim Tam by a head, but after a lengthy review the three Hialeah stewards concluded that the winner and his jockey, the fiery Manny Ycaza, had bumped Hartack's mount excessively through a long stretch drive. They awarded the first-place purse to Tim Tam. The deliberation lasted long enough for (a) Tim Tam to be returned by his handlers to his barn; (b) Lucille Markey of Calumet to leave the winner's circle and return to the Turf Club; and (c) Hartack to return to the jockeys' room, where he wandered to and fro, not wanting to speak or be spoken to until he knew whether he had won or had to settle for second money. Hartack was equally concerned about how Tim Tam would come out of the roughly run race. "My colt isn't big and he can't take the beating he had to take today," he said when his number was finally put up and Jewel's Reward was taken down. "But he's strong and willing. Best of all, he runs when it counts most, in the last part of the race. He has no bad habits and he gives everything he's got."[15]

Jewel's Reward would head to New York, avoiding Tim Tam until they met in the Kentucky Derby. By then, Tim Tam had run four more times, winning them all. In Kentucky, he won a minor race at Keeneland, seventy miles east of Louisville, and the Tuesday before the Derby he notched a win at Churchill Downs in the Derby Trial, which was a quarter of a mile shorter than the Derby. Hartack was not around for the Trial, however. Three days before the Trial, prior to the second race on a dark, rain-splattered day, he suffered a broken left leg when Quail Egg, a skittish 2-year-old filly, reared in the starting gate. Hartack was thrown backward, his leg striking the tailgate of the stall as he fell to the ground.[16]

An ambulance quickly appeared to take him to Saints Mary and Elizabeth Hospital. The driver drove his car through the tunnel that leads from the paddock to the track; then he took a lefthand turn, beeping his horn all the way, to reach the gate that would lead to Central Avenue. On a stretcher in the rear of the ambulance, with his agent Chick Lang sitting next to him, was Hartack, on his back with a tongue depressor sideways in his mouth, to keep him from biting his tongue or his lip when waves of pain from his leg shot through his body.[17]

After being thrown from his horse, Hartack was helped off the course at Tropical Park, 1958 (Herb Smith collection).

All Hartack could think about was Tim Tam and the Kentucky Derby, which was a week away. "Nothing heavy on this leg," he said to Lang. "Don't let them use a heavy cast. We got to ride that horse next week. If I can get a light cast, maybe I can still ride."[18]

A victory on Quail Leg, the horse that had unseated Hartack in the gate, would have been worth $50 to the jockey. A victory astride Tim Tam in the Derby would be worth about $11,000.[19]

George Dwyer, the doctor at the hospital, said that Hartack had a broken leg. Lang was told that there would be at least a six-week recovery before his client could resume riding. That meant that Hartack would miss all three Triple Crown races—the Derby, the Preakness and the Belmont Stakes.[20]

Back at Churchill Downs, news about Hartack was passed on to Jimmy Jones, who said he would wait until Monday, two days after the spill, to name a replacement on Tim Tam for the Derby Trial. An obvious choice, for some, was Dave Erb, who had been cast aside by Jones and his father in the Derby the year before, when Hartack's mount, Gen. Duke, was injured, and they chose Hartack to replace Erb and ride Iron Liege, the eventual winner. The mount on Tim Tam might have softened the bitterness that Erb felt toward the Joneses.[21]

Erb was an established rider; he had won the Derby with Needles in 1956.[22] When

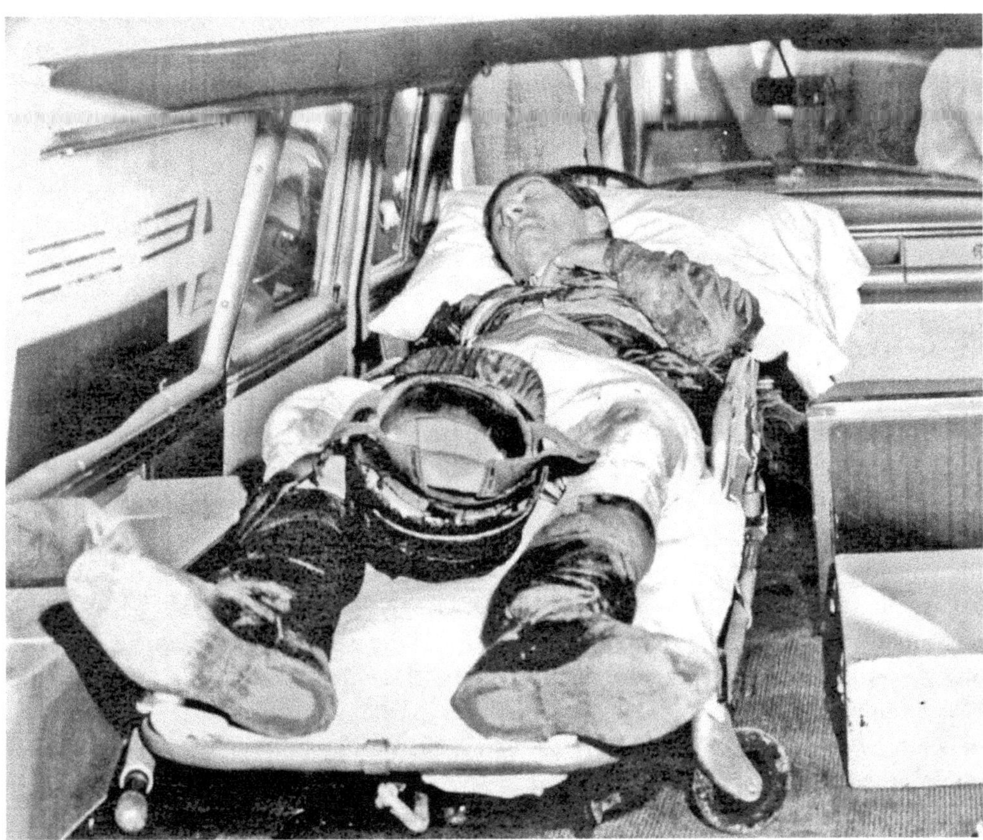

An ambulance took him to the hospital. Hartack suffered a broken leg just days before the 1958 Kentucky Derby, costing him the mount on Tim Tam, who won the race under substitute Milo Valenzuela (Herb Smith collection).

entries were due for the Derby Trial, the day before the race, Jimmy Jones wasn't required to name a jockey. Until the entry rule was tightened, it was not uncommon to see "no boy" next to a horse's name on an entry sheet. This was a designation, and a semantical distinction, that bugged Hartack early on. "We're not boys, we're men," he frequently complained. "If they want to put anything, they should put 'no rider' instead of 'no boy.'"[23]

Hartack didn't care about riding in the Derby Trial; it was the Derby itself that was his goal. He sent the hospital's X-rays to New York and Alexander Kaye, a physician who represented the Jockeys' Guild. Meanwhile, in case he got the green light from Kaye, the jockey called a company in Chicago that made special braces. "I want a real light one," Hartack said. "It needs to be aluminum. It has to go inside a riding boot. And I need it by Wednesday."[24]

Dr. Dwyer, who had treated Hartack when he was first brought to the hospital in Louisville, continued to pooh-pooh the jockey's chances to ride in the Derby. "He won't listen to me," Dwyer said. "The fibula is snapped and there are some ripped ligaments around it. That leg will need a long time."[25]

Jimmy Jones was already convinced he would need a new rider for both the Derby Trial and the Derby. The previous summer, Hartack, scheduled to ride Fabius for Calumet in the Arlington Classic, was nursing a sore back, but he had convinced Jones that he would be able to ride with a supportive corset. Jones had acquiesced, but Fabius finished second to Clem, leaving Jones second-guessing himself about using a jockey who wasn't 100 percent. It was unlikely that Jones would risk using Hartack under similar circumstances in the Derby.

Most of the top jockeys, of course, were already committed to other horses. Eddie Arcaro, seeking his sixth Derby win, was lined up to ride Jewel's Reward. Bill Shoemaker had come from California with Silky Sullivan, a horse who ran from so far back that he had become the darling of the television crowd, which had developed a newfound interest in the sport.

Jones tapped Milo Valenzuela. The Texas-born Valenzuela, one of twenty-two children, was a 23-year-old rider who was the hottest jockey in New York but had never ridden in a Derby. Not that this was a bugaboo; already in the 1950s two jockeys—Bill Boland and Henry Moreno—had won the race the first time they ever rode in it.[26]

Tim Tam and Valenzuela won the Derby Trial, after a harrowing trip in which the colt appeared to be stopped twice behind tiring horses. Hartack watched from a box seat near the finish line. The Derby, four days later, was an easier ride for Valenzuela. Tim Tam's closing punch made the difference, and he beat the long shot Lincoln Road by a half-length on a muddy track. Jewel's Reward finished fourth, but the biggest disappointment was Silky Sullivan, who was last among fourteen horses after three-quarters of a mile and ended up beating only two of them. The *Daily Racing Form*'s chart footnote told the tale: "…He made only a brief and effectual bid of less than one-sixteenth of a mile, and refused to extend himself thereafter."[27]

The *Daily Racing Form* hired Hartack to write a column about the race. He watched from the press box, and then he wrote, "The only horse Tim Tam had to run down was the horse [Lincoln Road] he beat in the Florida Derby, and he did it with good courage. I don't think Tim Tam was all out, because it looked as if he had his opponents measured to the wire."[28]

They practically ran the same race two weeks later in Baltimore. Tim Tam and Valenzuela again caught Lincoln Road in the stretch, and they got to the wire a length and a half the better. All that remained for Tim Tam to become the ninth Triple Crown champion, and the first since Calumet Farm's Citation in 1948, was a win in the Belmont Stakes on June 7.[29]

On May 28, Hartack, wearing a thin iron brace under his left riding boot, rode three races at Garden State Park and finished eighth, second and third.[30] A few days later, he met Jimmy Jones at Belmont Park. The story breaks down regarding what was said or not said. Hartack claimed that Jones gave him encouragement about riding Tim Tam in the Belmont. Reports of their conversation carried all the way to Paris, where Lucille Markey, the *grande dame* of Calumet Farm, was vacationing. She sent Jones a telegram telling him to make sure he had a physically fit jockey riding in the race.

A few days before the Belmont, Jones was scheduled to appear at a press luncheon, where he was going to say that Valenzuela would keep the mount, but both he and Hartack, in recalling what happened next, agreed that Jones wanted Hartack to submit a statement saying that he was not 100 percent and it would be better that he not ride in such a crucial race under those circumstances.

Hartack reportedly disagreed with the statement Jones proposed. According to Linn, Hartack said, "Mr. Jones, I'm not going to tell you what to do, but I don't think it's fair for me to come out and say I'm not physically fit to ride Tim Tam when I'm riding three or four horses for others every day.... How do you think that statement is going to make me feel?"

According to Chick Lang, Hartack's agent, Jones promised he would not mention Hartack's fitness at the press conference. Lang suggested to Jones that he tell the media he was sticking with Valenzuela because it would be unfair to drop him after he won the Derby and the Preakness. According to Lang, Jones thought this was a good idea.[31]

The *Morning Telegraph*, the sister publication to the *Daily Racing Form*, came out the next morning with a story that quoted Jones as saying that Hartack wasn't in peak physical condition to ride. Lang dreaded going over to Hartack's hotel and showing him the story. Hartack sat on the edge of his bed and read Jones' quotes.

"But he told me he wouldn't say that," Hartack said. "He promised me."

"All right, so he promised," Lang said. "That's the way things go sometimes. Forget it."

"I'll never ride for him again," declared Hartack, who claimed that he might have ridden Cavan, another horse running in the Belmont, if Jones had told him sooner that he wasn't riding Tim Tam.[32]

Questioned later, Jones said, "Apparently we just didn't understand each other. I don't recall that they ever suggested such a thing [using the reason Lang suggested for not using Hartack]. If I promised him one thing, I certainly wouldn't have done it another way. Hartack had only been riding for a week. Any other race [but a mile-and-a-half race] and we would have used him. I didn't do anything to hurt him, and I wouldn't for the world. If we misunderstood each other, I'm sorry. I like the boy, and I think he is a good rider, although I do think he needs a little coaching in his public relations."[33]

Jones said that he had offered Hartack at least a dozen mounts after the Belmont, and he turned them down.[34]

"Billy is wrong about being so stubborn about it," said Lang, who quit as Hartack's agent in 1960. Lang had lasted for six tumultuous years, the longest Hartack ever stayed with the same agent. Typical of their feuds was the time Hartack chewed out Lang in front of dozens of people. Later, Lang called Hartack aside and said, "You little son of a bitch. You do that again and I'll break your skull." Unfazed, Hartack just walked away.[35]

Tim Tam's Belmont was a disaster. In a weak moment, Jones allowed himself to be photographed with the Belmont trophy the morning of the race. Cavan, ridden by Pete Anderson, and Tim Tam were running 1–2 with a quarter of a mile to go when Valenzuela hit his mount with the whip. Tim Tam swerved to the left, almost crashing into the rail. Valenzuela hit him again, and Tim Tam overreacted once more, veering to the outside. Meantime, Cavan pulled away. Tim Tam finished second, beaten by six lengths. Valenzuela jumped off Tim Tam just past the wire. The colt had shattered a sesamoid bone in his right foreleg. He never ran again but was saved for stud duty. "At the time," the racing historian Edward L. Bowen wrote, "the fact that he could be saved was a major achievement for the veterinary profession."[36] Cavan ran only one more race before he, too, suffered a career-ending injury.[37]

Six weeks after the 1958 Belmont, they ran the Delaware Oaks in Stanton, Delaware. Hartack sent his mount, Idun, right from the gate and set obscenely fast early fractions that killed off not only his filly's chances but also those of A Glitter, a Calumet Farm runner who was ridden by Milo Valenzuela. "From the way Hartack rode, it seemed to me that he had made up his mind to beat A Glitter at any cost," wrote Audax Minor in the *New Yorker*. In the paddock before the race, Hartack and Jimmy Jones had bumped into one another for the first time since the Belmont brouhaha.

"Hello, Bill," Jones said, "how are you?"

"I'm fine, thank you, Mr. Jones," Hartack replied. Then he shook hands with Jones and walked toward Idun, who was being saddled. Hartack shook with his left hand.[38]

10

Cover Boys

In May 1948, as he was riding Citation to a sweep of the Triple Crown, Eddie Arcaro and his Jimmy Durante–size nose were splashed across the red-bordered cover of *Time* magazine.[1] Somebody from the horse-racing ranks had never before been so honored, and ten years later Henry Luce's magazine deigned to feature the sport once more, this time with a Bill Hartack cover. To Hartack's chagrin, his name on that cover was listed as *Willie* Hartack. Inside, the story, which was called "Bully & the Beasts," verily mocked its own choice of first names: "Hartack's only vocal complaint is that a lot of people, including sportswriters, call him Willie, a name he detests." After that, the unsigned piece couldn't seem to make up its mind. Talking about how the odds would frequently plummet on over-bet Hartack horses, the story said, "But thousands of [bettors] bet on Willie anyway. Their motivation is simple: Bill Hartack may not always win, but he always tries." By the end, it seemed as though the editors were determined to balance the books: Hartack was called Willie twenty times, Bill thirteen times, and they even threw in one Billy.[2] (Actually, a handful of close friends did call him Billy, without so much as admonishment or an arched eyebrow.)

Had *Time* delayed its Hartack story, he might have been downsized to only a few paragraphs, since he broke his leg in April, a week before the Kentucky Derby, and, as a hire of the *Daily Racing Form*, watched from the press box as his scheduled mount, Tim Tam, won the race under a ride by Milo Valenzuela. What followed was Hartack's spat with trainer Jimmy Jones and his voluntary departure from the payroll of Calumet Farm, the Kentucky monolith that was the linchpin for Hartack's sensational year in 1957. By walking away from Calumet, Hartack cost himself a lot of business, and that, combined with the time on the sidelines as his leg mended, added up to a sub-par year by what had already become known as Hartackian criteria. He won 226 races, more than a hundred less than 1957; his stakes total dropped sharply from the record forty-three to seventeen; and his horses earned \$1.3 million, compared to \$3 million the year before.[3]

In 1957, Hartack had several go-to horses that swelled his stakes total. A year later, there was no bell cow to be had. Tim Tim gave Hartack three stakes wins early in 1958, but then he lost the mount due to injury, and Tim Tam's career was finished after he was beaten in the Belmont Stakes.[4] Jones said that he sought out Hartack to ride after their tiff, but Hartack always seemed to have a scheduling conflict. The truth, Hartack's agent Chick Lang said, was that Hartack had closed the door on Calumet. It was Lang, trying to leave the door with Calumet at least ajar, who had made up the scheduling excuse.[5]

The year had almost seven months to go, and Hartack was forced to make himself available for whatever business came along. Bill Shoemaker had been riding the redoubtable

Round Table, but in mid-July Shoemaker wasn't available and Hartack took over for the Laurance Armour Memorial Handicap at Arlington Park. Undefeated on grass, Round Table gave twenty pounds to Clem and beat him by a nose. "He's all horse, a real pro," Hartack said after the race. Travis Kerr, the oilman who owned Round Table, had suggested to Hartack that he might be riding the horse again after the Arlington race.[6] But three weeks later, Shoemaker was riding Round Table, and Hartack never got another chance with the horse.

"The best thing to do in this racing business is to trust them once, maybe," Hartack said. "Kerr didn't keep his word to me about riding Round Table. Jimmy Jones and I had trouble over Tim Tam. That's what can happen to you if you believe everybody."[7]

The shoe was on the other foot the day in Chicago when Dave Feldman said that Hartack didn't keep his word. Feldman, the turf editor for *Chicago's American*, and later the *Chicago Daily News* and the *Chicago Sun-Times*, had conflicts of interest running out both ears: he both owned and trained horses; he once was president of a horsemen's organization that he also wrote about; and he was the track announcer at Sportsman's Park, which meant that he called races in which his horses ran and was on the payroll of a track that he wrote about. Curiously, none of these conflicts bothered the newspapers Feldman worked for. He had such a large following among racing fans, as a writer and handicapper, that the papers splashed his picture across the sides of their delivery trucks; at the *Daily News* his contract with the paper was so sacrosanct that it was secured in publisher Marshall Field V's vault.

One of Feldman's horses in the 1950s was Deux Moulins, whom he had claimed out of a race for $3,500 and developed into a steady marathon runner. Although Hartack rode Deux Moulins and didn't win, Feldman promised him the mount again in the mare's next race. In the meantime, Hartack was scheduled to ride Latches, another Feldman horse. Feldman shared with Hartack some quirks about Latches that he figured would be useful. But when the entries were taken for the Latches race, Hartack was named to ride another horse.

Hartack's horse beat Latches by a nose. Feldman thought that the private information he had shared with Hartack had been the difference between winning and losing. Feldman saw Hartack's agent, Chick Lang, the next day and angrily demanded, "Didn't I have the call on Hartack?"

Lang hemmed and hawed, but he never gave Feldman an answer. Then, when the Deux Moulins race came up, Feldman bumped Hartack and gave the mount to Bill Shoemaker, who rode the mare to victory at the seldom-run distance of two and one-sixteenth miles.

Now Lang and Hartack were livid. "You told me I had the mount on that horse of yours," Hartack said.

"What you did to me, with Latches, I did to you," Feldman told him.

"I didn't do it, Chick did it," Hartack protested.

"Well, dammit, I did it to him then," Feldman said.

"You did it to me," Hartack said.

By now, Feldman was tired of this hair splitting. "Who am I dealing with?" he asked. "Whoever did it to me the first time, that's who I did it to the second time."

Hartack quit talking to Feldman.[8]

By the fall of 1958, Hartack was shopping around for a 2-year-old who might develop into a solid horse for the Kentucky Derby in 1959, but he had fallen off just about everyone's radar—quite a comeuppance for a rider who had won the Derby in 1957 and might have repeated in 1958 had he not been injured. It appeared that the mounts on Sword Dancer, First Landing and Tomy Lee, who were among the best 2-year-olds, had been gobbled up by other jockeys. First Landing, the champion of the division after winning all but one of his eleven races, was Eddie Arcaro's to ride, and Arcaro's alone. Tomy Lee belonged to Bill Shoemaker, although Hartack did get one shot. Sword Dancer was a strange one. He kept losing races, and his trainer, Elliott Burch, kept searching for the right jockey combination. For his first twelve starts, which produced only three wins, Sword Dancer never had the same rider in two straight races. In the colt's fourteen races at two, ten jockeys rode him, none of them Hartack.

Hartack's one chance with Tomy Lee as a 2-year-old was a misadventure. In October, they finished second to First Landing in the Champagne Stakes at Belmont Park, and then Tomy Lee was demoted from second to third after Eldon Nelson, the rider of the third-place horse, Intentionally, claimed foul. Hartack really never had a chance. The headstrong Tomy Lee tried to bolt right from the start, and then he swerved madly to the outside at the half-mile pole.[9]

Two weeks later, with Shoemaker regaining the mount on Tomy Lee for the Garden State Stakes in New Jersey, Hartack said, "This is going to be something to see. I pulled my arms out of their sockets trying to get him to go around one turn. What's going to happen with Shoemaker when he tries to get him around two turns?"

On this rainy, muddy day, Shoemaker did have trouble controlling Tomy Lee, who finished second again, losing by a neck to First Landing. Shoemaker said that if they had navigated the turns better, they would have won.

Hartack, still shopping for a decent young horse, accepted the mount on Black Hills for the King Ranch. Although Black Hills had earned less money than any of the thirteen horses in the race, he went off a surprisingly low 8–1 fourth choice. That Hartack had won the race the two previous years might have had something to do with his horse becoming an underlay. However, Black Hills was never in the hunt and finished sixth. "The backers of Black Hills learned again a basic race-track lesson," James Roach wrote in the *New York Times*. "The horse, not the jockey, does the running."[10]

Although Shoemaker continued to ride Tomy Lee to start 1959, he doubted the horse's tractability and his potential to endure the mile and a quarter in the Kentucky Derby. Meanwhile, Sword Dancer was putting together some solid races despite a late start as a 3-year-old in Florida. Burch was going to make the Stepping Stone Purse, which was run at Churchill Downs, Sword Dancer's final Derby prep, and he called Shoemaker to ride, with the idea that he would also ride the colt in the Derby a week later. Shoemaker said that if everything went well in the Stepping Stone, that was a good possibility.

But when Shoemaker told his agent, Harry Silbert, about the possibilities with Sword Dancer, Silbert told him that he had already made a provisional commitment to Frank Childs, the trainer of Tomy Lee. Shoemaker was scheduled to ride Tomy Lee in the Blue Grass Stakes at Keeneland for his last pre–Derby race. "If Shoe wins the Blue Grass with your horse," Silbert had told Childs, "you got him for the Derby, too."

Shoemaker told Silbert that he thought Sword Dancer would win the Derby. "But Frank Childs is such a nice guy, I don't want you going back on your word," Shoemaker said. "So let's be loyal to Frank even though we're going to be on the wrong horse."

"Well," Silbert said, "that's the way it is."[11]

Leading up to the 1959 Derby, Hartack was riding several prospects, including Easy Spur and Dunce in Florida. Easy Spur was a gelding. At one time in the United States, castrated horses were prohibited from running in several major races, including the Belmont Stakes, but geldings were always welcome in the Derby. That is not to say that they ever did well. At the time, only seven geldings had won the Derby, and none since Clyde Van Heusen in 1929.[12]

Among the 1958 2-year-olds, Easy Spur was ranked twenty-sixth in the country, but after a slow start at Hialeah, he found a track he loved, Gulfstream Park, and under Hartack he won the Florida Derby, beating Sword Dancer a month before the Kentucky Derby.[13]

The day that Easy Spur and Hartack beat Sword Dancer by almost a length in the Florida Derby, the horse's owner was in Chicago, watching a hockey game. That was because James D. Norris, who owned Easy Spur, also was co-owner of the Chicago Black Hawks, who were losing to the Montreal Canadians and getting eliminated from the National Hockey League playoffs.[14]

Hartack was in an unusually chipper mood in the jockeys' room after the Florida Derby. Sensing this, a valet took a chance. "When did you think you had it won, Willie?" he shouted across the room. Hartack detested that question; he thought it was stupid, and he hated to be called Willie. But he rolled with the sarcasm and yelled back, "When I read the entries, of course."[15]

Based on the Florida Derby, Easy Spur was projected as the third choice for the Kentucky Derby, behind First Landing and Tomy Lee, who did indeed win the Blue Grass, forcing Shoemaker to reluctantly ride him in the Derby. Hartack had some options. He had promised Claiborne Farm to ride their Dunce, but now he asked for—and was given—permission to be excused. He was still not sold on riding Easy Spur, especially after they were beaten, at seven furlongs, by Sword Dancer in the Stepping Stone Purse.

"Easy Spur was injured a few days before the Derby," Hartack said years later. "His trainer [Paul Kelley] came to me and said that Easy Spur was not right, and if I could get the mount on Sword Dancer, he would release me. I tried to get on Sword Dancer, but I couldn't."[16]

By the time Hartack got to Elliott Burch, Sword Dancer's trainer had already hired Bill Boland. Sword Dancer had only been ridden once by Boland, but they had won together at Saratoga the year before, and Boland, while still a teenager, had won the Derby in 1950 with Middleground.[17]

What happened, of course, was something that reinforced that old saw about jockeys being the worst handicappers—Tomy Lee won the Derby, as Shoemaker nosed out Sword Dancer and Boland at the wire after a furious stretch drive. Easy Spur was too far back to make a difference and wound up thirteenth in the seventeen-horse field. Silver Spoon, that rare filly trying to defeat males in the race, finished a respectable fifth, beaten by less than four lengths.[18]

Years later, Shoemaker took a stab at rewriting history when he claimed that Sword Dancer would have won with a better ride from Boland.[19] Sword Dancer did at least prove Shoemaker right over the long haul: he won the Belmont Stakes and the Travers Stakes, then beat older horses repeatedly in the fall[20] and was voted Horse of the Year.[21] Plagued by injuries, Tomy Lee had a spotty career right up to the time he was seven; after the Kentucky Derby, he never won another important race.[22]

11

Chick Throws in the Towel

In August 1959, although he was only twenty-six, Bill Hartack led the voting and was elected into the Racing Hall of Fame in Saratoga Springs, New York.[1]

The Hall of Fame was founded in 1955, when twelve jockeys, mostly from another era, were enshrined. Five more were added the next year; Ted Atkinson was the lone inductee in 1957; and Bill Shoemaker, John Longden and Eddie Arcaro, all still riding, were admitted in 1958.[2] Then came Hartack, with 280 votes, and Johnny Loftus, with 175, in 1959. The media might not have been enamored with the taciturn Hartack, but that didn't bother them at the ballot box.[3]

Hartack's admission caused some titters of another sort, since he had been riding for only six full seasons, and there were older riders waiting their turn.[4] But his record spoke for itself:

- He had already won more than 2,100 races, 131 of them in stakes.
- At the time, only nine jockeys had won three hundred or more races in a year, and just six of those had done that more than once. Shoemaker had had six three-hundred-plus years, and Hartack five.[5]
- From 1953, his first full year, through 1957, Hartack's low win total was 323 in 1954.[6]

By the 1990s, jockeys needed to have ridden at least fifteen years in order to qualify for the Hall of Fame ballot. Still later, the requirement was changed to twenty years.[7] *Ex post facto*, as Hartack began to pile up Kentucky Derby wins—four more to go following his win aboard Iron Liege in 1957—the second-guessing about his early entry into the Hall of Fame disappeared.

Ironically, Hartack's enshrinement came only a few months before the wildly successful partnership with his dynamic agent, Chick Lang, would crash and burn. By the time Hartack won the 1960 Kentucky Derby with Venetian Way, a horse that Lang had found for him, Lang was gone, off to Maryland and a long career in race-track management.[8] One Howard "Scratch Sheet" Pestano was quickly hired by Hartack, the start of an unending series of short-term relationships with dozens of other agents. Pestano lasted four months before he was fired. For a while, Hartack even chucked all his agents and sought out mounts on his own.[9]

Officially, Lang's breakup with Hartack came at Gulfstream Park on the morning of March 29, 1960, just four days before Hartack was scheduled to ride Venetian Way, for the first time, in the Florida Derby.[10] Like most breakups, there had been bumps along the way, some minor, some Gulliverian, but *in toto* they were enough to drive Lang away.

An example of one of the small problems was the hot, steamy day at Arlington Park when Hartack was scheduled to ride all nine races. Lang suggested that he ride three races, skip a race, ride three more and skip another one. "I'm riding all nine," Hartack snapped. "You leave it up to me as far as when I ride or don't ride." Lang could overlook that outburst, because it was a *tête-à-tête*, but other Hartack tirades were less private. There was another day, after Hartack had been badly beaten on an ordinary horse, when he spotted Lang in the paddock in a group of dozens of horsemen. "Don't ever put me on a horse like that again!" Hartack shouted. Then, according to Lang's account, Hartack continued with his diatribe for about five minutes.[11]

Sometimes Lang would hear about Hartack's explosions second-hand. He and Shoemaker crossed paths during one racing day, and Shoemaker, who had a dry sense of humor, said, "Your guy just set a track record."

"What do you mean?" Lang asked.

"A track record for throwing a water bottle across the jocks' room," Shoemaker told him.[12]

Lang was once asked if he ever put Hartack on a "bad" horse. "I have to confess I did," Lang said. "When a boy rides from twelve hundred to seventeen hundred races a year, as Bill does, they can't all be good horses. There's another consideration, and this is something he never understood. There must be a certain give-and-take in a rider's relationship with owners and trainers. You can't accept the mounts on their handicap stars and turn them down when they have an ordinary horse in their stable running."[13]

Frank Merrill Jr. was a trainer who won races all over North America, including circuits in his native Canada, Florida and Chicago. When Merrill died in 1990, he had won almost four thousand races, some of them stakes but most of them with lesser horses who competed in the claiming ranks. Merrill, who was enshrined in the Canadian Racing Hall of Fame in 1981, seemed to be a bad match for the persnickety Hartack, since Merrill was known as "The Prince of Patch" for his ability to take someone else's sore horses, cure their problems and convert them into winners. Sore horses were the bane of Hartack's existence.

One day at Gulfstream Park, Hartack rode one of Merrill's reclamation projects, and after finishing far back the horse came off the track in much worse shape than when he'd started. Hartack was incensed. He sent word to Merrill that he wanted to talk to him in the jockeys' room before the day ended. When Merrill arrived, Hartack upbraided him for several minutes while other jockeys and their valets looked on in horror. A stunned Merrill finally walked away, and outside the room, near the paddock, he spotted Chick Lang and related what happened. Later, Lang said to Hartack, "If you had to talk to him about it, you should have waited until tomorrow morning, at the barn. You should have talked to him in private."[14]

In truth, Lang didn't think Hartack should have said anything to Merrill at all, but by then he knew that it was fruitless to lecture Hartack about manners— or punctuality. There was the time Hartack, while based in Florida, flew to California to accept an assignment in the San Juan Capistrano Handicap at Santa Anita. Before leaving, he agreed with Lang that he could get back to Florida in time to take seven mounts on the Monday after the Santa Anita race. On Sunday night, he called Lang and said he was in Las Vegas, unable to get a flight back to Florida for the Monday racing. "They run planes out of Las Vegas like they're streetcars," Lang said. "But that's what he tells me. Now I've got to get on the phone and tell seven trainers that Hartack can't ride. It embarrasses the hell out of me. I make commitments, and then I have to break them. It's terrible."[15]

A reporter once asked Hartack if he felt badly about not riding horses Lang had booked, including Hartack's scratching of horses in post parades, which required tracks to refund the money bet on them. "After all, Bill, you and Chick have had much success together," the reporter said, trying to make a case.

"Why should I feel bad?" Hartack asked. "I didn't pick the lousy horses, Chick did." He then took a couple of drags off one of the sixty cigarettes he smoked almost every day, still considering the question. "The hell with that," he finally said, indicating that the discussion was over.[16]

The day Lang walked away, he tried to explain what sent him over the brink. "Bill changed somewhere along the line, and it became harder and harder," Lang said. "The hardest part of the job became soothing people he insulted, to try to get him mounts. It's gotten to the point where almost everybody on the race track dislikes him. They don't criticize his riding, but he's got a warped sense of values about what's right and what's wrong. He told somebody that I had forgotten about who was the employer and who was the employee. When that got back to me, I knew I had to leave him. When I went to work for him, I was the man and he was the boy, but by the time we parted, it was the other way around."

For his part, Hartack felt that, more and more, Lang was putting him on horses that didn't have a chance to win. In particular, Hartack said that Lang put him on a horse whose habit was bolting on the turns, and when he declined to ride, his replacement was injured when the horse took off and dumped him. Hartack claimed that he felt responsible for his fellow rider's injuries. "When I'm paying the bills," he said, "I believe it's my right to decide which horses I ride."[17]

Lang said that an incident that occurred at Garden State Park in New Jersey in 1959 soured Hartack on virtually everyone around him, and he carried over the same saturnine disposition into 1960. When one of his horses broke poorly in a race, Hartack blamed the starter and his assistants. After the race, Hartack phoned the stewards from track level and unleashed a barrage of billingsgate. They suspended him for thirteen days, for the rest of the meeting, not because of his complaint but because of the salty language. Hartack appealed, but after a hearing, the stewards let the suspension stand.

"I didn't expect them to reverse the decision," Hartack said at the time. "They never do. But I wanted to go in there and let them hear me. Sure, I cursed. But I didn't direct it at anyone. I apologized. They must have taken it as a direct insult. They act like swearing is a crime. And the starters have been careless more than once. It's happened a couple of times."[18]

After leading the country in wins for three straight years, Hartack had fallen to fourth place in 1958. He had been determined to regain the crown in 1959, but the two-week suspension in May, at a track where he commanded the top mounts, was a setback. He missed the Jersey Stakes at Garden State and the Withers at Belmont Park. (Under racing's reciprocity rule, other tracks enforce suspensions.) Shoemaker was that year's champion, with 347 wins, while Hartack, with 275, finished fourth again. The next year, 1960, Hartack had an extra reason to shoot for the title: he wanted to prove that he could lead the country without Chick Lang's help.[19]

He did, too, with 307 wins, and leading the way was Venetian Way. Hartack had never ridden Venetian Way when the Florida Derby loomed in early April. Bally Ache had beaten Venetian Way earlier, at Hialeah, and he had beaten him twice the year before. He would also beat him two more times before the Kentucky Derby: in the Florida Derby by a nose and in the Stepping Stone Purse at Churchill Downs, a week before the Kentucky Derby.

Two mornings before the Florida Derby, Vic Sovinski, the trainer for Venetian Way, waited patiently at his barn for Hartack, who was supposed to get used to the horse with an easy three-furlong blowout. Hartack was a no-show. He didn't explain to Sovinski why he was missing, but the truth was that he was at a local hotel, playing cards until six in the morning.[20]

Bobby Ussery, who had never ridden in the Kentucky Derby, was Bally Ache's regular rider. When the horses were being pulled up after crossing the finish line in the hotly contested Florida Derby, Ussery looked over at Hartack and hee-hawed something about Venetian Way not being good enough. "Some guys would do that after races," Hartack said almost thirty years later. "It got picked up because it was a big race. He said something. I yelled back that he beat me because my horse wasn't fit."[21]

When Venetian Way got to Louisville for the Stepping Stone prep race and the Kentucky Derby itself, there was a controversy about the colt being sore and needing to run with Butazolidin, an anti-inflammatory drug referred to as *bute.* Bute was permitted in some states, including Kentucky, but banned in others, including Maryland (home of the Preakness) and New York (where they run the Belmont Stakes). Sovinski waffled when asked about the drug issue with his horse.[22] Eight years later, after Kentucky had joined other states by temporarily outlawing bute, Dancer's Image finished first in the Derby but was disqualified when a post-race test turned up positive for bute. After a prolonged court battle, the winning purse money of $122,600 was awarded to Calumet Farm's Forward Pass, who had finished second. The Dancer's Image jockey who was deprived of a share of the winning purse was Bobby Ussery.[23]

Sovinski, in his fifties, had been a dough mixer for the A & P grocery chain in Kankakee, Illinois, and served in the military during World War II before he took up horse training in 1945. In his only previous Derby, he had finished second, behind Tim Tam, with Lincoln Road in 1958.[24] Sovinski was having second thoughts about using Hartack, who had been second twice with Venetian Way. Eddie Arcaro, who had won a record five Derbys (later matched by Hartack), hadn't missed riding in the race since 1943, but this was a year when he didn't have a mount.

Sovinski was upset with Hartack after Venetian Way finished second in the seven-furlong Stepping Stone. The trainer asked Hartack to work the colt an extra furlong after they reached the wire. "He ran a horrible race that day," Hartack said many years later. "He couldn't get a hold of the track, and after the race was over he was practically in distress because he struggled the whole way, trying to get hold of the track. I just assumed that if I worked him out a mile, it was going to hurt him more than it was going to help him. So I didn't work him the extra distance. The trainer was quite unhappy about it. I don't know what he expected out of me. I had to use my own judgment; I didn't have a chance at the eighth pole to talk to him and explain why I wasn't going to work him out. I had to do it on my own, and he was very annoyed about it. I must have been right, because he ended up just walloping Bally Ache in the Derby."[25]

Sovinski eventually fired Hartack, after the Preakness, but with the Derby only a few days away, he decided to pass on the chance to hire Arcaro.

Not many handicappers picked Venetian Way to win. One who did was the *New York Daily News* cartoonist Leon O'Maelia, whose drawing on the day of the race was captioned "I'm pickin' Venetian Way!" O'Maelia turned in his cartoon, left the office, and went home to his wife. They watched some television and went to bed. That night, O'Maelia died in his sleep. He was seventy-six, and never got the chance to watch the race he had picked correctly.[26]

The drying-out track was listed as "good" for the Derby, which means it was not "fast" but not as slow as "muddy." The temperature was fifty-two degrees, the fourth coldest in Derby history. Hartack followed Sovinsky's instructions, which were to have Venetian Way laying third or fourth in the early going. Bally Ache made the lead, as expected, and after a mile he was still a length in front of Venetian Way. Tompion was in third place, but too far back to be a factor, and he also lost a shoe at some point. Venetian Way passed Bally Ache at the top of the stretch and won easily, by three and a half lengths.[27]

The press waited thirty minutes to interview Hartack in the jockeys' room, and not one fellow jockey came over to congratulate him. Hartack eventually cut the interview short, because he had to change silks for the next race. On Derby day, jockeys riding in the Derby usually don't take mounts in the next race, or else they cancel those engagements if

Venetian Way, with Hartack riding, was led into the winner's circle by his trainer, Vic Sovinski (hatless), after the 1960 Kentucky Derby. Sovinski fired Hartack two weeks later after criticizing his losing ride in the Preakness (Keeneland/Meadors).

they win the Derby. But not Hartack. He was in the jockeys' room after the TV interviews, answered a few questions and was gone again.

The first question began with "Willie ..." Hartack immediately cut the speaker off. "Haven't you learned yet that my name is Bill, not Willie?" he demanded. "Gentlemen, I'll answer anything you want to know, but I'll tell you now that I'll refuse to answer any stupid questions."[28]

Two weeks after the Derby, Venetian Way's next-to-last finish in the six-horse Preakness resurrected theories that the horse needed Butazolidin to be effective. Bally Ache, in winning the Preakness, beat Venetian Way by almost nine lengths at Pimlico, which meant there was a remarkable twelve-length swing between the two horses in only a fortnight.

Sovinski blamed Hartack for allowing Bally Ache to lope along on an easy early lead. The early fractions were the slowest for a Preakness in thirty years.

Coming off the track, Hartack said that he thought Venetian Way was sore. "I would like to have a barn full of broken-down horses like him," Sovinski said. "I was surprised that a rider like Hartack wouldn't realize there was such a slow pace. Hartack will never ride another horse for me again."[29]

Sometimes Hartack's alarm clock worked and sometimes it didn't, as demonstrated in this photo c. 1958. He missed a workout for Venetian Way, his Kentucky Derby winner, just before the Preakness. When Venetian Way lost the race the trainer fired Hartack (Nancy Lang collection).

When Hartack heard about Sovinski's comments, he was surprised. He said that he had had dinner with the trainer on the night of the Preakness, and there was no mention that he had ridden the colt poorly. "He trained that horse just like any baker would have done," Hartack remarked, a snide reference to Sovinski's pre-war job with the A & P.[30]

When Hartack said that Venetian Way didn't do much running, and that he thought he knew the reason but wouldn't divulge it, some observers speculated that he was talking about the absence of bute because of Maryland rules. Asked specifically about that, he said, "I don't know how a trainer trains his horse," he said. "I'm a rider."[31]

Red Smith, the syndicated columnist, was at the forefront of the pundits who believed that Venetian Way ran sore because he couldn't be treated with bute in Maryland. "It was no secret around Churchill Downs that Venetian Way was getting the [bute] before the Kentucky Derby," Smith wrote. "Presumably he was on the wagon when he went into the Preakness. Maybe there's no connection. Perhaps the sauce doesn't help a horse run fast. Yet it seems possible that W. Hartack had Butazolidin on his mind when he remarked after getting off Venetian Way in Baltimore."[32]

Just before the Preakness, Bally Ache was sold by Leonard Frutchman to a Kentucky syndicate of breeding investors for $1.25 million. Frutchman had bought the horse as a yearling in 1958 for $5,000. The colt's new owners planned to race him for the rest of 1960 and then turn him out to stud, which would mean he could be bred to about forty mares a year, for many years. The offspring could then be raced or sold. Either way, it seemed like a sound investment, but Bally Ache had physical issues. He won the Jersey Derby after the Preakness, but he came up lame for the Belmont and couldn't run. In early October, Bally Ache experienced a career-ending breakdown in a race. On October 29, he was put down after suffering an acute intestinal attack. He was insured for $1 million.[33]

Besides Bally Ache, three other horses headed for the Belmont also ran in the Jersey Derby. Bally Ache beat Tompion by a neck in New Jersey, where Hartack picked up the mount on Celtic Ash (they finished third). Steve Brooks rode Venetian Way to a fourth-place finish.

There was more jockey roulette for the Belmont. "I'm getting a jockey—Eddie Arcaro," Venetian Way's Sovinski said. "Hartack will be lucky to get some bum."[34] In the end, Hartack stayed with Celtic Ash. Arcaro, winner of six Belmonts, finally re-entered the Triple Crown mix via his assignment on Venetian Way. It was to be one of Vic Sovinski's last days in the glow of the klieg lights. At fifty-two, he suffered a fatal heart attack in Florida on December 19.

Per his instructions from the Irish trainer, Tom Barry, Hartack bided his time in the early going with the English-bred Celtic Ash. On the turn for home, Hartack roused his colt and they blew past Venetian Way and Arcaro.[35] This was Hartack's first Belmont mount. He never won the stake again.[36]

The winning margin was five and a half lengths. Hartack declined to crow about his victory. "Venetian Way had a light constitution," he said. "He could really run fast, but he just didn't have the endurance to put his good races back to back. He never came back to his Derby form again."[37]

12

Bill and Eddie: Don't Invite Them to the Same Party

In 1961, during a sixty-seven-day meeting at Arlington Park in suburban Chicago, Bill Hartack won an astounding one hundred races. He broke the record of eighty-one set by Johnny Sellers the year before.[1] Midway through the 1961 meet, Hartack was visited by a good friend, the broadcaster Larry King, who was on vacation. King, a hidebound horse-player dating back to his formative years in Brooklyn, had gotten to know Hartack in Miami Beach a few years before. Hartack was booting home winners by the bagful at the Florida tracks and King was just breaking in to local radio with a daily interview broadcast from Pumpernick's, a popular restaurant. The station paid him $50 a week; Charlie Bookbinder, who had won the deli in a poker game with restaurateur Wolfie Cohen, paid King another $50. The first day King was on the air in 1957, he looked around, and nobody had come to be interviewed, so he talked with a waiter to fill some air time. The next day, the crooner Bobby Darin, staying at the Fontainebleau Hotel, was on his way to the airport to pick up Sandra Dee when he came into the restaurant and, unannounced, went on with King. Darin's classic recording, "Mack the Knife," had been a big hit. The day after Darin, Hartack came in for a bite; King had him on, and he was off and running with his new show. Born Lawrence Harvey Zeiger, he changed his last name to King after he saw an ad in a newspaper for a liquor store with that name.

"Bill never gave me a horse," King said, meaning a horse that Hartack felt was worth a bet. "That just wasn't his style." King told the story about how Bookbinder, also a friend of Hartack's, came to the track one day, was told that Hartack's car was being repaired, and offered to give the jockey a ride home to Miami Springs after the last race. Hartack told Bookbinder that he would let him know. The time came for that last race, and Bookbinder was in the paddock, leaning on the fence in the midst of other spectators, when Hartack came out of the jockeys' room, ready to mount his horse. Hartack spotted Bookbinder and nodded without saying anything. Hartack's horse won and paid about $40 for a $2 bet.

After the race, Bookbinder waited outside the jockeys' room while Hartack showered. "What are you doing here?" Hartack asked when he came out.

"To give you a ride," Bookbinder said.

"I told you I would let you know," Hartack said. "I got a ride, but thanks."

"So why were you nodding to me in the paddock?" Bookbinder asked.

"That meant I wanted you to bet the horse," Hartack said. "How much did you make?"

Bookbinder hadn't bet a nickel.

While King was in Chicago to spend time with Hartack, he got a ride to the track one day in the jockey's dirty Cadillac. "Geez, Bill," King said, "this car looks like hell. I'll get it washed and cleaned during the races." Hartack left King the keys before he went off for a day of riding. After the races, King told Hartack that the car was now spic and span.

"Did you clean the ashtray?" Hartack asked. He was a heavy smoker, and the ashtray filled up in no time.

"Yeah, that too," King said.

"That's too bad," Hartack remarked. "I met this blonde yesterday, and she put her phone number on a piece of paper, and it was in the ashtray."[2]

Through Marje Everett, who ran Arlington Park, Hartack was able to rent a house for the season on the cheap on Euclid Avenue, across from the track. When the meet ended, Hartack took off, and a track official went to the house to make sure everything was in order. Under the bed he found seventy-six used condoms.[3]

Hartack and Shoemaker were favorites of Everett, who was determined that one or the other would win the meet title in 1957 (Hartack prevailed, with sixty wins). Another jockey, Larry Gilligan, recalled, "Marje ran me out of Chicago. I was running third in the standings that summer, and I thought I had a legitimate shot at winning the title. But Marje was determined that Shoe or Hartack win. Every time I'd win a race with a good horse, Marje would get word to the trainers to take me off, and put Shoe or Hartack on."

In June, Gilligan won the Modesty Handicap with Grecian Ayr, a 58–1 shot who had been running in $10,000 claiming company the year before. "I never got the chance to ride the filly the next time," Gilligan said. "Marje got word to the trainer, Jimmy Wallace, that she wanted Shoemaker or Hartack in the saddle. I finally had to leave Chicago and ride elsewhere. The way it went, I ran out of good horses to ride."

With 549 wins, Hartack ranks far down on the list of all-time leading jockeys at Arlington Park,[4] but when Phil Georgeff wrote his memoir, there were only three chapters devoted exclusively to jockeys—Hartack, Eddie Arcaro and Bill Shoemaker.[5] Georgeff was the premier announcer ("Here they come, spinning out of the turn," was one of his pet phrases) at Chicago race tracks from the 1950s to the 1990s. During his early years, Hartack and Shoemaker were the kingpins at Arlington, with the New York–based Arcaro dropping in intermittently to ride in an important stakes race. "They were three great riders, and three distinct personalities," Georgeff said. "They had three different riding styles. But nobody knew the shortest route to the winner's circle any better than those three. They each deserved a chapter, because for my money they're the three greatest of all time."[6]

Bill Nack, a future award-winning writer for *Sports Illustrated*, was a young Chicagoan when Shoemaker and Hartack were battling to see who would succeed the aging Arcaro as the country's preeminent rider.

"One of the advantages of growing up in Chicago in the 1950s," Nack wrote, "was that the tracks offered a front-row seat to witness the greatest show in all the Windy City—the hammer-and-tong battles fought there every summer between Hartack and Shoemaker. Heady Eddie Arcaro often said that Shoemaker was the guy who would take his place as the premier reinsman in America. Ultimately, Arcaro may have been right, but I must add that there was no smarter, tougher, or more competitive race rider in America than Bill Hartack. A marked visual contrast to Shoemaker, who sat very still and pretty on a horse, the bouncing, gyrating Hartack always came home looking as though the entire Sioux Nation was chasing after him."

Nack went on to say that while Hartack might be a thorn in the side of some owners, trainers and even veterinarians, he "rode the hair off of every horse I ever saw him on, and it didn't matter if it was Round Table or Majestic Prince in the major races or lowly claimers like Fast Dance or Fleet Argo in the daily double." On Kentucky Derby day, according to Nack, Hartack was one of only a few riders who "had the smarts, strength, and guts to get it done in that hottest of all pressure cookers. I have seen three: Arcaro, Hartack and more recently Gary Stevens." If he were forced to make a choice, Nack said, Hartack would be his "go-to guy. I will always remember the coalminer's kid, his lonesome honesty badly missed from the game."[7]

Hartack's best race at Arlington was one that he didn't even win. Three days before the running of the Arlington Classic, a $150,000 race, he was riding Smoke-Me-Now, who ran up on the heels of another horse and stumbled. Hartack was tossed in the air before he hit the ground. They were afraid to move him until the ambulance came. His spine appeared badly damaged, and there was a fear that Hartack might never ride again. The preliminary assessment of the X-rays was that there was a fracture of the twelfth dorsal vertebra, and a possible fracture of the tenth rib.

Phone calls and telegrams began to pour into St. Joseph's Hospital, where Hartack was recovering. Eddie Arcaro, who was never close to Hartack, on or off the track, was one of the first to call. An anonymous telegram said, "As one of your ardent admirers, I never bet on horses, only on you. Did very well in the Derby [Iron Liege at 8–1]. Get well soon so I can win again. But make a complete recovery."

At Iron Liege's barn, his trainer, Jimmy Jones, fretted about whether he'd need a substitute rider for the Classic. (One horse Iron Liege wouldn't have to beat was Bold Ruler, who had been pulled out of the race due to a splint injury. Bold Ruler had won the Preakness after running poorly in the Kentucky Derby.[8]) The word on Hartack the next day was better: his condition had gone from serious to good. Just in case, Jones lined up Dave Erb as a standby. Erb had won the Classic the year before, with Swoon's Son. But in the first race on the day before this Classic, Erb's left knee was a black-and-blue mess after one of his mounts bounced him off the wooden rail. "What are you gonna do?" Jones asked. "If Hartack is ready to ride, I'll send a horse over to pick him up."[9]

Released from the hospital, Hartack soaked himself for two days in a hot tub. The day before the race, at 8 o'clock at night, he went over to the track and got on one of Jones' stable ponies. "That is Mister Bill Hartack," one of Jones' exercise riders said when a security guard came by to inquire. "He has a fine feeling for money and right now he is teaching his back to feel the same way. He's strapped up like he's a fat old woman trying to keep the rolls in. But he's going to be riding Iron Liege tomorrow, and he'll be thereabouts when they pass out the money, too."

After forty-five minutes on the pony, Hartack got off and went to the phone to call Jimmy Jones. He told him that it hurt getting on and off the horse, but he would try to ride.[10]

The morning of the race, Hartack was at the track, blowing out Barbizon, another Calumet horse, at 6 o'clock. A few hours later, he galloped a horse named Crossland. He said he felt fine, but the truth was that it hurt like blazes every time he moved from side to side. He was wearing an elastic girdle when he appeared on the track for the post parade of the first race. He finished second.

Three hours before the Classic, there was concern in the jockeys' room because Conn McCreary, scheduled to ride Clem, was not there. Coming from New York, McCreary was on his way in from the Chicago airport when he got lost in traffic because of what was described as Chicago's heaviest rainstorm in seventy-two years. When McCreary finally walked through the jocks' room door, he said, "I could have swum here and made better time."

The rain stopped, but there was so much standing water on the track that the stewards made the official condition "sloppy." There was an asterisk next to Iron Liege's name in the *Daily Racing Form* past performances, which meant that the colt could handle off tracks, but in reality he had run three times in the mud and never been better than second. After Greek Game led most of the way, Hartack and Iron Liege collared him in the stretch. Then it was Clem's turn. McCreary turned him loose, and he won by about two lengths. Clem earned over $100,000, which was more than he had accrued in all twenty-two of his previous races. Iron Liege finished second, and his stablemate, Barbizon, finished ahead of only one horse.

Coming off the track, Hartack was furious at not having won. In the jockeys' room, one of the valets tried to console him. "You did great," he said. "You're lucky you can walk, much less ride."

"I don't care if I have one leg," Hartack barked. "That's no excuse. I got the lead and should have won."[11]

By the time the press got to him, Hartack had cooled off. William Leggett, of *Sports Illustrated*, suggested that it might have been the best race he ever rode.

"I don't think so," Hartack said. "Nope, that wasn't my best."

Leggett returned to the press box and wrote up his story. "Maybe Hartack was right," he wrote. "Maybe it wasn't his best race. But it may have been his bravest."[12]

Hartack still led the Arlington Park jockey colony that summer with sixty wins. It was his third straight riding title. The year before, he rode seventy-five winners in an abbreviated meeting of thirty-six days. In 1961 and 1962 he would win a hundred races each year, leading the way both times.

Shoemaker won only one title at Arlington, but overall he outrode Hartack in stakes wins, forty-eight to thirty-five.[13] "Many dyed-in-the-wool handicappers deplored their dominating ways," Phil Georgeff said. "Too often they rode the favorites, or the heavy second choices, making price shots few and far between. Real fans loved it. Shoe and Hartack were two of America's three finest riders, and to see them slug it out on a daily basis was a treat for the ages."[14]

A week after the Arlington Classic, Hartack had the mount on Sir Ruler as he tried to win the Arlington Futurity for the second straight year. The competition was stiff—Fred Hooper owned two horses in the race, the undefeated Alhambra and Olymar, who were running as a single betting entry. Hooper had won the Kentucky Derby in 1945 with Hoop Jr., named after his son and the first horse he ever owned, and was still trying to win the race a second time.[15] Alhambra and Olymar were both sons of Hooper's Olympia, who had been the odds-on favorite in the 1949 Derby but faded to sixth after leading the race for a mile.[16] Hooper died in 2000, never having won his second Derby. He was 102 years old.[17]

Hooper liked to run his own show, so before the 1957 Arlington Futurity, he helped his trainer, Chuck Parke, give the jockeys—Eddie Arcaro on Alhambra and Doug Dodson on Olymar—pre-race instructions. "Don't use the whip," Hooper told Dodson. "He'll jump the rail if you hit him."[18]

Alhambra, who had inherited the speed of his sire, led all the way. Arcaro eased him to the finish line as they won by about five lengths in a record time. After the winner, in order, came Leather Button, Rellim S.W., Olymar and Sir Ruler. But in midstretch, about a sixteenth of a mile from the wire, Dodson, ignoring Hooper's orders, hit Olymar righthanded, causing the horse to veer to the left, into the path of Sir Ruler. The rough stuff had nothing to do with the first three finishers, but Hartack had no choice but to claim foul against Olymar. As the three stewards began to interview Dodson and Hartack from a phone near the winner's circle, getting their versions of the interference, those aware of Illinois' racing rules knew that the stewards' decision could affect much more than who finished fourth or fifth. If the stewards disqualified Olymar and moved him back, they would also have to disqualify his entrymate Alhambra, an innocent bystander.

Arcaro knew the rule, which was also on the books in New York. Some states, however, gave the stewards more latitude in such cases. On the track, waiting to have their photos taken with Alhambra in the winner's circle, Arcaro and Parke, who had trained both Alhambra and Olymar, stood next to one another. It took fifteen minutes, an extraordinarily long time, for the stewards to come to a decision. A rule of thumb at the track is that the longer the stewards take, the more likely there will be a disqualification, and Arcaro could sense what was coming. He looked at Parke and said, "That'll teach you to run a bum with a champ."

Parke, unaware that the rule was unbending, replied, "They can't take you down. It wouldn't be fair."

"The hell they can't," Arcaro said, spitting his words. "You know that crazy rule. If Olymar did anything wrong, then we all suffer."

Dodson, the culprit for whipping Olymar, came over. He tried to calm Arcaro down. "I straightened him out immediately after he came over," Dodson said. "The judges will see that it wasn't my fault, certainly unintentional."[19] (The purpose of the rule was to prevent one part of an entry setting up the race for an entrymate.)

The articulate Hartack was usually good on the phone with the stewards. He was able to detach himself from the heat of the moment and calmly argue his case in a succinct way. He had an advantage over many other jockeys in this regard. His case against Olymar was clear cut, and he didn't have to say much. When the smoke had cleared, Alhambra, who was much the best horse in the race, was dropped to fourth place. His undefeated streak was officially no more. Leather Button, though no match for Alhambra, was moved up to first place and collected $104,874 for his owners. Rellim S.W. was awarded second place, with the rest of the order being Sir Ruler, Alhambra and Olymar.[20] It wasn't too long after the running that the entry-disqualification rule was broadened, to give the stewards more leeway, in several states, including Illinois and New York.[21]

Oddly, none of the Arlington Futurity combatants were around the next year for the Kentucky Derby. Alhambra had an eighty-race career (twenty-three wins and purses of more than $300,000), but Hooper accepted the reality that he was a sprinter, hardly a candidate for the mile-and-a-quarter demands of the Derby. (Ironically, it was Hooper who had been on the receiving end when the stewards made another reversal of a major Chicago race for 2-year-olds in 1956. After California Kid, ridden by Shoemaker, finished first in the Washington Park Futurity by a nose, the second-place finisher, Greek Game, ridden by Hartack and owned by Hooper, was moved up to the win following twenty minutes of film reviews and jockey interviews. The stewards said that Shoemaker, whipping lefthanded, had caused California Kid to drift to his right, knocking Hartack's mount offstride. After California Kid's number was taken down, one angry bettor on the track apron looked toward the stewards' perch high atop the track, shook his fist and screamed, "Nice going, Mister Capone."[22])

Hartack would eventually have an acrimonious falling out with Hooper over a horse, Greek Circle, that Hartack forced the stewards to scratch in the post parade in 1959. Eddie Arcaro defended Hartack over that one, even saying, "He thought the horse was sore, and he was right. It took a little guts, too."[23]

Arcaro retired from riding at the end of 1961. At the 1962 Derby (the one Hartack would win with Decidedly), Arcaro was invited to Louisville to speak at the National Turf Writers' Association's annual dinner. Arcaro was going to be in Louisville anyway, because he was a commentator on ABC TV for the national telecast of the race (a gig that Hartack would also have in later years).

Surprisingly, much of Arcaro's speech at the turf writers' dinner was about Hartack. "Jockeys are under great tension, frequently after major stakes races," Arcaro said. "When writers descend on them, they often give terrible answers. I am thinking of one rider in particular. You all know who I mean. You fellows knocked him down. Now, you should help pick him up."

Afterward, Arcaro confirmed that the jockey he had referred to was Hartack. Asked if he had discussed his speech with Hartack beforehand, Arcaro said, "No. No chance of that. We haven't spoken to each other for years."

Arcaro related how the feud started. It was years before at Belmont Park. According to Arcaro, the Hall of Fame jockey Ted Atkinson said some horrible things about Hartack in the jockeys' room. Atkinson was loud enough that almost everybody in the room—dozens of jockeys—heard him.

"I wasn't even in the room," Arcaro said. "When the word got back to Hartack about what was said, somehow it was wrongly attributed to me. I tried to explain that to Hartack, several times. He wouldn't listen. After a while I gave up. So he's never talked to me again. I couldn't care less."[24]

According to Chick Lang, however, Hartack had other reasons to feud with Arcaro. Lang said that whenever Arcaro was asked to name the best jockeys of his era, he would mention Shoemaker, Braulio Baeza and maybe two or three others, but never Hartack.[25]

Arcaro might have sloughed off the snubs most of the time, but the winner of the 1962 Derby was Decidedly, ridden by Hartack, and it was Arcaro's job to interview the winning jockey on ABC TV.

A minute after Decidedly crossed the finish line, the network cut to a commercial. Off the air, Arcaro turned to his broadcasting partner, Chris Schenkel. "Can you get somebody else to do Hartack?" he asked.

"What are you talking about?" Schenkel asked.

"Hartack," Arcaro said. "He hates my guts."

"We can't do that," Schenkel told him. "It's too late. You'll just have to take your chances."

After the commercial break, Hartack went on camera with Arcaro and treated him like he was his best friend. Step by step, he took Arcaro and the audience through a replay of the race. It was a very informative exercise. That was the last time Hartack ever spoke to Arcaro.[26]

Hartack once said there was a disconnect between him and most jockeys. "I wasn't cut out to be a jockey," he said. "My ideals are different from those of other riders. I don't think it's good to get too friendly with your rivals. Once away from the track, I see little of them. Just because we're in the same business doesn't mean I have to hang around with them after hours."[27]

Hartack's long-running feud with Churchill Downs was connected to Arcaro. The track had once forced Hartack to pose with Arcaro for a publicity photo. It was taken with both riders standing on an empty race track, and although it doesn't show, Hartack reportedly was gritting his teeth. He never forgave Churchill Downs and resisted their promotional entreaties for the rest of his life.[28]

Arcaro could be thankful to Hartack and his agent at the time for getting the mount on Kelso, the five-time Horse of the Year from 1960 through 1964.[29] The Belmont Stakes and the Triple Crown were over before Kelso made his first start as a 3-year-old. Steve Brooks rode him in his first stakes start, the Arlington Classic, and they finished eighth. Leaving the gate, Kelso reared, hit his head hard against the steel barrier and was left with a crease for the rest of his life. Hartack rode Kelso a couple of weeks after Arlington for a win in the Choice Stakes in New Jersey, and Carl Hanford, Kelso's trainer, thought he would retain Hartack's services when the horse returned from Chicago for an eastern campaign late in the year. But Hartack, Hanford sensed, was angling for the mount on Tompion. (Indeed, Hartack won the Travers at Saratoga with Tompion in August.) Nevertheless, Hanford called several times, hoping to land Hartack. "They didn't give us the time of day," Hanford said. "They didn't even bother to return my calls. So I said, 'The hell with them.'"[30]

Although Arcaro was nearing retirement, he still rode well all the way to the end. "I don't know why I didn't think of Arcaro before," Hanford said. "He was 'The Master.' There were few riders in his league."[31] So Arcaro got the mount. From September 1960 through November 1961, they were inseparable, and out of fourteen races, Kelso won all but two.[32]

While Arcaro could go either way on the fickle Hartack and be open-minded enough to judge him on a case-by-case basis, Manny Ycaza, another Hall of Fame jockey, felt quite differently. Fred Hooper, instrumental in bringing Braulio Baeza and Laffit Pincay Jr. to the United States from Panama, had an affinity for Panamanian jockeys, which led him to also using Ycaza on his horses. In fact, Ycaza rode Alhambra, and in 1961–1962 he and Hartack both had multiple flings with Ridan, who won his first eight races as a 2-year-old. It was Ycaza's turn in the 1962 Derby, but Ridan finished third as Hartack won his third of five Derbys with Decidedly, who was 8–1.[33]

In 1965, Ycaza rode Bold Lad to a third-place finish in the Wood Memorial, two weeks before the Derby, but the colt's trainer, Bill Winfrey, switched to Hartack for the Derby Trial. While Bold Lad won in a canter, becoming the Derby favorite, Ycaza scrambled to get the mount on Hail to All, a horse he had never ridden and who had never won over a distance of ground.[34] The shuffling was moot; Bold Lad finished next to last and Hail to All ran fifth, neither a challenge to the victorious Lucky Debonair, ridden by Shoemaker.[35] By the time Hail to All won the Jersey Derby, the Belmont and the Travers, Ycaza had again been forgotten; Johnny Sellers was his jockey for all three races. Ycaza never did win a

Derby,[36] but in 1964, when Hartack and Northern Dancer, with the Derby and Preakness already theirs, ran third in the Triple Crown windup, it was Ycaza who won the Belmont Stakes with Quadrangle.[37]

The first serious flare-up between Hartack and Ycaza came in the 1958 Flamingo Stakes. Jewel's Reward, with Ycaza, finished first, and Tim Tam, with Hartack, ran second, but not after they had bumped six times in the stretch run. The horses were so close together barreling down the lane that Ycaza, on the inside, didn't have room to whip righthanded, and Hartack wasn't able to whip lefthanded, his natural hand. When Ycaza, out of desperation, went to his left hand, Jewel's Reward shied to the right and began slamming into Tim Tam. The crowd booed Hartack for claiming foul immediately afterward, but in fact the stewards had flashed their own "inquiry" sign on the tote board seconds after the horses reached the wire. Tim Tam's number was ultimately moved up to the win position, and Elizabeth Arden Graham, owner of Jewel's Reward, beat an embarrassed retreat from the winner's circle, where she had gone to pick up the bric-a-brac that went to the winner.[38]

Asked once about Hartack, Ycaza said, "One of these days, I'm going to run him into the rail. No, I take that back. I'm going to run him *through* the rail. That's if some other jock doesn't beat me to it."[39]

(Author's disclosure: Several years ago, Manny Ycaza and I discussed doing his biography. Joe Hirsch of the *Daily Racing Form* came up with what I thought was a brilliant title: *Blinking Lights: The Story of Jockey Manny Ycaza.* It was a reference to the horses' numbers that blink on the tote board while the stewards are considering a foul claim, something that often happened during the career of the fiery Ycaza. Manny didn't particularly like the title, and he liked my ideas for the biography even less. After a civil lunch with Hirsch at P.J. Clarke's in New York, we talked one more time on the phone and mutually agreed to drop the project.)

Others jockeys' dislike for Hartack took on groundswell proportions in 1964, after an incident involving Milo Valenzuela at Arlington Park. Here, improbably, was Hartack, defending Valenzuela, the jockey who had replaced him on Tim Tam in the 1958 Kentucky Derby.[40] Valenzuela was hired by Mary Hecht, the owner of Sadair, to ride her crack 2-year-old in what had become the Arlington-Washington Futurity. The winning jockey in the rich race would earn 10 percent of the purse—$13,492. The day before the race, I'm Nashville was scratched because he was running a fever, which left his jockey, Bill Shoemaker, available to ride another horse. Hecht and her trainer, Les Lear, unceremoniously told Valenzuela to go home; Shoemaker would ride Sadair instead.

Valenzuela was furious, especially since he had given up a mount in an important race in New York, at Aqueduct, in order to be at Arlington Park to ride Sadair. Valenzuela appealed his losing the Sadair mount to the Arlington stewards. One of them, the former rider Ted Atkinson, suggested a compromise, by which they would get Hecht to pay Valenzuela $2,500 not to ride. Valenzuela nixed that idea; he was in town, he said, for the chance to earn more than five times that much. On race day, Valenzuela tried to get into the jockeys' room, to ask the other riders to boycott the race in support of his argument. He was denied admittance by the stewards. They ran the race, Sadair won and Shoemaker collected the big bucks. Valenzuela received $25 for what is known as a "mount fee."[41] He sued Hecht and Lear for $2 million. A year later, the suit was dropped. Valenzuela said the lingering legal action was hurting his business.[42]

What did the malaprop-prone Samuel Goldwyn, the movie mogul, say? "A verbal contract isn't worth the paper it's printed on"?[43] Then and now, racing has operated on verbal contracts in many ways. Hartack felt Sadair's camp had reneged on the agreed-upon deal and that Valenzuela was entitled to redress. Valenzuela, like many of the riders at Arlington Park, was a dues-paying member of the Jockeys' Guild, which declined to get involved. Bert Thompson, executive director of the guild, didn't think the case was worth the fight. Hartack had been down Valenzuela's path with the guild before. In Florida, he had been fined $100 for missing a stewards' meeting to review film of a race. The guild said he was wrong to appeal. So did the state racing commission. But a judge agreed with Hartack, and he was refunded the money.[44]

"Hartack was a very opinionated guy," a fellow Hall of Fame rider, Laffit Pincay Jr., said after Hartack died in 2007. "He had his own ideas, and I'll tell you, he could have been a lawyer. Nobody could beat him in an argument. I don't know why he didn't become a lawyer, because he would have been very good at that."[45]

Hartack quit the guild over the Valenzuela furor. "It wasn't because of Shoemaker riding the horse, and it wasn't because of Valenzuela not riding the horse," Hartack said. "But when Milo was trying to establish his case, and he had to be in the jocks' room to show that he was there and ready to ride, they wouldn't allow him into the room. The guild does not want to enter into any argument that will cause notoriety."[46]

A couple of years later, sixty-two jockeys, including Hartack, resigned from the Jockeys' Guild to form the Jockeys Benefit Association. They said that there were several reasons for the schism, including "weak representation." However, the movement was short lived.[47]

As for Milo Valenzuela, not all his breaks in racing were bad. Ten years after his serendipitous Kentucky Derby win with Tim Tam, Providence was at his doorstep again. No one broke his leg, as Hartack had done in 1958, but Don Brumfield ate some bad chicken salad and came down with a nasty case of food poisoning, and suddenly Forward Pass needed a new rider for the 1968 Blue Grass Stakes, taking place the week before the Derby. With Valenzuela taking Brumfield's place, they won the race, and Valenzuela kept the mount for Churchill Downs. Dancer's Image beat Forward Pass, but then Valenzuela lucked out again: Dancer's Image flunked the post-race drug test, and after a long court battle by Peter Fuller, the owner of Dancer's Image, they gave the win to Forward Pass and Valenzuela. Calumet Farm's Lucille Markey paid both jockeys—Valenzuela and Brumfield—10 percent shares of the purse. That came to more than $12,000 apiece. For Valenzuela, it beat the hell out of the $25 he got that dastardly day in Chicago.[48]

Since 1950, Santa Anita has honored jockeys "whose careers and personal character earn esteem for the individual and the sport of thoroughbred horse racing" with the George Woolf Award. Woolf, who rode Seabiscuit and many other famous horses of that era, died in 1946 after a spill at Santa Anita.

In 1956, when Johnny Adams was the seventh winner of the Woolf Award, Hartack made the presentation. But, for whatever reason, Hartack never won the award, which through the years has been given to jockeys following votes by media, or fans, or riders who belong to the Jockeys' Guild.[49] The guild has done the voting, it is believed, since the 1990s. It is debatable whether Hartack's contentious relationship with the guild was related to his exclusion. The Woolf Award has never been presented posthumously.[50]

Wayne Harris, who rode against Hartack when they both competed in California and went hunting with him all over the United States, said that one year Robyn Smith's name was placed on the ballot at the expense of Hartack. "That was the end of the George Woolf as far as I was concerned," Harris said. "I quit going to the ceremony even though some of my close friends were winners. I wanted nothing to do with the award after they kept snubbing 'Tack."[51]

Smith was at the forefront of the movement to allow women to ride, and in 1969 she became the first female to win a major stakes race. But, like other women, she had trouble getting mounts on a regular basis, and today she is better known for having married Fred Astaire than for any race she won.[52] Julie Krone is another female who has never won the George Woolf Award, even though she holds the record—3,704—for wins by a female jockey and her horses earned $90 million.[53]

13

Put the *Schadenfreude* on Hold

From about 1961 on, it was *de rigueur* for many journalists to bury Bill Hartack. "Hartack's Losing His Riding Touch," headlined a Florida newspaper.[1] "Big Stables Don't Look for Hartack Anymore," the *Washington Star* announced.[2] "Whatever Happened to Bill Hartack?" asked *Sports Illustrated*.[3] Even Chick Lang, the agent who had spearheaded Hartack's rise during those halcyon years before their messy split in 1960, thought his former client was slipping. "I doubt if he is as good as he used to be," Lang said to the *Star*. "He may have lost some of his wonderful determination as he began to lose popularity. Anyway, he's not getting the good mounts anymore. He did it to himself. I mean, Bill didn't get heavy or have a bad spill. Nothing of the sort. He lost out because of his tantrums and his attitude."

One problem for these naysayers was that Hartack kept winning the Kentucky Derby. On a day-to-day basis, his business turned turtle; some years he wouldn't even win a hundred races. But at Derby time, he was still the jockey of choice, in demand for many of the major trainers. He won his third Derby with Decidedly in 1962; he won number four with Northern Dancer in 1964; and he tied Eddie Arcaro's record with number five—on Majestic Prince in 1969—when he was thirty-six years old. Of the five Derby winners, only the last, the undefeated Majestic Prince, went into the race favored.[4] By 1968, though, Hartack's annual win percentage had sunk to 13.6 percent, down from the 20 percent and higher that he had registered from 1952 through 1962.[5] Johnny Longden, trainer of Majestic Prince, paid the numbers no mind; he was confident that Hartack still knew how to win at Churchill Downs. "You don't need to tell a jockey with Hartack's experience what to do," Longden said. "He knows what's going on."[6]

The bandwagon to derail Hartack's career gained momentum in 1961, when Carry Back and Crozier, two horses he had ridden, finished one-two in the Kentucky Derby while Hartack sat on the sidelines. He had ridden Carry Back six times the year before and then, according to Jack Price, was evasive about riding the colt when he turned three. Carry Back was a rags-to-riches, mom-and-pop deal all the way. He ran in the name of Katherine Price, the wife of Jack Price, who had both bred and trained the horse. Price took Carry Back's dam, whose name was Joppy, as *partial* payment for a $265 boarding bill at his small Ohio farm. He bred Joppy to Saggy, a Maryland stallion who stood for a $750 fee (Price got a discount by breeding three mares instead of one). When Price first saw Carry Back, the result of one of those matings, he was so unimpressed that he was inclined to turn him over to his daughter Leslie as a riding horse.[7]

Price ran Carry Back twenty-one times as a 2-year-old. A horse hadn't been subjected to a more grueling early campaign and gone on to win the Derby since 1910. Hartack rode Carry Back in four sprint races in Florida; then he got another chance with the horse in two year-end races in New York. They won the Cowdin Stakes together, but then, in his first start beyond seven-eighths of a mile, Carry Back flubbed the start, and they ran last as the favorite in the Champagne.[8]

"We did everything to get Hartack to ride Carry Back," Price said. "But he had other horses. Even my daughter Kay, who dated Hartack, tried to influence him to ride my horse."[9] Price ultimately gave the mount to Johnny Sellers, who in a year would lead North America in races won, breaking up a monopoly that Hartack and Shoemaker had enjoyed for eight years.[10]

"I wanted Hartack to continue riding Carry Back," Price said later, "but he kept stalling me. He had been riding Itsa Great Day and apparently thought he was a better horse. He was entitled to that opinion, but what I didn't like was that he stalled me by saying he had another commitment he had to keep. Hartack simply does what he pleases, when he pleases. I know he has promised to ride horses for me and then the day of the race pulled himself off."[11]

Sellers won both the Derby and the Preakness with Carry Back; then they finished seventh in the Belmont.[12] Hartack didn't ride in any of those races.[13] Crozier, who finished second in the Kentucky Derby and third in the Preakness, was ridden by Hartack in the Florida Derby a month before Kentucky, after Fred Hooper's first choices, Braulio Baeza and Manny Ycaza, were unavailable. Baeza, Hooper's contract rider, had a broken shoulder, and Ycaza was sitting out a suspension. Sellers was now ensconced as Carry Back's rider, and Itsa Great Day suffered cartilage damage to a foreleg and had to be retired. Thus, five days before the Florida Derby, Hartack, with hat in hand and wearing contrition on his sleeve, went to the office of Hooper's construction company to try to patch up their two-year-old feud. Hooper had said he would never ride Hartack again after Hartack questioned the fitness of Hooper's Greek Circle and asked the stewards to scratch the horse only minutes before the running of the Widener Stakes. Hooper ran Greek Circle a couple of days later, with another jockey, and he won the race.

While rounding off final training preparations for Carry Back to run in the Florida Derby, Price was asked about the Hooper-Hartack détente. "That's the way things happen," Price said. "I've fired a lot of jocks in my time, and when I let them go, I always said that I would never hire them back—not unless I needed them."[14]

On a sloppy track, Carry Back beat Crozier by a head after the two of them bumped repeatedly in a furious drive to the finish line. Crozier came over after Hartack had smacked him with a lefthanded whip. "He had no reason to hit him," Hooper complained. He went back to Baeza, his rehabilitated contract rider, for the Kentucky Derby and the Preakness.[15]

A seventy-nine-year-old Jimmy Winkfield, rider of Derby winners in 1901 and 1902, attended the 1961 Derby. "It's hard to understand that Hartack doesn't have a horse," Winkfield said. "He's the best in the business. Some owner has sure missed the boat."[16]

Sellers won 328 races in 1961, exactly 100 more than Hartack, who finished fourth in the standings. But Sellers rode in 334 more races than Hartack. Pointing out that he had won 157 of his races at the Chicago tracks, Hartack said, "I knew I still had it. But I had to prove it to the public, and the writers. And I proved it by the way I rode in Chicago."

Hartack declared that he had never geared himself up for winning the title in 1961. "I didn't get to Florida until mid-January," he said. "I was in Hawaii, taking it easy. Does that look like a guy who is gunning for another championship? I went through hell last year to lead the country, and I promised myself that I'd never do it again." Hartack said that he had taken up water-skiing and wouldn't ride much during the last couple of months of 1961. He talked about endurance skiing, from Florida to Bimini, and from Florida to Nassau and back.[17]

Moody Jolley and his son Leroy, who shared the training of Ridan, shut down on the 2-year-old colt in September 1961 after he had reeled off seven straight wins. None of the wins was beyond six and a half furlongs, however, and the divisional title went to Crimson Satan, even though Ridan had beaten him twice early in the year. Hartack rode Ridan from July on—the last three of his wins. Ridan's season ended because of a peach-sized splint on his right foreleg, but those around him felt that time off would be an effective cure. Hartack said that Ridan was not only the best 2-year-old he ever rode but also the best 2-year-old he had ever seen. He thought of Ridan as a solid contender for the 1962 Kentucky Derby.

Down in Florida, as 1962 began, Hartack could be seen every day at the Jolleys' barn. Ridan had a bad habit of bearing out in his races, and Hartack was determined to work with the horse in the mornings to get him to run straight.[18]

In January, Ridan started off with his eighth straight win, but the streak ended a couple of weeks later when Sir Gaylord handed him his first loss. Then, in the Everglades Stakes at Hialeah, Sir Gaylord and Decidedly ran one-two, and Ridan, a well-beaten third, was demoted to fourth place for interference both early and late in the race.[19] Moody Jolley was not thrilled with Hartack's ride in Ridan's first loss, and less enamored with the way he handled the colt in the Everglades. He wanted to replace Hartack with Manny Ycaza for the Flamingo, but Ycaza was committed elsewhere.[20] Before Jolley could fire Hartack, however, the stewards effectively took him off Ridan, issuing a ten-day suspension for causing interference in the Everglades.[21] So the Jolleys hired Milo Valenzuela, but his ride also didn't please them, as Ridan finished third but was moved up to second on a foul. Sunrise County finished first but was demoted to third, and Prego was moved up to the win spot.[22]

For the Florida Derby at Gulfstream Park, the Jolleys could have gone back to Hartack, but Moody Jolley scotched that idea. "Hartack is riding poorly," he said. "I don't know the reason for it. But it's a fact. He didn't follow instructions and I think he used poor judgment. He charged out of the gate and used up the horse early. You can't do that when you're asking a horse to go a mile and an eighth [the distance of the Florida Derby]. Just as soon as you give Hartack his riding instructions, you know perfectly well that he has no intention of following them."[23]

A sometimes insensitive Hartack could infuriate trainers after races. Bill Raymond was a trainer who campaigned significant horses like Oink and Freetex. Coming off the track after one of his horses had been beaten, Raymond asked Hartack if anything went wrong. "Why ask me?" Hartack wanted to know. "You got binoculars. You could see for yourself." That was the last time Hartack rode a Raymond horse.[24]

The Jolleys were able to get Ycaza to ride in the Florida Derby, and Ridan won the race by a nose over the brilliant filly Cicada (albeit after the stewards took ten minutes to review a possible foul by the winner). Nine days before the Kentucky Derby, Ycaza won with Ridan again, in the Blue Grass at Keeneland, and Leroy Jolley said, "He gave us the kind of ride we've been waiting for all season to get."[25]

Hartack was left without a Derby mount going into early April. There was a chance that he might miss the race for the second straight year. On the other hand, going into March, Bobby Ussery, the leading rider in the country at the time, thought he was set to ride Decidedly right on through to the Derby.[26] But before the Florida Derby, George Pope, the lumber and shipping executive who owned Decidedly, hired Bill Shoemaker without telling his trainer, Horatio Luro. Ussery was not a happy camper; he said he missed the ride on Sunrise County in the Flamingo and missed out on the Florida Derby altogether. Shoemaker didn't ride Decidedly in the Florida Derby, either—the colt came down with colic and missed the race. When Decidedly recovered, Pope still wanted Shoemaker for two races at Keeneland before the Kentucky Derby, but Shoemaker hedged his bets, and Pope told Luro to hire Hartack. Decidedly finished second twice under Hartack, including a far-back second behind Ridan in the Blue Grass.

Hartack said that the mount on Decidedly came to him like manna from heaven. He thought that there were only four or five horses who could win the Derby, and Decidedly was one of them. In the first prep race at Keeneland, Decidedly, an odds-on favorite, was beaten by five lengths; Hartack said that after he had improved his position, from fifth to second, the horse lost interest in chasing the winner. When Hartack suggested that blinkers be added for the Blue Grass, Luro went ballistic. "I tried blinkers with him as a 2-year-old," the trainer said. "He got so riled that he dumped the jockey in the post parade, ran off, and I had to scratch him. I can't put blinkers on him this close to the Derby, because I can't take the chance of having him explode again."

Ridan beat Decidedly by four lengths in the Blue Grass. "He beat us by a street," Hartack said. "He beat me just as easy as a horse could beat me."

Again, Luro was open to suggestion. Again, Hartack mentioned blinkers. "I should have taken your advice and used blinkers in the Blue Grass," Luro conceded. "I'll use them in the Derby."[27]

Sir Gaylord, bred and owned by the Christopher C. Chenery family, which would win back-to-back Derbys with Riva Ridge and Secretariat in 1972–1973, had won four straight races and was going to be favored in the Derby. But the morning before the race, Sir Gaylord came back from a breeze favoring his right foreleg. X-rays showed that he had fractured a bone, and he was immediately retired. Chenery was tardy getting to the track because his train from Virginia to Louisville was two and a half hours late. He had entered Cicada, the filly who ran second to Ridan in the Florida Derby, in both the Kentucky Oaks (which was restricted to fillies) on May 4 and the Kentucky Derby on May 5. They ran her on May 4, and she won the Oaks, but Chenery was left without a starter in the Derby. (Had she run in the Derby, Cicada would have had an outside post in a big field.) On the revised morning line, the Churchill Downs handicapper made Ridan the new favorite at 2–1; he would go off at less than that.[28]

As though it was any consolation to Hartack, Leroy Jolley complimented him (sort of) a few days before the race. "In spite of the criticism of Hartack and the fact that we changed riders, let me tell you something about Bill Hartack," the younger Jolley said. "Bill was convinced he could break Ridan of that habit of trying to get out in his races. He did what he said he would with the horse. Hartack isn't going to benefit, but he did a fine job for us."[29]

Jolley could hardly imagine just how much Hartack would benefit from riding Decidedly. Hardly an impressive colt, he was smallish, like his sire, Determine, who had won the Derby in 1954. Seventeen years later, I interviewed Andy Crevolin, who had bankrolled his racing interests at the start with some very successful car dealerships. He remembered how he had bought Determine at a yearling auction at Keeneland for $12,000. "He didn't weigh a lot, and he wasn't very tall," Crevolin said. "I must have been standing in a hole when I saw him."

A breeding syndicate paid $1 million for Determine and Imbros, another stakes winner of Crevolin's, after they had run their last races. The day Decidedly broke his maiden at Saratoga, in August 1961, Crevolin said that he and Allaire du Pont offered $100,000 for him, with the understanding that Luro would remain his trainer, but George Pope wasn't selling.[30]

Determine was the first gray to ever win a Derby. Decidedly was the second.[31] The best gray *not* to win the Derby was Native Dancer, who in 1953 was roughed up in the early going, fell far back, and then lost by a head to Dark Star. That was the only race Native Dancer lost in 22 lifetime races.[32]

There were reasons not to bet Decidedly: he had won only one of his most recent six starts, and none of his wins had come in a stakes race. Still, Hartack didn't think lightly of his chances. "I thought he had the makings of a great horse, and could go a distance," he said.[33]

At 8–1, Decidedly was the third betting choice, behind Ridan and Sunrise County, in a field of fifteen. On the far turn, Decidedly still had seven horses to beat, but Hartack could tell that most of them were already winded. At the top of the stretch, Decidedly had moved into third place, with only Roman Line and Ridan to beat. Inside the eighth pole, Decidedly took the lead. Ridan, up to his bad old tricks, was trying to bear out, and Ycaza knew that it wasn't going to be their day.[34] In an interview with Larry King long after the Derby had been run, Hartack said that Ridan would have been the winner had he behaved and run straight.[35] Not only did Decidedly win by two-plus lengths, but his time of 2:00 2/5 also broke the record (by a full second) of Triple Crown champion Whirlaway, set twenty-one years earlier. Northern Dancer, another colt ridden by Hartack and trained by Luro, would beat Decidedly's record only two years later.[36]

Years later, Hartack sniffed at Decidedly's accomplishment. "I personally am against setting track records," he said. "The first preference is to win the race. To win by four or five lengths just to set a record, that's foolish. I don't believe in making a horse run 100 percent if he can win by giving only 95 percent. If you can do that, your horse is going to last longer. You're taking a chance when you're running a horse full out, because you're forcing the horse to extend. If you don't have to do it, why do it?"

In one of Ridan's races, Hartack said beforehand that the colt could break the track record, but he wasn't going to let him.[37] Ridan ran the fastest time in the twenty-seven-year history of the stake, but he was two-fifths of a second short of the Hialeah record.[38]

Traditionally, there is at least one more race run after the Derby. Jockeys in the Derby (especially those with leading contenders) frequently don't book themselves to ride in that extra race, or they ask the stewards to excuse them if they win the Derby. But Hartack was scheduled to ride Kentucky Warbler, a cheap claiming horse, for a $3,000 purse, and he was not going to skip the race. "Put away the cameras, boys," he told photographers in the jockeys' room after the Derby. "I gotta take off my pants."

He had time for a brief interview. "For many personal reasons, this was a very important Derby to me," he said. "The people in the racing game know why. This was a double thing; winning the Derby and beating Ridan."[39]

At the end of the long day, Hartack was asked to pose with the Derby trophy.

"Where's Moody Jolley?" he asked, referring to the trainer of Ridan.

"Why do you want him?" someone asked.

"Because I want to take this trophy and stick it up his ass," Hartack said.[40]

Hartack thought the blinkers—his idea—had helped Decidedly win. But, he said, Decidedly was such a smart horse that he quickly understood why he was wearing them, and after the Derby he ignored them, thereby reducing their effectiveness.[41] Two weeks later, at the Preakness in Baltimore, the public was skeptical about the Derby winner and sent off Decidedly as the third choice again, behind Ridan and Jaipur. Third in the Derby, Ridan was second in the Preakness, behind Greek Money, whose jockey, Johnny Rotz, engaged in a slam-bang duel with Ycaza and Ridan for the last sixteenth of a mile. The Belmont Stakes went to Jaipur as Decidedly finished fourth. For the rest of the year, Decidedly ran in seven races after the Derby, not winning any of them.[42]

Kentucky Warbler finished far back in the race after the Derby. In the jockeys' room before that race, after Hartack had put on a new pair of white pants to ride him, the photographers got their cameras ready again. "Give us a big smile, Bill," one of them said.

"Don't you know that I never smile?" Hartack asked, and he headed for the door that led to the paddock.[43]

14

Hard Times

On June 21, 1963:

- Bill Hartack was flying from Chicago to Philadelphia, in order to ride in a race at Delaware Park the next day.[1]
- Editors at *Sports Illustrated* in New York were putting together the final touches on a story that would be titled "Whatever Happened to Bill Hartack?"[2]
- William Hartack Sr., the jockey's father, was shot to death.[3]

The magazine story was written by Jack Olsen, who tried to balance his report but found it difficult to locate anyone, except Hartack's agent of the month, who had anything good to say. Even the agent, Duane Murty, who had been fired and rehired in less than a year's time, had to plumb deep to find a few compliments. "He's a very high-tempered person," Murty said.

The magazine with the unflattering story about Hartack hit the newsstands in the middle of the week in which Hartack's father was buried.[4] His father, who was fifty-five, was killed on a Friday afternoon at a farm four miles west of Charles Town, West Virginia, after an argument with his 47-year-old girlfriend involving a handgun.[5] The magazine was put to bed, as they used to say in the business, that Sunday night, but neither the editors nor Olsen apparently knew about the death, since the article didn't refer to it. "If they had known," said Bill Nack, a senior writer at the magazine in the 1980s, 1990s and 2000s, "I know Jack Olsen, who was such a great reporter, would have rushed to the funeral to talk to Hartack. He would have insisted to the editors that they hold the story or let him re-do the story on deadline."[6]

Authorities in West Virginia had trouble catching up with Hartack—they didn't know where he was staying—and it wasn't until the next day that he was told his father was dead.[7] Based at Arlington Park in the Chicago suburbs, he had gone to Delaware Park to ride Chieftain, a 2-year-old colt who began coughing several hours before the race and was scratched. So Hartack, in the jockeys' room, got two phone calls—one from Frank Whiteley Jr., Chieftain's trainer, saying Hartack had wasted a trip, and the other with word of his father's death.[8] Hartack was not close to his coalminer father, but at least they were on speaking terms, which was not the case with his two sisters.[9]

Other jockeys riding at Delaware Park were unaware that Hartack's father had died.[10] "He was always a guy who kept his own counsel," said Walter Blum, a Hall of Fame jockey who rode against Hartack in Florida, Chicago and other venues. "He hardly said anything to anybody when he was in the [jockeys'] room. And personal stuff, you could forget about him talking about any of that."[11]

After starting 1963 on the wrong foot in Florida, Hartack was threatening to resurrect himself in Chicago, if only Blum, a formidable roadblock, weren't there.[12] It was less than a year since Hartack had won his third Kentucky Derby with Decidedly,[13] but one slump after ten mostly brilliant years brought on widespread scrutiny. Not riding in any of the 1963 Triple Crown races, a series that had been Hartack's oyster, further fueled the skeptics' negativity. "This is a winner's business," Duane Murty said.[14]

Instead of having his pick of Derby horses, which was the case in most years, Hartack had ridden only one of the nine horses that ran at Churchill Downs. That lone horse, Investor, really had no business in the Derby. By May, he had won only two of twenty-five starts, and he had lost eleven straight prior to the Derby. Hartack was one of eighteen jockeys who had ridden him.[15] Investor finished next to last in the Derby, like he was supposed to.[16]

Chateaugay, a 9–1 shot who won the race,[17] could have been ridden by Hartack instead of Braulio Baeza, if Murty was to be believed.[18] Baeza rode Chateaugay to victory in the Blue Grass at Keeneland, nine days before the Derby, but he had already promised Fred Hooper, the owner of Admiral's Voyage, that he would ride his horse in a stake in New York on the same day as the Derby. Baeza told Jimmy Conway, trainer of Chateaugay, that riding Conway's colt in the Blue Grass had to be a "one-time deal."

Eventually, Hooper told Baeza that he would find another jockey for New York, that he wouldn't stand in the way of a jockey having a good shot at a Derby win.[19] But before that happened, the way Murty told the story, the Derby assignment on Chateaugay could have belonged to Hartack. "He ignored the meeting at Churchill Downs," Murty claimed. "If we had been in Kentucky, we'd at least have had a chance to ride the Derby winner."

Hartack wasn't as optimistic as Murty about landing the mount on Chateaugay. "I didn't see any point to going to Kentucky just to break even," Hartack said. "And there was another reason—I wanted a rest to get ready for the long Chicago season. There were three long meets at Washington Park, Arlington and Hawthorne coming up. I figured that if I didn't rest before I started in Chicago, I might get sour there and take off right in the middle of it."

Even before their disagreement about whether Hartack should have been at Churchill Downs in case a Derby mount opened up, he and Murty were at odds early in the year in Florida. At Hialeah, where the winter season began, Hartack finished sixth in the standings with twenty-two wins, nine less than the leader, Bobby Ussery. When the racing moved to a longer season at Gulfstream Park, Hartack did even worse. He won twenty-one races; the season's leader, Howard Grant, won more than twice as many. Murty said that their business was damaged because trainers had read in the *Daily Racing Form* that Hartack wasn't going to ride until his appeal of a $100 fine by the stewards, for missing a hearing, had been settled. Trainers, Murty said, didn't want to risk naming Hartack on horses unless they were sure he would show up to ride.

Hartack said that he had been too successful for too long to attempt an attitude adjustment. He maintained that he wasn't capable of being anything less than forthright, no matter the consequences. Other horsemen made him pay for his candor. "He doesn't have a friend in the jockeys' room," said one. "His attitude costs him mounts. Trainers are fed up with the flippant way he talks and answers questions. It doesn't cost anything to be polite."

Murty was fired toward the end of the Gulfstream meet. Hartack then went into seclusion for three weeks.

When Hartack showed up for the start of the meeting at Washington Park, he patched up things with Murty and had him booking his mounts again. In a rare concession, Hartack allowed that he needed to turn over a new leaf and began working more horses in the mornings. He even made an effort to be punctual in coming to the barns to exercise horses. He told Murty (as though Murty didn't know already) that he had many long-simmering fires to put out. And he was smart enough to know that Murty, who was twenty-seven, almost the same age as Hartack, didn't have the clout of a Chick Lang to unburn the bridges.

The somewhat reconstructed Hartack was also displaying an élan on the track that his critics thought had deserted him. He was looking for room on the rail with his mounts, to shorten the distance between gate and wire; once more, he was unafraid to seek holes between horses that, without split-second timing, could close dangerously. Hartack was winning with long shots, getting unaccomplished horses to extend themselves. But there were times when he would regress, when diplomacy would leave his vocabulary again. Once, when riding a heavy favorite, Hartack was unseated leaving the gate when the ground broke out from underneath the horse. While the horse, as horses do, instinctively continued his run around the oval, an uninjured Hartack picked himself up and walked dejectedly toward the jockeys' room. When he got close enough to the crowd, four disgruntled bettors shouted obscenities. Hartack wheeled in their direction but was stopped in his tracks by the clerk of scales, who bear-hugged him into submission. He undeniably saved Hartack from a bad beating; all four of the husky agitators outweighed him by about a hundred pounds apiece. "Sometimes," Hartack said later, "you have to be made of iron to disregard the stuff you hear. This was one of those times."[20]

Herb Hinojosa won six races the first day of the Washington Park meeting, but by the end of the season, Hartack was atop the standings. At Arlington Park, however, Walter Blum, was unstoppable. He won 121 races, demolishing Hartack's record and setting a new record that would go uncontested for thirteen years. Blum had such a rousing start at the Arlington meeting that there was little Hartack or any other rider could do to overtake him. In mid-July, for instance, Hartack won four races on the same card and Blum was shut out. But at the end of the day, Hartack still trailed Blum by twenty-one wins.[21] At year's end, Hartack's important stakes wins could be counted on one hand. His horses won just over $1 million in purses, not much of a total for a jockey whose mounts had earned three times as much just a few years before.[22]

By the end of the year, Duane Murty was gone again, replaced by the veteran Lenny Goodman, whose time with Hartack was also short lived. The future agent for such stars as Braulio Baeza and Steve Cauthen, Goodman had been booking mounts since the late 1940s. He would last just over five months with Hartack.

Hartack was on a bad losing streak at the time that Goodman was sacked.[23] Hartack was good at denial. "Bad streaks?" he said. "I don't run into bad streaks. It's not like other sports. In baseball, you stop hitting. It's you. You're up there with the same bat. If you're not hitting, you're not producing. You're not being asked to hit with a bat only half as long. But a jockey doesn't govern what he has to work with. I could be on or off, and it would have no bearing on whether I was winning or losing races—it would be the horse. I always ride good. I ride good, and I ride better, but I don't ride bad."[24]

For a time, Hartack was counting on Chieftain to be his Kentucky Derby horse in 1964. From July 1963 until a couple of weeks before the 1964 Derby, Hartack rode the colt nine straight times and won three stakes. Three months before the Derby, at three-quarters of a mile, Chieftain and Hartack beat Northern Dancer by two lengths at Hialeah. Northern Dancer, making his first start of 1964, had won seven of nine races, with two seconds, the year before. With the Derby looming, Hartack had a choice of riding Chieftain or Quadrangle in the Wood Memorial at Aqueduct. He picked Quadrangle, who won the race as Chieftain ran a disappointing fifth.[25] The Derby was two weeks off, and Hartack had another win at Churchill Downs in his future. But it wasn't going to be with Quadrangle.[26]

15

What's His Line? Winning the Derby

John Charles Daly: "OK, panel, get your blindfolds in place. If our first challenger will enter and sign in, please."

Bill Hartack appeared from behind a curtain in the New York television studio, went to a chalkboard, and with his left hand signed "Bill Hartack." As he took a seat next to Daly, the words appeared on the screen: "Four Time Kentucky Derby Winner."

"Our guest is self-employed and deals in a service," Daly said, and with that another edition of the popular TV show *What's My Line?* was under way.[1] Hartack's most recent Derby win, with Northern Dancer, had come just eight days before.[2] That made it fairly easy pickings for the astute panel, which consisted of the regulars Dorothy Kilgallen, Arlene Francis and Bennett Cerf, plus Allan Sherman, the comic songwriter. Kilgallen and Sherman never got a chance to try their luck. Francis, leading off the questioning, needed only four questions to establish that Hartack was a sports figure, but she lost her turn after guessing that his profession might be golf. Cerf, who was next, asked if Hartack was from the world of baseball or horse racing. When Hartack said yes, Cerf asked if it was horse racing. When Hartack said yes to that, the game was over. Cerf quickly identified him. With the chance to win $50, Hartack went home with $5.[3] But no tears, please. His share from Northern Dancer's Derby had been more than $11,000.[4]

After the applause subsided, Daly turned to Hartack and remarked that he had won his fourth Derby in a record time.

"Well, the horse did," Hartack said.

"That's very nice," Daly commented, "that he gives the horse credit."

Hartack was asked if the Derby was his favorite race. "They all are," he said, repeating what he had said many times. "I treat them all alike. I want to win every one of them."

Cerf asked him if he and Northern Dancer were going to win the upcoming Preakness at Pimlico in Baltimore. Daly, known for his puckish humor, cut off Hartack in the middle of his answer. "The FCC has rules against us imparting that information," Daly said.[5]

A couple of weeks later, after Northern Dancer won the Preakness to reach the cusp of the Triple Crown, Hartack repeated almost the same thing he had said to Daly.

"Thank you for another great ride," Winnie Taylor, the wife of Northern Dancer's owner, said to Hartack in the winner's circle.

"Thank the horse, ma'am," Hartack said.[6]

Three weeks after the Preakness, before sixty-one thousand fans at Aqueduct in New York, Northern Dancer finished third in the Belmont Stakes as Hartack's chance to ride a

Triple Crown champion went south. There was mild criticism of Hartack's Belmont ride, but by and large his canny handling of Northern Dancer in the Kentucky Derby and his workmanlike ride with the colt in the Preakness returned him to racing's firmament, just when the skeptics were bullhorning that he was a has-been.[7]

Not only did the two Triple Crown wins get Hartack back in the limelight, but they also reinforced his reputation as an opportunist *par excellence.* Hartack's first Derby win, with Iron Liege in 1957, came after the horse he was supposed to ride was injured; his 1960 Derby win came with Venetian Way, a colt he had never ridden until a month before the race; Decidedly, his 1962 Derby winner, came his way about two weeks before the Derby; and Northern Dancer's trainer, the estimable Horatio Luro, turned to Hartack after the renowned Bill Shoemaker walked away from the mount in early April.[8]

There was a game of musical chairs at work among the jockeys like no other going into the ninetieth running of the Derby. Shoemaker had made an odd handshake agreement with Rex Ellsworth, who owned The Scoundrel and who also had owned Swaps, Shoemaker's first Derby winner in 1955. Shoemaker told Ellsworth that he would ride The Scoundrel as long as he didn't have a chance to ride the Derby favorite. But as the spring wore on, Hill Rise, a colt out of California, where Shoemaker was based, began piling up wins, and George Pope told his trainer, Bill Finnegan, that he wanted Shoemaker instead of Don Pierce for his Derby jockey. "If Shoe gets into trouble in the Derby," Pope reasoned, "we can always say that we had the best going for us. But if Pierce messes up when we could have had Shoemaker, we'd never forgive ourselves."

Eventually, Shoemaker told Ellsworth that he had been offered Hill Rise, who was going to be the Derby favorite, and that their agreement gave him that leeway. When Horatio Luro called E.P. Taylor, Northern Dancer's owner, and said that Shoemaker was going to ride Hill Rise, Taylor was livid. Lenny Goodman, who had been Hartack's agent for only three months, was somehow privy to these machinations, and he quickly called Luro, offering him Hartack's services aboard Northern Dancer. This piqued Hartack, who had won the Wood Memorial with Quadrangle and had told Elliott Burch, that colt's trainer, that he would ride the horse in the Derby. Hartack was either painted into a corner or left with a Hobson's choice (or maybe both). "I feel badly about this," he said after he had made an awkward call to Burch. "They can say what they want about me, but one thing I am is honest. If I give my word, I keep it. But my agent committed me to Northern Dancer, and that is that."[9]

Out of such mixups, winning Kentucky Derby mounts are acquired.

At first glance, Hartack didn't seem to be the right rider for Northern Dancer, since he was notorious for whipping his horses. Luro had trained Northern Dancer's sire, Nearctic, as well as his dam, Natalma, who was a daughter of the redoubtable Native Dancer. Both parents, Luro said, did not respond well to whipping, and according to him Northern Dancer was the same way.[10] Luro took the horse away from the jockey Bobby Ussery after he had disobeyed instructions and used his whip in a race at Hialeah in February.[11] Shoemaker whipped Northern Dancer in winning the Florida Derby and said that the horse "didn't like it much." But Luro felt that he would work with Hartack on this—they had one more Derby prep race together, the Blue Grass Stakes—and besides, the Argentine-born trainer was still indebted to Hartack for helping Decidedly win the Derby by virtually forcing him to add blinkers for the race. Luro became Hartack's staunchest defender when some of Taylor's top advisors—Joe Thomas was one—began pooh-poohing Hartack. A couple of days before the Derby, Thomas gave an interview in which he questioned the choice of Hartack. When asked about Thomas' comments, Luro said, "I am running the stable!"[12]

The Blue Grass at Keeneland, seventy miles east of Churchill Downs, was eight days before the Derby, and it was Hartack's first chance to familiarize himself with Northern Dancer. The five-horse race was little more than a paid workout for the colt; while the victory margin was only a half-length, the chart footnotes of the race said that he won "with complete authority."[13]

Despite that win, Hill Rise, on an eight-race winning streak that included the Santa Anita Derby, was a 7–5 favorite in the Derby, with Northern Dancer a tepid second choice at more than 3–1.[14] Northern Dancer also was not favored in the Preakness.[15]

By then, Northern Dancer should have been used to lefthanded compliments. Fully grown, he was fifteen hands, which was a smallish five feet at the withers. Hill Rise was four inches taller, and he weighed about three hundred pounds more.[16] At least one horseman said that Northern Dancer reminded him of a quarter horse. E.P. Taylor had tried to unload Northern Dancer when he was a yearling, and Luro tried to have him gelded before he ran at two (to settle him down so he could be manageable to train). Taylor talked Luro out of the gelding notion.[17] Castrating the colt would have cost his owner and the rest of the breeding syndicate an estimated $115 million in stud fees by the time his trysting days were over, at age twenty-six. Taylor's practice was to sell half of his yearlings every year, saving the rest to race, but when Northern Dancer was run through the sales ring with a reserve (minimum price) of $25,000, the bidding stopped well short of that mark. "Who wants to buy a midget?" said one of the buyers at the sale.[18]

In 1990, the same year that Northern Dancer died, Alex Harthill, the veterinarian to the stars at Churchill Downs (his practice jump-started with Citation, the Triple Crown winner, in 1948), told a colleague that before the Derby he had treated Northern Dancer with Lasix, which was then illegal in Kentucky. Lasix, a diuretic commonly given to horses that bleed from pulmonary stress, was injected into Northern Dancer, Harthill said, because he was hot-blooded and high strung.[19] In an interview with the *Daily Racing Form* twelve years later, Harthill elaborated, saying that he sent another veterinarian with a loaded syringe to Northern Dancer's stall, the better to throw off security snoops.[20] In 1968, Harthill was fined by the Kentucky racing commission in the wake of that year's Derby, which was marred by the disqualification of the winner, Dancer's Image (a son of Native Dancer), after the colt tested positive for an illegal anti-inflammatory agent.[21]

Harthill died in 2005 at the age of eighty. Jimmy Croll, who trained Holy Bull, the favorite who finished twelfth in the 1994 Derby, thought his horse was sluggish going into the race and told me early in 1995, during an interview at Gulfstream Park, that he suspected Harthill. I had known Harthill since the 1968 Derby. I interviewed him a couple of days after that Derby, and he obliquely implicated himself. As we were driving in his station wagon through the infield tunnel at Churchill Downs, en route from the front side to the backside of the track, he said, "You know where *they* [italics mine] made the mistake, don't you? They gave the horse the [Butazolidin] by tablet instead of syringe. If they had used the needle, it wouldn't have stayed in his system as long." I always had the feeling, when Hartack used the word *they*, that he was talking about himself. I wrote the story for the *Louisville Times* and never got a reaction from Harthill.

There was a good reason Northern Dancer was dwarfed by the eleven other horses in the Derby field. Impregnated as a breeding afterthought, Natalma had foaled the colt on May 27, 1961, so Northern Dancer didn't really turn three until after the Derby and Preakness were run.[22]

"[Winning the Derby] was always a question of stamina, because he was so small," Hartack said. "It was fortunate in the Blue Grass that there was so little competition. I didn't have to worry about taking a chance trying to rate him and then jeopardizing his chance of winning. The chance that he might lose was very slight. Although I was in front most of the way, the time was so slow that I was actually rating him and slowing him down. It was similar to what I hoped to do in the Derby."[23]

At the time, a Canadian-bred horse had never won a Triple Crown race. "By dint of his resolve and power, the stocky colt compelled an entire country to fall in love with him," Kevin Chong wrote.[24]

Chieftain, who was Hartack's Derby hope early on, had beaten Northern Dancer in a dash at Hialeah in February, but when they stretched out some two weeks later and Northern Dancer turned the tables by a wide margin, the Chieftain camp decided to send their horse in another direction.[25]

After winning the Blue Grass, Hartack said he was puzzled that Shoemaker would have abandoned Northern Dancer. He was unaware of the pact between Shoemaker and Rex Ellsworth. Shoemaker, according to his agreement with Ellsworth, couldn't ride a horse besides The Scoundrel in the Derby unless a call on the favorite was available, and that opportunity materialized with Hill Rise. Four days before the Derby, Shoemaker's decision looked sound when Hill Rise won the Derby Trial in a solid time.[26]

There is always such a mob at the Derby that Churchill Downs could announce almost any attendance and get away with it. This time, the figure was ninety-seven thousand, and there might have been even more. Quadrangle, third choice in the betting, got none the best of the break when he was squeezed between horses. A 179–1 shot, Royal Shuck, broke quickly from the outside and led the race for a quarter of a mile. He would finish last, beaten by more than thirty lengths.

Northern Dancer and Hill Rise settled into the middle of the pack, and down the backstretch, with Northern Dancer hugging the fence, Shoemaker thought he and Hill Rise had Hartack's horse trapped on the inside. There was a wall of three horses ahead of Northern Dancer. Hartack, sensing a blockade, eased Northern Dancer off the rail. They passed Hill Rise on the outside, also clearing the three leaders. With a quarter mile to go, Northern Dancer held a narrow lead. Hill Rise was in fourth place, but only two lengths back. Shoemaker caught a tough break at the half-mile pole, when Royal Shuck ran out of gas, and the horse behind him, Mr. Moonlight, was forced to change lanes. Mr. Moonlight swerved to the outside, right into Hill Rise's path.

Hartack had one more crucial decision to make. Disregarding Luro's caveats about the whip, he tapped the horse, who responded. At the top of the stretch, all bets were off. This was the Derby, and Hartack began laying in to Northern Dancer with his strong left hand. He hit him ten times the rest of the way, and he needed every stroke. Shoemaker was whipping Hill Rise, and he was gobbling up ground. The wire came up just in time for Hartack. Northern Dancer won by a long neck, in a record time of two minutes flat for the mile and a quarter. Unofficially, but of little consolation to Shoemaker, Hill Rise also broke the record.[27]

There was something unprecedented about the immediate order of finish. The

At Keeneland, Northern Dancer, in his final 1964 Kentucky Derby prep, won the Blue Grass Stakes. Left to right: groom Bill Brevard, trainer Horatio Luro, owner E.P. Taylor and Hartack (Keeneland/ Meadors).

Scoundrel was third, Roman Brother fourth and Quadrangle fifth—and none of them were bred in Kentucky.[28] It was a long night for the Kentucky hardboots, and it got even worse two weeks later in the Preakness. There were no Kentucky-breds in the race at all, as the first five Derby horses, in a six-horse field, returned for a rematch.[29]

Luro thought that the race was won between the quarter and the eighth poles, when Hartack, with the help of the whip, increased his lead to two lengths. Obviously, the first question for Shoemaker after the race was whether he regretted giving up Northern Dancer. He said he would do the same thing if he had a second chance. He thought the bad luck Hill Rise had on the far turn could have been the difference. It was the fourth time he had been beaten with a Derby favorite.[30]

Regarding the whip, Hartack said that he didn't hit Northern Dancer hard, but enough that he felt it. Hartack believed that while Northern Dancer was a willing horse, it didn't hurt to tap him every now and then—gentle reminders that he should keep running.[31]

It was suggested that there were two scoundrels in the race—The Scoundrel, who had four legs, and Hartack. With about fifty antsy writers waiting in the jockeys' room for a post-race interview, Hartack lingered outside for forty-five minutes, signing autographs. Hartack never met a newspaper deadline that he didn't hate.[32]

"I got $200 worth of tickets on your horse," one of the autograph seekers said. "You're the greatest."

"Where's my half?" Hartack said. "I did all the work."[33]

16

Peaks and Valleys with Northern Dancer

Two days after he won the Kentucky Derby, Northern Dancer was loaded on to a van for a fourteen-hour ride to Baltimore for the Preakness, the middle race of the Triple Crown, which would be run in less than two weeks. Bill Hartack took a red-eye flight from Louisville to New York, where he had been named to ride a couple of horses at Aqueduct on the Monday after the Derby. Hartack reached his Central Park South apartment in Manhattan at 5 in the morning, slept for a few hours, and was at Aqueduct by 11. His first date with a quadruped was in the second race.

"They talk about you, Hartack, but you win the races, kid," yelled one of the leather-lunged spectators as Hartack, aboard a cheap claiming horse, came on the track for the post parade. The thirty-five thousand fans gave him loud applause, and he tipped his cap a couple of times. In the press box, where many of the residents were more accustomed to the back of Hartack's hand, there was surprise all around.

"I didn't win the Derby in New York," Hartack said later. "They didn't have to give me an ovation. This wasn't part of my job. They were giving me a welcome back, and it deserved an acknowledgment."

Asked if he might take a short breather before heading to Pimlico Race Course for the Preakness, Hartack said, "Why take a vacation unless you need one? You get your laurels by riding, not resting. I'm riding well now. I'm refreshed."[1]

Traditionally, Pimlico reserved just one stakes barn for all the Preakness horses. At Churchill Downs, the Derby horses would be stabled at several different barns. Pimlico's stakes barn was the first barn that credentialed media and racing officials would see when they parked in a small lot along Hayward Avenue and entered the track through a gate attached to a cyclone fence that had barbed wire on the top to discourage interlopers. Thus there was heavy foot traffic around the stakes barn, and some trainers of visiting Preakness horses chose barns among the general training population, on the other side of the track. Horatio Luro, who trained Northern Dancer, passed up the Pimlico stakes barn to give his colt more privacy.[2] Thirty-six years later, Neil Drysdale, who worked for Charlie Whittingham (who worked for Luro), also chose the Pimlico outback for his Derby winner, Fusaichi Pegasus.[3]

So the stall reserved for the Derby winner at the Preakness stakes barn was empty. Eighteen years later, it would be empty again, for a different reason. Eddie Gregson, the trainer of Gato del Sol, the Derby winner, elected to skip the Preakness and save his late-running colt for the longer distance of the Belmont. You could have fried an egg on the head of Chick Lang, Hartack's former agent, who by then had become the general manager of Pimlico. Not having the Derby winner run in the Preakness would cost Pimlico tens of thousands in attendance. Lang couldn't contain himself: for a day or two, he placed a symbolic donkey in the stall that had been reserved for Gato del Sol. Three years later, Lang went apoplectic again when Spend a Buck, the Derby winner, skipped the Preakness because there were more greenbacks to be banked if he won the Jersey Derby, and his camp concluded that he couldn't run in both races. That time, Lang saved his diatribes for Bob Brennan, the proprietor of Garden State Park, who was dangling the bonus.[4]

In 1964, Pimlico got not only the Derby winner for its Preakness but also the four horses who had finished immediately behind Northern Dancer at Churchill Downs—Hill Rise, The Scoundrel, Roman Brother and Quadrangle. The first five Derby finishers running in the Preakness had happened only twice before, in 1947 and 1958.[5] This time, Pimlico would get only one other horse besides those five, a local horse by the name of Big Pete who had what was derisively known as "cheap speed"—the ability to briefly set the pace in a race but not the ability to carry that speed much farther than a half-mile.[6]

Lang, who had been working in the Pimlico front office for only four years since his departure as Hartack's agent, had made peace with his former client, and vice versa. In November 1963, Hartack was enshrined in the National Jockeys Hall of Fame and honored at a dinner in the New Clubhouse at Pimlico. Hartack was on the ballot for the first time in 1962, and when Steve Brooks had outvoted him, there were suggestions that in a vote of national turf writers the unpopular Hartack would never achieve a plurality. Then, when Hartack was elected in 1963, he declined to pose for the portraitist who did the likenesses of the previous riders who were enshrined. The portrait of Hartack hanging at Pimlico with his fellow honorees had been drawn from one of his photos.

On the day of the dinner, Hartack rode Quadrangle to victory in the Pimlico Futurity, but when asked after the race whether he would attend the banquet in his honor that night, he parried the question. However, when the dinner started a few hours later, Hartack appeared. Chick Lang, his wife Nancy and their daughter Debi were seated at a table with a few friends. The Langs brought Debi along because she adored Hartack through his thick and thin with her father: "He was her Babe Ruth," Chick Lang once said. During his happy days with Lang, Hartack had been a frequent visitor at his agent's Baltimore home, and he took a liking to both the Langs' son Chickie and Debi. He played checkers and Ping Pong with them, he took them for ice cream, he brought them memorabilia from the track, he sent Christmas gifts, and while he wasn't their uncle, he sure acted like it.

At the dinner, Hartack made a moving acceptance speech. "I'd like—I'd really like, to uphold the honor that you've given me tonight," he said. "If not personality-wise, through ability."

When he had finished speaking, Hartack asked eleven-year-old Debi if she would join him on the stage to help unveil his portrait. When the ceremony was over, and she returned to her table, Hartack came over, pecked her on the cheek and signed her program. She had gotten the signatures of Eddie Arcaro, Steve Brooks and a few other star jockeys earlier in the evening. Next to all of those names, Hartack signed his name and wrote, "To Debi, my only true love."[7] In 2015, Debi Lang Tessier, now a grandmother, recalled that night: "I was speechless when Bill called me up there. You can imagine, a large roomful of people. Then when Northern Dancer won the Preakness, too, I was rooting so hard for him to win the Triple Crown. When Northern Dancer lost the Belmont, I was devastated. I locked myself in my room for a week."[8]

In 1964, Hartack was riding in his sixth Preakness. His record at Pimlico had been spotty. He won the Preakness in 1956 with Fabius, but with his three Kentucky Derby winners he ran second, fifth and eighth. Since 1957, jockeys seldom went into a Triple Crown race without riding at least a couple of races on the undercards. Why 1957? That year, Shoemaker, not one for excuses, said after misjudging the Derby finish line with Gallant Man (as Iron Liege, ridden by Hartack, won the race) that he had made a mistake by not riding at least one early race on the card. Shoemaker said that he hadn't ridden at Churchill Downs in a year and he misread the distance poles as the horses thundered toward the wire. Going into that Derby, Shoemaker claimed that his agent, Harry Silbert, tried to line up another mount or two for Derby day but was unsuccessful.[9] Other jockeys in subsequent Triple Crown races took heed.

The 1964 Preakness was the eighth race, and Hartack rode in the fifth and sixth races, so as to familiarize himself with the track. In the hours before his first mount, he played pool in the jockeys' room to pass the time. Shoemaker allowed a few reporters interview time—a card game called race-horse rummy, not pool, was his favorite jockeys' room pastime, but there was no rummy game to be found. Asked to rehash the Derby, Shoemaker said that the race was won and lost when Hartack, seemingly pinned on the rail and behind a trio of horses approaching the final turn, was able to swing Northern Dancer to the outside.[10]

The bettors, perhaps feeling that the Derby wasn't a true bill, sent Hill Rise off as the odds-on favorite, and they made Northern Dancer the 2–1 second choice. A New York newspaper ran the selections of twelve handicappers, only one of them picking Northern Dancer to win.

There was nary a Kentucky-bred horse in the race; not many Preaknesses, if any, had been run that way. When the gate opened, Hartack took back slightly with Northern Dancer. He fixed one eye on Quadrangle, up ahead, and the other on Hill Rise. He wanted to make sure Hill Rise was outside of his horse all the way. Leaving the backstretch, Hartack hit Northern Dancer once and he accelerated. Shoemaker tried to move with Hill Rise but couldn't keep up.

"Shoemaker was forced to use different tactics because he was criticized for the ride in the Derby," Hartack said. "I anticipated he would have to do this. Mind you, I think he rode a good race, but the trouble was that he took up pursuit when I still had a fresh horse."[11]

Northern Dancer had a three-length lead at the top of the stretch, and Hartack just hand-rode him to the finish. He won by two and a quarter lengths. The Scoundrel edged out Hill Rise for second place.[12]

No one had won the Triple Crown since 1948, when Citation had become the eighth horse to sweep the series. Neither Hartack nor Luro sounded confident about Northern Dancer winning the Belmont on June 6. Hartack said that the colt "is not really the Belmont type." Luro put it better: he felt that Northern Dancer's best distance was between a mile and a mile and an eighth, and none of the Triple Crown distances, especially the mile and a half of the Belmont, were in that range.

E.P. Taylor said after the Preakness that his horse was bound for the Belmont, but on the night of the race, at a party at Pimlico, Luro shocked Taylor and the rest of the room by saying that he was not going to run in New York. The trainer questioned the short-striding colt's ability to win at a mile and a half. Taylor was aghast, and he tried to deflect Luro's comments by saying that he and the trainer would make a decision in the next day or two. The next day, Luro was still unbending, but after meeting with Taylor he agreed to ship the horse to New York and decide whether to run after watching the horse train for two-plus weeks. There was a method to Taylor's strategy: he knew that once he got his trainer and Northern Dancer to New York, he could break down Luro's resistances and running in the Belmont would be inevitable.

Meanwhile, Hartack, like Luro, continued stating that he didn't think Northern Dancer would be effective at the Belmont distance; in addition, he feared Quadrangle, the horse he rode to victory in the Wood Memorial, two weeks before the Derby. Quadrangle was fifth in the Derby and fourth in the Preakness, but Hartack sensed that he might be peaking in time for the Belmont. Between the Preakness and the Belmont, Quadrangle ran a good second in the Metropolitan Handicap.

Three days before the Metropolitan, on May 27, Northern Dancer reached his third birthday. The youngest horse to ever win the Derby, he was finally as old as the horses he had been running against. Frank and Betty McMahon, the Canadians who would win the 1969 Derby and Preakness with the Hartack-ridden Majestic Prince, sent a bunch of carrots, shaped like a cake and topped by the Canadian flag, to barn thirty-one at Belmont Park, where Northern Dancer was stabled. An estimated three hundred birthday cards and telegrams were also delivered to the barn, many of them from Canadians who were proud of the colt's derring-do. Hardly Canadian, there was even a telegram from Princeton University in New Jersey that read, "HAPPY BIRTHDAY AND MAY ALL YOUR TURNS LEAD TO SHORT STRETCHES." It was signed, "Princeton U. Northern Dancer Syndicate."[13]

The morning of the Belmont, Hartack and his agent of five months, Lenny Goodman, parted company. Chick Lang, the agent who had lasted the longest with Hartack, once said that he could name at least twenty-four agents whom his former rider had used from 1953 to 1967. Publicly, neither Hartack nor Goodman ever discussed the reasons for their separation. Hartack had been in a slump, losing twenty-five straight races in New York. A week before Hartack won the Derby with Northern Dancer, Goodman got a phone call from Braulio Baeza, who asked the agent to take his book. Goodman declined, but after the Belmont, he did indeed partner up with Baeza, a union that would last twelve years. Many years later, Goodman said that it was he who had dropped Hartack. "I never enjoyed a minute of the six months I worked for Hartack," Goodman explained. "The only reason I lasted six months was that I was dying to win the Derby. I spent three months getting Hartack the mount on Northern Dancer, and I knew he couldn't lose." At the time of the Belmont, Goodman still had Baeza's offer on the table. "Braulio was the rider of my dreams," Goodman said.[14]

There were 61,215 fans at Aqueduct, a record crowd for the Belmont Stakes. The race was run at Aqueduct, Belmont's sister track, because Belmont Park was being rebuilt.[15] With eight horses to choose from, bettors made Northern Dancer the favorite for the first time in the series. However, Quadrangle tracked Orientalist from the start, overtook him with a half-mile to run and sped to a two-length victory. Roman Brother finished second, four lengths in front of Northern Dancer, and Hill Rise was fourth. E.P. Taylor was not happy with Hartack's ride, claiming that he should have put Northern Dancer into the race sooner, and George Pope, who owned Hill Rise, thought Shoemaker could also have done better. "Both jockeys were watching each other, and ignored the slow pace," Pope said. "They underestimated Quadrangle and they paid for it."[16]

Luro thought Hartack did the best he could, since his pre-race instructions were followed to the letter. After the race, Hartack said that the grueling distance wore down his mount, but later he saw Ron Turcotte, the Canadian rider who had been yanked by Luro after he rode Northern Dancer as a 2-year-old, and said something very chilling: "It wasn't the instructions that beat him, it was the soundness."[17]

Luro furiously drove away from Aqueduct several hours after the Belmont. He was angry that the Triple Crown had been lost. Frances Luro, his wife, and Jim Proudfoot, the Toronto columnist, were also in the car. Years later, Proudfoot reminded Luro of that terrifying ride. "You were never in danger, my friend," Luro said. "Argentina has produced two great drivers. Juan Manuel Fangio [four-time winner of the Argentine Grand Prix][18] was one, and I don't need to tell you the other."[19]

Northern Dancer would run only one more race, going home to Woodbine in suburban Toronto to win the Queen's Plate, Canada's premier race for 3-year-olds. He destroyed the opposition, winning by more than seven lengths. When Northern Dancer blew by another horse in the race, the jockey, Hugo Dittfach, hopelessly beaten, yelled, "Hey, Bill, loan me your whip!" In the jockeys' room later, Hartack walked over to Dittfach's locker with his whip in hand. "Here's that thing you asked for out there," Hartack said.

Avelino Gomez, the iconic Canadian rider who was fifth with Pierlou in the race, playfully yelled over to Hartack from his locker, "Hey, Bill, how come you ain't mad at nobody today?"

"Canadian sportswriters are better to talk to than Americans," Hartack yelled back. "But I like Americans better than Cubans." That was a sarcastic reference to Gomez's lineage.

Gomez wouldn't let up. "You were shaking pretty good before the race."

"I always shake before a race," Hartack said. "You do your shaking *during* the race."

"You not gonna leave town without paying me eighty bucks I win at pool? I beat you pretty good last night."

"I beat you pretty good today."

"When you think you had it won?" Gomez had done his homework—that question would infuriate Hartack when it came from the press.

"Right from the start," Hartack said. "When I saw a burrhead like you was on the second choice."[20]

Before the year was out, Northern Dancer was retired from the track because of a tendon injury. He went on to become the world's most valued stallion, at times commanding a stud fee of $1 million for a mating to just one mare. Just one of the horses he sired was Nijinsky II, who in 1970 became England's first Triple Crown champion in thirty-five years. No horse since has swept the English triple.[21]

Eventually, Taylor moved Northern Dancer from Canada to stand stud at his farm in Maryland, and it was there that one of his handlers captured the essence of the horse. "He was small all right," Junior Clevenger said, "but I don't think he knew he was small."[22]

In July 2007, Hartack, who had ridden his last horse in Hong Kong in 1980, was working as a steward at Louisiana Downs, but he took time off to accept an invitation from the Woodbine track to attend the Queen's Plate, which Northern Dancer and he had won forty-three years before. The main reason Hartack went to Canada was Sandy Hawley, the Hall of Fame jockey from Canada who also overlapped with Hartack on the Southern California circuit. Hawley was one of the few jockeys Hartack ever socialized with. They had been friends since 1969, when Hawley, still an apprentice, was riding against Hartack at Oaklawn Park in Hot Springs, Arkansas. "He looked like a kid who was going to make it," Hartack said. "He was fearless on a horse."

Another race on Queen's Plate day was named after Northern Dancer. A couple of days before, Hartack had helped with the draw for post positions. "It's the Dancer," he said; then, one by one, he shook the numbered pills out of what looked like a rubber milk bottle.

"I remember every one of the last five races I rode Northern Dancer," Hartack said. "They were great memories. He was always the underdog. I don't know if that was because he was from Canada, or because of his small size. I liked underdogs. He'd be in my top-five favorites of all times."

Hawley remembered Hartack as a cool poker player. "Just like on a horse, he had great anticipation," Hawley said. "He seemed to just know when every card was coming. He almost always won."[23]

17

Westward Ho

One white foot, run him for his life.
Two white feet, keep him for your wife.
Three white feet, that's the way it goes.
Four white feet, feed him to the crows.[1]

If it had not been for Northern Dancer, 1964 would have been the worst year of Bill Hartack's career. Even though he rode the Kentucky Derby–Preakness winner, Hartack dropped off the national leader board in races won. He rode in six hundred fewer races than two years before, and his 115 wins were easily his lowest in the twelve full years he had been riding. He was still in demand as a stakes rider, and his horses earned $1.4 million, which meant that he was still earning six figures. But without Northern Dancer, Hartack's purse total would have sunk below the million-dollar mark.[2]

As 1965 began, Hartack, at thirty-two, was in need of another Big Horse (a figurative term in the case of the dwarfish Northern Dancer). It didn't look like that horse was going to come from the crop of burgeoning 3-year-olds in Florida, so Hartack moved west to Santa Anita, Charles Strub's picturesque track. Santa Anita was a doorstop for the breathtaking San Gabriel Mountains in Arcadia, California, just northeast of Los Angeles. Strub, a San Francisco dentist, had launched Santa Anita on Christmas Day 1934, and the track was quickly able to draw the best horses from all over the country. The Seabiscuit phenomenon had helped carry Santa Anita into the 1940s, and after a closure for World War II (when the track, for a time, was used for what became a politically unpopular Japanese internment camp), the track reopened in 1945 by averaging a spectacular thirty thousand fans a day. Santa Anita not only became a must-attend site for the two-dollar bettor but also served as a familiar respite for the movie-star crowd. Seeing box-office icons like Al Jolson, Don Ameche, Betty Grable and Bing Crosby (one of the owners of the Del Mar track, a hundred miles to the south) at the races on the same day was commonplace.[3]

Hartack's arrival at Santa Anita in 1965, with all his Kentucky Derby press clippings, was met with a yawn. Santa Anita had its established riding stars, starting with Bill Shoemaker, who had led the track in races won for an incredible fourteen consecutive seasons. Shoemaker not only won meet titles but also marginalized the opposition; one year he finished fifteen wins ahead of the second-place jockey, Manny Ycaza.[4] Tony DeSpirito, who had won the national riding title in his apprentice year, 1952, had a fling at Santa Anita and didn't stay long. "They should call it Santa Shoemaker," he said.[5]

By the 1960s, Hartack was aware that his career was flagging. "There's no question," he said, "that I'm lacking good horses to ride.... I'm riding lots of long shots. But as far as the caliber of horses there are to ride, I'm pretty much out in left field.... If owners and trainers of good horses are mad at me because of my honest opinion, what's the use of giving an honest opinion? I could be just like an average rider, go back and say: 'This horse got in a lot of trouble,' when he really didn't get in a lot of trouble. 'This horse ran straight and kind,' when he didn't. Or, 'This horse is perfectly sound,' when he wasn't perfectly sound. That's all I have to do. But I can't do that. Man, I've got to live with myself."

While Hartack might have had a good grasp of the big picture, he was not one to dwell on short-term slumps. Approaching him about slumps was an automatic turnoff, not any different from addressing him as "Willie." "I don't want to talk about slumps," he peevishly said. "How would I know why I'm losing? If I knew why, I'd be winning. I just don't want to talk about any slump. If that's what you want to know, forget it."[6]

Hartack rented a house in Hollywood, not far from the famed Sunset Strip. The mat at the front door read, "GO AWAY." He won more than twenty races at Santa Anita, finishing well behind Shoemaker, who bagged sixty-nine.

"I didn't expect much when I came out here," Hartack said toward the end of the season. "And I was right. I've ridden a lot of horses, and I've ridden a lot of losers."[7]

Hartack's opportunities in stakes races were scant. Trainers stayed loyal to Santa Anita–based jockeys who had latched on to young horses the year before. Hartack didn't land a mount for the nine-horse Santa Anita Derby. Lucky Debonair, ridden by Shoemaker, soundly defeated Jacinto in a Santa Anita Derby upset and went to Louisville as the West Coast's best hope to win the Kentucky Derby.[8]

Although none of his wins as a 2-year-old had come beyond a mile, Bold Lad was declared the champion juvenile for 1964.[9] Braulio Baeza appeared to have the mount on Bold Lad in his hip pocket, closing out 1964 with five straight wins on the chestnut son of Bold Ruler. Baeza's agent was the estimable Lenny Goodman, who had split with Hartack, after only five months, on the morning of the 1964 Belmont Stakes, the one Hartack would lose with Northern Dancer.[10]

Besides Bold Lad, other preeminent Kentucky Derby contenders for 1965 also seemed to be spoken for, with Hartack on the outside looking in: Johnny Sellers, winner of the 1961 Derby with Carry Back, was the regular rider for Hail to All, an honest horse, though yet to win around two turns; Ron Turcotte was part and parcel with Tom Rolfe, who ran true no matter the track; and Shoemaker was riding Lucky Debonair, who, after getting a late start as a 2-year-old, had won virtually everything in sight at Santa Anita.[11]

Hartack, as usual, was turning over agents like they were flapjacks in a hash house. His agents were clocked in months, not years, after Chick Lang ended a six-year partnership with him in early 1960. Hartack's penchant for changing agents was so furious that one of the racing magazines said, "Jockey Bill Hartack is parting company with his agent, Duane Murty, who recently succeeded Bud Aime, who took over after Jimmy Bracken, etc." *Etc.* was a euphemism for the names of many agents.[12]

Like many of Hartack's Derby mounts, Bold Lad was happenstance. His trainer, Bill Winfrey, had eased the horse back into training after he was sidelined by a splint injury in January and February. Bold Lad won his first start of 1965 at Aqueduct on April 3, a month before the Derby, but two weeks later, with Manny Ycaza substituting for the suspended Baeza, the Wood Memorial distance of a mile and an eighth proved daunting as he ran third behind Flag Raiser and Hail to All.[13]

Winfrey hadn't been to a Derby since 1953, when his heavily favored Native Dancer, in the only loss of his career, had a nightmarish trip and was nipped by Dark Star.[14] To get Bold Lad to the Derby, Winfrey needed him to rebound in the Derby Trial, a mile race only four days before the main event. Baeza was back from his suspension, but he was the contract rider for Darby Dan Farm, and that Ohio outfit was expected to run either Bugler or Country Friend in the Derby (as it turned out, it did neither, leaving Baeza without a Derby mount).[15] So the mount on Bold Lad went to Hartack, who had won the last three Derbys he had ridden in (1960, 1962, 1964) and had taken the race four times out of six tries overall.[16]

With only four horses to beat, Hartack rode Bold Lad to a facile win in the Trial. "He did everything right in the Trial," Hartack said. "I knew that he had problems and Winfrey was trying to catch up with the others, but after the Trial I thought he had done that."[17]

The morning line for the Derby had Bold Lad favored at 8–5, Tom Rolfe at 4–1 and Lucky Debonair at 5–1. Some handicappers shied away from Bold Lad because he was sired by Bold Ruler. The *Daily Racing Form*'s Horse of the Year in 1957, Bold Ruler won the Preakness, but he was beaten badly in the Derby and the Belmont Stakes, the longest races in the Triple Crown and was not thought to be a stamina sire whose get would win at classic distances.[18] As late as 1973, Bold Ruler still bore that stigma. Leading up to the 1973 Derby, the knowledgeable Dave Feldman, writing about the favorite in a Chicago newspaper, repeatedly said that the colt wouldn't win because he was sired by Bold Ruler. They ran the race, and afterward I was part of a gaggle of turf writers who poured into the jockeys' room to interview the winning rider.

"Hey, Dave," said Ron Turcotte, who was sitting on a wooden bench, wearing only a towel and smoking a cigar that was as long as Argentina. "Still think Bold Rulers can't go a mile and a quarter?" Turcotte had just ridden Secretariat, the future Triple Crown champion. Together they had broken Northern Dancer's Derby record with a time of 1:59 2/5.[19]

Bold Lad looked like he had been whitewashed. Around all of his lower legs, he had what they call white stockings. Horses with four white stockings, so the hoary backstretch superstition went, were supposed to be jinxed. But four white stockings didn't stop Charismatic (1999)[20] or California Chrome (2014) from winning the Derby.[21] Hartack was not much for black cats or talismans, although he did insist that a friend wear a black derby hat when he won at Churchill Downs with Majestic Prince in 1969.[22]

The night before the 1965 Derby, Art Rooney went to dinner with Jimmy Cannon and a few others. Rooney, the avuncular owner of the Pittsburgh Steelers, who had basically bought the football team with some extraordinary betting scores that he had made at two New York tracks during one wild week in the 1930s, hadn't missed a Derby since 1926. Cannon, an old friend of Rooney's, was an immensely popular, curmudgeonly sports columnist from New York. He bemoaned to Rooney how rickety Churchill Downs was, how it was still mostly made out of wood—rotting wood—and was a firetrap that could turn into a conflagration if a blaze ever got started. "Jimmy," Rooney said, "why is the world always coming to an end for you?"[23]

The next day, two hours before the Derby, a careless smoker in Section L on the fourth-floor grandstand, just opposite where the horses would run into the clubhouse turn, flipped a lit cigarette. It caught between two sections of floorboard and started a fire. Flames shot ten feet into the air. Heavy smoke, black as anthracite, billowed upward. Racegoers scrambled but didn't panic. The crowd of a hundred thousand was aghast. Firemen rushed to the scene with their trucks and equipment. They extinguished the flames, and no one was injured. Then Churchill Downs announced that the Derby would be run a half-hour late. A clever headline the next day said, "Run for the Roses Turns to Run for the Hoses."[24]

The broadcaster Jack Drees and the rest of the CBS television crew were preparing for the race. The fire had badly damaged their cables, and for a while there was doubt that they would even be able to go on the air. The broadcast started on schedule, but mostly with pictures and no sound. The broadcasters still went ahead with their comments, in case sound was restored in mid-broadcast. "You prepare for weeks, even months, for the Derby," Drees said. "And then the only one who heard what I said was the guy standing next to me."[25]

(I didn't get to my first Derby until three years later. On Derby day 1965, I was in Baltimore, in the throes of a newspaper strike. Several of us out-of-work journalists, in the interests of making ends meet, published a daily sports newspaper out of a vacant downtown garage. I was in charge of Derby coverage, so to speak, and was going to bootleg my story from the CBS telecast. Fat chance. All I had at my disposal was, sans sound, the small pictures on a flickering black-and-white TV set. Like the rest of the country, I couldn't hear a thing. I hadn't been smart enough to bring along a radio as a backup.)

At Churchill Downs, it was already hot before the fire. The temperature hit an unseasonable eighty-four degrees, with high humidity as well.[26]

One of the spectators who caused a stir was Connie Francis, the pop singer, who was at the height of her popularity. Her relationship with Hartack had been an item for gossip columnists,[27] although Larry King, who knew them both and was a good friend of Hartack's, said, "I don't think Connie and Bill were ever that serious."[28]

Warming up Bold Lad, Hartack sensed something amiss.[29] When the gates opened, his concern became reality. Bold Lad, favored at 2–1, usually put himself in the thick of contention early in his races, but this day he was in sixth place after a half-mile, four lengths off the pace. It got worse from there. He was never better than fifth and "gave way badly in the final drive," according to the official chart footnotes. He finished tenth, ahead of only a 92–1 shot in the eleven-horse field, and was beaten by twelve lengths.

"We never had a shot," Hartack said. "At first I thought it might be the track cupping out from under him, but that wasn't it. He was trying to run all the way, but wasn't going anywhere. Something is bothering him. He had a reason not to run. I think I know what it is, but that's not for publication."[30]

Bold Lad was a big horse, more than sixteen hands (at four inches to the hand), but sometimes big horses can be hard on themselves. He was suffering from calcium deposits and was also diagnosed as anemic. He didn't run in the other Triple Crown races, the Preakness and the Belmont Stakes, and in fact didn't run again in 1965. He was brought back in 1966, without Hartack and without Winfrey as his trainer, and won four races, but he was retired after a poor finish on the Fourth of July, when a weighty 135-pound impost took its toll.[31]

Hartack didn't pick up another horse to ride in either the Preakness or the Belmont. He rode at Hollywood Park and Del Mar, the next stops on the Southern California circuit. Astoundingly, he was the leading rider at Del Mar, with forty-five wins during the forty-two-day season.[32] In only seven weeks, he won 30 percent of all the races he would win all year. Hartack rode nine more years and led only one more meet—an abbreviated second Del Mar season in 1967.[33]

Decades later, there were several opinions about Hartack's resurgence. Harry "The Hat" Hacek, a veteran agent, put forth this theory: "In those days, they didn't run the kind of meets that Del Mar has now. Del Mar turned a competitive corner in the 1980s or thereabouts. Crowds increased, purses shot up, the horses got better, and it got a lot tougher to win races there. Before that, they didn't have meets that were at the same level as Santa Anita or Hollywood Park. I took Darrel McHargue there in 1975, and he won the title. I'm not saying it was easy, but the jocks' colony got better later on."[34]

When Hartack arrived at Del Mar in 1965, Shoemaker was riding in New York. Shoemaker already had won seventeen stakes races at Del Mar, as well as six riding titles, but from 1959 through 1970 he concentrated his summer efforts in Chicago and New York, where the purses were more appealing and the more important horses were running.[35] Don Pierce, a Hall of Fame jockey who is among the leaders in career stakes wins at Del Mar, also rode in New York in 1965. When Pierce did butt heads with Hartack, whether it was on the track or in race-horse rummy, he was determined to beat him. Pierce remembered the four-handed game in which he was certain that he held one of Hartack's key cards. He refused to give up the card, just because he wanted to beat Hartack. Pierce said that he held the card to the end, even though it didn't fit in his hand. Pierce lost the game, costing him $50 or $60, but he had the satisfaction that Hartack didn't win, either.

"He might have been able to ride, but as a guy he was a turkey," Pierce said. "You would see him around the track, and say hello to him, and he'd just look right through you and not say hello back. You always wondered what you had done to deserve that. After a while, you just said, 'Screw him,' and you gave him the same thing back. He must have been dead six months before I found out about it. I was sorry to hear that nobody in the family came forward. Nobody deserves that. If I had known, I would have paid to get him buried."[36]

Vince DeGregory began booking jockeys' mounts almost sixty years ago. Included among his clients were Hall of Famers Laffit Pincay Jr., Angel Cordero Jr., and Chris McCarron. DeGregory, who never worked for Hartack, also played cards with him when they overlapped in New York. Hartack, DeGregory said, was cordial during the games.

"Let me ask you something," DeGregory said to Hartack one night. "How come you are all right with me tonight, in this game, but when I see you around the track, you ignore me?"

Hartack thought for moment. "Maybe it's because we were never introduced," he said.[37]

Kenny Church was a riding contemporary of Hartack's. Church didn't finish among the leaders during the 1965 Del Mar meeting, partly because he was also taking mounts out of town, but he won four stakes races there, two of them with the 2-year-old Coursing, who was considered one of the best juveniles in the country. Other jockeys, including Hartack, coveted the mount on Coursing, in the event that something happened to Church. Some pundits thought that Coursing had the goods to win the 1966 Kentucky Derby. Bob Hebert of the *Los Angeles Times* said at the time that Coursing might be the best California-bred 2-year-old of them all.

Coursing was a son of Fleet Nasrullah and grandson of the prepotent sire Nasrullah. Fleet Nasrullah had two Kentucky Derby winners—Count Fleet and Reigh Count—in his family. Coursing was trained by Clyde Turk. In a prep race before the Del Mar Futurity, Church had a conflict with a horse he was to ride in New York, and Hartack took over in California, with the understanding among all concerned that it was a one-race commitment. Coursing won by seven lengths.

According to Church, during the two-plus weeks between that race and the Futurity, Hartack used several ploys in an attempt to ride the horse again. At one point, Church said, Hartack offered to pay Turk for the mount: "It was either cash up front or he offered to share his commission with Clyde, depending on what the horse did in the Futurity." This might not have been against the rules, but it was unethical, in Church's judgment. He said that this—another jockey trying to buy his way onto a horse that he was riding—had happened only one other time during his long career. Turk, Church said, rejected Hartack's offer out of hand and firmly said, "Kenny Church is Coursing's jockey."

With Church in the saddle, Coursing won the Del Mar Futurity by five lengths as he extended his undefeated streak to five in a row. He won "as his rider pleased," according to the *Daily Racing Form*'s chart footnotes. Hartack, settling for a 31–1 shot, finished fifth with Winkover. But Coursing never made it to the Kentucky Derby; he was sidelined after shattering a sesamoid bone, attempted a comeback and never won another race.

Church, who had ridden against Hartack often, said that he already had a low opinion of him before the Del Mar Futurity incident. "He had no class," Church said. "He was egotistical. He couldn't hit a horse with his right hand. He was left-handed all the way, and was unable to switch sticks. The way he sat on a horse, there was no rhythm between him and his horses. But on the other hand, he was a very clever rider. He had a knack for keeping his horses out of trouble. He was also a very hard tryer, he would doing anything to win. Those were his hole cards."[38]

Hartack skipped a year; then he returned to ride at Del Mar in 1967 and 1968. Wins were not hanging from the trees; he won sixteen races at the main meets each year.[39] In October 1967, prior to the second race on the opening day of a twenty-day abbreviated second meet, he witnessed the accident that killed Freddie Robertson. A thirty-one-year-old jockey, Robertson sustained fatal injuries in the post parade when Dublin Hearts, a 2-year-old filly, reared as the field neared the starting gate. Dublin Hearts threw Robertson against the inner wood rail, and he suffered a broken neck and fractured skull. Robertson was known around the track as "Fearless Freddie" because of his willingness to ride even the most obstreperous of horses. Dublin Hearts was on the track without a lead pony, a familiar precaution at U.S. tracks that is taken to settle down fractious horses.[40]

After an ambulance sped Robertson to Scripps Memorial Hospital in nearby La Jolla, it was left to Dan Smith, a young member of Del Mar's public relations department, to call the jockeys' room for details. He asked for Hartack, since he and his horse had been closest to Dublin Hearts when she tossed her rider.

Hartack picked up the phone and didn't even say hello. "That jock's dead," he announced.[41]

18

Taxing Problems

There were published reports as early as 1960 that suggested Bill Hartack and the Internal Revenue Service were not exchanging Christmas cards. "Uncle Sam's getting ready to swat Willie Hartack across his jodhpurs," Murray Olderman wrote in his syndicated column. "Tax problems ... Willie's the neglectful sort who carries around checks and forgets about them.... But worries haven't kept him from rebuilding his Miami-area house with Japanese tiles decorating the walls."[1]

Later, it came to light that Hartack had a laundry list of debts to the U.S. government, starting with his second full year of riding. The red ink on his ledger spilled over like this[2]:

1954: $79,917
1955: $86,286
1956: $134,770
1957: $209,039
1958: $80,322
1959: $71,723
1960: $89,323

These numbers, based on Hartack's estimated earnings, which in turn were based on the purse money his horses won, suggested that Hartack was not paying federal taxes at all. In 1968, Hartack admitted to the government that he owed $751,303 from 1954 through 1960. Interest charges were also piling up. They were averaging $142 a day, or $51,830 a year. In 1978, Howell Melton Sr., a federal judge in Jacksonville, Florida, entered a summary judgment in favor of the IRS that said Hartack owed $1,065,822. Three weeks before the judgment, Hartack had been a no-show at a pre-trial hearing.[3] In 2015, the Jacksonville court could not find a copy of the judgment,[4] and Howell Melton Jr. said that his father, retired from the bench, did not recall the case.[5]

Chick Lang once said that his former client's cash-flow situation wasn't promising. Lang claimed that Hartack was banking only about eight to ten cents out of every dollar he earned. "Here's a guy who's winning everything in sight, and he still isn't getting any money," Lang added.[6]

Some of the math didn't add up. In 1957, the year Hartack won his second Kentucky Derby with Venetian Way, his mounts earned slightly more than $3 million, which set a record at the time.[7] A rule of thumb is that a jockey's earnings can be estimated at 10 percent of his purse total. Based on that formula, Hartack would have collected about $300,000, minus 20 percent for his agent. Lang said that he earned $50,000, give or take, during each year he was with Hartack.[8] In 1957, Lang might have done even better, since 20 percent of Hartack's total would have been $60,000. That would have left Hartack with $240,000. Yet in 1978, when the IRS dropped the hammer, his taxes exceeded $200,000 for 1957 . It was not conceivable that he was paying almost all of his income toward taxes. I asked Eddie Sapir, a former New Orleans judge who was one of Hartack's best friends for more than forty years, about this apparent anomaly. Sapir said that he was never familiar with Hartack's finances and didn't even know him in 1957. Sapir theorized that Hartack, perhaps through endorsements, speaking appearances and other sources, could have earned more than $300,000 that year.[9]

By 1980, Hartack's tax morass got worse. There were reports that the IRS had filed three lawsuits against him for back taxes, bringing the total (with interest) to $2.3 million. The government filed liens against his home in Miami Springs, Florida, along with some of his other possessions.[10] The home was eventually bought by Canadian horse breeder George Gardiner. The co-owner of Miami Springs Villas, the hotel complex across the street from Hartack's home, Gardiner also bought the properties on both sides of the Hartack place and converted the three parcels into an opulent estate.[11]

According to Evelyn "Dolly" Hartack Ferguson, "When Sonny [her nickname for her brother] died, [Gary Condra] called me to ask if I would waive any inheritance. I did so willingly, because it didn't make any difference. I didn't expect anything, and there was nothing left to speak of. Sonny had nothing left."[12]

Friends said that while Hartack was astute in many ways—another jockey, Laffit Pincay Jr., said that he won so many arguments, he could have been a lawyer[13]—he had little interest in pecuniary matters. Hartack thought he had been paying his taxes all along. At tax time, he would write a check and send it to his accountant.[14]

While he was riding at Arlington Park in Chicago, Hartack and Bill Thayer, a track executive, were in a card game with a few friends. At the end of the night, Hartack went to his car to give Thayer a ride home. He also wanted to show Thayer a new whip that he had just bought. When Hartack opened the trunk of his car, several uncashed checks flew out. Thayer grabbed one before it was lost to the wind. The amount was $5,000, on a Calumet Farm account.

"Why haven't you cashed this?" Thayer asked.

"I'm never going to cash it," Hartack said. "They gave me that when all that shit came up about Tim Tam."

Hartack, scheduled to ride Calumet's Tim Tam in the 1958 Kentucky Derby, had broken his leg shortly before the race. He was replaced by Milo Valenzuela, who won both the Derby and the Preakness with the colt. Then Hartack told Jimmy Jones, who trained for Calumet, that he had recovered and was fit enough to ride Tim Tam in the Belmont Stakes with the Triple Crown on the line. Jones, however, wasn't ready to make a jockey change at that juncture. There was a bitter squabble, and Lucille Markey, who ran Calumet Farm, gave Hartack the check for $5,000 to assuage his injured feelings. An unforgiving Hartack filed the check away and quit riding for Calumet.

"Screw Calumet," Hartack said. "I don't need their horses and I don't need their money." He took the check out of Thayer's hand, wadded it up, and threw it back in the trunk.[15]

Dolly Ferguson said that she had heard that the accountant went to prison and died there.[16] Hartack, according to Penny Pierce, the wife of the jockey Don Pierce, paid all of his IRS debts, but it took years for them to settle. Federal agents were seen outside the jockeys' quarters at Santa Anita, waiting for Hartack to make a payment as he departed at the end of the day.[17] When agents showed up at Hartack's home in Miami Springs, he turned loose his house dog, a German shepherd. They ran to their car and didn't return.

Hartack sent payments to the IRS while he rode in Hong Kong during the late 1970s.[18] Tad Dowd, a friend of Hartack's, said that Zayle Bernstein, a Florida attorney, was conversant with Hartack's tax struggles.[19] Bernstein was a field agent for the IRS for eight years in the 1960s. In 1987, he was indicted by a grand jury on racketeering and drug charges and turned himself in to police in Tampa, Florida.[20] Attempts to reach Bernstein were unsuccessful. Twice, through a former business associate, Irene De Camp-Ultimo, Bernstein declined interviews.[21]

For someone in need of money, Hartack repeatedly bargained his way out of lucrative opportunities. In the early 1970s, Woodbine Race Track, near Toronto, sent its public relations manager, Bruce Walker, to Arkansas to ask if Hartack would relocate to Canada and ride. Woodbine's jockey colony was reduced when Avelino Gomez retired to train horses and Sandy Hawley moved his tack to Southern California. John Mooney, the president of Woodbine, believed that jockeys were longer-lasting drawing cards than horses. Horses, Mooney said, come and go, and many times they are retired early because of their stud value. Jockeys have extended careers and are what the public better identifies with. Mooney thought Hartack could help fill the gap that Gomez and Hawley had created.

This was during Hartack's Wild West period. Away from the track, he dressed in buckskin jackets, sporting a cowboy hat and pointed-toe boots. He let his hair grow long and wore a mustache and a small goatee. Walker hadn't seen him for a while, and when they met at Oaklawn Park in Hot Springs, he hardly recognized him. They talked briefly in the jockeys' room after the races, and Hartack said to meet him at a bar across the street from the track. "The place was a dump," Walker said. "I made sure I sat at a table with my back to the wall."

Hartack sat down with a list of his requirements, should he come to Woodbine. "The money part, the retainer, was completely out of line," Walker declared. "He was asking for the kind of money that Bill Shoemaker would have commanded in his prime. This was a Bill Hartack who had seen better days. We were giving him a chance to climb back on top. He could have won a lot of races in Canada, because the two top guys weren't there anymore. But I knew Hartack was asking for the kind of money that John Mooney wasn't willing to pay. We shook hands but never made a deal."[22]

Later on, after Hartack's IRS debts had escalated because of the interest charges, he quit buying new cars. His good friend in Florida, Gary Condra, was in the car-leasing business and provided him with several vehicles. The Cadillac Hartack once drove had a couple hundred thousand miles on it. Churchill Downs, to promote the Kentucky Derby, invited the winning jockeys to Louisville. Hartack told them he would come if they bought him a new car. The track countered by offering all expenses for his trip, plus $5,000. This was more than the other jockeys were going to be paid. However, Hartack insisted on the new car. Churchill Downs said that it would run the promotion without him.

As it turned out, Hartack was in Louisville by chance at the time of the promotion anyway. He was there for business reasons. "Are you crazy?" a friend asked. "You're there. Take the money."

"They should have given me the car," Hartack said. "Fuck 'em."[23]

Hartack might have increased his income by renting out his luxurious home on Deer Run in Miami Springs. The only time he was there was when he rode at the Florida tracks. Hartack allowed race trackers to stay at his house free of charge. Harry "The Hat" Hacek, the jockeys' agent, and his rider, Craig Perret, once shared the Hartack residence. Perret was riding at Hialeah and Gulfstream Park at the time.

When Hartack handed them the keys, he said, "It's always been a safe neighborhood. I thought it was so safe that I never even locked the front door. But one night a couple of guys came in with guns. They pushed me around a little. They had done some of their homework, but in another way they were kind of stupid. I had had a big day at the track, two or three winners, one of them a stake. But these clowns figured I got paid in cash, right on the spot, and carried all that money home. So all they got was six hundred bucks. And they didn't realize that a lot of my trophies were in boxes up in the attic. They probably wouldn't have known what they had anyway."

Hartack mentioned that he had had a peephole installed in the front door after the robbery. But he didn't tell Hacek and Perret about the unique wall that separated the living room and the master bedroom. You could push a button and the wall would slide out of sight. One night Hacek and Perret were watching television in the living room when they noticed the button. They pushed it, and the wall receded.

"Damnedest thing I ever saw," Hacek said. "We didn't know what to think. Kind of kinky, when you think about it. For two bachelors who were straight, it wasn't the answer. And there was one other thing. Bill's bedroom was painted entirely in black. Black walls, black ceiling. Who goes to sleep like that? We tried to, but it took some getting used to. I meant to ask Bill about that but never did."[24]

Tommy Roberts, a racing telecaster, stayed at Deer Run for an entire race track meeting. It saddened Roberts to see Hartack's decline. "He once had that fantastic drive to win," Roberts said in 1968. "I don't think he has that anymore."[25] The 1969 Triple Crown, with Majestic Prince, served as a rejuvenation for Hartack, but it was only a temporary fix.

19

Bus Stop

In 1966, a young jockey from Panama, Laffit Pincay Jr., arrived in the United States as a contract rider for the Fred Hooper stable. Pincay, only 19, broke in sensationally, winning with eight of his first eleven mounts at Arlington Park near Chicago. Many of the jockeys in the Arlington colony cheered Pincay on. But not Bill Hartack. "He wasn't friendly at all," Pincay said. "He would mind his own business, play his own card games, but he would never look at you or nothing."[1]

Pincay would go on to win more than 9,500 races, breaking the record held by Bill Shoemaker before Pincay himself was displaced in the record books by Russell Baze, the Old Man River of jockeys.[2] Eventually, Pincay and Hartack became friends, their relationship given a quantum boost because one of Hartack's girlfriends, Roseann Williams, had been a friend of Linda Pincay, Laffit's first wife.[3]

"I thought [Hartack] would never speak to me," Laffit Pincay said. "But once I got to know him, I could have a pretty good conversation with him. But I definitely would never dare to argue with him, and since I don't like to argue, anyway, he had no problem with me."[4]

By 1966, the choleric Hartack was an equal-opportunity shunner. His stakes winners had all but dried up. Each year, trying to secure a Kentucky Derby mount was a hardship. Instead of being forced to make hard choices among several Derby prospects, as was his dilemma in the good old days, he had to campaign for whatever he could get. "Scrounging" was a more callous word for it. That he had won the Derby—his fourth—just two years before didn't seem to matter. He would spend many idle hours in jockeys' rooms around the country, waiting for the few chances a handful of trainers might give him. In 1966, fifteen horses ran in the Derby, none of them ridden by Hartack. In 1967, he settled for riding a long shot, a horse he regretted aligning himself with as race day got closer.[5]

While the field for the Derby was heating up in Florida, New York and Southern California, Hartack was riding at Bay Meadows and Golden Gate Fields, near San Francisco. Those were hardly the places to find a viable Derby contender. Hartack's already minimal chances of securing a Derby candidate in Florida, which was once his stronghold, were cut even thinner when Braulio Baeza, who had been the contract rider for Fred Hooper—who had given Pincay his start—decided to freelance. This meant that the talented Baeza was available to all trainers, not just the conditioners who worked for Hooper. It was an expensive decision; Baeza wanted out before his contract with Hooper expired, and the owner was adamant that he not leave even a day early. To go out on his own, Baeza had to pay Hooper $100,000, an astronomical amount. Fortunately, Baeza quickly recouped that outlay. In his first year away from Hooper, he rode Buckpasser, and that horse alone gave Baeza earnings that totaled more than half of his escape fee.[6]

Hartack began the 1966–1967 season in Florida. He won with only three of thirty-four mounts at Tropical Park, and even though Hialeah was well under way in January, he had found only three races to ride.[7] So he took to nickel-and-diming his way around Northern California.

"I couldn't get mounts in Florida," Hartack said. "That's exactly true. It was very easy for me to have principles when I was on top. Now's the time to see if I can take it."[8]

For the 1967 California Derby at Golden Gate, he took the assignment on Dr. Isby, a colt trained by Frank Childs, who had won the Kentucky Derby with Tomy Lee in 1959.[9] "[Other trainers] weren't exactly knocking down my doors seeking my services," Hartack said. "It was strictly a case of an owner who was a personal friend and wanted to give me a chance. P.L. Grissom had Royal Native [a champion filly] and I had ridden her for him before he sold her. We had been friends for years. He called me up and said he had a 3-year-old who might be a Derby colt and would like me to ride him."[10]

Dr. Isby, named after a surgeon in Detroit, had been ridden by seven different jockeys in his fifteen races. Hartack rode him twice and finished no better than fifth. The California Derby, two weeks before the Kentucky Derby, was Dr. Isby's thirteenth race in twelve weeks. At Santa Anita, Childs ran him three times in ten days. Dr. Isby ran fourth in the California Derby, but he closed willingly after lagging at the start, and he had four wins at a mile or longer on his record. That was enough reason for Childs to ship him to Kentucky. "Fourth in the California Derby might not have sounded exciting," Hartack said. "But I was hoping. It can happen."[11]

In the Stepping Stone, Dr. Isby finished a good late-running second to Ruken, the Santa Anita Derby winner.[12] Four days later, under vigorous lefthanded whipping from Hartack, Barbs Delight won the Trial. Getting off Barbs Delight, Hartack said to the trainer, Hal Steele, Jr., "I like your horse. He ought to win the Derby."

"Then you'll ride him?" Steele asked.

"I can't," Hartack said. "I'm already committed." He was talking about Dr. Isby.

That was a private conversation. Minutes later, in the jockeys' room, a peevish Hartack declined to answer questions about his Derby plans. Although Damascus would go off the favorite, there was widespread interest in Hartack's Derby plans. With four wins in the race, and a chance to tie the retired Eddie Arcaro with a fifth, he had built a reputation for picking the right horse at the right time.

"You can't guarantee me that what I say will come out the way I say it," Hartack said. "Unless you can give me a legal, written guarantee, I'm not talking."

In his column, Shirley Povich asked, "The next time we want to talk to Hartack, should we bring a notary public?"[13]

Dr. Isby would go off at slightly lower odds than Barbs Delight in the Derby, but both were long shots and it was obvious which horse Hartack preferred. Be that as it may, he was loyal to P.L. Grissom, the owner, and rode Dr. Isby. Barbs Delight might have discouraged the public because of his drinking habits. He liked wine, either straight from the bottle (Italian Swiss Colony, a domestic Chianti) or mixed with his fodder. His groom, Bill Whaley, made sure that he didn't imbibe at least two days before a race; a positive post-race test for alcohol would disqualify the horse from any purse money earned.[14]

Damascus had won the Wood Memorial by a gaping margin. His only loss out of eight races came against Dr. Fager. That was a race at a mile, a distance that was in Dr. Fager's wheelhouse. Since the Derby was a quarter-mile longer, Dr. Fager skipped the race.

Proud Clarion drew little attention. His trainer, Lloyd "Boo" Gentry, appeared to have a sprinter on his hands, and after a poor workout four days before the Derby, he had neither a jockey to ride his colt nor an inclination to run. John Galbreath's Darby Dan Farm seemed to be in a Derby funk. In 1966, their highly regarded Graustark broke down the week before the race, and in 1967 their best Derby prospect, Cup Race, was sidelined with sore shins. Galbreath had shopped Proud Clarion around, but his asking price of $60,000 brought no takers.

In 1963, Darby Dan had won the Derby with Chateaugay, a horse who also didn't figure, so Galbreath figured there was room for more lightning in the bottle. He entered Proud Clarion, who went off at 30–1. Braulio Baeza, once the contract rider for Darby Dan, had passed up Proud Clarion to ride Successor. Who could blame him? Before Proud Clarion only two horses in Derby history had won at higher odds. On entry day, two days before the race, Gentry hired the veteran Bobby Ussery, who had ridden the sire, Hail to Reason, but had never been on Proud Clarion's back, not even for a workout. Ussery had been shopping around, and he'd hoped to ride a horse with a better chance, such as Reason to Hail or Cool Reception. But after losing to Barbs Delight in the Derby Trial, Cool Reception dropped out of the Derby.

On Derby day, it rained intermittently. There were hundreds of demonstrators outside the track, part of a movement to change the open-housing law in Louisville. State officials, concerned that the brouhaha might disrupt the races, brought in more than two thousand National Guardsmen as a precaution. Churchill Downs' long stretch was surrounded by helmeted soldiers. The crowd, estimated at eighty-five thousand, was much smaller than what the Derby had drawn in previous years.

The rain didn't subside for the race, but the track was still listed as fast. Barbs Delight, with Kenny Knapp riding because Hartack had honored a promise, ran the fastest opening quarter mile in Derby history. At the top of the stretch, Barbs Delight was still turning aside challengers, including the favored Damascus. Dr. Isby, with Hartack, was never a threat and would wind up twelfth, beating only two horses.

Barbs Delight was undefeated in four starts at Churchill, but Proud Clarion, once ten lengths behind, was swung to the outside by Ussery upon leaving the quarter pole. This was one rival Barbs Delight failed to turn aside. Proud Clarion outgamed his rival to the wire, winning by one length.[15]

Although Knapp had never ridden in a Derby, he was an experienced rider. Two years before, he had set the record at Arlington Park when he won eleven stakes races. But that didn't discourage speculation after the Derby that if Hartack had ridden Barbs Delight instead of Knapp, the order of the first two finishers might have been reversed. Hal Steele, Jr., didn't give Knapp's ride a ringing endorsement: "He gave him a cool ride, but maybe he did become a little nervous when Proud Clarion caught up with him in the stretch."

It was going to take an extra $10,000 to make Barbs Delight eligible for the Preakness in two weeks. Had the colt been nominated for the race ahead of time, it would have only cost his owners $100. It was mentioned to Steele that Barbs Delight had already earned $25,000 for running second in the Derby. "That's money that's already been spent," said Steele, who owned 25 percent of the horse.

While the Barbs Delight camp debated whether the Preakness was worth a $10,000 gamble, Knapp told them that he had a commitment to ride at Garden State Park that day and wouldn't be available even if they wanted him. That opened the door for Hartack, and when he said he would ride the horse, the owners wrote the check.[16]

"Knapp didn't ride a bad race in the Derby," wrote Shirley Povich, "but he did not ride a Hartack race. The switch of riders for the Preakness must be viewed as significant. Hartack is not a popular figure with the public, trainers or the racing press, but he does have virtues, particularly as a rider on front-runners. No jockey can hold a horse together better than Hartack, whose style may appear to be floppy, but who rides in concert with his mount."[17]

Frank Whiteley, the trainer of Damascus, ran a second horse, Celtic Air, in the Preakness. Whiteley, who said that the clamor at the Derby had distracted Damascus, trained him for the Preakness in relative privacy at Laurel Race Course, twenty-five miles away. Damascus didn't arrive at Pimlico until the morning of the race.[18] He and his entrymate, coupled in the betting, went off the favorite, with Barbs Delight the second choice. There was little respect for Proud Clarion; the Derby winner was third in the betting. He also finished third in the race. Celtic Air kept Barbs Delight busy in the early part, and in fact he led for three-quarters of a mile. Damascus was in eighth place out of ten until Bill Shoemaker got him to kick in at the quarter pole. They circled the field and won by two-plus lengths in a time that was only three-fifths off the record. For all the hub-bub about Hartack improving Barbs Delight's chances, the colt faded badly in the stretch and finished sixth. Proud Clarion, Barbs Delight and Hartack were not around for the Belmont Stakes. Damascus scored another convincing win, finished the year with twelve wins in sixteen starts and was voted Horse of the Year.[19]

Hartack finished 1967 with sixty-six wins, easily the lowest full-season total of his career.[20] Shoemaker was thirty-six years old, and Hartack thirty-five; yet Shoemaker showed no signs of slowing down while Hartack languished. Shoemaker had reached almost 6,000 wins, while Hartack was 255 wins short of 4,000. Shoemaker was closing in on the record of 6,032, held by the retired Johnny Longden.[21] When he was averaging three hundred wins a year, Hartack looked like a lead pipe to at least reach the four-thousand mark, but not anymore.

"I'm getting tired of offering my services," Hartack said a few weeks before the 1967 Derby. "I'm getting tired of fighting and not accomplishing anything.... Tomorrow's not going to be a better day, unless you make it a better day or attempt to make it a better day. The bus just isn't going to come over and pick you up. You've got to find the station and go get on. If you wait for the next bus, you might not catch that one, either. It's not as easy as that."[22]

There would be another bus for Hartack, but it was two years away. That's a long time in the business of race riding.

20

Any Horse in a Storm

Although he was small enough to be a jockey, Gil Stratton never rode horses for a living. Stratton did almost everything else: He was on Broadway at nineteen, kissing Judy Garland; he was on dozens of broadcasts during the Golden Age of Radio; and in the movies, he acted alongside Mickey Rooney (*Girl Crazy*), Marlon Brando (*The Wild One*) and William Holden (*Stalag 17*). He was a bombardier during World War II. He was a professional baseball umpire. He was a pro football announcer. He even worked with John Forsythe (when Forsythe had black hair), broadcasting the races from Hollywood Park, Santa Anita and Del Mar.[1] Then one day the diminutive Stratton hoped to interview Bill Hartack after Hartack won a race. That was one of the few things Stratton couldn't do.

Two days before the running of the 1968 Hollywood Derby, Hartack called the congenial Stratton, telling him that if he won the race, he would not be doing a TV interview on Stratton's hour-long Los Angeles show. Stratton, who never had a cross word with Hartack, on or off the air, asked for the reason. Hartack said that he knew there was no fee for doing an interview, but he thought it was about time jockeys got paid.

Riding Poleax, Hartack won the race. As promised, he didn't give Stratton an interview, and he didn't go to the winner's circle for the post-race photo, either. The photo included the horse, the owner, the trainer and Jackie Gleason, who presented the trophy, but no Hartack. "That's hard old Hartack, a true beauty," John Hall wrote. "There had been concern he might have mellowed. No chance."[2]

They ran that Hollywood Derby in July, after the Triple Crown races had passed Hartack by. His win total for 1968 improved from 66 to 105, but it was still far from the bar he had set during his banner years. Hartack's career in the mainstream was hanging by a thread. What saved him was a long-winded California gelding named Quicken Tree and that phone call in November from Johnny Longden, asking Hartack to ride Majestic Prince in his 2-year-old debut.

At the start of his career, no jockeys were clamoring to ride Quicken Tree, who won only two of his first sixteen starts. Clyde Turk, who trained the horse, tried addressing Quicken Tree's rambunctious ways by gelding him, but that didn't seem to help. Before one of Quicken Tree's races at Santa Anita, he threw the jockey in the paddock, ran through a flower bed, and scattered people in the walking ring as though Godzilla had come to town. Lou Rowan, who bred and owned him, risked losing Quicken Tree by running him in claiming races for $15,000 and lower. Rowan thought he had sold Quicken Tree when he packaged him with another horse for $25,000, but the buyer backed off and later claimed the other horse out of a race for $15,000. Instead of selling all of Quicken Tree, Rowan sold a piece of him to Wheelock Whitney, a horseman from Minneapolis. Whitney was the smart one—by the end of Quicken Tree's career, the horse had earned more than $700,000.

In addition to being a plodder and pigheaded, Quicken Tree was homely. "He's got a U-neck," said one horseman. "He's got a dropped hip. He's got that white spot on his neck. And he's got a slab head."

In 1966, Rowan gave in to a whim and ran Quicken Tree in the Del Mar Derby. This was a grass race, which would turn out to be the horse's best surface. At 53–1, Quicken Tree closed from far back to finish a respectable fourth, and a little later he won a small stake at Del Mar.

In 1967, they ran Quicken Tree far, wide and often. He went to the post twenty times, including four trips to New York, where the longest—and therefore more favorable—races were being carded. One of those cross-country excursions paid off when Quicken Tree won the Display Handicap, a two-mile marathon.[3]

In 1968, which would be Quicken Tree's best year, the veteran jockey Kenny Church thought he had the mount sewn up. Church and Turk had a good history together. In 1965, Church had won a pair of stakes with Turk's 2-year-old Coursing, including the Del Mar Futurity. Hartack had irked Church, however, when he allegedly tried to coerce Turk into letting him ride Coursing. Church said that Hartack had made a cash offer to Turk then, and he repeated the tactic—this time successfully—to get Turk to ride him on Quicken Tree.

"It didn't make any sense," Church said. "I had a good relationship with Clyde and was continuing to ride his horses. But then Hartack comes along and gets Quicken Tree."[4]

Fernando Alvarez also rode Quicken Tree, but it was Hartack who won the Manhattan Handicap,[5] the Del Mar Handicap and the Jockey Club Gold Cup with the horse. After Quicken Tree came from twenty-five lengths behind to win the Del Mar race, Hartack tried a different strategy in the two-mile Gold Cup. He rushed Quicken Tree into contention going down the backstretch, opened a clear lead with a quarter mile to go, and won by a length and a quarter. Two things played into Hartack's hand: Damascus, the favorite and the 1967 Horse of the Year, suffered a career-ending tendon injury early in the race, and Funny Fellow, a one-eyed horse who ran second, took a clod in his good eye during the stretch run.[6]

Church said that apart from the scramble over mounts with Hartack, he had a personal reason to dislike him. Church said that his wife Nancy, who worked in the Del Mar Turf Club, came home one night and told him that Hartack had made a romantic overture. "I was hot," Church admitted. He said that the next day he confronted Hartack in the jockeys' room and told him, "Look, you son of a bitch, if you ever walk by my wife, or even say hello to her, we're going to have serious problems."[7]

In 1967, Hartack's earnings dipped to an estimated $52,000. Mainly because of Quicken Tree, he was able to boost his income to about $80,000 in 1968.[8] Late in 1967, the Internal Revenue Service clamped down and placed a lien of more than $800,000 on Hartack's home in Miami Springs, Florida. The federal government said Hartack was in arrears for several years on his taxes from the 1950s.[9]

When Johnny Longden was ready to start Majestic Prince for the first time on Thanksgiving Day 1968, his first choice to ride, Bill Shoemaker, was still recovering from a hip injury. Longden located Hartack, then on a hunting trip in Montana, and brought him to

Bay Meadows for the race.[10] Majestic Prince won that race, and every other race, including the Kentucky Derby and Preakness,[11] until he ran, against Longden's wishes, in the 1969 Belmont Stakes, where he was beaten by Arts and Letters. Hartack was the only jockey Majestic Prince ever had.[12]

It was a mild surprise that Longden would have chosen Hartack in 1968. Sure, Hartack had won the Derby four times, but none in four years.[13] Since he and Northern Dancer had finished first at Churchill Downs in 1964, his career had waned.[14] Because Longden was planning a California campaign to ready Majestic Prince for the 1969 Derby, he needed a West Coast rider, and any number of jockeys seemed better positioned than Hartack. Just a partial list included Alvaro Pineda, Laffit Pincay Jr., Jerry Lambert, Don Pierce and Rudy Rosales.[15]

"You don't get dumb overnight," Don Pierce said, talking about Hartack. "You don't have to win a lot of races to be good. They start giving you good horses and you start winning races again, and suddenly you've gone from dumb to smart? That's not the way it works. Hartack was still a very smart rider, even when the record didn't show it. He didn't make many mistakes when he rode a horse. And he was always a top big-race rider."[16]

During the Del Mar meets, Hartack spent the off days hunting for quail at the old Fairbanks Ranch with fellow jockeys Bill Harmatz, Jerry Lambert and Dean Hall. It was important to Hartack that he bring home the most birds. Whether playing checkers, chess, race-horse rummy, sandlot softball, bowling, or water-skiing, it was important that he finish on top.[17]

"I was surprised Johnny got a hold of me," Hartack said when he recalled Longden's phone call about Majestic Prince. "I thought he was going to ride Shoemaker, but I forgot that Shoe wasn't quite ready to come back yet. I hadn't ridden in two months."[18]

Hartack and Longden overlapped as jockeys during a few summers in Chicago. Marje Everett, who ran Arlington Park for her father, Ben Lindheimer, had a house on the grounds, and it was made available to her favorite riders. One summer in the 1960s, Hartack shared the house with Longden and his thirteen-year-old daughter, Andrea.

"The women were after him like crazy," Andrea remembered. "I spent a lot of time on the phone with them when they called. Bill had me answering the phone. Around the house, Bill taught me how to play race-horse rummy. But then if he saw me around the track, he might not even talk to me. He got focused once he got to the track and didn't have time for anybody or anything else. They would get on him, calling him 'Willie,' which he hated, just to get his goat. My dad would tell them to leave him alone, and they paid attention when he said it. I think that was what forged a bond between the two of them. My dad liked him, and [Frank McMahon, owner of Majestic Prince] liked him, too. But my dad wouldn't have hired him to ride Majestic Prince if he wasn't a good fit for the horse."[19]

Hartack and Longden also rode together in California. "I remember Johnny about the time when he was ready to retire," Hartack said. "But he hadn't changed. He was violently opposed to anybody getting through on the inside. I liked to get through on the rail, and we clashed several times. I was as mean as John, but that was only on the track."[20]

They were also at odds with each other, in the beginning, about how Hartack was to work Majestic Prince. Longden didn't want his horse going too fast in the mornings. One morning, during a six-furlong workout, Longden sat on his pony and waved to Hartack to slow down. Hartack ignored him. He explained to Longden afterward that the colt was still breathing easily after the workout, and that a good horse just naturally works fast. Finally, Longden accepted that.[21]

The day after Christmas, as Santa Anita opened its season, Majestic Prince made his first start since his debut on Thanksgiving and won on a sloppy track. Majestic Prince and Hartack would win seven more races together, taking them all the way through the Kentucky Derby and the Preakness.[22] Hartack's ride in the Belmont, with the Triple Crown on the line, drew mixed reviews, but what counted was that Longden thought he did the best he could with a horse who would have been better off staying in the barn.[23]

Sometimes a Kentucky Derby win will resuscitate a jockey's career, but such was not the case with Hartack. Despite his record fifth Derby win, opportunities for the remainder of 1969 were scant. He rode Quicken Tree, now a 6-year-old, to another stakes win at Santa Anita[24]; he won a small stake at Pimlico; toward the end of the year, he won the Del Mar Futurity with George Lewis.[25] But for the seventh straight year, he didn't finish in the top ten nationally in either purses or races won.[26] Mostly through Majestic Prince, his earnings were near the $100,000 mark.[27]

George Lewis catapulted Hartack into one more Kentucky Derby in 1970. George Lewis was trained by Buster Millerick, who because of the inimitable Native Diver was branded with an unfair one-horse-trainer label. Millerick was finally elected into the Racing Hall of Fame in 2010, twenty-four years after his death.[28] In 1970, he was well past Derby fever. At sixty-four, he had never started a horse in the race and never thirsted to win it. But George Lewis and Hartack dragged him to Louisville. Through mid-April, the colt was either first or second in ten straight races, the last of which was a spiffy win in the California Derby at Golden Gate Fields. George Lewis was even shipped across the country, and he won there too. In January, Hartack went along as the horse won the Hibiscus Stakes at Hialeah.[29] The trip was necessitated by a mutuel clerks' strike that had closed down Santa Anita.[30] Millerick stayed back in California; his good friend, the Florida-based Allen Jerkens, saddled the horse.[31]

Alan and Phyllis Magerman, who owned George Lewis, had become Hartack's biggest boosters. "He has all the things I look for in a person," Alan Magerman said. "Maybe he doesn't communicate, but everybody who knows him well respects him. He's so straight. Because of the world we live in, we get used to little white lies. Bill tells the truth. Ask him what he thinks of your wife, and if he thinks your wife is ugly, he'll tell you so."

Magerman also defended Hartack's penchant for avoiding the press. "He loves to win," he said. "He's dejected and remorseful when he loses. He wants to hide."

Punctuality was something else. A couple of days before the Derby Trial, a one-mile prep taking place on the Tuesday of Derby week, Millerick scheduled a five-furlong workout at Churchill Downs. The trainer waited until well past 9 a.m., but Hartack had yet to arrive at the barn. There was a chance the track would be closed for renovation and George Lewis might miss the important workout. Finally, Millerick sent word to another barn, and one of its riders, Charles Donnelly, was loaned out. Unfortunately, Donnelly botched the workout. He pulled up the horse too soon, and George Lewis only covered four furlongs.

Nevertheless, Millerick's confidence in Hartack was unwavering. "He's the best money rider in the world if he gets enough horse," the trainer said.[32]

Millerick had more pressing problems in the days leading up to the Derby. George

Lewis was beaten in the Derby Trial—Admiral's Shield, four lengths behind at the top of the stretch, ran him down—and the horse was also bothered by a cough. Magerman had only been in racing for two years, and he was determined not to miss his first Derby. He insisted that the decision about running would be up to Millerick ("He's the smartest man in the world"), but the trainer's comments told a different story.

"Hell, you know the horse will run," Millerick said a couple of days before the race. "He'll run if they have to carry him out there on a stretcher. But you can bet if he was my horse, he wouldn't run."[33]

George Lewis drew the inside post position in a seventeen-horse field.[34] The Derby had been won by a horse with the No. 1 post only once in the previous thirteen years.[35] George Lewis did what he needed to do: He broke sharply, put himself in immediate contention and was only a half-length from the lead with a quarter mile to run. After that, fatigue overcame him. He finished fourteenth as Dust Commander, a $6,500 horse, won by five lengths.[36]

Several weeks before the race, in discussing the Kentucky Derby in general, Hartack said, "Sometimes they can jump up and run a big race. That's why they have racing."[37]

Dust Commander paid $32.60.[38] Hartack's comment fit this Derby to a T.

21

A 4,000th Win, the Hard Way

The Arlington Classic was run six weeks after the 1970 Kentucky Derby. The top contenders in the eight-horse field were George Lewis and Corn Off the Cob, both of them found badly wanting at Churchill Downs. Angel Cordero Jr., Corn Off the Cobb's usual jockey, was sitting out a ten-day suspension, so Eddie Belmonte, who was having a stellar year, flew in from New York to take the mount. Bill Hartack, as he had in the Derby, rode George Lewis.

They ran in a drizzle in suburban Chicago. The finish was a three-horse battle to the wire, with Corn Off the Cob winning by a nose over Tenacious Jr. and George Lewis coming in third, only a half-length behind the first two horses. Hartack rode under a boil all the way around. His horse had acted up in the gate, and Hartack charged that the official starter, James Thompson, had sprung the latch at the wrong time, seriously compromising George Lewis' chances. After the finish, Hartack reached the unsaddling area, dismounted without talking to his trainer, Buster Millerick, and headed straight to the stewards' phone near the winner's circle. The stewards told him to put his protest in writing. Even if Hartack was right, they couldn't disqualify either of the two horses that ran ahead of him.

Hartack had run afoul of official starters before. At Garden State Park he had been suspended for the balance of a season—roughly thirteen days—because of "unbecoming conduct." The stewards said that he had defamed the starter and his gate crew in lodging an appeal.

The day after the Arlington Classic, Hartack delivered a letter to the stewards that said, "I refuse to accept that what happened was unavoidable. I am either right in my protest or I am wrong. In either case, I or the starter should be reprimanded. My horse reared in the gate. Then he began to rear again, and as he did that, the starter opened the gate."

The stewards quickly dismissed Hartack's complaint. "It is clearly evident," they said, "that George Lewis was accompanied and assisted by an assistant starter. The videotapes do not support the Hartack contention that George Lewis reared up before the break and again just as the break was being taken. The tapes disclose that George Lewis reared only on the break."[1]

Later in the summer of 1970, the Hall of Fame trainer Frank Whiteley hired Hartack to ride Tatoi, a horse he was running in the West Virginia Derby at Waterford Park. For Whiteley and Hartack, it was a return to a track of their youth. Whiteley had raced horses at Waterford in its inaugural year, 1951, and the next year Hartack rode his first winner there.[2] In 1963, Hartack had been scheduled to ride one of Whiteley's horses at Delaware Park when he learned that his father had been fatally shot.[3]

Waterford, forty miles west of Pittsburgh, later became Mountaineer Park. It never emerged from minor-league status during the Hartack era.[4] Hartack rode there one day in 1966. He won two of his three races, but otherwise the trip didn't go well. There was an uneasy interview with a Pennsylvania newspaper and a headline that suggested his career was moribund. In the middle of the interview, another reporter from Johnstown, Pennsylvania, not far from where Hartack grew up, asked if Hartack would make an appearance in his town.

"I can make no promises," said Hartack, who was riding at Tropical Park in Florida at the time. "I've got to break back in. I haven't been riding too many horses. I can't take a day off. One day can make a difference in fourteen or fifteen horses. The position I'm in, I've got to get back and ride more often. I have to convince the trainers that I'm working steady. If I promise to appear and then something happens, I'll be criticized for breaking appointments. And I'm tired of the criticism, especially when it's not true."

A TV crew pulled Hartack aside and, with the camera rolling, asked him flatly if he owed a debt to racing. "I don't owe racing a thing," he said. "Racing is not a one-way street. I feel I've given to racing as much as I've taken out."

George Stidham, Hartack's loyal sidekick, had also ridden at Waterford Park. He approached Hartack and said that another drink was waiting for him at the bar. "I can use one," said Hartack, who immediately turned in the direction of the bar, leaving a reporter at a table with a few more questions that he never got the chance to ask.[5]

The 1970 West Virginia Derby, a $25,000 stake, was advertised as the biggest race in the twenty-year history of the track. The attendance was almost seven thousand, a couple of thousand more than what Waterford usually drew on a summer Friday night. One newspaper referred to Hartack as being "in the twilight of his brilliant seventeen-year career." He was supposed to ride two early races on the card, but he called to cancel when his flight from Atlantic City, New Jersey, was late arriving.

Hartack had won twice with Tatoi in New Jersey, but this night, as the favorite, he ran eighth in a ten-horse field. Hartack left immediately after the race without giving any interviews. He was due back at Atlantic City to ride the next afternoon.[6]

One of Hartack's few stakes wins in 1970 came in the Kelly-Olympic Handicap, a $41,000 race run over Labor Day weekend. The 6-year-old Fort Marcy, twice the national grass champion, was favored. Elliott Burch, Fort Marcy's trainer, was using the race as a prep for the United Nations Handicap, worth three times as much, later in the meeting.

Fort Marcy, who drew the outside gate in the thirteen-horse field, was, unlike most of his races, far back early. Both Hartack, riding Red Reality, and Jorge Velasquez on Fort Marcy made strong late runs, and at the wire Red Reality had his nose in front. Red Reality carried eleven pounds less than Fort Marcy.[7] The loss might have damaged Fort Marcy's late-season bid for Horse of the Year honors, but he finished with convincing wins in the United Nations, in the Man o'War at Belmont Park, and in the Washington, D.C., International at Laurel, clinching the title.[8]

It had been eight years since Hartack had reached the three-thousand mark in career wins. Finally, the four thousandth winner was in his sights. He was nonchalant as he closed in on this rare milestone. Only four jockeys before him—Bill Shoemaker, Johnny Longden, Eddie Arcaro and Steve Brooks—had reached four thousand, and all but Shoemaker had retired. He treated the day at Arlington Park when he won No. 3,000—July 7, 1962, astride a horse named Big Steve in the fifth race—like it was just another day at the office. He didn't smile in the winner's circle. In the jockeys' room, somebody broke the silence by asking Hartack to say something.

"It's hard to say how proud I really am to get this one," he said. "But back of those three thousand wins are almost ten thousand losers. I rode every one of those losers as hard as I did this winner."

Someone asked if he was going to try to get four thousand wins.

"Let me put it this way," he said. "I'm going for three thousand and one, three thousand and two, three thousand and three—one by one, one at a time."

At that time, there were seven jockeys ahead of him in total wins: Longden, Ted Atkinson, Arcaro, Johnny Adams, Brooks, Ralph Neves and Shoemaker. Shoemaker passed them all.[9] Russell Baze and Laffit Pincay Jr. would eventually pass Shoemaker.[10]

On December 11, 1970, two days after his thirty-eighth birthday, Hartack was sitting on 3,999 wins and had four chances. But the best he could manage at Tropical Park was one third-place finish. On December 13, which was the next racing day at Tropical, Hartack had another shot. In the seventh race, which had a $4,500 pot and was called the Bardstown Purse, the jockeys were riding for their share of the winner's share, which would come to $270. Hartack was riding Roart, a horse who had been beaten in eleven of thirteen starts. Roart, who drew the No. 3 post, had to wait in his stall while the assistant starters loaded the other nine 2-year-olds. Roart reared before the break, slamming Hartack into the side of the steel gate. The jockey and the horse recovered and were soon back in stride, but by the time they got rolling they were in ninth place. That was a familiar early position for Roart, but this was a short race, only six furlongs, and he was left with much ground to make up.[11]

The pain ran up and down Hartack's right leg. The worst pain was in his ankle, which he said bothered him for the rest of his riding career. He was also diagnosed with a bruised hip. After the field had cleared the chute and began running in earnest down the backstretch, Roart was still far back. But as the field rounded the far turn, Hartack's mount began to pick up the leaders.

At the top of the stretch, Shifty Woolie held the lead, while Famous Gun was second, and Roart, with Hartack going to his whip, began to gain on them with every stride. Roart won by two lengths. The crowd of about six thousand responded with polite applause. Perhaps they were waiting for Hartack and his horse to reach the winner's circle before they offered a major ovation, but they didn't get the chance. Out of necessity, Hartack quickly pulled up his mount on the clubhouse turn, while the other jockeys galloped past him with their horses. Hartack dismounted, turned his horse over to an outrider, and signaled to one of the patrol judges that he was in distress. The station wagon that picks up the patrol judges at their stations around the track gave Hartack a ride back to the trackside scale. It is necessary for a jockey to weigh in before a race result can be declared official.

After limping to the scale, Hartack was driven to the first-aid room for X-rays and treatment. His injuries were diagnosed as minor, and he was released. In the meantime, the ceremony in the winner's circle, where track officials had gathered with a sterling-silver tray emblematic of the achievement, had to be postponed.[12] There appears to be no record of Hartack discussing his reaction upon joining the pantheon of Shoemaker and the others. "Typically," said the *Daily Racing Form*, alluding to Hartack's well-known reticence, "he had little comment on this latest milestone, but he surely must have reflected on the interval [about eight years] between his 3,000th and 4,000th winners."[13]

Roart was scheduled to carry 113 pounds, but Hartack couldn't make that weight and the colt carried one pound extra. The third choice, Roart paid $11.60 for a $2 bet.[14]

Finishing last in the race was the only filly, Harrods Creek. She was ridden by Diane Crump, who was the only female jockey in the field. On February 7, 1969, at Hialeah, a twenty-year-old Crump had become the first woman rider to win a parimutuel race in the United States.

Hartack was among a legion of male jockeys around the country who were opposed to women riding. "He wouldn't even talk to me," Crump said. "He'd see me all the time and just ignore me. After a while, he was all right. But I think it was not until he came home one of those years he rode in Hong Kong [1974–1980]. It was kind of funny. Hartack got along quite well with my husband then [Don Divine]. They got to know each other when Hartack was riding for Calumet Farm and my ex was working for them. So Hartack would be friendly [with Divine] but wouldn't say hello to me. I think Hartack resented what I was trying to accomplish."[15]

In 1970, Crump became the first woman to ride in the Kentucky Derby when she finished fifteenth with Fathom, a horse trained by Divine.[16]

Two months after Hartack's four thousandth win, Saul Silberman, the owner of Tropical Park, died. A year after that, Tropical Park, built on the site of an old greyhound race track six miles south of Miami International Airport, closed down. Silberman never denied that he was the biggest bettor at his own track.[17]

At the time of Hartack's four thousandth winner, he was finishing his eighteenth full season. Those ahead of him had these totals:

- Shoemaker: 6,067 wins, 22 seasons
- Longden: 6,032 wins, 40 seasons
- Arcaro: 4,779 wins, 31 seasons
- Brooks: 4,447, 32 seasons

Shoemaker's last ride came in 1990, at age fifty-eight, after almost nine thousand winners. Russell Baze retired on June 13, 2016, well ahead of Pincay and Shoemaker in career wins:

- Russell Baze: 12,842
- Laffit Pincay Jr.: 9,530
- Shoemaker: 8,833

Hartack was in fifty-sixth place, with 4,272 winners, plus 72 wins in Hong Kong, where he rode seasonally from 1974 to 1980.[18]

"Christmas is no reason for recriminations," David Alexander wrote a couple of weeks after Hartack hit four thousand, "and I would have no reason to recriminate a jockey named Bill Hartack in any season, even though he is a young man who has gone out of his way to snarl a bit at people, especially the press, for very little reason.... A lack of graciousness and common courtesy cannot detract from his ability as a rider.... I was delighted to read that he had become one of five jockeys to ride 4,000 winners. I thought it highly appropriate that he should have brought his 4,000th home during the Christmas season. That's when all good things should happen. Congratulations, Bill, and, somewhat belatedly, a merry Christmas and happy New Year. And please note carefully, I didn't call you Willie."[19]

Alexander can be excused for not knowing that Christmas 1970 was the thirtieth anniversary of Hartack's mother's death. Following the accident that claimed his mother's life, young Bill (then eight years old) couldn't even look at a Yuletide tree for a long time afterward. Christmas remained a time of sadness for him, as opposed to a season of joy.[20]

22

Winding Down

Johnny Nerud, the Hall of Fame trainer, once said that if you name a horse after somebody you know, make sure the horse is a good one. Nerud applied that maxim to Dr. Charles Fager, the Boston neurosurgeon who saved his life, and whose four-legged namesake, just plain Dr. Fager, was ranked the ninth-best horse of all time.[1] For every Dr. Fager, however, there may be a Dr. Hing, a pitiable horse who raced around Philadelphia in the early 1970s. The eponymous Dr. Hing had lost all seventeen of his races the day Bill Hartack rode him at Liberty Bell Race Track. This was 1971, and while the Hartack name no longer carried the clout it once did, bettors sent off the winless Dr. Hing as the 5–2 favorite. In other words, the other eleven horses were just as bad, or worse.

Only a few years before, Hartack wouldn't have tarried with a horse of Dr. Hing's ilk. Low-caliber horses, Bill Shoemaker once told me, are usually sore horses, and sore horses are the kind that can get a jockey hurt.[2] But Hartack no longer had his pick of mounts, so there he was in Philadelphia for the second race on the card. Caution wasn't in the equation.

For most of the race, Dr. Hing raced with the leaders. But he ran out of gas through the stretch and finished last. Coming off the track, Hartack was bombarded with billingsgate. One fan was especially abusive. In response, Hartack grabbed a handy cup of water and emptied it on the miscreant.

The story breaks down after that. Liberty Bell officials said that Hartack was called before the stewards the next day for a lecture. Hartack claimed that the stewards didn't summon him, that he went to their offices of his own volition. According to the track, Alex Stokes, one of the stewards, said, "He's in trouble if it happens again."[3]

In 1971 and 1972, Hartack had 164 wins. In the 1950s and early 1960s, he would have topped that total in just one year. In 1973, he won 81 races. In 1974, starting out the year, he won 22 races, riding in only 226, and his win percentage, which was .198 lifetime, dropped to 10 percent. At Tropical Park in 1974, he won with only two of his first thirty-five mounts.[4] This was thirty-five mounts in fourteen days of racing: he wasn't winning very many, and he wasn't riding in very many, either. Before 1974 was over, he quit riding for good in the United States, and Hong Kong was just around the corner.

Toward the end of 1970, Hartack was riding a young colt named Crave who had Kentucky Derby potential for 1971. He was a son of Candy Spots, who won the Florida Derby, the Santa Anita Derby and the Preakness, an indication that he could pass on stamina to his offspring. But Candy Spots was lackluster at stud, and Crave was one of the reasons why. In Florida in December 1970, Crave won by seven lengths going a mile and seventy yards. Then he ran into Highbinder, who had the same parents as the Nerud-trained Dr.

Fager, the 1968 Horse of the Year. In late December, at the same distance that he had run before, Crave was ten lengths in front with three-eighths of a mile to go. Highbinder caught him and won by three-quarters of a length. Crave won five insignificant races in his career, earning less than $35,000. Neither he nor Highbinder made it to the 1971 Kentucky Derby.[5]

Not by choice, Hartack was becoming a part-time jockey. He took time out to ride in a quarter-horse race at a track in Orange County, California.[6] At Arlington Park, where he had once thrived, he spent as much time playing in the track's informal softball league as he did around the horses. His play on the softball diamond brought scrutiny, too. With the championship on the line, in the last inning of the last game, Hartack's team led by one run. He was a lefthander playing second base, a position usually occupied by righthanded throwers. On a ball hit deep to the outfield, with two runners on base, the outfielder threw to Hartack as the relay man. One runner was bound to score. Instead of conceding that run, Hartack threw wildly over the catcher's head. Both runners came across, and Hartack's team lost by one run.

Neil Milbert, a turf writer for the *Chicago Tribune*, was the captain and first baseman on Hartack's team. "My enduring memory of Hartack should be the five Kentucky Derbys he won," Milbert said. "Instead, I remember this Hall of Fame jockey for the bonehead play that cost us the league championship."[7]

Riding in New York, Hartack became friends with Joe Namath, the bachelor quarterback for the New York Jets. One of Namath's favorite hangouts, after he sold his own place under pressure from Pete Rozelle, commissioner of the National Football League, was the Tittle Tattle Pub on Manhattan's East Side. On Sixty-fourth Street at Second Avenue, a block away from the Tittle Tattle, was the more upscale Maxwell's Plum, but the Namath crowd preferred the clubbishness of the Tittle Tattle. Some of the singles bars on Second Avenue—Adam's Apple was one—would hand out chips for free drinks to passing women if they were attractive, but the Tittle Tattle pulled them in without that inducement. Having customers like Namath didn't hurt.[8] He wasn't the only football player who might be seen there. John Hicks and Jack Gregory, teammates who shared a rented house on Long Island, once exchanged punches in the men's room only a few hours after they had helped the Giants win a game.[9]

One night at the Tittle Tattle, Namath, Hartack and Jimmy Walsh, Namath's agent, shared a table with Ed Marinaro and Eddie Sapir. Marinaro, who had starred at Cornell University, was a New Jersey native playing for the Minnesota Vikings, and later he undertook an acting career. Sapir, a lawyer, was in the early stages of a career that would include a long judgeship in New Orleans and three stints on the New Orleans City Council. Sapir was also a friend, and later the long-time agent, of Billy Martin, who played for and managed the New York Yankees and other teams.

The night at the Tittle Tattle launched a friendship between Hartack and Sapir that would last for the rest of Hartack's life. After Hartack's death in 2007, Sapir was one of the founders of the Bill Hartack Foundation, a charity organization that annually honors the winning jockey in the Kentucky Derby.

At the Tittle Tattle, Hartack waxed sentimental, which was uncharacteristic for him. Bereft of good horses, he had time on his hands. He talked about visiting maybe a half-dozen race tracks that had given him some of his best memories. Sapir was also single, and in no hurry to return to New Orleans. "Why don't you and I do it?" Sapir suggested.

They left the next day. Driving all the way, they stayed at Holiday Inns and other moderately priced hotels.[10] Their first stop was on the New Jersey shore, at Monmouth Park, where Hartack rode Royal Native to victory in the 1960 Molly Pitcher Handicap. Royal Native, the champion older female that season, won eighteen races overall, and Hartack was aboard for fourteen of them. They loaded 130 pounds, including Hartack, on her one day at Gulfstream Park, and she still won by three lengths.[11]

From Monmouth, Hartack and Sapir headed down the New Jersey Turnpike to Delaware Park. Hartack brought along a set a dominos. "God forbid if you beat him," Sapir said. "If you started beating him, he wouldn't let you go to bed. If you wanted to go to bed, you had better let him win a game."

In Maryland, they hit all three of the major tracks—Pimlico (the home of the Preakness), Laurel Race Course, and Bowie. The way it worked was that the two idle tracks were used as training centers, which helped fill the races for the track that was in business. Hartack introduced Sapir to several jockeys, including Bill Passmore, Don Brumfield and Gregg McCarron. They were on the road for about ten days.

One night, Sapir asked Hartack whether he might become a racing official, such as a steward, if he ever quit riding. Hartack usually parried such inquiries—he wasn't much for looking ahead—but he had gotten comfortable enough with Sapir that he gave him a thoughtful answer.

"I'm too progressive to be a steward," Hartack said. "The rules are outdated, and it doesn't look like anybody really wants to improve them. They vary from state to state, even from racing association to racing association, and there's no consistency in that. The trainer-responsibility rule is also outmoded. There's no way in the world that a trainer can watch over each and every horse twenty-four hours a day. It's a physical impossibility. Yet if a horse comes up with a drug positive, the trainer is automatically responsible. And they usually gang up on the little guy. The big stables, they give them the edge. But the little guy, the guy with only a handful of horses, he's out of luck."

In the 1980s, after his six seasons in Hong Kong, Hartack would indeed become a racing official, and he spent some time at the Fair Grounds in New Orleans, Sapir's hometown track. Sapir, who at times considered running for mayor but never did, helped Hartack get a favorable lease at the Cotton Mill, a prestigious downtown condominium complex not far from Bourbon Street.[12] In 2005, Hartack was still living there when the flooding from Hurricane Katrina devastated the city.[13] Hartack lost most of his belongings and many of his most valued possessions.[14]

While Hartack and Sapir traveled up and down the mid-Atlantic seaboard, a 39-year-old Bill Shoemaker was beginning a year that would leave him with the record for stakes wins, breaking the record of forty-three that Hartack had set in 1957. Shoemaker collected twenty-nine of his stakes for trainer Charlie Whittingham's powerful barn, which included Ack Ack (the Horse of the Year), Cougar II and Turkish Trousers. There was no drama attached; Shoemaker rode his forty-fourth stakes winner on November 13, 1971—it was Royal Owl in the Junipero Serra Stakes at Bay Meadows.[15]

Hartack didn't have a Kentucky Derby mount in either 1971 or 1972, the first time he had gone two straight years without a horse in the race. His last try in the Derby would be 1974.[16] A week after the improbable Canonero II won the 1971 Derby, and a week before the Preakness, Hartack rode Royal J.D. to a fourth-place finish in the Preakness Prep. Going into Preakness week, the Royal J.D. camp was undecided on a rider. Vegas Vic, winner of the Derby Trial but sixth in the Derby, had been ridden by Howard Grant, who was replaced by Hartack for the Preakness. Hartack might not have been in demand anymore, but he still had three wins in the Baltimore race.[17]

Hartack being weighed, 1956. Late in his career, weight became a problem for Hartack. One of the reasons he went to Hong Kong in 1974 was that jockeys were allowed to ride at higher weights (Nancy Lang collection).

In the end, all of the jockey shuffling was moot, since the Preakness turned into a two-horse race; Canonero II beat Eastern Fleet by a length and a half. Vegas Vic, Hartack's mount, ran a poor tenth.[18] (Canonero II missed out on the Triple Crown when he finished fourth as Pass Catcher won the Belmont[19]).

Hartack would ride in only four more Triple Crown races—two Derbys, one Preakness and one Belmont—and his best finish would be a distant third with Cloudy Dawn in the 1974 Belmont.[20] His weight was going up a few pounds every year, to the point of being an untenable 118 pounds by 1973.[21] Hartack was much taller than, say, Johnny Longden and Bill Shoemaker, and after a while that worked to his disadvantage. At four-foot-ten, Longden was six inches shorter than Hartack and consequently was not constricted by weight. Shoemaker was four-foot-eleven. Weighing only two and half pounds at birth, he had almost died, but throughout his career he was a natural lightweight. In many big races, he thought he had a psychological advantage over some of the opposing riders. While they might have had to diet hard to make the weight their horses were assigned to carry, "I had to eat just to make a hundred pounds," Shoemaker said.[22]

Shoemaker had one other advantage over Hartack: He and his agent, Harry Silbert, were inseparable from the year he started, 1949, until Silbert died in 1987. They thought alike most of the time and formed a mutual admiration society. By contrast, the turnover among Hartack's agents was fierce. Chick Lang lasted more than six years, but nobody else came close. "I don't think," Lang said, seven years after their breakup, "that there has ever been a jockey who's had half as many agents as Hartack has had."[23]

23

9,000, Give or Take a Mile

Bill Hartack's final Kentucky Derby ride was in 1974. It was also one of his last rides anywhere in the United States.[1]

It was the one hundredth Derby, a historical priority for horsemen and fans alike, including owners of practically every 3-year-old in the United States and beyond. Raymond Guest, former U.S. ambassador to Ireland, was not given to running token horses in the Derby, but in 1974 he imported to Louisville one of his Irish-breds that was training in France. "I just want to see what he can do with these horses," Guest said before his Sir Tristram ran in a prep race at Churchill Downs, a week in advance of the Derby. "I want to have a little fun, being part of the hundredth Derby."[2]

As late as a week before the Derby, thirty-one horses were still considered possibilities for the race. Churchill Downs, which had two starting gates, announced that twenty-six horses could be shoehorned into the stalls if necessary. The track said that its racing secretary, Tommy Trotter, would determine the field if more than twenty-six wanted to run. This was news to Trotter, who had never played God in his life. "If you want me to tell a man that he can't run his horse in the Kentucky Derby, then you better find yourselves another racing secretary," Trotter told his bosses.[3]

Among the owners, sanity set in. The Meadow Stable's Penny Chenery, who had won the two previous Derbys with Riva Ridge and Secretariat, had a promising 3-year-old in Capital Asset, but when the colt failed to build any Derby momentum in New York, she withheld him from the race.[4] By entry time, the field was pruned to a record twenty-three starters.[5] Raymond Guest went ahead with his plans to run Sir Tristram, who was well bred and had the bloodlines to run a mile and a quarter, although in his first race on dirt the horse had run a dismal seventh, far behind Cannonade, in the Stepping Stone Purse at Churchill Downs.

Hartack rode Sir Tristram for the first time in the Stepping Stone.[6] He and Guest went far back; in the early 1960s, Hartack rode the stakes-winning, Guest-bred Chieftain. Hartack was at Delaware Park to ride Chieftain (although the colt was scratched) on the 1963 weekend when his father, 150 miles away, was shot dead by his girlfriend.[7]

"That was [Sir Tristram's] first time on dirt, and he had never run on a track with left-hand turns, either," Hartack said after the Stepping Stone. "He acted like he could run, but he didn't know anything about the gate. He broke bad, and the dirt hit him in the face, and after that he didn't run at all."

Hartack, frequently testy in the run-up to some of his previous Derbys, was chipper at the barn in the mornings. A few days before the Derby, he went over to Lexington, Kentucky, to ride one of Guest's horses in a one-mile hunt competition. "As they say in England, I had a merry go at it," Hartack said when he got back to Louisville.

Sir Tristram's English trainer, Charles Milbank, and Hartack worked with the colt in the mornings, trying to get him acclimated to the starting gate and the dirt surface.[8]

Princess Margaret of England came to the hundredth Derby, as did Lord Snowden, Bob Hope and the broadcaster Eric Sevareid. The crowd of 163,000 broke the old attendance record by almost 30,000.[9]

Sir Tristram hardly ran a step. Despite breaking from one of the outside posts, he was a contending third after a half-mile. But he dropped out of contention and finished eleventh, far behind Cannonade, who won the race even though his entry mate, Judger, had been considered the stronger horse.

Hartack's sixth Derby win, which would have broken his tie with Eddie Arcaro, was not to be. "I taught [Sir Tristram] as much as I could, leading into the race," Hartack said. "He was a learner, but he couldn't learn everything that quickly. He wasn't that mature of a horse. The Derby was only his fifth race."[10]

Hartack never rode Sir Tristram again. The colt ran fourteen more times, all in Europe, and won one race. He was not an attractive horse, being on the light side and what they called cow-hocked in the rear, so when Patrick Hogan, a New Zealand breeder, came looking for a stud prospect, Guest sold Sir Tristram for about $200,000. Hogan caught the gold ring, for Sir Tristram became one of the world's most prolific sires. When he died in 1997, after breaking his shoulder in a paddock accident, he had sired forty-five horses that won major races. At his breeding peak, when Hogan was mating him to eighty mares a year, Sir Tristram's one-time stud fee had risen to $200,000. Hogan once turned down an offer of $15 million for the stallion.[11]

Hartack's last Triple Crown race was the 1974 Preakness. Darrel McHargue, only nineteen, had ridden J.R.'s Pet to a fourth-place finish in the Derby, but on Preakness day McHargue was already committed to another stake out of town, so the colt's trainer, Harold "Baldy" Tinker, gave the assignment to Hartack. J.R.'s Pet, third choice on the Pimlico morning line, was a viable pickup mount. But he didn't run a step; he finished seventh as Little Current, a hard-luck horse in the Derby, won the race and Cannonade finished third.[12]

In 1972, Stan Freedman had asked Hartack to come to Hong Kong and ride. Freedman, a friend of Hartack's from Miami, had gone to Hong Kong in the 1960s to open a textile mill, and he ended up staying. He raced a small stable in Hong Kong and told Hartack how purses had mushroomed and how much money there was to be made. Initially, Hartack said no. In 1973, Freedman asked again, and he also sent Hartack a $1,300 first-class airline ticket. Hartack put it in a desk drawer, and it expired.[13]

In 1971, the Calder Race Course had opened in Florida, giving the Miami area another track to complement Hialeah and Gulfstream Park.[14] In the summer of 1974, Calder gave Hartack his best riding opportunities, although the purses were not competitive with the other tracks on the Florida circuit. Hartack had no trouble making the standard 126 pounds that horses were assigned for the Triple Crown races, but the run-of-the-mill races at tracks like Calder were for horses carrying less weight, and that became a burden. Hartack once spent four hours in a sweatbox when he had to lose nine and a half pounds.

Hartack's final Calder days were not noteworthy. In seven weeks' time, he won with nine of eighty-two mounts.[15] Once more, Freedman asked him to try Hong Kong. Hartack was still not enthusiastic. Hong Kong was about nine thousand miles away. There would be adjustments required, not the least of which was riding on a track with righthanded turns. Horses in Hong Kong ran clockwise, like they did in England, which was the opposite of the United States.[16]

Gary Condra, Hartack's best friend, told him that he could adjust to the cultural differences. Condra, who had known Hartack since the 1950s, had spent some time in Hong Kong when he was in the Air Force, and he had liked his duty there.[17] Freedman was a member of the exclusive Royal Hong Kong Jockey Club, so named because Hong Kong had been a British colony for more than a century. He said he could be influential in helping Hartack get licensed.[18] The Jockey Club, which was nonprofit, maintained a tight control over racing. It was—and still is—Hong Kong's biggest taxpayer. Owners of horses needed to be Jockey Club members in order to race them. The Jockey Club licensed only thirty-two jockeys to ride during its twice-weekly season, which started at the Happy Valley track in October and ran until May. Happy Valley had been in business since 1846, but the sport didn't really turn professional until 1971. Soon after, dozens of off-track betting shops were opened in order to supplement wagering at the track. Happy Valley was accustomed to drawing crowds of more than thirty thousand fans every time it opened its doors.[19]

"The Chinese are the greatest gamblers in the world," Freedman said. "It's in their nature. Toss a coffee cup in the air, and they'll place a bet on it."[20]

Hartack's money troubles, which dated to the 1950s, hadn't gone away. His appeal to the Internal Revenue Service was rattling around in the courts, and if he lost, the damage would be close to $1 million, including interest and penalties. He was already paying the IRS some of the debt, in the event that his final appeal might be overturned (which it was, in 1978).[21] Hartack was articulate in front of a microphone, but the networks were using Eddie Arcaro as the jockey expert for their Triple Crown coverage, and there were no indications that the door might open for anybody else. From 1963 through 1981, Arcaro did more than twenty telecasts for CBS and ABC, including eight Derbys. In the 1980s, after Hartack returned from Hong Kong, ABC used him four years for both the Derby and the Preakness, and he also worked one Belmont for ABC.[22]

Toward the end of the 1974 Calder meeting, Hartack called Freedman and said he was coming.[23]

Duke Fanaro, the latest in a long list of Hartack agents, had once been the barber at the Miami Springs Villas, where Hartack and Condra first met about twenty years before.[24] "I hate to see him go," Fanaro said when he learned that Hartack was bound for Hong Kong. "He said the money was so fabulous that he couldn't turn it down. It's American money that gets deposited in an American bank."[25]

Hartack's last two mounts in the United States came at Calder on September 28, 1974. There was no fanfare. The crowd of ten thousand was typical for a Saturday. It had been reported that Hartack was going to Hong Kong to ride, but the conventional assumption was that after he rode over there for a season, he'd be back riding in the United States. His commitment to Hong Kong was year to year.

His penultimate race was the first one on the Calder card. Hartack rode Dr. Taylor, who was favored but finished seventh. There was a four-hour wait for his last ride in the ninth race, which was the $23,000 Cypress Handicap.[26] Hartack's horse, Tastybit, was owned by the Tartan Stable. As a rule of thumb, John Nerud of Tartan didn't like to use Hartack, because Nerud felt he whipped his horses too much.[27] But there Hartack was, in his finale, riding for Tartan. Tastybit was favored but finished fifth. "Tastybit moved menacingly leaving the backstretch," the *Daily Racing Form*'s chart footnotes said, "came slightly wide in the stretch, and steadily gave ground through the stretch run."[28]

In early October, with a seventeen-hour flight ahead of him, Hartack was driven by Condra to the Miami airport.

"I'm still not so sure about this," Hartack said in the car.

"You can't back out now," Condra told him. "Stan Freedman is waiting for you at the other end."

"I should take more time to think about it," Hartack said.

"The season's almost beginning over there," Condra said. "Try it out, and see how it goes."

Hartack got on the plane. Stan Freedman met him at the Hong Kong airport, which was on the mainland.[29] It was a half-hour cab ride to the dock of the Star Ferry, which took them across Victoria Harbor to Hong Kong Island. Another short cab ride, and they were at the Hong Kong Hilton,[30] which would be Hartack's on-again, off-again home for the next six months and for parts of the next six years. Lodging and meals were part of the deal.[31]

Another new jockey in Hong Kong in 1974 was Bill Burnett, a native of Scotland who had begun riding in Australia, where his family had moved when he was a young boy. Burnett and Hartack had adjacent lockers at Happy Valley and became pals. Opposites attracted: Hartack was a lifetime loner, whereas Burnett, who had a fun-loving reputation, met people easily and was quick with a wisecrack.

In 1978, Burnett, on Hartack's suggestion, tried riding in Florida while the Hong Kong tracks were between seasons. Hartack, after watching Burnett ride in Hong Kong, thought his riding style would fit U.S. tracks. "You're a good gate jockey," Harack said. "You break horses well. That's what it takes to win races back home."

The first horse Burnett rode in Florida was an 80–1 shot for the trainer Eddie Plesa, who was a friend of Hartack's. Hartack had also lined Burnett up with an agent, Mike Stidham, who was then twenty. (Mike was the son of George Stidham, who rode with Hartack during the early days in West Virginia and later became Hartack's business agent and interim agent.)

Hartack himself was not riding. Because Burnett was riding for the first time in the United States, where the horses run counter-clockwise instead of the way they do in Hong Kong and Australia, Hartack focused on his friend. He found a valet who could tend to Burnett's needs in the jockeys' room. In the paddock, Hartack, smoking one menthol cigarette after another, was a wreck. He had ridden in all those Kentucky Derbys, and now here he was, a bundle of nerves before a cheap race with a small crowd.

Burnett broke his mount quickly, put him on the lead, and they were still ahead with fifty yards to run before settling for a fourth-place finish. "I told you this guy could ride," Hartack told Plesa afterward.

The next time Burnett rode for Plesa, he won the race. Hartack, grinning widely, arrived in the winner's circle to congratulate his friend. "He was beside himself," Burnett recalled.[32]

Other wins didn't come that easily. After modest success, it was time for Burnett to return to Hong Kong, where by the early 1980s he had won 143 races, twice as many as Hartack.[33] In 1978, Burnett told friends in Australia that if he could continue for four more seasons in Hong Kong, "I will be set for life." In 1985, he returned to Australia, where he built and ran a 387-acre ranch. In 2004, at sixty, Burnett retired and became a willing slave to the golf course.[34]

Hong Kong, once known as a "backwater trading post," was a different place by the time Hartack got there. It was being reinvented by Murray MacLehose, a lanky Scotsman who had been installed as governor in 1971. MacLehose's Operation Bootstraps was in full swing in 1974. Government spending increased by 50 percent as he rebuilt mass transit; launched an overhaul of the public health system; started a ten-year housing project that would rid Hong Kong of many of its slums; and passed a law that would guarantee children nine years of free education. After a while, the people lovingly called him "Big Mac." He would stay until 1982, the longest-serving governor in Hong Kong history. (Chinese control of Hong Kong wouldn't happen until 1997.)[35]

Another of MacLehose's projects was the Independent Commission Against Corruption (ICAC), whose goal, in part, was to rid the police and fire departments of the rampant graft that had become an international embarrassment. Decades later, the ICAC would shatter the reputations of the renowned Gary Moore, who was implicated in a widespread jockey scandal, and Stan Freedman, Hartack's friend, who would be caught, *in flagrante delicto*, trying to deceive the Hong Kong Jockey Club.[36]

Some critics saw the Jockey Club as a body in need of sweeping changes. "[The Jockey Club was] an arrogant club and loathed by many locals who saw it being a law unto itself," one of them wrote. "Ex-pat jockeys seemed to [belong to] a Get Out of Jail Free Club, until the formation of the [ICAC], which ... brought down many sacred cows."[37]

Despite its detractors, the Jockey Club was the biggest component in the Hong Kong economy, besides being one of the colony's largest charitable contributors. Ten percent of Hong Kong's budget came from racing revenues. Racing would get even bigger in the decades to come. By the mid-1990s, annual betting averaged $1,500 for every man, woman and child; in 2015 there were eighty-three days of racing, which drew on-track attendance of 2 million for the third straight year. Betting totaled almost $14 billion in American dollars.[38]

Four million people lived in Hong Kong in the mid-1970s. There was a stifling heat most of the time. Even during the winter, Hong Kong is hot and sticky. The temperatures are not much different from those in Miami, but besides temperatures in the mid-eighties, the humidity is never lower than seventy, and it frequently runs as high as 80 percent. "Hong Kong is a concrete jungle that closes in on you," said another American jockey, who was happy to leave Hong Kong after two seasons.[39]

Happy Valley was the only track operating in Hong Kong, but ground had been broken, twelve miles away, for Sha Tin, which had a tentative opening date of the fall 1978. A century before, Happy Valley had been built on a marshland, but now it was in the heart of Hong Kong's teeming central business district. Stall space for the horses was at such a premium that the barns were located on three levels, with the second and third floors reachable by freight elevator. Rather than being sent to the overcrowded track, some of the horses exercised on the roof, half a football field above ground level. To give the horses relief from the heat, the track opened daily for training at 4 a.m., and the last group of horses finished by 7. Trainers expected jockeys who rode the horses in the races to also work them out. In the United States, Hartack sometimes worked his stakes mounts, but most times he left the rest of a barn's stock to exercise riders, many of them former jockeys who had gotten too heavy to ride in races.[40]

Freedman predicted that Hartack would be successful: "I think Bill has mellowed. And he's smart, smart enough to realize that he has reached a time in his life when he has to get along. He realizes that if it's necessary to go out to dinner with an owner in order to ride one of his horses, he'll go out to dinner."[41]

Some thought that Hartack had reached the point of no return as a jockey. "Hartack loves the game," said a racing correspondent in Hong Kong, "and this is the only place in the world where he can still ride."[42]

More than weight, Hartack said that the cloying, uninformed U.S. media drove him to Hong Kong. "They're so stupid in the U.S.," he complained. The *Washington Post* requested an interview while Hartack was in Hong Kong, and he turned them down.[43]

Hartack was riding against many jockeys whose names were much shorter than his. They included P.F. Yiu, K.S. Ho, C.C. Chan, M.C. Tam and A.K. Cheam. British jockeys, their flat-racing seasons having ended, would ride in Hong Kong until it was time to return for another English season the following spring. The great Lester Piggott was one, and he was joined by Pat Eddery, Willie Carson, Mick Kinane and Kieren Fallon.[44]

Also riding in Hong Kong was Dennis Elliott, who had ridden at bush tracks in Canada, the United States and several other countries. Elliott and Hartack bonded from the start, in part because Hartack liked Elliott's young son, Stewart, who surprised his father one night, in conversation in Hartack's hotel suite, when he said that he wanted to be a race rider.[45] Stewart Elliott has gone on to win almost five thousand races; he rode Smarty Jones to victories in the Kentucky Derby and Preakness in 2004, and in 2015 he was elected into Canada's Racing Hall of Fame.[46]

On one of Hartack's December 9 birthdays, Dennis Elliott walked into the jockeys' room wearing a Texas-size Stetson. "I got a big hat just like that back at the hotel," Hartack commented. Later, the jockeys brought out a chocolate cake and put it on a table in the center of the room. It finally registered on Hartack that the joke was on him. "That's my cake," he said. "That's my hat, too."

One of them, sneaking into Hartack's hotel suite, had come away with the cake and the hat. While amused, Hartack put his fellow riders on notice: he wouldn't let them hoodwink him a second time. The jockey Geoff Lewis, a well-known prankster, bet Hartack that they could get into Hartack's suite again. The next night, returning from dinner, Hartack entered his suite to find the Lewis and three other riders playing cards.

"How the hell did you get in?" Hartack demanded. Lewis told him that they had bribed somebody in the hotel's laundry department. One man was wheeled into the suite concealed in a big canvas basket, and then he let the others in.

Hartack was never a good loser, whether it was race riding, dominos or cards. He threatened to sue the Hilton for poor security. Finally, after a couple of days, he laughed about the stunt right along with Lewis and the others.[47]

Not so funny was Hartack's relationship with Gary Moore. The racing was dominated by the Australian father-son team of George and Gary Moore, one a famous ex-rider turned trainer, the other a nineteen-year-old horsebacking *wunderkind.* Hartack, twenty-three years older than Gary Moore, resented the family's stranglehold on the industry. There was a mutual respect between Hartack and George Moore because of their riding accomplishments, but Hartack begrudged Gary Moore his riding success and didn't extend him the courtesies that he displayed for Gary's father. Hartack tangled with young Moore several times on the track. In the 1978 Pokfulam Gap Handicap, Hartack won by a head with Minotaur, edging out Moore's Very Best Wishes, but Moore claimed foul because he felt Hartack's mount had interfered in the stretch run. The stewards disallowed the protest but reprimanded Hartack for excessive use of the whip. Hartack questioned the stewards' reasoning: "How can you throw out the claim, but still give me a lecture?" Their answer, he felt, was not satisfactory.

Another time, in a race Hartack won with Welsh Villain, Moore claimed that Hartack had crossed over in front of him at the start, compromising his chances. Again, the stewards supported Hartack, but this time there was no reprimand. The rift between the two riders was exacerbated when a trainer switch resulted in Hartack losing the mount on Silver Lining, the best horse he ever rode in Hong Kong. Gary Moore rode Silver Lining after his father took over as the horse's trainer.[48] "Before I leave," Hartack said, "I'm going to hit [Gary Moore] so hard that his head is going to go through his locker and come out the other side."[49]

At first, when contacted about this book, Moore indicated by email that he was willing to discuss Hartack. But he didn't respond to subsequent interview requests.[50]

Moore won eight riding titles in Hong Kong. When he retired from riding in 1997, to follow his father into the training ranks, he had averaged fifty-three wins a year there. He won more races (eighty-four) in one season, 1980–1981, than Hartack won (seventy-two) in all six of his Hong Kong campaigns. In eight of his seasons, Moore rode between 261 and 311 races; the most races Hartack ever rode in a season was 152.[51]

Jerry Ng, Peter Supple and Fred Carr were trainers who frequently put Hartack on winning horses. Ng, from Shanghai, was known as "The Silver Fox" for his heaping shock of silver hair. He still had that movie-star hair when he died in 2014. Ng's stable was better known for betting coups than the horses it ran. His best horse was Silver Lining, who won three Horse of the Year titles, the first of which was for Ng (the other two came when the horse was transferred to George Moore's stable).[52]

In 2015, Gary Moore ranked Silver Lining and Super Win as the best that he had ever ridden. He put them ahead of Gold River, who won the 1981 Arc de Triomphe for Moore.[53]

Hartack won four races with Silver Lining before Gary Moore got his chance with the durable gray horse. One of the Hartack wins came on October 7, 1978, as part of the opening program at Sha Tin,[54] which had cost $100 million to build.[55] Silver Lining was a short price, but in many other races the duo of Ng and Hartack, absent a pattern, confounded punters all the way to Beijing. "The two of them were impossible to follow," said one horseplayer. "Their horses backed and tipped, and somehow, almost always, flopped. But when [there was a long shot], they'd pop up."[56]

Incredibly, Silver Lining was such a horse once, winning under Hartack at astonishing 8–1 odds. If Hartack was privy to any of Ng's betting coups, it was not for him to let on. Asked about the honesty of the races in Hong Kong, he said, "It's no concern of mine. I don't concern myself with anything that doesn't concern me. I lead what I think is a clean life. There's a stigma on racing wherever you go. I'm not going to worry about it if I can't change it. The only thing I'm responsible for is what I do personally."[57]

In the 1980s, during the government's investigation into Gary Moore and other jockeys for alleged race fixing (Moore was granted immunity in exchange for his cooperation), a jockey testified that he had been paid $13,000 American for preventing his horse from winning.[58]

Once, in the lobby of the Hong Kong Hilton, a punter complained that it was impossible to make any money on Ng-trained horses ridden by Hartack.

"You can't wait and wait to bet," Hartack said, "but that's what you do. Then when you put your money down, the price is next to nothing."[59]

Hartack was known to bet, even though technically that was *verboten*. He once discussed his betting strategy: "When I think a horse is getting near his peak, I like to try my luck straight away. I'll risk half my stake, but I'll get four times the price. And then I've still got a little left to back him up next time, anyway."[60]

One of the best ways for Hong Kong jockeys to ingratiate themselves with the horse owners was to evaluate horses in such a way that winning bets could be cashed. The purses were moderate, even skimpy, by some international standards, but because of the large pools, betting with first-hand information could be lucrative.

"I cannot stress how important a jockey's judgment dictated his success or failure," said ex-jockey Bill Burnett. "Bill [Hartack] was one of the best, and it was not unusual for him to land big betting plunges."[61]

There was one time, however, when Hartack's instincts failed him. As the 1976 Hong Kong Derby approached, the trainer Peter Supple planned to run two horses. One of them was the estimable Corvette, a smallish, average-looking filly who proved that racing isn't a beauty contest. Corvette was one of the best horses that Supple campaigned in Hong Kong, and she was Hartack's to ride in the big race. But Hartack told Supple that the distance would be Corvette's undoing, and he tried to dissuade the trainer from running her.

"I have no choice," Supple said. "The owner is determined to run, and there's nothing we can do about it. My hands are tied."[62]

Hartack rode Supple's other horse and finished far back as Corvette won the race.[63]

Although Supple and Hartack were successful together, the trainer found it difficult to rouse Hartack in the mornings to exercise his stock. "Sometimes, you didn't even know where Bill was," Supple said. "He would disappear for a couple of weeks at a time. I would ask Stan Freedman where he was, and he said that he didn't know, either. Sometimes it got pretty ticklish, trying to explain to owners why he wasn't around. This was just a habit Bill had brought with him from the States. He was past forty, he wasn't going to change in midstream. He brought an infallibility with him; he couldn't see anything wrong with himself. In a sense, it was something that had made him great, but it also worked against him."[64]

In 1976–1977, Hartack won twenty races, his best Hong Kong season numerically.[65] On May 7, 1977, he was almost ten thousand miles away from Churchill Downs, the scene of his epic wins. In Louisville, Seattle Slew won the Derby en route to his Triple Crown sweep. At Happy Valley, an American standing on the outside of the walking ring couldn't resist shouting, "Hey, Bill! You should be in Louisville today!" Hartack didn't even blink. Steely eyed and focused as always, he rode his horse out to the track.[66]

One of Hartack's sweeter wins for Stan Freedman came the next year with Cincinnati Kid. The colt was a neck better than Chop-Chop, ridden by Pat Eddery.[67] Years later, Freedman would be disgraced following a sting operation by the Independent Commission Against Corruption. He was part of a small ring that was found guilty of conspiring to defraud the Jockey Club. Freedman had endorsed the membership of two applicants whom he had never met. The applicants, according to court documents, paid close to $100,000 for the favors, although Freedman reportedly didn't see any of the money. The eightyish Freedman, battling cancer and unable to digest solid foods, appeared in court in a wheelchair. The judge acknowledged his condition and commuted his nine-month sentence. Others in the scheme were sentenced to more than eight years in prison.[68]

Cincinnati Kid was trained by Frank Carr, an Irishman. The same day that Hartack won with Cincinnati Kid, he won a second handicap for Carr, also by a slim margin. Hartack worked hard for Carr. He would gallop eight or more of Carr's horses during the early-morning hours. Despite the heat, Hartack would arrive at the track wearing a turtleneck top, a nylon windbreaker and thick leather pants. The other riders would be dressed much lighter, usually in short sleeves. Hartack said that Hong Kong's trainers, as a rule, worked their horses slower than they did in the United States. That might have been, Hartack said, because the horse population was smaller and there was a need to supply the races with full fields.[69]

Hartack and Carr were copacetic for a while, but then there was an ugly split. "It was wild and tempestuous," someone familiar with the breakup said. "As tempestuous as one of Hong Kong's force-10 typhoons."[70]

Even when the second track opened in Hong Kong, jockeys without families there had much free time on their hands. Happy Valley raced on Wednesdays, and Sha Tin on Saturdays. There were morning workouts to be honored, but they were conducted so early because of the heat that on non-racing days a jockey's work was finished long before noon, with nothing to do at the track until the next morning. There was no gambling except on horses in Hong Kong, but in Macau, only forty miles away, casinos thrived. Macau (pronounced m'KAW), across the Pearl River Delta from Hong Kong, is a densely populated peninsula connected to the Chinese mainland. By the 1970s, Macau was well on its way to shifting from Portuguese to Chinese control.

Hartack began going to the Macau casinos and developed a passion for blackjack. His income at the track was so good that he was able to send some money back to the United States, keeping the IRS at bay, and still have enough left over to live stylishly. While he didn't win races by the bushel, as he once did in the United States, bonuses from owners, for tipping them toward substantial betting propositions, were not uncommon. Hartack would occasionally organize trips to Macau with other jockeys. Bill Burnett remembers the time he, Hartack and five others made the trip. They put up $1,000 apiece to get started at blackjack. Burnett didn't know the game, but Hartack said he would signal him on how to play. They went home with $76,000. Another time, the same group won $80,000.

Burnett said that there was a good side to Hartack that flew in the face of his reputation as a "guy who only cared about himself." Burnett and Supple both agreed that the pressure to win from the Hong Kong Jockey Club was intense. "There was an English jockey who had a long run of outs," Burnett recalled. "He needed to win a race badly, to keep the jockey club off his bag. Bill was scheduled to ride a horse at Happy Valley who looked like a sure winner. He had the trainer take him off the horse and put the English jockey on, and they won, to bring the other rider out of his slump."[71]

By the 1979–1980 season, which ended his six years in Hong Kong, it was Hartack who needed outside help to find winners. An ankle injury didn't help. He rode in forty-nine races, winning five.[72] His last win came in January.

Peter Supple did his best to renew rapport with owners who had turned to other jockeys. "Bill wasn't much for golf, but he did like to play tennis," Supple said. "One of my best owners, a very influential man in Hong Kong, was married to a woman who liked to play tennis. So I arranged a doubles match. Bill's partner was the wife. She wasn't playing particularly well, and we were only five minutes or so into the match when Bill reacted. He really tore into her. I thought, good heavens, what is he doing? It was the worst possible time to be starting an argument. But this was Bill Hartack. You always knew where you stood with him, but there was another side to that. He didn't have a diplomatic stick in his body."[73]

On Hartack's last day at Happy Valley, Bill Burnett watched him clean out his locker. "It was full of unopened mail," Burnett said. "He went through it and kept the bills that had to be paid. But he threw all the personal things in the trash, unopened. He certainly was a strange character."[74]

24

Quo Vadis?

Some will argue that other Breeders' Cup races were better, but for my money the most dramatic Breeders' Cup race of them all came in 1984. That was the first year in which racing's multi-million-dollar, year-end extravaganza was held. Bill Hartack had little to do with the running of the Breeders' Cup Classic, which was worth a record $3 million. He was a patrol judge at Hollywood Park. Patrol judges work from elevated platforms around the track. They watch, with binoculars and the naked eye, the field of horses as it passes their location. Should there be an objection by a jockey or an inquiry into the running of the race by the stewards, patrol judges may be consulted for their opinions on incidents that may or may not be recorded on videotapes of the race. There are blind spots around the track, small pockets that are not picked up by the cameras, and in this event the patrol judges' assessments come into play. When the stewards make the decisions about the validity of a foul claim, they wait until they've talked to the jockeys and (sometimes) the patrol judges before they vote on the merits of the case.

After the furious three-horse photo finish of the 1984 Classic, the stewards had to sort out multiple issues. They didn't need the help of Hartack and the other patrol judges, because the question of whether there had been interference in the race related to the final fifty yards of the stretch run. The stewards, whose stand is high above the track, with the finish line beneath them, had a front-row seats. After ten minutes of give and take, and reviewing the video of the stretch run, they ruled that Wild Again, who had prevailed by a narrow margin, would be allowed to keep his win.[1] They decided that Gate Dancer, who had finished second, lugged in and fouled the third-place horse, Slew o' Gold. Gate Dancer was thus dropped from second to third, and Slew o' Gold, who was wedged between Wild Again on the rail and Gate Dancer on the inside, was moved up to second place. The stewards ruled that Wild Again was blameless.[2]

Then the you-know-what hit the fan. The owners of Slew o' Gold, Mickey and Karen Taylor and Jim and Sally Hill, and Ken Opstein, the owner of Gate Dancer, were not happy campers. Slew o' Gold's camp contended that Wild Again, a party to the crowding near the wire, should also have been disqualified, which would have given the win to Slew o' Gold. By contrast, Opstein didn't feel that Gate Dancer had fouled anyone. If his second-place finish had been allowed to stand, and Wild Again had been disqualified, Gate Dancer would have come away with the win.

The owners of both runner-up horses appealed the stewards' ruling. The appeal process, had it run its course, would have begun with a hearing before the stewards, followed by a hearing before an administrative law judge representing the California Horse Racing Board; eventually, if no one was satisfied or had given up by then, a trial before a judge in a court of law would have been in order. In theory, this process could have stretched out for years.

Enter Bill Hartack, stage right.

The morning after the race, the stewards invited the owners of the horses to a hearing at Hollywood Park.

"Is the press welcome?" asked Jack Mann of the *Baltimore Evening Sun.*

"Of course," said Marje Everett, who ran Hollywood Park. "Hollywood Park has no secrets." (This was the same Marje Everett who, many years before, was the tell-tale witness and equivalent of an unindicted co-conspirator in a trial about a Chicago race-track scandal that sent the governor of Illinois, Otto Kerner, to prison.[3])

As I entered the room, along with a few dozen others, I was surprised to see Hartack standing in front, next to a big TV screen. The stewards, employees of the State of California, were Pete Pedersen, Alfred Shelhamer and Hubert Jones. Arguably, there was no finer officiating crew extant. Pedersen, a race-track lifer, enjoyed an impeccable reputation. Gene Autry, in "I'm Back in the Saddle Again," sang about "the only law is right,"[4] and this is what Pedersen lived by. Shelhamer and Jones were ex-jockeys, long enough removed from the riding end of the game that they played no favorites, all the while in full grasp of the nuances of race riding. Jones once rode seven winners in one afternoon at the track in Tijuana, Mexico.

"Hubert," I once asked him, "anything special you remember about that day [in Tijuana]?"

"Yes," he said. "I smoked more cigarettes than I ever have in my life. The pressure kept building, race by race, to win one more. I was never so nervous in my life."

This is how smart Pedersen, Shelhamer and Jones were: They knew the best guy at the track to break down footage of a race was Bill Hartack. They stepped aside, and the floor was his, with their blessing.

It was a *tour de force.* For forty-five minutes, he took us through the intricacies of that slam-bang stretch run, getting inside the heads of the three warring jockeys, explaining how this horse or that horse reacted to a whip here, a nudge there. Because of Hartack's brilliance, and the way he delineated the race, both appeals were dropped, and the result of the race, arrived at the day before, could be chiseled in stone instead of prolonged in the courts.

"I still don't agree with what happened," said Ken Opstein, the owner of Gate Dancer, as he left the room. "But the way Hartack laid it out, I gotta go along with it."[5]

In late 1985, Hartack got his first steward's job at Tampa Bay Downs—the same track, when it was called Sunshine Park, where he had broken in as an apprentice in 1952.[6] Then, early in 1986, when Walter Blum took off a week at Hialeah, Hartack filled in as state steward. But for the most part it was more of the same—lesser jobs at scattered tracks. Many former jockeys quickly broke into the stewards' ranks, and several, such as Blum, Ted Atkinson, Johnny Rotz and Warren Mehrtens, had regular schedules at major tracks not long after they retired from riding. Rotz's nickname, "Gentleman John," was indicative of his easygoing style as a rider, and that same even-handed temperament carried him through stewards' jobs in other states before he spent many years in New York.[7] Atkinson was held in such high esteem that sometimes he was called in as an expert witness in hearings that involved appeals in states other than where he was officiating.[8]

"I'm not politically minded when it comes to racing," Hartack said. "I wasn't politically minded when I was a rider, otherwise I might have gotten along a little better. My ambition is to become a good steward. Not just a steward, but a good one. I want to be fair, objective and consistent. I've got to learn. I will not prostitute myself."[9]

Blum, a Hall of Fame jockey, rode his last race in 1975, and he almost immediately became a steward at Garden State Park and Atlantic City in New Jersey, despite the fact that he was sightless in his right eye. (When he was two, he had fallen from a wooden hobby horse, and the eye had been pierced by the toy's pointed ear as he dropped to the floor.) Two years after working at the New Jersey tracks, Blum applied for the state steward's job at the major Florida tracks. He came so highly recommended that it was a foregone conclusion that the post would be his.

"Do you have any physical defects?" he was asked at the interview.

"Well, I'm blind in one eye," Blum said.

"Anything else?"

Blum hesitated. "No, nothing that I can think of."

"Well, Mr. Blum, the job is yours then."

Blum had a long career at the Florida tracks.[10]

While Hartack's efforts to become a steward gained little traction for several years, his television career seemed promising. In 1982, Chet Forte of ABC-TV was instrumental in using him on the telecast of the Preakness, the middle jewel of the Triple Crown.[11] Hartack's opportunity as a race analyst came about after the firings of Eddie Arcaro and John Veitch. Arcaro's 1981 Kentucky Derby was his last. He had done the race for five straight years and eight times overall. The network said that he had lost touch with the game and didn't keep himself current with the annual turnover of the 3-year-old crops. Veitch was an unusual hire, in that he was still active as a trainer for Calumet Farm.[12] From the start, the critics were not kind. "Howard Cosell [Veitch's broadcast partner] still knows nothing about the game," Bernie Dickman wrote, "and Veitch isn't even close to being polished enough on a live show to make any intelligent statements."[13]

Veitch and Cosell were a disarming pair. Veitch shaved his head, giving him a Yul Brynner look. Cosell wore a floppy hairpiece, which was fair game on windy days at the tracks. At the 1983 Derby, Hartack tried in vain to protect Cosell from the elements with a giant umbrella. One wag, Dick Young, said that Cosell and his flying rug reminded him of Tattoo, the mop-headed character played by Hervé Villechaize in the TV show *Fantasy Island*.[14]

When Arcaro, and then Veitch, went to the sidelines, Roone Arledge, who ran ABC Sports, wanted another race-track name. Arledge and Forte, a roll-the-dice director, had been wildly successful with ABC's *Monday Night Football*, which was launched in 1970, so when Forte mentioned Hartack, Arledge liked the idea. Hartack had no broadcasting experience, but Arledge, always on the prowl for controversy, liked the idea that the ex-jockey was an ogre to many in the media, and he thought that Hartack, like Arcaro, would be highly opinionated. One of Arcaro's most opinionated telecasts was the 1969 Belmont. With the Triple Crown at stake, Majestic Prince was beaten, and Arcaro had blamed Hartack's ride for the defeat.

Hartack got along with the strident, cocksure Cosell, who was characterized as difficult by others who worked with him. Cosell liked Hartack, and he tried to draw him out on camera by asking pointed questions. Horsemen, some of whom knew Hartack from his riding days, and others who simply respected his reputation, were bent on sharing information. Hartack's salary, said a friend, "was too good for him to pass up." Besides Cosell, Hartack also blended with the production crew. He would crack them up, for instance, with his imitation of the Chinese dialect, which he had picked up from his Hong Kong years. "Hartack," said someone who worked on those telecasts, "was smart enough to know that being nice to the little guys made everyone's life easier."[15] Somewhere, Chick Lang, Hartack's old agent, might have been saying, "Finally!"

At pre-race production meetings, however, Hartack would sometimes bite his lip when brainstorming producers and assistant producers ran what he thought were cockamamie ideas up the proverbial flagpole. Afterward, among friends, his spleen would be showing. "Do you know what those dumb [expletive] want me to do?" he asked one night in Louisville. "These ignorant [expletive] want me to go on national TV before the race with some kind of [expletive] graphic and say where all twenty horses are going to be. Have you ever heard of anything more ridiculous? [Expletive] idiots. It can't be done. Nobody's got a clue how a race like this will unfold. But I've gotta think of something to tell 'em without looking too stupid."[16]

Hartack's best Derby as a broadcaster came in 1986, when the long shot Ferdinand came from last place to win under Bill Shoemaker. ABC wisely put an isolation camera on Ferdinand from start to finish, and shortly after the race ended, Hartack did a two-minute commentary on the complete replay. Whether a racing official or a TV analyst, it's what Hartack did best—dissect film. "Shoe's winding it up a bit," Hartack said as Ferdinand began to pass horses from back in the pack. Then, when Shoemaker made an adroit move coming out of the last turn, zigging instead of zagging to find a hole toward the inside, Hartack underscored that the maneuver was both clever and crucial.[17]

The beginning of the end for Hartack on the ABC Triple Crown telecasts came when Chet Forte crashed at the network. Forte grew up in Hackensack, New Jersey. He was starring in high-school basketball during a time when several schools in the New York City area were at the center of college basketball's most widespread point-shaving scandal.[18] By the time Forte got to Columbia University, however, the stench had gone. Though only 5-foot-7, he led the country in scoring, beating out Wilt Chamberlain, the 7-foot skyscraper at Kansas.

At ABC, Forte was *sui generis*. But he had an insatiable gambling habit. His debts totaled $4 million, he was in trouble with the Internal Revenue Service, and he stood accused of mail fraud. Arledge had no choice but to let him go.[19]

Arledge thought it was time for a woman to be added to the racing telecasts. He didn't have to look far. Charlsie Cantey, who trained horses and once exercised the great filly Ruffian, had come up through the ranks, first for a weekly from-the-track show for an independent New York channel, and then for CBS.[20]

Hartack didn't have Forte as an ally anymore. It turned out that Hartack won one more Derby as a jockey than he covered as a broadcaster. His fourth Derby for ABC (1986) was his last. Cantey, who did interviews on horseback, shared that broadcast, but in 1987 she was back and Hartack wasn't.[21]

He took a job as a steward at Hawthorne, which would lead to more jobs at upscale Arlington Park, another Chicago track.[22] At Arlington, Hartack ran afoul of Tommy Trotter, another steward. "He is widely considered to be one of history's legendary racing officials," it was once said of Trotter. "Trotter's contribution to the sport exceeds the sum of everyone currently drawing a salary from the New York Racing Association."[23]

When this particular Arlington season ended, Trotter would move on to Florida to work as the director of racing at Gulfstream Park. One of the duties of a director of racing is to ensure that a track will have enough horses on hand to fill the races throughout the course of a season. Generally, a racing department assigns barn space to trainers whose stock is plentiful enough, and healthy enough, to put on the show on a daily basis.

While working alongside Trotter at Arlington, Hartack complained to the Illinois racing board that Trotter was spending a lot of time on the phone, recruiting trainers and their horses for the upcoming Gulfstream season. Trotter was called on the carpet and asked to defend himself. Because Trotter's credentials preceded him, Hartack's accusation was quickly dismissed.

"He tried to knife me in the back, and I don't know why, because we never had any disagreements, not ever," Trotter said. "He could have come to me first. During that entire Arlington meet, I didn't make one phone call on behalf of Gulfstream on Arlington's time. I've been in the game long enough to know where my priorities lie. It was embarrassing. I was at a stage in my career where I shouldn't have been put in that position. It was all very regrettable."[24]

In the fall of 1993, Hartack was hired as the state steward at the historic Fair Grounds in New Orleans.[25] Of all the tracks in the United States, only Pimlico in Baltimore and Saratoga in upstate New York are older.[26] The Fair Grounds season opened on Thanksgiving day that year. Less than three weeks later, the track burned down.[27]

The Friday afternoon racing program was over, and Hartack had finished his duties in the stewards' stand and gone home, when an electrical fire broke out in the ceiling above the empty jockeys' quarters. There were no sprinklers, since they were not required by law. The seven-alarm blaze spread quickly, and it was over in less than an hour. Both wooden buildings, the grandstand and the clubhouse, burned to the ground. The executive offices were also wiped out. More than a thousand horses, stabled on the other side of the racing oval, survived. When firefighters were able to reach the main floor of the clubhouse, they saw only one thing standing: the track's giant Christmas tree.[28]

Financially, the fire was devastating. Insurance only paid $18 million, and it cost twice as much for a rebuilding program that was completed in 1997. In the meantime, the Fair Grounds made do with temporary facilities, and attendance suffered badly. Losing a lawsuit to horsemen, who sought revenues from video-poker machines that had been installed at the track, was the last straw. The Krantz family, which had bought the track in 1990, sought bankruptcy protection in 2003, and they sold out a year later to Churchill Downs Incorporated for $47 million.[29]

In August 2005, Hurricane Katrina struck, less than a year after Churchill Downs' purchase. The track was flooded, and the roof was blown off; as a result, the season, moved to Louisiana Downs in the northwest corner of the state, was reduced to thirty-seven days.[30] Hartack, who lived in a ground-floor dwelling in downtown New Orleans, near the French Quarter, lost most of his possessions in the storm (the back of his apartment faced a canal that overflowed). After being unable to gain access for several weeks, he was greeted by overwhelming mold. Until he could find other lodgings, he lived with Larry Munster, a former jockey who worked for the state racing commission.

In 2006, not surprisingly, Hartack's Fair Grounds contract was not renewed by Churchill Downs. Hartack and Churchill Downs had been enemies for years; he felt they were niggardly when it came to paying for personal appearances to promote the Derby. Because of his issues with track management, whenever asked to return for the Derby, he declined, usually not very politely.[31] Hartack's last steward jobs in Louisiana were at the separately owned Louisiana Downs in 2006 and 2007.[32] Louisiana Downs ran the Super Derby, a rich race, every fall, but otherwise the track near Shreveport was hardly a blip on the national screen. Hartack was back in the game's minor leagues again.

At the Fair Grounds, there were no incidents to rival Hartack's run-in with Tommy Trotter in Chicago, but neither did Hartack sail through his years in New Orleans without an occasional cloudburst. One controversy was bagatelle in the grand scheme of things, but it reveals how intransigent Hartack could be when he felt like it.

Louisiana-born Joe Talamo, only seventeen, was moving to California in early 2007 after being the leading rider at the Fair Grounds. Talamo's agent, Ron Ebanks, remembered a Louisiana rule that allowed riders an extension of their apprenticeship if they were furthering their education online. (Horses ridden by apprentices are allowed to carry less weight than horses ridden by journeyman jockeys—a significant benefit.) California officials were willing to grant Talamo this consideration as long as the Louisiana stewards could certify that he was doing the school work.

Hartack refused Ebanks' request. "I don't think he deserves the extra time, no matter what the rule says," Hartack said.

Ebanks went to Eddie Sapir, a former New Orleans judge who, during his lawyering days, had represented Ebanks when he was an apprentice rider. Sapir was also a good friend of Hartack's. But Hartack would not be moved. Sapir appealed to Bob Wright, chairman of the Louisiana commission; however, Wright was reluctant to usurp Hartack's authority.

"Look, Bill," Sapir finally said to Hartack, "you were the valedictorian of your high school class. It came easy for you."

Talamo started in California without the added apprentice advantage that Ebanks had sought. Talamo told Sapir later that while he appreciated the intervention, he thought he would do just as well on the West Coast without the extra days.[33]

Roy Wood, who shared the stewards' stand in Louisiana with Hartack, was not surprised about how his colleague handled the Talamo matter. "At times," Wood said, "Bill was the Hartack that people knew about and wrote about. He could be standoffish and he could go his own way. He did have that side of him, and people who got to know him saw that side."[34]

That side surfaced when the Fair Grounds honored Laffit Pincay Jr., the Hall of Fame jockey who once held the record for most career wins. At the reception, Hartack sat across the room from Pincay with his good friend Gary Palmisano and Palmisano's young son. Hartack had been the guest of Palmisano at his home, going fishing many times with the father and son for redfish and speckled trout in Lake Pontchartrain. There is the dog-eared family snapshot of Hartack, wearing a cap that says "Mr. Lucky," standing with young Palmisano, then about ten, and both of them holding loads of fish. (The Palmisanos called Hartack "Mr. Lucky" because they said that no one could win five Kentucky Derbys *and* catch all those fish every time he went to the lake.)

Young Palmisano, also named Gary, spoke about wanting Pincay's autograph. His father, since Hartack and Pincay were friends, kept egging Hartack on, asking him to go over and get the signature. Finally, Hartack relented. For his part, he detested giving out autographs and was known to harshly reprimand fans before turning them down. The occasion after one of his Derby wins, when Hartack signed dozens of autographs before giving an interview, was interpreted as more of a ploy to spite the press than to accommodate fans.

As Pincay gladly signed for Hartack, a photographer from the *New Orleans Times-Picayune* took their picture. The caption in the newspaper the next day said that Pincay was such a racing icon that even another Hall of Famer, Bill Hartack, wanted his autograph. Hartack was livid. "He never let me hear the end of it," the elder Palmisano said.[35]

Roy Wood knew what he had when Hartack, after saying no a few times, finally signed a photo of Northern Dancer, Hartack's 1964 Derby winner. Hartack inscribed it, "To a big man and a big friend."[36]

Eddie Sapir wasn't as lucky. Sapir, who knew Hartack for the last forty years of his life, had a copy of Bill Shoemaker's book, written with Dan Smith and signed by Shoemaker. Before Sapir gave the book to his son, he thought it would be nice to have it also signed by Hartack, a family friend and another Hall of Fame jockey.

Hartack looked at the book quizzically. "What's this?"

Sapir took that as a no. He still has the book, signed only by Shoemaker.[37]

"I think," said Roy Wood, "that he just didn't want people making a lot of to-do about him. That's just the way he was. It's a shame, when you think about what a valuable asset to the sport he could have been, as a spokesman, for a lot of years. But his personality just wouldn't let him do it."[38]

In 1995, as the Fair Grounds season was winding down, an apprentice named Jimmie Ward Jr. caught Hartack's eye. Ward was twenty-six, which was awfully old to start a riding career, and he didn't win many races, but Hartack still liked his potential. Moreover, Ward was constantly asking the veteran riders at the track about riding intricacies, and he even went to Hartack once with a few questions about how he could improve on his whipping of horses. Keith Dickey, a young trainer, was moving east with his ten-horse stable, and when he asked Ward to come along, Hartack made it a threesome by becoming Ward's agent.

Two years before, Ward had been working in a print shop in Dallas, helping produce the weekly issues of *TV Guide.* Now he was riding for substantial prize money at Garden State Park, Philadelphia Park and Pimlico, where Hartack, decades before, had won the Preakness three times. At Pimlico, Ward rode the winner of a $38,000 stakes race.[39] Dickey asked Hartack to join them and the horse for the winner's circle photo. It was Ward's first stakes win. Hartack refused. "He woudn't sign the photo for a while, either," Dickey said. "He wasn't much for signing. But finally, he agreed to sign it. Then, wouldn't you know, I lost it."

When the stable reached Monmouth Park in late summer, the wins started to dry up. Monmouth was Hartack's card-playing track. It was not unusual, Dickey said, for Hartack to start playing, in a shady nook near the jockeys' quarters, at 10 in the morning, after workouts were over, and not quit until 7 at night, after the last race was run. By the time Ward decided to try New York, it was time for Hartack to return to New Orleans, where his steward's job was waiting.[40]

Ward rode twenty-six times in New York without winning a race.[41] Ironically, the agent who replaced Hartack was Joe French Jr. French's mother was Hartack's younger sister Maxine, who went from the 1960s until 2007, when Hartack died, without speaking to her brother.[42]

As a steward, Hartack rarely went out of his way to help a rider. He had seen Zoe Cadman ride at Hawthorne, where she became the first woman to lead an Illinois track in wins for a season. Before she became a racing broadcaster, Cadman continued her career at the Fair Grounds, where one day a horse of hers was disqualified and she faced a suspension for careless riding.

Hartack called Cadman to his office, where he gave her a reprimand, plus some advice: there were ways to do what she did in the race without being detected by the stewards. He told her that there are blind spots on track where the stewards are blocked from view, as well as blind spots that go undetected by the patrol cameras. He suggested that she try that tactic next time. It was chapter one, audio version, of the cheaters' handbook.[43]

In front of the Galt House hotel in downtown Louisville is "Gallop to Glory," a concrete collection of jockeys' handprints and signatures from dozens of winners of the Kentucky Derby. Hartack had been asked to add his prints and name to the display in 2005, and again in 2006. Both times he declined, saying that he wanted nothing to do with anything related to Churchill Downs, even though the Galt's exhibit was independent of the track. Finally, in 2007, he told Jane Dempsey, who had been instrumental in bringing many of the Derby winners back to Louisville, that he would come.

"I will do the prints and so forth at the Galt, and I will do the oral history for the [Kentucky Derby] Museum," Hartack said. "But I won't go to the track or attend the Derby."

Dempsey scheduled Hartack for Louisville for the spring of 2008, the week of the Derby.[44] Hartack's fatal hunting trip to Texas came a few months before.[45] The Galt House will have to do without his handprints forevermore.

25

Iberia

The trainer Gary Palmisano had come from New Orleans with a horse to run at Churchill Downs. Bill Hartack, in Louisville for no special reason, was a good friend of Palmisano's.

"You look white as a sheet," Palmisano said upon seeing his friend.

Hartack said that he felt all right.

"When you get back, I want you to go to the doctor," Palmisano insisted.

Hartack went into the sundries shop at the hotel and got a package of Tums. "I feel better already," he said by the time he returned to the hotel lobby, having popped a couple of tablets into his mouth.

"See a doctor, will ya, 'Tack?" Palmisano urged.

Back in New Orleans, where Hartack was working as a steward at the Fair Grounds, Palmisano asked him what the doctor had said. The report was not good: Hartack's blood pressure was off the charts. He was a candidate, the doctor said, for a stroke, if he did not start taking precautions. He was a chain smoker, sometimes going through as many as three packs of cigarettes a day. While most times he didn't smoke a cigarette all the way down, there was usually a fresh one between his fingers while he was butting the old one.

Palmisano told his family that he believed Hartack had what he called "an episode."[1]

Johnnie Johnson, a jockey about Hartack's age, had met him when they were just breaking in at tracks in Ohio. Johnson took a quick dislike to the teenage Hartack, who had strong, unyielding opinions about everything, from Dwight Eisenhower to stud poker. "Years later, his career took off," Johnson said. "When it did, I said to myself, 'How could a guy like that do so good?'"

Like Hartack, Johnson became a steward in Louisiana, and they worked together harmoniously for a couple of years. "It was a joy," Johnson recalled. "He was funny, he had knowledge and the respect, he was a good steward. The only disagreements we had were mainly on procedural matters."

But Hartack had an unhealthy pallor about him. "He didn't look like he was feeling good," Johnson said. "Around Hartack, you didn't broach the subject, and he didn't bring it up, either. It looked like he had lost some weight."[2]

Hartack didn't go back to the doctor. He traded Tums for Nexium, which he began consuming like candy, but his stomach wouldn't stop churning.[3]

"He was never much for doctors," said Roseann Williams, a Los Angeles realtor who had dated Hartack in the 1970s. "There was a good chance that he could have had something or other and not even known it."[4]

When Hartack no longer worked the Fair Grounds meet and moved on to Louisiana

Downs, it meant that his winters were free.[5] In Texas, about seventy miles north of the Mexican border town of Laredo, he had found more than a thousand miles of hunting ground that kept drawing him back, year after year. Deer and wild boar roamed the territory. In 2006, Hartack had bagged a handsome buck, worthy of mounting.

During the Thanksgiving weekend of 2007, Hartack was packed and ready to make the six-hundred-mile trip from New Orleans—across Louisiana, past Houston—to tiny Freer, the town nearest to the hunting sprawl.[6] Freer, Texas, population about three thousand, has been known for a half-century for its Rattlesnake Roundup. It's a wing-ding that was inspired by a Texaco gas station that showed off rattlesnakes in cages, and it has grown in attendance from hundreds to thousands. As the event has grown, it's the country singers Trisha Yearwood, Chris Cagle and Mark Chestnutt, not the fried rattlesnake, that keep the roundup humming.[7]

In late November 2007, Hartack was several months too early for the roundup. He pulled into the hunting site in his gold Ford Explorer SUV but neglected to sign in at the registration area, eight miles from the mobile home where he would be staying. He was towing a small white cargo trailer.

Jim Beale, a retired game warden from Harlingen, Texas, was working the grounds in a freelance capacity. One of his main functions was to guard against illegals who might have crept across the Mexican-U.S. border near Laredo.

On Sunday, November 25, Beale noticed the SUV, with Louisiana plates, and the attached trailer parked in front of one of four one-bedroom mobile homes that formed a horseshoe. On his cellular phone, he called David Kitner in the front office.

"I don't know who that can be," Kitner said. "There's nobody on the books. I wouldn't worry too much about it. Check again in the morning."

At 10 o'clock on the morning of November 26, sixteen hours after he had seen the SUV the first time, Beale went by the mobile homes again. He noted that Hartack's car hadn't been moved. He tried to look in the windows of the mobile home, but they were too dirty to see through clearly. He thought he saw a body lying on the floor of the big living room but couldn't be certain. Beale knocked on the door several times, but there was no answer. He decided to force his way in. It took a few minutes. Hartack, besides locking the door from the inside, had also secured it by propping up a chair against the handle.

Finally, Beale broke through. He saw Hartack, motionless, on his back, fully clothed. High on the wall was the head of a deer, which Beale learned later was one that Hartack had killed the previous year. The deer seemed to be looking down on Hartack, who appeared to be looking up at the deer. It struck Beale immediately that this was an odd finish to Hartack's life: an avid hunter, his last living sight was something he had killed.[8]

Beale called the county sheriffs, notified the local police and contacted the coroner. In less than a half-hour, seven or eight people joined him. Hartack, who would have turned seventy-five on December 9, was declared dead by Corinne Stern, the chief medical examiner for Webb County. Her examination showed that Hartack had suffered from heart disease and died of natural causes. It was unclear whether Hartack was awaiting the arrival of friends or had come to Texas to hunt alone. Over the years, he had done both. After dozens of interviews, I found nobody who knew of anyone who was supposed to join him.[9]

Someone notified Michael Stidham, who had been a young boy when he went to Louisville in 1969 to see Hartack win his fifth Kentucky Derby with Majestic Prince. The son of George Stidham, Michael had followed his father into training horses. George Stidham was still a jockey when Hartack first began riding, and he later became Hartack's business manager and sometime agent. "Bill Hartack was my idol," Michael said. "He was a great person to grow up around. He was a kid at heart."[10]

Michael Stidham and other friends of Hartack, including Eddie Sapir and Tad Dowd, quickly launched the Bill Hartack Charitable Foundation, which honors the Derby-winning jockey every year with a diamond ring. "He touched all of our lives," said Sapir. "The whole idea is to raise money in his name for racing-related charities, in the interest of keeping Bill Hartack's legacy alive."[11]

Johnny Longden, who won more than six thousand races before he went from jockey to trainer, had given Hartack the mount on Majestic Prince; then the three of them combined to win the 1969 Derby. Shortly after Longden's six thousandth riding winner in 1965, he ranked Hartack as the sixth best jockey—after George Woolf, Eddie Arcaro, Sonny Workman, Don Meade and Bill Shoemaker.[12]

"Hartack was the greatest Derby rider ever," columnist Joe Hirsch said. "Think about it. He won the race for the fifth time with only his ninth mount. He went 5-for-12 lifetime. Arcaro also won the Derby five times, but it took him twenty-one mounts overall, and he didn't get to the fifth win until his thirteenth try."[13]

Chick Lang, who had lasted the longest as Hartack hopscotched from one agent to the next, recalled a conversation between Hartack and Calumet Farm's trainer, Jimmy Jones, at Keeneland. Jones was starting a horse who had been assigned a lot of weight, and he figured that if the horse didn't win, the racing secretaries might be kinder in assigning weight down the line, when the races would be more important.

"You know," Jones said. "It's all right if he gets beat. It wouldn't bother me."

"It might not bother you, but it will bother me," Hartack replied. "I'm going to try to win by a nose or by a mile, whatever it takes."[14]

Tommy Kelly, the trainer who had jump-started Hartack's career by introducing him to his first big stable, gave a stirring eulogy after his death, speaking at a Lutheran church just down the street from where Hartack once owned a home in Miami Springs, Florida.[15] A couple hundred mourners attended, many of them race trackers like Bobby Ussery, who rode against Hartack in five Kentucky Derbys.

It was through Kelly that Hartack and Paul Hornung had become friends.[16] Hornung, who starred in football at Notre Dame and later with the Green Bay Packers, was a Louisville native not opposed to betting horses through bookmakers. The National Football League suspended him for a full season for consorting with gamblers. "My favorite jockey was Bill Hartack," Hornung said. "Because he never pulled [restrained] a horse."[17]

Hornung was known for picking up checks, but when he was with Hartack, that became impossible. He said that no matter the size of the party, Hartack would be there at the end to pay the bill. "He would fight you for it, if you tried to get it," Hornung recalled. "I told him to cut it out. I told him there was no rule that said he had to pay all the time."[18]

When Gary Condra, Hartack's best friend for about fifty years, heard about his death, he called the jockey's two sisters.[19] He barely knew them. Evelyn "Dolly" Hartack Ferguson, who was seventy-six, was living in Las Vegas.[20] Maxine Hartack Shadrach, sixty-eight, was in Charles Town, West Virginia. Neither of the sisters had spoken to their brother in at least forty years. Nor could they explain why he had spent all that time shutting them out.

"I was still getting over the death of my son Joe," Maxine said. "The whole conversation [with Condra] came and went. All that I remembered was that Bill had died. I was in a fog by the time I hung up."[21]

Dolly was in Cleveland, visiting friends, and missed Condra's call. When she got home a couple of days later, the message on her answering machine was garbled. She made out that someone had died but couldn't understand who it was. A day or two after that, a cousin called to confirm that it was her brother, whom Dolly always called "Sonny."[22]

Condra, who was living in Hialeah, Florida, grew up in Iberia, a Central Missouri town with a population of about seven hundred, and a cemetery with thirteen hundred graves. Dozens of Condra's relatives are buried there, among unmarked graves (probably those of slaves) from the Civil War. Condra flew to Houston, rented a car and drove to Freer, Texas, where he claimed the body. Hartack's remains were flown to St. Louis, more than nine hundred miles away, and then driven the final 140 miles to Iberia. Hartack had never lived in Missouri, never ridden a horse there.

"I imagine that if I asked around Iberia, not many would know who Bill was," Condra said. "All a lot of people would tell you is that there's a famous jockey, and he's buried out there. But I'm glad I did what I did. I know Bill is happy there."

Condra revealed that he and Hartack had planned a fishing trip to Costa Rica to take place a couple of weeks after he returned from hunting in Texas. The sailfish and grouper were supposed to be good, and Condra, who was in car leasing, also had a little business there.

Gary Condra, Bill Hartack's friend of almost a half-century, buried him near the Condra family plot in a cemetery that dated back to the Civil War in Iberia, Missouri (Gary Condra collection).

"The two of us had never talked about dying," Condra said. "But if we had, I can imagine how it would have gone. He would have said to me, 'Where you gonna get buried?' I would have said, 'Back home.' And he would have said, 'Well, that's good enough for me.'"[23]

Jim Beale, the game warden, theorized that Hartack had probably died on November 25, the day before he discovered the body.[24] Eleven days after the body was found, Hartack was buried. A small gathering attended the services, which were not well publicized.[25]

Jay Ferguson (not related to Evelyn Hartack Ferguson), curator of the Churchill Downs Museum, was the only racing official to attend. When Ferguson walked into the funeral home after making the seven-hour drive from Louisville, he was mistaken for the minister. It was freezing rain that day. Conditions stayed so bad that Ferguson was unable to drive all the way home; he spent the night in St. Louis.[26]

Georgianna Reid, an old friend of Hartack's, came from Kansas City with a friend. No one at the funeral knew her. Online, she said that she had donated a poster of Hartack, done by LeRoy Neiman, to the Kentucky Derby Museum. "Bill, I will never forget you," Reid wrote.[27]

LeRoy Neiman was a good friend of Hartack, who was the first jockey that the artist put on canvas. Neiman was active in the Bill Hartack Foundation until his death in 2012 (Bill Hartack Foundation).

Reid said that she had met Hartack, twenty years her senior, at a race-track affair in San Diego when she was a schoolgirl. Johnny Alessio, Reid's godfather, ran the Agua Caliente track in Tijuana, Mexico, and her grandfather, Frank Blando, worked in the front office. Hartack had asked Reid to dance, and her grandfather didn't like it. He sent Johnny Longden to the dance floor to cut in; Hartack told Longden to take a seat. Exasperated, Blando cut in on his granddaughter and sent Hartack to the sidelines.

Reid left soon afterward for a Catholic girls' school in Mexico City. Hartack phoned her a few times, but the nuns wouldn't put the calls through. Eventually he got the idea of saying he was her brother and was able to talk to her that way. Then they drifted apart. Reid said that she wrote to Hartack in 2007, the year he died, and they had begun to talk on the phone again.[28]

Alongside an eight-foot-long granite bench is Hartack's headstone. It reads, "William 'Bill' Hartack. Born Dec. 9, 1932. Died Nov. 26, 2007. Winner of Five Kentucky Derbys. One of the World's Greatest Jockeys. Dedicated to Honesty and Integrity in Racing."

If it is not the biggest marker in the cemetery, it is close. "I didn't want it to be the biggest," Condra said. "That would be too much like putting on the dog. But I want it to justify the life Bill led, and all the accomplishments he had."

On Memorial Day weekend in 2015, Condra, still living in Florida, went home to Iberia and visited the graves of his parents and Hartack. Condra had been born in Iberia eighty years before in a remodeled log cabin, the son of a cattle-and-wheat farmer. The mayor of Iberia, a hundred-dollar-a-month part-time job, now knew who Hartack was, because other workers in his office had been talking about the grave.

Condra went out to the cemetery. Somebody had left a wreath that said, "Waterford Park." Condra didn't know who had put it there, nor did the only flower shop in town.[29] On October 14, 1952, Hartack had ridden his first of more than four thousand winners at Waterford Park, the leaky-roof West Virginia track that changed its name to Mountaineer Park in 1987.[30]

Although no one truly knows why, the Kentucky Derby has been called "The Run for the Roses" since 1925.[31] At the cemetery, Condra checked out the rose bush that he had planted at Hartack's grave in 2014. "It was blooming like crazy," he said.[32]

Chapter Notes

Chapter 1

1. Chuck Corolla, telephone interview with author, September 25, 2012.
2. Joseph C. Nichols, "Majestic Prince Scores Easily in Non-Betting Louisville Dash," *New York Times*, April 27, 1969.
3. Chuck Corolla.
4. *Kentucky Derby Media Guide* (2011), 93, 97.
5. *The American Racing Manual* (New York: Daily Racing Form Press, 2011), 672.
6. *Kentucky Derby Media Guide* (2011), 239, 241.
7. "Racing's Angriest Man," *True*, April 1960.
8. Chuck Corolla.
9. "Jack Mann," *Washington Star*, October 28, 1968.
10. "Jack Mann," *Washington Star*, May 1, 1969.
11. Tad Dowd, telephone interview with author, August 21, 2014.
12. *Kentucky Derby Media Guide* (2012), 212.
13. Tad Dowd.
14. Steve Nagler, telephone interview with author, June 24, 2013.
15. "The Prince and the Peasant," *New York Times*, May 4, 1969.
16. Joe Hirsch, telephone interview with author, November 5, 2008.
17. "Hartack (Don't Call Me Willie) Enters Jockeys' Club," *New York Times*, September 18, 1958.
18. "The Prince and the Peasant."
19. Chuck Corolla.
20. "Racing's Angriest Man."
21. Maxine Hartack Shadrach, telephone interview with author, September 12, 2014.
22. Gary Condra, telephone interview with author, August 20, 2014.
23. B.K. Beckwith, *The Longden Legend* (Cranbury, NJ: A.S. Barnes, 1973), 218–19.
24. "San Juan Capistrano Day Afforded Longden Fond Memories," *Post Time USA*, March 2003.
25. Cathy Schenck, Keeneland Association Library (Lexington, Kentucky), letter, February 26, 2013.
26. Gary Condra.
27. Nancy Lang, telephone interview with author, May 18, 2014.
28. *Kentucky Derby Media Guide* (2011), 97; *Maryland Jockey Club Media Guide* (2012), P-56; *New York Racing Association Media Guide* (2013), B35.
29. "Whatever Happened to Bill Hartack?" *Sports Illustrated*, June 24, 1963.
30. Beckwith, *The Longden Legend*, 219.
31. Jerry Lambert, telephone interview with author, August 15, 2014.
32. Beckwith, *The Longden Legend*, 219.
33. Vince DeGregory, telephone interview with author, October 1, 2013.
34. Jerry Lambert.
35. Vince DeGregory.
36. Jerry Lambert.
37. Beckwith, *The Longden Legend*, 208.
38. "95th—Kentucky Derby—95th," *Daily Racing Form*, May 3, 1969.
39. Beckwith, *The Longden Legend*, 218.
40. "The Princes and the Rose," *The Blood-Horse*, April 20, 1985.
41. *The American Racing Manual* (2011), 672.
42. Beckwith, *The Longden Legend*, 218.
43. "95th—Kentucky Derby—95th."
44. "The Princes and the Rose."
45. "95th—Kentucky Derby—95th."
46. "It May Be a Two-Horse Derby," *Sports Illustrated*, April 7, 1969.
47. Beckwith, *The Longden Legend*, 221.
48. Ibid., 92.
49. Johnny Bucalo, telephone interview with author, March 8, 2015.
50. Biff Lowry, telephone interview with author, April 22, 2014.
51. "It May Be a Two-Horse Derby."
52. Bill Shoemaker and Barney Nagler, *Shoemaker: America's Greatest Jockey* (New York: Doubleday, 1988), 114–15.
53. "It May Be a Two-Horse Derby."
54. Jim Bolus, *Derby Fever* (New Orleans: Pelican, 1995), 169, 171–72.
55. *Kentucky Derby Media Guide* (2011), 18.
56. "Flower Child," *Los Angeles Herald-Examiner*, May 4, 1969.
57. Joe Hirsch.
58. "Flower Child."
59. "My Old Kentucky Home," Kentuckyderby.com, accessed March 20, 2015.
60. "A Royal Neck for Bill's Fifth," *Sports Illustrated*, May 12, 1969.
61. "The Prince Almost Too Perfect," *Los Angeles Herald-Examiner*, May 4, 1969.
62. "A Royal Neck for Bill's Fifth."
63. "Majestic Prince—1969 Kentucky Derby (In Color)," YouTube, accessed March 20, 2015.

64. *Kentucky Derby Media Guide* (2011), 211.
65. Gary Condra.
66. Jim Bolus, *Kentucky Derby Stories* (New Orleans: Pelican, 1993), 159.
67. "The Prince and the Peasant."
68. Chuck Corolla.
69. "Hartack (Don't Call Him Willie) Enters Jockeys' Club."
70. Joe Hirsch.
71. "Persecution Complexes," *New York Times*, May 6, 1969.
72. Eddie Sapir, telephone interview with author, June 8, 2015.

Chapter 2

1. *Thoroughbred Times Racing Almanac 2009* (Lexington, KY: Thoroughbred Times Books, 2008), 123.
2. "Man in the Middle Jewel," *Sports Illustrated*, May 21, 1973.
3. "Agent Lang Walks Out on Jockey Bill Hartack," *Pittsburgh Post-Gazette*, March 31, 1960.
4. Bill Hartack career record, *The American Racing Manual* (New York: Daily Racing Form Press, 1952–1975).
5. "Man in the Middle Jewel."
6. Nancy Lang, telephone interview with author, May 18, 2014.
7. "A Hard Ride All the Way," *Sports Illustrated*, March 27, 1967; "My Feuds with Officials and the Press," *Sports Illustrated*, April 3, 1967; "The Days of the Roses," *Sports Illustrated*, April 10, 1967.
8. "Bully & the Beasts," *Time*, February 10, 1958.
9. *Maryland Jockey Club Media Guide* (2012), P-75.
10. "Racing's Angriest Man," *True*, April 1960.
11. Ed Linn, "What Makes Willie Hartack Burn?" *Sport*, June 1959.
12. B.K. Beckwith, *The Longden Legend* (Cranbury, NJ: A.S. Barnes, 1973), 219.
13. Vinnie Perrone, "Recalling Clem Florio's Matchless Gift for Life," *The Maryland Horse*, July 2008.
14. *Maryland Jockey Club Media Guide* (2012), P-75.
15. "Bully & the Beasts."
16. "The Prince Ducks the Big One," *Sports Illustrated*, May 26, 1969.
17. "Majestic Prince—1969 Preakness," YouTube, accessed January 20, 2013.
18. "The Prince Ducks the Big One."
19. Dave Johnson, telephone interview with author, January 20, 2013.
20. Beckwith, *The Longden Legend*, 227.
21. *Maryland Jockey Club Media Guide* (2012), P-75.
22. "The Man Takes Charge of His Horse," *Sports Illustrated*, June 2, 1969.
23. Dale Austin, telephone interview with author, June 25, 2013.
24. "The Man Takes Charge of His Horse."
25. "Majestic Prince Gallops and Walks at Belmont," *New York Times*, May 23, 1969.
26. "Racing's Angriest Man."
27. "Arts and Letters and Majestic Prince Show High Speed in Workouts," *New York Times*, May 28, 1969.
28. "Saturday Night," *New York Times*, June 9, 1969.
29. Tad Dowd, telephone interview with author, August 24, 2014.
30. Mark Kriegel, *Namath: A Biography* (New York: Penguin Books, 2005), 325.
31. Joe Hirsch, "The Front Runner," *Sports Illustrated*, September 15, 1956.
32. Kriegel, *Namath*, 326.
33. Tad Dowd.
34. Biff Lowry, telephone interview with author, April 22, 2014.
35. Linn, "What Makes Willie Hartack Burn?"
36. Dave Johnson, telephone interview with author, September 18, 2014.
37. Tommy Trotter, telephone interview with author, August 31, 2015.
38. Bruce Walker, email, December 1, 2012.
39. Biff Lowry.
40. *New York Racing Association Media Guide* (2013), B64.
41. "Revenge Was Sweet," *Sports Illustrated*, June 16, 1969.
42. "Arts and Letters Easily Beats Majestic Prince," *New York Times*, June 8, 1969.
43. Jerry Bailey, Belmont Stakes telecast, NBC-TV, June 6, 2015.
44. *New York Racing Association Media Guide* (2013), B35.
45. Ibid., B64.
46. "Revenge Was Sweet."
47. "Was It Won or Lost?" *New York Times*, June 8, 1969.
48. *Thoroughbred Champions: Top 100 Race Horses of the 20th Century* (Lexington, KY: Blood-Horse Publications, 2000), 140, 182.
49. "Was It Won or Lost?"
50. "The Belmont," *Thoroughbred Record*, June 10, 1969.
51. "The Princes and the Rose," *The Blood-Horse*, April 20, 1985.
52. "Jockey in a Million," *New York Times*, June 9, 1969.
53. "Revenge Was Sweet."
54. "Saturday Night."
55. Georgianna Reid, telephone interview with author, September 3, 2015.
56. "Conversation Piece: Lady Liz of Llangollen," *Sports Illustrated*, June 9, 1958.
57. "Saturday Night."

Chapter 3

1. Evelyn "Dolly" Hartack Ferguson, telephone interview with author, April 2, 2013.
2. "History of Coal in Cambria County," Johnstown Discovery Network (website), accessed August 18, 2015.
3. Evelyn "Dolly" Hartack Ferguson, telephone interview with author, August 27, 2012.
4. "Bully & the Beasts," *Time*, February 10, 1958.
5. Evelyn "Dolly" Hartack Ferguson.
6. Evelyn "Dolly" Hartack Ferguson, telephone interview with author, August 11, 2015.
7. Tad Dowd, telephone interview with author, June 15, 2014.
8. Alkie Darlington, telephone interview with author, February 10, 2015.
9. Author's recollection.

10. Evelyn "Dolly" Hartack Ferguson.
11. Maxine Hartack Shadrach, telephone interview with author, September 12, 2014.
12. Walter Blum, telephone interview with author, August 10, 2013.
13. "Raymond Guest, 84, Ambassador, Polo Player and Breeder of Horses," *New York Times*, January 1, 1992.
14. Joe Hirsch, telephone interview with author, November 5, 2008.
15. "Mrs. Brant Will Be Charged with Murder of William Hartack Sr.," *Spirit of Jefferson Farmers Advocate*, June 27, 1963.
16. Tad Dowd.
17. "Mrs. Brant Will Be Charged with Murder of William Hartack Sr."
18. Walter Blum.
19. Alkie Darlington.
20. Maxine Hartack Shadrach.
21. Evelyn "Dolly" Hartack Ferguson.
22. Maxine Hartack Shadrach.
23. "Slayer Gets 1 to 5 Years," *Pittsburgh Post-Gazette*, October 15, 1963.

Chapter 4

1. Maxine Hartack Shadrach, telephone interview with author, September 12, 2014.
2. Evelyn "Dolly" Hartack Ferguson, telephone interview with author, April 2, 2013.
3. Maxine Hartack Shadrach.
4. Evelyn "Dolly" Hartack Ferguson.
5. Maxine Hartack Shadrach.
6. Cathy Schenck, Keeneland Association Library (Lexington, Kentucky), email, March 31, 2015.
7. Evelyn "Dolly" Hartack Ferguson.
8. "Blacklick Township Senior Class of 1950" (photograph), *Johnstown, Pennsylvania, Tribune*, June 1950.
9. "A Hard Ride All the Way," *Sports Illustrated*, March 27, 1967.
10. Joe Verrone, telephone interview with author, August 2, 2014.
11. "Troubled Waters Deep in Life of Torquato Sr.," *Pittsburgh Post-Gazette*, July 27, 1984.
12. Joe Verrone.
13. "Why Didn't Truman Run for Re-election in 1952?" Answers.com, accessed September 3, 2015.
14. Alkie Darlington, telephone interview with author, August 8, 2014.
15. Melvyn Bragg, *The Soldier's Return* (London: Hodder & Stoughton, 1999), 79.
16. Joe Verrone.
17. Alkie Darlington.
18. *Thoroughbred Times Racing Almanac 2009* (Lexington, KY: Thoroughbred Times Books, 2008), 697–99.
19. "The Waterford Wizard," *Pittsburgh Post-Gazette*, April 16, 1973.
20. "A Pioneer Woman Jockey Recalls Her Tough Ride to Finish Line," *New York Times*, March 21, 2009.
21. Joe Verrone.
22. "Mountaineer Park on Speed Course with Slots," *Mid-Atlantic Thoroughbred*, October 2002.
23. "A Hard Ride All the Way."
24. Alkie Darlington.
25. Chuck Corolla, telephone interview with author, September 25, 2012.
26. Alkie Darlington.
27. Joe Hirsch, "The Front Runner," *Sports Illustrated*, September 15, 1956.
28. Joe Verrone.
29. "Racing's Angriest Man," *True*, April 1960.
30. Nancy Lang, telephone interview with author, March 1, 2014.
31. "A Hard Ride All the Way."
32. John Nerud, telephone interview with author, February 17, 2014.
33. *Kentucky Derby Media Guide* (2011), 185, 188, 190, 192, 197.
34. Phil Georgeff, *And They're Off! My Years as the Voice of Thoroughbred Racing* (Lanham, MD: Taylor Trade, 2002), 141.
35. "Racing's Angriest Man."
36. Gary Condra, telephone interview with author, August 20, 2014.
37. Ed Linn, "What Makes Willie Hartack Burn?" *Sport*, June 1959.
38. Alkie Darlington.
39. Joe Verrone.
40. *Daily Racing Form Chart Book* (New York: Triangle, 1952).
41. "A Hard Ride All the Way."
42. *Daily Racing Form Chart Book.*
43. Alkie Darlington.
44. "Racing's Angriest Man."
45. "A Hard Ride All the Way."
46. *Daily Racing Form Chart Book.*
47. Alkie Darlington.
48. "A Hard Ride All the Way."
49. *Daily Racing Form Chart Book.*
50. "A Hard Ride All the Way."
51. Cathy Schenck.
52. *Daily Racing Form Chart Book.*
53. Cathy Schenck.

Chapter 5

1. Alkie Darlington, telephone interview with author, September 4, 2015.
2. Joe Verrone, telephone interview with author, August 2, 2014.
3. *Daily Racing Form Chart Book* (New York: Triangle, 1952).
4. "A Hard Ride All the Way," *Sports Illustrated*, March 27, 1967.
5. Alkie Darlington.
6. "Hartack Rides Hard in Every Race," *Daytona Beach, Florida, Morning Journal*, October 5, 1958.
7. Alkie Darlington.
8. "He Wants to Stay Put," *Life*, October 5, 1953.
9. "Today's Racing at Wheeling Off," *Pittsburgh Press*, June 4, 1941.
10. "Wheeling Island Fire Is Raging," *Pittsburgh Post-Gazette*, February 3, 1936.
11. "The 1950 Snowstorm Was in a Class by Itself," InterMountain.com, February 7, 2009.
12. "Jockeys Strike at Wheeling," *Beaver Valley, Pennsylvania, Times*, May 26, 1953.

13. *Daily Racing Form Chart Book* (New York: Triangle, 1953).
14. *Hollywood Casino at Charles Town Races Media Guide* (2014), 22.
15. "Remember Me," *The Blood-Horse*, September 9, 2001.
16. Cathy Schenck, Keeneland Association Library (Lexington, Kentucky), email, March 31, 2015.
17. Bill Shoemaker and Barney Nagler, *Shoemaker: America's Greatest Jockey* (New York: Doubleday, 1988), 221–22.
18. Cathy Schenck.
19. *The American Racing Manual* (New York: Daily Racing Form Press, 2007), 704.
20. "The Remarkable Mr. Hartack," *Thoroughbred Record*, April 15, 1961.
21. *The American Racing Manual*, 704.
22. *Kentucky Derby Media Guide* (2011), 93.
23. Shoemaker and Nagler, *Shoemaker*, 223.
24. "My Feuds with Officials and the Press," *Sports Illustrated*, April 3, 1967.
25. Chuck Corolla, telephone interview with author, September 25, 2012.
26. "The Feud," *The Blood-Horse*, May 1, 2010.
27. Ibid.
28. "Eddie Arcaro, 'The Master,' Is Dead at 81," *Los Angeles Times*, November 15, 1997.
29. "The Feud."
30. "Hartack Target of Second Guessing," *Victoria, British Columbia, Advocate*, June 9, 1969.
31. Nancy Lang, telephone interview with author, September 5, 2015.
32. Alkie Darlington.
33. Nancy Lang.
34. Sam "The Genius" Lewin and Frederick C. Klein, *The Education of a Horseplayer* (New York: Hawthorn Books, 1969), 135.
35. Oliver Cutshaw Jr., telephone interview with author, September 5, 2015.
36. "Man in the Middle Jewel," *Sports Illustrated*, May 21, 1973.
37. Nancy Lang.
38. "That's Mr. Preakness," *The Blood-Horse*, May 20, 2003.

Chapter 6

1. "That's Mr. Preakness," *The Blood-Horse*, May 20, 2003.
2. Nancy Lang, telephone interview with author, September 5, 2015.
3. Alkie Darlington, telephone interview with author, September 2, 2015.
4. Joe Hirsch, "The Front Runner," *Sports Illustrated*, September 15, 1956.
5. Nancy Lang.
6. "Chick Lang, Star Jockey, Is Dead," *Wilmington, Delaware, Sunday Morning Star*, June 15, 1947.
7. "Man in the Middle Jewel," *Sports Illustrated*, May 21, 1973.
8. "Chick Lang, Star Jockey."
9. Nancy Lang.
10. "Man in the Middle Jewel."
11. "New Golden Boy," *Saturday Evening Post*, May 3, 1958.
12. Maxine Hartack Shadrach, telephone interview with author, September 12, 2014.
13. "A Hard Ride All the Way," *Sports Illustrated*, March 27, 1967.
14. Alkie Darlington.
15. "Man in the Middle Jewel."
16. "Hard Riding Jockey Wins Many Races," *St. Petersburg, Florida, Evening Independent*, December 16, 1960.
17. "Pet Bully 1st in Garden State Opening Event," *Chicago Tribune*, May 2, 1954.
18. Tommy Trotter, telephone conversation with author, September 1, 2015.
19. "Imbros Wins Rich California Stakes; Ties World Mark," *Sarasota, Florida, Herald-Tribune*, June 13, 1954.
20. *Daily Racing Form Chart Book* (New York: Triangle, 1954).
21. "Pet Bully Wins Rich Handicap in Record Time," *Sarasota, Florida, Herald-Tribune*, September 7, 1954.
22. "Pet Bully Defeats Dutch Lane in Highweight Handicap," *New York Times*, September 23, 1954.
23. "Joe Jones Beats Pet Bully by 2 Lengths in Vosburgh Handicap," *New York Times*, October 12, 1954.
24. "Pet Bully Takes $24,050 Princeton," *New York Times*, October 21, 1954.
25. Tommy Trotter, telephone interview with author, September 1, 2015.
26. "Hall of Fame Trainer T.J. Kelly Dead at 93."
27. Gary Condra, telephone interview with author, August 27, 2015.
28. "Tim Tam, 50 Years Later," *New York Times*, April 25, 2008.
29. *Kentucky Derby Media Guide* (2011), 62, 97.

Chapter 7

1. Bill Shoemaker and Barney Nagler, *Shoemaker: America's Greatest Jockey* (New York: Doubleday, 1988), 195.
2. "Jockey Agents Are Group of Nice Guys," *Daily Racing Form*, September 3, 1957.
3. Nancy Lang, telephone interview with author, September 5, 2015.
4. "Racing Legend Bill Shoemaker Dies," *Thoroughbred Times*, October 18, 2003.
5. "The Feud," *The Blood-Horse*, May 1, 2010.
6. *The American Racing Manual* (New York: Triangle, 1954, 1955).
7. "Hartack Moody But Well Paid," *Baltimore News American*, March 1, 1958.
8. "Racing Legend Bill Shoemaker Dies."
9. Nancy Lang.
10. "Bully & the Beasts," *Time*, February 10, 1958.
11. Willie Shoemaker and Dan Smith, *The Shoe* (Chicago/New York/San Francisco: Rand McNally, 1976), 174.
12. *The American Racing Manual* (New York: Triangle, 1956).
13. "Hartack Moody But Well Paid."
14. *The American Racing Manual.*
15. "82nd—Kentucky Derby—82nd," *Daily Racing Form*, May 5, 1956.

16. "Hero at Pimlico," *Sports Illustrated*, May 28, 1956.
17. "82nd—Kentucky Derby—82nd."
18. *Kentucky Derby Media Guide* (1981), 9.
19. "Fabius Wins Derby Trial," *Palm Beach Post*, May 2, 1956.
20. "Hero at Pimlico."
21. *Kentucky Derby Media Guide* (1981), 146.
22. "Needles Outruns Fabius in Derby," *New York Times*, May 6, 1956.
23. *Kentucky Derby Media Guide* (1981), 13.
24. Ibid., 146.
25. "Needles Outruns Fabius in Derby."
26. "Hero at Pimlico."
27. Herb Smith, telephone interview with author, July 25, 2014.
28. *New York Racing Association Media Guide* (2013), B62.
29. "His Strong Desire to Win..." *Lakeland, Florida, Ledger*, March 24, 1963.
30. "Barbizon Wins Rich Garden State Race," *Miami News*, October 27, 1956.
31. "With 19 2-Year-Olds Running for $319,210, the Garden State Was Barbizon's Day," *Sports Illustrated*, November 5, 1956.
32. Pedigreequery.com, accessed September 8, 2015.
33. *Kentucky Derby Media Guide* (1981), 147.

Chapter 8

1. "Top Horse Race Sire, Bull Lea, Dead at 29," *Milwaukee Journal*, October 17, 1964.
2. "82nd—Kentucky Derby—82nd," *Daily Racing Form*, May 5, 1956.
3. *Kentucky Derby Media Guide* (1981), 146.
4. Ed Linn, "What Makes Willie Hartack Burn?" *Sport*, June 1959.
5. "My Feuds with Officials and the Press," *Sports Illustrated*, April 3, 1967.
6. "Gen. Duke Triumphs in Florida Derby," *Danbury, Connecticut, Sunday Herald*, March 31, 1957.
7. "Say Hello to Jimmy Jones," *Sports Illustrated*, March 17, 1958.
8. "Arcaro to Be Highest-Paid Star in World of Sports," *Palm Beach Times*, October 10, 1952.
9. "Hartack Owes a Million in Back Taxes," *St. Petersburg, Florida, Evening Independent*, June 21, 1978.
10. Roseann Williams, telephone interview with author, March 18, 2015.
11. Bill Thayer, telephone interview with author, October 30, 2014.
12. "82nd—Kentucky Derby—82nd."
13. "Bold Ruler Wins Flamingo," *Chicago Tribune*, March 3, 1957.
14. "Hartack's Agent Is a Bright Guy," *Miami News*, March 31, 1957.
15. "Double Trouble," *Sports Illustrated*, April 8, 1957.
16. John Nerud, telephone interview with author, February 1, 2014.
17. "How You, Willie?" *Sports Illustrated*, May 13, 1957.
18. "82nd—Kentucky Derby—82nd."
19. "Federal Hill Wins Derby Trial," *Palm Beach Post*, May 1, 1957.
20. Joe Hirsch, telephone interview with author, November 5, 2008.
21. Dave Erb, telephone interview with author, June 10, 2013.
22. "Picking the Derby," *Sports Illustrated*, May 6, 1957.
23. "Gen. Duke Scratched in Derby," *Gadsden, Alabama, Times*, May 1, 1957.
24. Dave Erb.
25. "The Baby Comes Into His Own," *Sports Illustrated*, May 13, 1957.
26. *Kentucky Derby Media Guide* (1981), 147.
27. "The Baby Comes Into His Own."
28. John Nerud.
29. Bill Shoemaker and Barney Nagler, *Shoemaker: America's Greatest Jockey* (New York: Doubleday, 1988), 75.
30. John Nerud.
31. "Hirsch Recalls '57," *Daily Racing Form*, April 27, 1999.
32. "The Baby Comes Into His Own."
33. "82nd—Kentucky Derby—82nd."
34. Linn, "What Makes Willie Hartack Burn?"
35. Shoemaker and Nagler, *Shoemaker*, 73–74.
36. *Kentucky Derby Media Guide* (1981), 147.
37. Ibid., inside front cover.
38. "8–1 Shot Triumphs: Iron Liege Gains Nose Victory for Sixth Calumet Derby," *New York Times*, May 5, 1957.
39. "The Princes and the Rose," *The Blood-Horse*, April 20, 1985.
40. "The Baby Comes Into His Own."
41. Willie Shoemaker and Dan Smith, *The Shoe* (Chicago/New York/San Francisco: Rand McNally, 1976), 61.
42. Red Smith, "Red Smith's Views of Sports" (syndicated column), May 5, 1957.
43. "8–1 Shot Triumphs."
44. John Nerud.
45. "Red Smith's Views of Sports."
46. "The Princes and the Rose."
47. John Nerud.
48. Dave Erb.
49. Shoemaker and Nagler, *Shoemaker*, 73.
50. John Nerud.
51. Shoemaker and Nagler, *Shoemaker*, 74.
52. John Nerud.
53. Shoemaker and Nagler, *Shoemaker*, 74.
54. "The Princes and the Rose."
55. "Hartack Tells How Iron Liege Scored in 83rd Kentucky Derby," *Daily Racing Form*, May 7, 1957.
56. *Maryland Jockey Club Media Guide* (2012), P-72.
57. *New York Racing Association Media Guide* (2013), B62.
58. *Thoroughbred Champions: Top 100 Race Horses of the 20th Century* (Lexington, KY: Blood-Horse Publications, 2000).
59. Shoemaker and Nagler, *Shoemaker*, 239–40.
60. "The Remarkable Mr. Hartack," *Thoroughbred Record*, April 15, 1961.
61. "New Golden Boy," *Saturday Evening Post*, May 3, 1958.
62. Larry King, telephone interview with author, March 27, 2015.
63. Nancy Lang, telephone interview with author, September 5, 2015.

Chapter 9

1. *The American Racing Manual* (New York: Daily Racing Form Press, 2007), 704.
2. "The Remarkable Mr. Hartack," *Thoroughbred Record*, April 15, 1961.
3. Robert F. Kelley, *Racing in America, 1937–59* (New York: Jockey Club, 1960), 226.
4. "Women: Hold Fast to Life & Youth," *Time*, October 28, 1966.
5. "84th Kentucky Derby," *Daily Racing Form*, May 3, 1958.
6. "Bill Hartack Sets New Mark as Nadir Wins Richest Race," *Spokane, Washington, Spokesman-Review*, October 27, 1957.
7. "Mrs. Graham Is Provoked by Hartack," *Gettysburg, Pennsylvania, Times*, October 23, 1957.
8. Larry King, telephone conversation with author, March 27, 2015.
9. "Mrs. Graham Is Provoked by Hartack."
10. Ed Linn, "What Makes Willie Hartack Burn?" *Sport*, June 1959.
11. *Kentucky Derby Media Guide* (2011), 62.
12. Linn, "What Makes Willie Hartack Burn?"
13. "84th Kentucky Derby."
14. "Tumult, Shouting in Flamingo," *Miami News*, March 3, 1958.
15. "84th Kentucky Derby."
16. "Silky Sullivan Runs 4th; Hartack Breaks Leg," *New York Times*, April 27, 1958.
17. "Racing's Angriest Man," *True*, April 1960.
18. "Silky Sullivan Runs 4th."
19. *Kentucky Derby Media Guide* (2011), 186.
20. "Silky Sullivan Runs 4th."
21. "Erb Looms as Tim Tam's Rider in Kentucky Derby on Saturday," *New York Times*, April 28, 1958.
22. *Kentucky Derby Media Guide* (2011), 184.
23. Tad Dowd, telephone interview with author, March 15, 2014.
24. "Erb Looms."
25. "Valenzuela Will Ride Tim Tam in Trial Today," *New York Times*, April 29, 1958.
26. "Texan Replaces Injured Hartack," *New York Times*, May 1, 1958.
27. "Tim Tam, 50 Years Later," *New York Times*, April 25, 2008.
28. "Tim Tam Only One of Big Three to Run His Race," *Daily Racing Form*, May 4, 1958.
29. *Maryland Jockey Club Media Guide* (2012), P-73.
30. "Hartack Returns After Injury, Finishes in Money in 2 Races," *New York Times*, May 29, 1958.
31. Linn, "What Makes Willie Hartack Burn?"
32. "Racing's Angriest Man."
33. Linn, "What Makes Willie Hartack Burn?"
34. "The Race Track: Down They Go," *New Yorker*, July 19, 1958.
35. "Man in the Middle Jewel," *Sports Illustrated*, May 21, 1973.
36. "Cavan Captures $114,600 Belmont; Tim Tam, 3–20, Lame After Finishing Second," *New York Times*, June 8, 1958.
37. "Cavan Wins, Turn Lame," *Palm Beach Post*, June 29, 1958.
38. "The Race Track: Down They Go."

Chapter 10

1. "Man on a Horse," *Time*, May 17, 1948.
2. "Bully & the Beasts," *Time*, February 10, 1958.
3. "The Remarkable Mr. Hartack," *Thoroughbred Record*, April 15, 1961.
4. "Tim Tam," gallopoutblogspot.com, January 28, 2011.
5. Ed Linn, "What Makes Willie Hartack Burn?" *Sport*, June 1959.
6. Phil Georgeff, *And They're Off! My Years as the Voice of Thoroughbred Racing* (Lanham, MD: Taylor Trade, 2002), 148.
7. "Press Box," *Detroit News*, January 29, 1959.
8. Dave Feldman, with Frank Sugano, *Woulda, Coulda, Shoulda* (Chicago: Bonus Books, 1989), 137–38.
9. "Tomy Lee Beaten; Drops from 2d to 3d as 2–1 First Landing Wins Champagne," *New York Times*, October 12, 1958.
10. "Triumph of Class Over Mud," *New York Times*, November 3, 1958.
11. Bill Shoemaker and Barney Nagler, *Shoemaker: America's Greatest Jockey* (New York: Doubleday, 1988), 85–87.
12. *Kentucky Derby Media Guide* (2011), 10.
13. "Bill Hartack," *Florida Derby Souvenir Magazine* (1988), 78–83.
14. "Big Happy Week for Jim Norris," *Sports Illustrated*, April 6, 1959.
15. "Two for the Big Money," *Sports Illustrated*, April 13, 1959.
16. "The Princes and the Rose," *The Blood-Horse*, April 20, 1985.
17. *Kentucky Derby Media Guide* (2011), 178.
18. Ibid., 187.
19. Shoemaker and Nagler, *Shoemaker*, 86.
20. *Champions: The Lives, Times, and Past Performances of America's Greatest Thoroughbreds* (New York: Daily Racing Form Press, 2005), 170.
21. *The American Racing Manual* (New York: Daily Racing Form Press, 2007), 12.
22. "Tomy Lee," Wikihorseworld.com, accessed September 10, 2015.

Chapter 11

1. "Calumet Trio Elected Into Turf Hall of Fame," *New York Times*, August 16, 1959.
2. *Thoroughbred Times Racing Almanac 2009* (Lexington, KY: Thoroughbred Times Books, 2008), 112–13.
3. "Calumet Trio Elected Into Turf Hall of Fame."
4. Tad Dowd, telephone interview with author, August 15, 2014.
5. *The American Racing Manual* (New York: Daily Racing Form Press, 2007), 705.
6. Cathy Schenck, Keeneland Association Library (Lexington, Kentucky), email, March 3, 2015.
7. Brien Bouyea, National Museum of Racing and Hall of Fame, email, April 22, 2015.
8. "Hartack Gets New Agent," *Miami Herald*, March 30, 1960.
9. "Turf Official Gives Hartack Clinical Eye," *Miami News*, August 7, 1960.

10. "Agent Resigns, Lashes Hartack," *Miami News*, March 30, 1960.
11. "Heartache and Bally Ache," *Sports Illustrated*, April 11, 1960.
12. "Unique Talent," *Thoroughbred Times*, December 8, 2007.
13. "Big Stables Don't Look for Hartack Anymore," *Washington Star*, May 19, 1963.
14. Ed Linn, "What Makes Willie Hartack Burn?" *Sport*, June 1959.
15. "Racing's Angriest Man," *True*, April 1960.
16. "Heartache and Bally Ache."
17. "Agent Resigns, Lashes Hartack."
18. "Will It Happen Again?" *Miami News*, May 19, 1959.
19. "Agent Resigns, Lashes Hartack."
20. "Tough—That's Hartack!" *Chicago Tribune*, July 31, 1960.
21. "Bill Hartack," *Florida Derby Souvenir Magazine* (1988), 82.
22. "The Drugstore Derby," *Turf & Sport Digest*, June 1960.
23. "The 1968 Kentucky Derby: The Victory That Wasn't," *Los Angeles Times*, May 1, 1988.
24. *Kentucky Derby Media Guide* (2011), 87.
25. "The Princes and the Rose," *The Blood-Horse*, April 20, 1985.
26. "1960 Kentucky Derby Brought Mixture of Sadness and Joy," *New York Daily News*, May 1, 2010.
27. *Kentucky Derby Media Guide* (2011), 188.
28. "Venetian Shows the Way," *Sports Illustrated*, May 16, 1960.
29. "Trainer Vic Sovinski Fires Jockey Hartack," *Sarasota, Florida, Herald-Tribune*, May 21, 1960.
30. "Tough—That's Hartack!"
31. "The Drugstore Derby."
32. "Maybe Venetian Way Was On the Wagon?" *Philadelphia Inquirer*, May 23, 1960.
33. Richard Sowers, *The Kentucky Derby, Preakness and Belmont Stakes: A Comprehensive History* (Jefferson, NC: McFarland, 2014), 185–86.
34. "Tough—That's Hartack!"
35. *New York Racing Association Media Guide* (2013), B63.
36. Ibid., B35.
37. "The Days of the Roses," *Sports Illustrated*, April 20, 1985.

Chapter 12

1. *Arlington Park Media Guide* (2009), 33.
2. Larry King, telephone interview with author, March 27, 2015.
3. Phil Georgeff, telephone interview with author, April 27, 2015.
4. *Arlington Park Media Guide* (2009), 32.
5. Phil Georgeff, *And They're Off! My Years as the Voice of Thoroughbred Racing* (Lanham, MD: Taylor Trade, 2002), 93, 119, 135.
6. Phil Georgeff.
7. "Remembering Hartack," *The Blood-Horse*, December 8, 2007.
8. *Champions: The Lives, Times, and Past Performances of America's Greatest Thoroughbreds* (New York: Daily Racing Form Press, 2005), 142.
9. "$427,000 in Two Minutes," *Sports Illustrated*, July 22, 1957.
10. "Racing's Angriest Man," *True*, April 1960.
11. Phil Georgeff.
12. "$427,000 in Two Minutes."
13. *Arlington Park Media Guide* (2009), 32.
14. Georgeff, *And They're Off!* 124.
15. *Kentucky Derby Media Guide* (2011), 65.
16. Ibid., 177.
17. "Horse Racing, Fred W. Hooper," About.com, August 4, 2000.
18. "On the Dawn Patrol," *New York Times*, May 4, 1961.
19. Georgeff, *And They're Off!* 162–63.
20. "Disqualification Rule Costs Alhambra Win," *Eugene, Oregon, Register-Guard*, July 21, 1961.
21. Tommy Trotter, telephone interview with author, September 1, 2015.
22. "In Chicago: Greek Game Wins Futurity on Foul," *Sports Illustrated*, September 10, 1956.
23. "Racing's Angriest Man."
24. "Hartack Makes Unique Plea," *Miami News*, May 4, 1962.
25. "The Feud," *The Blood-Horse*, May 1, 2010.
26. Tad Dowd, telephone interview with author, March 15, 2015.
27. "The Strange Case of Willie (Oops, Bill) Hartack," *Baltimore News-Post*, May 21, 1960.
28. Georgianna Reid, telephone interview with author, September 7, 2015.
29. *Thoroughbred Racing Associations Directory & Record Book* (2015), 81.
30. "Kelso—'King Kelly,'" About.com, accessed September 12, 2015.
31. "Kelso," *Daily Racing Form*, December 21, 2011.
32. *Champions*, 208.
33. Richard Sowers, *The Kentucky Derby, Preakness and Belmont Stakes: A Comprehensive History* (Jefferson, NC: McFarland, 2014), 190–92.
34. "88th—Kentucky Derby—88th," *Daily Racing Form*, May 5, 1962.
35. *Kentucky Derby Media Guide* (2011), 193.
36. Ibid., page unnumbered.
37. *New York Racing Association Media Guide* (2013), B63.
38. "Tumult, Shouting in Flamingo," *Miami News*, March 3, 1958.
39. "Tough—That's Hartack!" *Chicago Tribune*, July 31, 1960.
40. "My Feuds with Officials and the Press," *Sports Illustrated*, April 3, 1967.
41. "Top Prize at Arlington to Pay $134,925," *Chicago Tribune*, September 14, 1964.
42. "French Horses Are Cutting It Close," *Los Angeles Times*, November 9, 1987.
43. "Samuel Goldwyn Quotes," brainyquote.com, accessed September 11, 2015.
44. "The Feud."
45. "By Any Name But Willie, Bill Hartack Was a Winner," *Gaming Today*, December 4, 2007.
46. "My Feuds with Officials and the Press."
47. "Riders Revolt, Organize New Association," *St. Petersburg, Florida, Times*, July 23, 1966.

48. Milton C. Toby, *Dancer's Image: The Forgotten Story of the 1968 Kentucky Derby* (Charleston, SC: History Press, 2011), 42.
49. *Santa Anita Park Media Guide* (2011–2012), 10.
50. Terry Meyocks, telephone interview with author, February 8, 2014.
51. Wayne Harris, telephone interview with author, September 20, 2015.
52. "From Ace Jockey to Fred's 'Baby,'" *Los Angeles Times*, May 17, 1997.
53. *The American Racing Manual* (New York: Daily Racing Form Press, 2011), 673.

Chapter 13

1. "Hartack's Losing His Riding Touch," *Miami News*, May 9, 1960.
2. "Big Stables Don't Look for Hartack Anymore," *Washington Star*, May 19, 1963.
3. "Whatever Happened to Bill Hartack?" *Sports Illustrated*, June 24, 1963.
4. *Kentucky Derby Media Guide* (2011), 185, 188, 190, 192, 197.
5. Cathy Schenck, Keeneland Association Library (Lexington, Kentucky), email, March 3, 2015.
6. B.K. Beckwith, *The Longden Legend* (Cranbury, NJ: A.S. Barnes, 1973), 92.
7. William H. Rudy, *Racing in America, 1960–1979* (New York: Stinehour Press, 1980), 20.
8. *Champions: The Lives, Times, and Past Performances of America's Greatest Thoroughbreds* (New York: Daily Racing Form Press, 2005), 199–200.
9. "Kentucky Derby Notes," *Los Angeles Times*, May 1, 1986.
10. *The American Racing Manual* (New York: Daily Racing Form Press, 2007), 705.
11. "Hartack's Losing His Riding Touch."
12. Richard Sowers, *The Kentucky Derby, Preakness and Belmont Stakes: A Comprehensive History* (Jefferson, NC: McFarland, 2014), 187–88.
13. *Kentucky Derby Media Guide* (2011), 189; *Maryland Jockey Club Media Guide* (2012), P-73; *New York Racing Association Media Guide* (2013), B63.
14. "Hartack Admitted Mistake," *Miami News*, March 30, 1961.
15. "Carry Back Outruns Crozier, Wins Muddy Florida Derby," *Miami News*, April 2, 1961.
16. "Bill Hartack Derby Slight Shocks Vet," *Toledo Blade*, May 5, 1961.
17. "Odd Project Lures Hartack on Vacation," *Miami News*, September 21, 1961.
18. "All But Forgotten—By a Nose," *Thoroughbred Times*, July 13, 2002.
19. "88th Derby—Kentucky Derby—88th," *Daily Racing Form*, May 5, 1962.
20. "Jolley Stews on Hartack's Ride of Ridan," *Miami News*, February 22, 1962.
21. "Hartack Suspended," *Miami News*, February 22, 1962.
22. "88th Derby—Kentucky Derby—88th."
23. "Leroy Jolley Finds Derby Grind Rough," *Miami News*, May 3, 1962.
24. Tommy Trotter, telephone interview with author, April 23, 2015.
25. "Leroy Jolley Finds Derby Grind Rough."
26. "Ussery Makes Advance Plan for Big Stake," *Miami News*, March 14, 1962.
27. "The Princes and the Rose," *The Blood-Horse*, April 20, 1985.
28. "Injury Costs Sir Gaylord; Ridan Favored," *Daytona Beach, Florida, Morning Journal*, May 5, 1962.
29. "Leroy Jolley Finds Derby Grind Rough."
30. "Determine," *Kentucky Derby Souvenir Magazine* (1991).
31. *Kentucky Derby Media Guide* (2011), 8.
32. *Champions*, 159.
33. "A Day of Vindication," *New York Times*, May 6, 1962.
34. *Kentucky Derby Media Guide* (2011), 190.
35. Larry King, telephone interview with author, March 27, 2015.
36. *Kentucky Derby Media Guide* (2011), 190, 192.
37. "The Princes and the Rose."
38. "88th—Kentucky Derby—88th."
39. "A Day of Vindication."
40. Gary Condra, telephone interview with author, August 27, 2015.
41. "'We Had It, Didn't We?'" *Palm Beach Post*, May 6, 1962.
42. Sowers, *The Kentucky Derby*, 190–91.
43. "Day of Vindication."

Chapter 14

1. "Big Pete's Record Still Unblemished," *Miami News*, June 23, 1963.
2. "Whatever Happened to Bill Hartack?" *Sports Illustrated*, June 24, 1963.
3. "Elder Hartack Killed by Shots," *Miami News*, June 22, 1963.
4. "Mrs. Brant Will Be Charged with Murder of William Hartack Sr.," *Spirit of Jefferson Farmers Advocate*, June 27, 1963.
5. "Elder Hartack Killed by Shots."
6. Bill Nack, email, September 17, 2015.
7. Don Brumfield, telephone interview with author, November 1, 2014.
8. John C. Skinner Jr., telephone interview with author, July 15, 2013.
9. Evelyn "Dolly" Hartack Ferguson, telephone interview with author, April 17, 2015.
10. Don Brumfield.
11. Walter Blum, telephone interview with author, August 10, 2013.
12. "Whatever Happened to Bill Hartack?"
13. *Kentucky Derby Media Guide* (2011), 190.
14. "Whatever Happened to Bill Hartack?"
15. *Daily Racing Form*, May 4, 1963.
16. *Kentucky Derby Media Guide* (2011), 191.
17. "Unusual Plea Gave Baeza Derby Chance," *Miami News*, May 6, 1963.
18. "Whatever Happened to Bill Hartack?"
19. "Unusual Plea Gave Baeza Derby Chance."
20. "Whatever Happened to Bill Hartack?"
21. *Arlington Park Media Guide* (2009), 33.
22. Cathy Schenck, Keeneland Association Library (Lexington, Kentucky), email, March 3, 2015.
23. "Lenny Goodman, Jockeys' Agent, 76," *New York Times*, September 26, 1996.

24. "Uncompromising Idealist," *The Blood-Horse*, May 30, 1964.
25. *Daily Racing Form*, May 2, 1964.
26. *Kentucky Derby Media Guide* (2011), 192.

Chapter 15

1. "What's My Line?, May 10, 1964," YouTube, accessed May 6, 2015.
2. *Kentucky Derby Media Guide* (2011), 192.
3. "What's My Line?"
4. *Kentucky Derby Media Guide* (2011).
5. "What's My Line?"
6. "Three for the Triple Crown," *Sports Illustrated*, May 25, 1964.
7. "Taken for a Virginia Reel," *Sports Illustrated*, June 15, 1964.
8. "The Princes and the Rose," *The Blood-Horse*, April 20, 1985.
9. "The Tyranny of the Little Men," *Sports Illustrated*, April 27, 1964.
10. Avalyn Hunter, *The Kingmaker: How Northern Dancer Founded a Racing Dynasty* (Lexington, KY: Eclipse Press, 2008), 110.
11. Ibid., 96.
12. Ibid., 106.
13. *Daily Racing Form*, April 24, 1964.
14. *Kentucky Derby Media Guide* (2011), 192.
15. *Maryland Jockey Club Media Guide* (2012), P-74.
16. Kevin Chong, *Northern Dancer: The Legendary Horse That Inspired a Nation* (Toronto: Viking Canada, 2014), 102.
17. Ibid., 51.
18. Ibid., 49–50.
19. "The Long History of Horse Racing's Addiction to Doping," ProPublica.com, May 2, 2014.
20. "The Doc's Legacy at the Derby," *New York Times*, April 30, 2009.
21. "The 1968 Derby: The Victory That Wasn't," *Los Angeles Times*, May 1, 1988.
22. Chong, *Northern Dancer*, 44.
23. "The Princes and the Rose."
24. Chong, *Northern Dancer*, xiii.
25. "90th—Kentucky Derby—90th," *Daily Racing Form*, May 2, 1964.
26. Bill Shoemaker and Barney Nagler, *Shoemaker: America's Greatest Jockey* (New York: Doubleday, 1988), 103.
27. "The Dancer Dazzles Old Kentucky," *Sports Illustrated*, May 11, 1964.
28. "90th—Kentucky Derby—90th."
29. "Three for the Triple Crown."
30. "The Dancer Dazzles Old Kentucky."
31. "The Princes and the Rose."
32. "Did The Scoundrel Win After All? Ask Writers," *Miami News*, May 3, 1964.
33. "Hartack Obliges His Fans, But Keeps Press Waiting," *Louisville Courier-Journal*, May 3, 1964.

Chapter 16

1. "Bill Hartack, as Seen by Hartack," *New York Times*, May 5, 1964.
2. "Three for the Triple Crown," *Sports Illustrated*, May 25, 1964.
3. "It's No Laughing Matter to Funny Cide's Trainer," *Los Angeles Times*, May 19, 2003.
4. "Triple Crown," *Los Angeles Times*, May 9, 1985.
5. *Maryland Jockey Club Media Guide* (2012), P-71, P-73.
6. Ibid., P-74.
7. "The Morning After," *Baltimore Sun*, November 25, 1963.
8. Debi Lang Tessier, telephone interview with author, September 22, 2015.
9. Bill Shoemaker and Barney Nagler, *Shoemaker: America's Greatest Jockey* (New York: Doubleday, 1988), 71, 73.
10. "Three for the Triple Crown."
11. *Maryland Jockey Club Media Guide* (2012), P-74.
12. "Ride Clear to Hartack," *Baltimore Sun*, May 17, 1964.
13. "One More to Make It Nine," *Sports Illustrated*, June 1, 1964.
14. "Cauthen's Agent Sets High Goals," *Toronto Star*, May 2, 1977.
15. *Thoroughbred Times Racing Almanac 2009* (Lexington, KY: Thoroughbred Times Books, 2008), 112–13.
16. "Taken for a Virginia Reel," *Sports Illustrated*, June 15, 1964.
17. Kevin Chong, *Northern Dancer: The Legendary Horse That Inspired a Nation* (Toronto: Viking Canada, 2014), 166.
18. "Obituaries: Juan Manuel Fangio," *The Independent*, July 18, 1995.
19. "Dance Smartly One in a Line of Northern Dancer's Legacies," *Toronto Star*, November 1, 1992.
20. Chong, *Northern Dancer*, 182–85.
21. Avalyn Hunter, *The Kingmaker: How Northern Dancer Founded a Racing Dynasty* (Lexington, KY: Eclipse Press, 2008), 132–33.
22. "Northern Dancer," Pinterest.com, accessed September 14, 2015.
23. "Hartack Still Rides Hard," *Toronto Star*, July 20, 2007.

Chapter 17

1. "From Claim to Fame," *Los Angeles Times*, June 2, 1999.
2. Cathy Schenck, Keeneland Association Library (Lexington, Kentucky), email, March 3, 2015.
3. *Santa Anita Park Media Guide* (2011–2012), 15–16, 23.
4. Ibid., 118.
5. "Hartack Stays Mad at World," *Los Angeles Times*, April 21, 1965.
6. "My Feuds with Officials and the Press," *Sports Illustrated*, April 3, 1967.
7. "Hartack Stays Mad at World."
8. "Lucky Debonair Upsets Jacinto," *Ocala, Florida, Star-Banner*, March 7, 1965.
9. *Thoroughbred Times Racing Almanac 2009* (Lexington, KY: Thoroughbred Times Books, 2008), 110.
10. "Backtracking with Agent Lenny Goodman," *Miami News*, January 17, 1980.

11. "91st—Kentucky Derby—91st," *Daily Racing Form*, May 1, 1965.
12. "News of the Week," *The Blood-Horse*, April 13, 1963.
13. William H. Rudy, *Racing in America, 1960–1979* (New York: Stinehour Press, 1980), 77.
14. *Kentucky Derby Media Guide* (2012), 89, 181.
15. Rudy, *Racing in America*, 82.
16. *Kentucky Derby Media Guide* (2012), 97.
17. "Bold Lad, Hartack Up, Takes Derby Trial by 4 Lengths," *New York Times*, April 28, 1965.
18. Richard Sowers, *The Kentucky Derby, Preakness and Belmont Stakes: A Comprehensive History* (Jefferson, NC: McFarland, 2014), 175–77.
19. "Penny Chenery's Life, Unscripted," *Daily Racing Form*, September 30, 2010.
20. "Overlooked Horse Has Nice Timing," *Los Angeles Times*, June 3, 1999.
21. "Sherman Compares California Chrome with Hall of Famer Swaps," thehandicappersedge.com, accessed September 14, 2015.
22. Tad Dowd, telephone interview with author, May 26, 2015.
23. "Art Rooney Sr. Enjoys Kentucky Derby from Up Close," *Pittsburgh Post-Gazette*, May 9, 1988.
24. "Roses for the Shoe," *Sports Illustrated*, May 10, 1965.
25. Jack Drees, interview with author, Louisville, May 2, 1968.
26. Sowers, *The Kentucky Derby, Preakness and Belmont.*
27. "Tower Ticker," *Chicago Tribune*, May 2, 1965.
28. Larry King, telephone interview with author, July 22, 2015.
29. "He Comes Up Roses," *Thoroughbred Record*, May 2, 1970.
30. "Roses for the Shoe."
31. Rudy, *Racing in America*, 65.
32. *Del Mar Media Guide* (2015), 8.
33. Mac McBride, email, May 26, 2015.
34. Harry Hacek, telephone interview with author, May 27, 2015.
35. *Del Mar Owners, Trainers, Jockeys Source Book* (2015), 62, 69.
36. Don Pierce, telephone interview with author, May 27, 2015.
37. Vince DeGregory, telephone interview with author, May 27, 2015.
38. Kenny Church, telephone interview with author, May 28, 2015.
39. Mac McBride, email, June 2, 2015.
40. "Hovdey: Del Mar Hoping 1967 Was Just a Bad Trip," *Daily Racing Form*, November 5, 2014.
41. Dan Smith, emails, May 26–27, 2015.

Chapter 18

1. "Between You 'n' Me," *Ocala, Florida, Star-Banner*, February 1, 1960.
2. "No Gold in Bronze," *Eugene, Oregon, Register-Guard*, June 21, 1978.
3. "Hartack Owes a Million in Back Taxes," *St. Petersburg, Florida, Evening Independent*, June 21, 1978.
4. U.S. Tax Court, Jacksonville, Florida, conversation with author, June 3, 2015.
5. Howell Melton Jr., telephone message for author, June 9, 2015.
6. "Success Costs Hartack Cash," *Milwaukee Journal*, October 24, 1957.
7. *The American Racing Manual* (New York: Daily Racing Form Press, 2007), 704.
8. "Man in the Middle Jewel," *Sports Illustrated*, May 21, 1973.
9. Eddie Sapir, telephone interview with author, June 9, 2015.
10. "Round-the-Clock Guards Ran Up Tuna Trial Cost," *Miami News*, February 8, 1980.
11. Gary Condra, telephone interview with author, August 27, 2015.
12. Evelyn "Dolly" Hartack Ferguson, telephone interview with author, April 17, 2015.
13. Penny Pierce, telephone interview with author, May 27, 2015.
14. Evelyn "Dolly" Hartack Ferguson.
15. Bill Thayer, telephone interview with author, October 30, 2014.
16. Evelyn "Dolly" Hartack Ferguson.
17. Penny Pierce.
18. Gary Condra.
19. Tad Dowd, telephone interview with author, August 21, 2014.
20. "Broward Lawyer Indicted, Faces Racketeering and Drug Charges," *Fort Lauderdale, Florida, Sun-Sentinel*, April 18, 1987.
21. Irene De Camp-Ultimo, telephone conversation with author, August 5, 2015. (The second time, I called and left her a voice mail and she never returned the call).
22. Bruce Walker, email, November 30, 2012.
23. Gary Palmisano, telephone interview with author, June 4, 2015.
24. Harry Hacek, telephone interview with author, June 10, 2014.
25. "The Glitter's Gone," *Miami News*, May 23, 1968.

Chapter 19

1. "Spotlight Stays on Pincay Family," *Daily Racing Form*, January 9, 2014.
2. *The American Racing Manual* (New York: Daily Racing Form Press, 2007), 705.
3. Roseann Williams, telephone interview with author, March 18, 2015.
4. "Spotlight Stays on Pincay Family."
5. *Kentucky Derby Media Guide* (1981), 156–67.
6. "Horse Racing: Look for a Triple," *Time*, February 25, 1966.
7. "Hartack Enters Hialeah Race," *Ocala, Florida, Star-Banner*, January 31, 1967.
8. "Field of 13 Seen for Coast Derby," *Reading, Pennsylvania, Eagle*, April 20, 1967.
9. "The Days of the Roses," *Sports Illustrated*, April 10, 1967.
10. "93rd—Kentucky Derby—93rd," *Daily Racing Form*, May 6, 1967.
11. "Favorite First," *Reading, Pennsylvania, Eagle*, April 23, 1967.

12. "Jockey Rides Seven Firsts at Woodbine," *Montreal Gazette*, May 17, 1967.
13. "93rd—Kentucky Derby—93rd."
14. "Dr. Isby Is the Runner-Up in Stepping Stone Purse," *New York Times*, April 30, 1967.
15. "Room to Run," *Washington Post*, May 19, 1967.
16. "Barbs Delight: A Chaser for Dr. Fager," *New York Times*, September 2, 1967.
17. "93rd—Kentucky Derby—93rd."
18. "Clarion Call: $62.20!" *Sports Illustrated*, May 15, 1967.
19. *Kentucky Derby Media Guide* (2011), 195.
20. "Clarion Call: $62.20!"
21. "Barbs Delight's Owners Take $10,000 Gamble," *Miami News*, May 17, 1967.
22. "Room to Run."

Chapter 20

1. "Anchor and Sportscaster Was Also an Actor," *Los Angeles Times*, October 1, 2008.
2. "Hard Old Hartack," *Los Angeles Times*, July 7, 1968.
3. Mary Fleming, *A History of the Thoroughbred in California* (Arcadia: California Thoroughbred Breeders Association, 1983), 175–80.
4. Kenny Church, telephone interview with author, May 28, 2015.
5. "Quicken Tree, Coast Invader, Wins Manhattan," *New York Times*, August 10, 1968.
6. "A Cup Goes West," *New Yorker*, November 2, 1968.
7. Kenny Church.
8. Cathy Schenck, Keeneland Association Library (Lexington, Kentucky), email, March 3, 2015.
9. "U.S. Charges Hartack Owes $805,250 on Tax Lien on House," *New York Times*, October 13, 1968.
10. B.K. Beckwith, *The Longden Legend* (Cranbury, NJ: A.S. Barnes, 1973), 219.
11. "95th—Kentucky Derby—95th," *Daily Racing Form*, May 3, 1969.
12. "The Princes and the Rose," *The Blood-Horse*, April 20, 1985.
13. *Kentucky Derby Media Guide* (2011), 97.
14. Cathy Schenck.
15. *Santa Anita Park Media Guide* (2011–2012), 97.
16. Don Pierce, telephone interview with author, May 27, 2015.
17. Andrea Longden, telephone interview with author, June 18, 2015.
18. "Hartack Remembers Longden," *Daily Racing Form*, February 19, 2003.
19. Andrea Longden.
20. "Hartack Remembers Longden."
21. Johnny Buccalo, telephone interview with author, March 25, 2014.
22. "95th—Kentucky Derby—95th."
23. "He Comes Up Roses," *Thoroughbred Record*, May 2, 1970.
24. Fleming, *A History of the Thoroughbred in California*, 179.
25. *Del Mar Owners, Trainers, Jockeys Source Book* (2015), 69.
26. *The American Racing Manual* (Chicago: Triangle, 1970), 138.
27. Cathy Schenck.
28. National Museum of Racing and Hall of Fame.
29. "George Lewis Muddles 3-Year-Old Scene," *Miami News*, January 22, 1970.
30. "Strike Halts Opening at Santa Anita," *Toledo Blade*, December 27, 1969.
31. "96th—Kentucky Derby—96th," *Daily Racing Form*, May 2, 1970.
32. "By George, He'll Run," *Pittsburgh Press*, May 1, 1970.
33. "Sailstone Withdrawn; George Lewis Looks for Derby Position," *St. Petersburg, Florida, Times*, April 27, 1970.
34. *Kentucky Derby Media Guide* (2011), 198.
35. Ibid., 11.
36. Ibid., 198.
37. "George Lewis Muddles 3-Year-Old Scene."
38. *Kentucky Derby Media Guide* (2011), 198.

Chapter 21

1. "Hartack's Race Protest Denied," *Los Angeles Times*, June 24, 1970.
2. "Hartack Returns to Waterford Park," *Washington, Pennsylvania, Observer-Reporter*, August 19, 1970.
3. "Elder Hartack Killed by Shots," *Milwaukee Journal*, June 22, 1963.
4. *Thoroughbred Times Racing Almanac 2009* (Lexington, KY: Thoroughbred Times Books, 2008), 698.
5. "Days Growing Shorter for Jockey Hartack," *Beaver County, Pennsylvania, Times*, August 22, 1970.
6. "Hartack's Night a Nightmare," *Pittsburgh Press*, August 22, 1970.
7. *Champions: The Lives, Times, and Past Performances of America's Greatest Thorouhghbreds* (New York: Daily Racing Form Press, 2005), 265.
8. *Thoroughbred Racing Associations Directory & Record Book* (2015), 81.
9. "Hartack in Chicago," *Thoroughbred Times*, July 14, 1962.
10. *The American Racing Manual* (New York: Daily Racing Form Press, 2010), 686.
11. *Daily Racing Form Chart Book* (Chicago: Triangle, 1970).
12. "Hartack Joins Elite, Gets 4,000th Win," *Rome, Georgia, News-Tribune*, December 15, 1970.
13. "Hartack Rides 4,000th Winner," *Daily Racing Form*, December 15, 1970.
14. *Daily Racing Form Chart Book.*
15. Diane Crump, telephone interview with author, July 10, 2015.
16. "Sad Anniversary: 20 Years After Making History, Jockey Diane Crump Is Injured in Fall," *Los Angeles Times*, March 1, 1989.
17. "Saul Silberman, 75, Race Track Owner," *New York Times*, February 20, 1971.
18. Equibase.com, accessed September 18, 2015.
19. "Post Parade," *Thoroughbred Record*, December 26, 1970.
20. Gary Condra, telephone interview with author, June 23, 2015.

Chapter 22

1. "The 100 Greatest Horses of the 20th Century," *Thoroughbred and Harness Racing Action*, December 22, 1987–January 4, 1988, 9.
2. Bill Shoemaker, interview with author, c. 1990.
3. "Hartack Reprimanded After Abusing Fan," *Montreal Gazette*, July 27, 1971.
4. Cathy Schenck, Keeneland Association Library (Lexington, Kentucky), email, March 3, 2015.
5. Pedigreequiry.com, accessed September 8, 2015.
6. "Hartack-Longden in Last Place," *Reading, Pennsylvania, Eagle*, July 1, 1969.
7. Neil Milbert, telephone interview with author, April 28, 2015.
8. Mark Kriegel, *Namath: A Biography* (New York: Penguin Books, 2005), 325, 327.
9. "Giants Playing Down Hicks-Gregory Brawl," *New York Times*, December 8, 1977.
10. Eddie Sapir, telephone interview with author, June 8, 2015.
11. *Champions: The Lives, Times, and Past Performances of America's Greatest Thoroughbreds* (New York: Daily Racing Form Press, 2005), 222–23.
12. Eddie Sapir.
13. "Collateral Damage of Hurricane Katrina," *Bangor, Maine, Daily News*, September 4, 2007.
14. Gary Condra, telephone interview with author, June 23, 2015.
15. Bill Shoemaker and Barney Nagler, *Shoemaker: America's Greatest Jockey* (New York: Doubleday, 1988), 239.
16. *Kentucky Derby Media Guide* (2011), 97.
17. "Jim French Tests No. 11 Jinx Today," *Fredericksburg, Virginia, Free Lance-Star*, May 5, 1971.
18. *Maryland Jockey Club Media Guide* (2012), P-58.
19. *New York Racing Association Media Guide* (2013), B65.
20. *Kentucky Derby Media Guide* (2011), 97; *Maryland Jockey Club Guide* (2012), P-56; *New York Racing Association Media Guide* (2013), B35.
21. Shoemaker and Nagler, *Shoemaker*, 184.
22. Ibid., 239.
23. "19th Hole: Foul Claim," *Sports Illustrated*, May 1, 1967.

Chapter 23

1. *Kentucky Derby Media Guide* (2011), 97.
2. "The Cannon Takes Aim," *Sports Illustrated*, May 14, 1974.
3. Tommy Trotter, telephone interview with author, September 1, 2015.
4. "Double-Barreled Derby Threat," *Sports Illustrated*, May 7, 1974.
5. *Kentucky Derby Media Guide* (2011), 5–6.
6. "100th—Kentucky Derby—100th," *Daily Racing Form*, May 4, 1974.
7. "Elder Hartack Killed by Shots," *Milwaukee Journal*, June 22, 1963.
8. "Cannonade Takes Giant Derby Step," *New York Times*, May 4, 1974.
9. "Horse Becomes Royalty on Kentucky Derby Day," *New York Times*, May 4, 1974.
10. "The Cannon Takes Aim."
11. "Sir Tristram—A Four-Leg Goldmine," *The Age* (Melbourne, Australia), February 1, 1988.
12. "Little Current Runs Away with Preakness," *Spartansburg, South Carolina, Herald-Journal*, May 19, 1974.
13. Gary Condra, telephone interview with author, July 19, 2015.
14. *Thoroughbred Times Racing Almanac 2009* (Lexington, KY: Thoroughbred Times Books, 2008), 633.
15. "Hartack Heading for Hong Kong," *Miami News*, September 26, 1974.
16. *Thoroughbred Times Racing Almanac 2009*, 951.
17. Gary Condra.
18. "Heavy Hartack Light in Hong Kong," *Chicago Tribune*, February 23, 1975.
19. "Gateway to Fortune," *The Blood-Horse*, January 6, 1996.
20. "Hartack: Happier in a Hong Kong Saddle," *Washington Post*, February 12, 1977.
21. "Hartack Owes a Million in Back Taxes," *St. Petersburg, Florida, Evening Independent*, June 21, 1978.
22. "List of Kentucky Derby Broadcasters," Wikipedia.org, accessed September 19, 2015; "List of Preakness Broadcasters," Wikipedia.org, accessed September 19, 2015; "List of Belmont Stakes Broadcasters," Wikipedia.org, accessed September 19, 2015.
23. Gary Condra.
24. "Gourmets and Gourmands," *Miami News*, March 21, 1959.
25. "Hartack Heading for Hong Kong."
26. *Daily Racing Form Monthly Chart Book* (Chicago: Triangle, 1974); Keeneland Association, email, July 20, 2015.
27. John Nerud, telephone interview with author, February 1, 2014.
28. *Daily Racing Form Monthly Chart Book.*
29. Gary Condra.
30. Worldweatheronline.com, accessed July 9, 2015.
31. Gary Condra.
32. Bill Burnett, email, July 26, 2015.
33. Hong Kong Jockey Club, email, July 13, 2015.
34. "Bill in Clover," *Sydney Morning Herald*, June 16, 1978.
35. "Lord MacLehose, 82, Governor of Hong Kong and Chinese Scholar," *New York Times*, June 12, 2000.
36. "Brosnan Bitter Over Scandal," *Singapore New Straits Times*, May 28, 1988; "Jockey Club Fraudsters Guilty," *Hong Kong Standard*, January 4, 2013.
37. "Remembering the Silver Fox," Fasttrack.hk, June 22, 2014.
38. "Gateway to Fortune."
39. Gary Stevens, *The Perfect Ride* (New York: Citadel Press Books, 2002), 119–22.
40. "Hartack Revisited," *Horseman's Journal*, June 1979.
41. "Hartack: Happier in a Hong Kong Saddle."
42. "Bill Hartack Was a Fierce Competitor," *The Telegraph* (Great Britain), December 6, 2007.
43. "Hartack: Happier in a Hong Kong Saddle."
44. "A Hero Who Has Gone On to Happy Valley," *Sports Illustrated*, May 23, 1977.
45. "Local Family, Friends Had Influence on Jockey," *Ocala, Florida, Star-Banner*, May 15, 2004.
46. "From Rock Bottom, Jockey's Unlikely Ride to Top," *New York Times*, May 23, 2004.

47. "Great and Good Celebrate Lewis' 70th," *The Telegraph* (Great Britain), December 22, 2005.
48. Hong Kong Jockey Club.
49. "Bill Hartack Was a Fierce Competitor."
50. Gary Moore, email, July 3, 2015.
51. Hong Kong Jockey Club; Garymooreracing.com, accessed July 11, 2015.
52. "Remembering the Silver Fox."
53. Garymooreracing.com.
54. Hong Kong Jockey Club.
55. *Thoroughbred Times Racing Almanac 2009*, 951.
56. "Remembering the Silver Fox."
57. "Heavy Hartack Light in Hong Kong."
58. "Brosnan Bitter Over Scandal."
59. "Heavy Hartack Light in Hong Kong."
60. "Hartack Revisited."
61. Bill Burnett.
62. Peter Supple, telephone interview with author, August 15, 2015.
63. Hong Kong Jockey Club.
64. Peter Supple.
65. Hong Kong Jockey Club.
66. "A Hero Who Has Gone On to Happy Valley."
67. Hong Kong Jockey Club.
68. "Jockey Club Fraudsters Guilty."
69. "Hartack Revisited."
70. "Bill Hartack Was a Fierce Competitor."
71. Bill Burnett.
72. Hong Kong Jockey Club.
73. Peter Supple.
74. Bill Burnett.

Chapter 24

1. Bill Christine, "Shelhamer Left a Legacy of Talent and Tales," *Los Angeles Times*, November 13, 1986.
2. *Breeders' Cup Statistics* (2005), 170.
3. Bill Dwyre, "Marje Everett Dies at 90," *Los Angeles Times*, March 24, 2012.
4. "*Back in the Saddle Again* lyrics," metrolyrics.com, accessed August 25, 2015.
5. Bill Christine, "A 20-Year-Old Blur," horseraceinsider.com, October 19, 2010.
6. "Hartack Hired at Tampa Bay Downs," *St. Petersburg, Florida, Evening Independent*, November 12, 1985.
7. "Carry Back Carries Cleveland on Thrilling Run at Triple Crown," *Cleveland Plain Dealer*, June 11, 2011.
8. Bill Christine, "A Filly Mugging Recalled: Lukas' Codex Was the Culprit in 1980," *Los Angeles Times*, May 21, 1988.
9. "Ex-Jockey Bill Hartack Makes Return as Racing Official," *Kingman, Arizona, Daily Herald*, September 9, 1981.
10. Walter Blum, telephone interview with author, July 25, 2014.
11. Steve Nagler, email, July 21, 2015.
12. "ABC-TV Set for Eighth Derby Telecast," *Ocala, Florida, Star-Banner*, April 29, 1982.
13. "ABC Telecast of Wood Memorial a Disgrace," *Ocala, Florida, Star-Banner*, April 20, 1982.
14. Dick Young, "Young Ideas," *New York Daily News*, May 13, 1983.
15. Steve Nagler.
16. Cliff Guilliams, "Bill Hartack Excelled at Winning Races, Not Friends," *Evansville, Indiana, Courier & Press*, December 2, 2007.
17. "TV Sports: On Target with Ferdinand," *New York Times*, May 5, 1986.
18. "Explosion: 1951 Scandals Threaten College Hoops," ESPN.com, November 19, 2003.
19. "Chet Forte Dies of Heart Attack," *Prescott, Arizona, Daily Courier*, May 19, 1996.
20. William Leggett, "She Can Handle This Field," *Sports Illustrated*, June 7, 1976.
21. Steve Nagler.
22. "Bill Hartack Comes Aboard as Steward at Hawthorne," *Chicago Tribune*, September 18, 1987.
23. Paul Moran, "The Saratoga Season," ESPN.com, September 6, 2000.
24. Tommy Trotter, telephone interview with author, October 1, 2013.
25. Larry Munster, email, July 10, 2015.
26. *Thoroughbred Times Racing Almanac 2009* (Lexington, KY: Thoroughbred Times Books, 2008), 654.
27. Ibid., 73.
28. "Fire Rakes New Orleans Fair Grounds," *Florence, Alabama, TimesDaily*, December 18, 1993.
29. *Thoroughbred Times Racing Almanac 2009*, 654.
30. Ibid., 73.
31. Gary Palmisano, email, August 20, 2015.
32. Larry Munster.
33. Eddie Sapir, telephone interview with author, August 17, 2015.
34. Randy Moss, "The Bill Hartack You Didn't Know," NTRA.com, November 28, 2007.
35. Gary Palmisano.
36. Moss, "The Bill Hartack You Didn't Know."
37. Eddie Sapir.
38. Randy Moss, "The Bill Hartack You Didn't Know."
39. Jay Searcy, "An Odd Couple at Garden State Park: Jimmie Ward Is a Bug Rider. Bill Hartack Is a Legend. Together, They Win," *Philadelphia Inquirer*, May 1, 1995.
40. Keith Dickey, telephone interview with author, August 24, 2015.
41. Bill Finley, ESPN.com, January 5, 1996.
42. Keith Dickey.
43. Zoe Cadman, speech at Arcadia, California, April 17, 2013.
44. Jane Dempsey, email, August 4, 2015.
45. "Five-Derby Winner Bill Hartack Dies," *Daily Racing Form*, November 27, 2007.

Chapter 25

1. Gary Palmisano, telephone interview with author, June 4, 2015.
2. Randy Moss, "The Bill Hartack You Didn't Know," NTRA.com, November 28, 2007.
3. Gary Palmisano.
4. Roseann Williams, telephone interview with author, March 15, 2015.
5. Larry Munster, email, July 10, 2015.
6. *National Geographic Atlas of the World*, Fourth Edition (Washington, DC: National Geographic Society, 1975), 34–35.

7. "Freer Rattlesnake Roundup Is in Existence Since 1965," *Alice Echo News*, April 17, 2014.
8. Jim Beale, telephone interview with author, May 25, 2015.
9. "Five-Derby Winner Bill Hartack Dies," *Daily Racing Form*, November 27, 2007.
10. Bill Hartack Charitable Foundation, dinner journal, spring 2013.
11. Eddie Sapir, telephone interview with author, June 18, 2015.
12. "Longden's Top All-Time," *The Blood-Horse*, August 21, 1965.
13. "Five-Derby Winner Bill Hartack Dies."
14. "Unique Talent," *Thoroughbred Times*, December 8, 2007.
15. Gary Condra, telephone interview with author, August 20, 2014.
16. Paul Hornung, telephone interview with author, August 21, 2015.
17. "The Golden Boy," *Los Angeles Times*, February 24, 1986.
18. Paul Hornung.
19. Gary Condra.
20. Evelyn "Dolly" Hartack Ferguson, telephone interview with author, April 2, 2013.
21. Maxine Hartack Shadrach, telephone interview with author, September 12, 2014.
22. Evelyn "Dolly" Hartack Ferguson.
23. "Hall of Fame Jockey Bill Hartack Found His Final Resting Place in a Small Missouri Town," *Riverfront Times*, July 29, 2015.
24. Jim Beale.
25. Gary Condra.
26. Jay Ferguson, telephone interview with author, August 24, 2015.
27. Legacy.com, September 10, 2008.
28. Georgianna Reid, telephone interview with author, September 3, 2015.
29. Gary Condra.
30. *The American Racing Manual* (New York: Daily Racing Form Press, 2007), 859.
31. "Why Run for the Roses? Kentucky Derby Moniker History," Examiner.com, accessed September 6, 2014.
32. Gary Condra.

Bibliography

About.com. "Horse Racing, Fred W. Hooper," August 4, 2000; "Kelso—'King Kelly,'" accessed September 12, 2015.

The Age (Melbourne, Australia). "Sir Tristram—A Four-Leg Goldmine," February 1, 1988.

Alice Echo News. "Freer Rattlesnake Roundup Is in Existence Since 1965," April 17, 2014.

The American Racing Manual. New York: Triangle, 1952–1975.

The American Racing Manual. New York: Daily Racing Form Press, 2007.

The American Racing Manual. New York: Daily Racing Form Press, 2010.

The American Racing Manual. New York: Daily Racing Form Press, 2011.

Answers.com. "Why Didn't Truman Run for Re-election in 1952?" accessed September 3, 2015.

Arlington Park Media Guide. 2009.

Bailey, Jerry. Belmont Stakes telecast, NBC-TV, June 6, 2015.

Baltimore News American. "Hartack Moody But Well Paid," March 1, 1958.

Baltimore News-Post. "The Strange Case of Willie (Oops, Bill) Hartack," May 21, 1960.

Baltimore Sun. "The Morning After," November 25, 1963; "Ride Clear to Hartack," May 17, 1964.

Bangor, Maine, Daily News. "Collateral Damage of Hurricane Katrina," September 4, 2007.

Beaver County, Pennsylvania, Times. "Days Growing Shorter for Jockey Hartack," August 22, 1970.

Beaver Valley, Pennsylvania, Times. "Jockeys Strike at Wheeling," May 26, 1953.

Beckwith, B.K. *The Longden Legend*. Cranbury, NJ: A.S. Barnes, 1973.

Bill Hartack Charity Foundation. Dinner journal, Spring 2013.

The Blood-Horse. "News of the Week," April 13, 1963; "Uncompromising Idealist," May 30, 1964; "Longden's Top All-Time," August 21, 1965; "The Princes and the Rose," April 20, 1985; "Gateway to Fortune," January 6, 1996; "Remember Me," September 9, 2001; "That's Mr. Preakness," May 20, 2003; "Remembering Hartack," December 8, 2007; "The Feud," May 1, 2010.

Bolus, Jim. *Kentucky Derby Stories*. New Orleans: Pelican, 1993.

_____. *Derby Fever*. New Orleans: Pelican, 1995.

Bouyea, Brien. Email to author, April 22, 2015.

Bragg, Melvyn. *The Soldier's Return*. London: Hodder & Stoughton, 1999.

brainyquote.com. "Samuel Goldwyn Quotes," accessed September 11, 2015.

Breeders' Cup Statistics. 2005.

Burnett, Bill. Email to author, July 26, 2015.

Cadman, Zoe. Speech at Arcadia, California, April 17, 2013.

Cape Girardeau, Missouri. "Damascus Training in Secret; Among Favorites for Preakness," May 16, 1967.

Champions: The Lives, Times, and Past Performances of America's Greatest Thoroughbreds. New York: Daily Racing Form Press, 2005.

Chicago Tribune. "Pet Bully 1st in Garden State Opening Event," May 2, 1954; "Bold Ruler Wins Flamingo," March 3, 1957; "Tough—That's Hartack!" July 31, 1960; "Top Prize at Arlington to Pay $134,925," September 14, 1964; "Tower Ticker," May 2, 1965; "Heavy Hartack Light in Hong Kong," February 23, 1975; "Bill Hartack Comes Aboard as Steward at Hawthorne," September 18, 1987.

Chong, Kevin. *Northern Dancer: The Legendary Horse That Inspired a Nation*. Toronto: Viking Canada, 2014.

Christine, Bill. "A Filly Mugging Recalled: Lukas' Codex Was the Culprit in 1980." *Los Angeles Times*, May 21, 1988.

_____. "Shelhamer Left a Legacy of Talent and Tales." *Los Angeles Times*, November 13, 1986.

_____. "A 20-Year-Old Blur." horseraceinsider.com, October 19, 2010.

Cleveland Plain Dealer. "Carry Back Carries Cleveland on Thrilling Run at Triple Crown," June 11, 2011.

Daily Racing Form. "82nd—Kentucky Derby—82nd," May 5, 1956; "Hartack Tells How Iron Liege Scored in 83rd Kentucky Derby," May 7, 1957; "Jockey Agents Are Group of Nice Guys," September 3, 1957; "84th Kentucky Derby," May 3, 1958; "Tim Tam Only One of Big Three to Run His Race," May 4, 1958; "88th—Kentucky Derby—88th," May 5, 1962; "90th—Kentucky Derby 90th," May 2, 1964; "91st—Kentucky Derby—91st," May 1, 1965; "93rd—Kentucky Derby—93rd," May 6, 1967; "95th—Kentucky Derby—95th," May 3, 1969; "96th—Kentucky Derby—96th," May 2, 1970; "Hartack Rides 4,000th Winner," December 15, 1970; "100th—Kentucky

Derby—100th," May 4, 1974; "Hirsch Recalls '57," April 27, 1999; "Hartack Remembers Longden," February 19, 2003; "Five-Derby Winner Bill Hartack Dies," November 27, 2007; "Penny Chenery's Life, Unscripted," September 30, 2010; "Kelso," December 21, 2011; "Spotlight Stays on Pincay Family," January 9, 2014; "Hovdey: Del Mar Hoping 1967 Was Just a Bad Trip," November 5, 2014.

Daily Racing Form Chart Book. New York: Triangle, 1952.

Daily Racing Form Chart Book. New York: Triangle, 1953.

Daily Racing Form Chart Book. New York: Triangle, 1954.

Daily Racing Form Chart Book. Chicago: Triangle, 1970.

Daily Racing Form Monthly Chart Book. Chicago: Triangle, 1974.

Danbury, Connecticut, Sunday Herald. "Gen. Duke Triumphs in Florida Derby," March 31, 1957.

Daytona Beach, Florida, Morning Journal. "Hartack Rides Hard in Every Race," October 5, 1958; "Injury Costs Sir Gaylord; Ridan Favored," May 5, 1962.

Del Mar Media Guide. 2015.

Del Mar Owners, Trainers, Jockeys Source Book. 2015.

Dempsey, Jane. Email to author, August 4, 2015.

Detroit News. "Press Box," January 29, 1959.

Dwyre, Bill. "Marje Everett Dies at 90." *Los Angeles Times,* March 24, 2012.

Equibase.com, accessed September 18, 2015.

ESPN.com. "Explosion: 1951 Scandals Threaten College Hoops," November 19, 2003.

Eugene, Oregon, Register-Guard. "Disqualification Rule Costs Alhambra Win," July 21, 1961; "No Gold in Bronze," June 21, 1978.

Examiner.com. "Why Run for the Roses? Kentucky Derby Moniker History," accessed September 6, 2014.

Fasttrack.hk. "Remembering the Silver Fox," June 22, 2014.

Feldman, Dave, with Frank Sugano. *Woulda, Coulda, Shoulda.* Chicago: Bonus Books, 1989.

Finley, Bill. ESPN.com, January 5, 1996.

Florida Derby Souvenir Magazine. "Bill Hartack," 1988.

Fleming, Mary. *A History of the Thoroughbred in California.* Arcadia: California Thoroughbred Breeders Association, 1983.

Florence, Alabama, TimesDaily. "Fire Rakes New Orleans Fair Grounds," December 18, 1993.

Fort Lauderdale, Florida, Sun-Sentinel. "Broward Lawyer Indicted, Faces Racketeering and Drug Charges," April 18, 1987.

Fredericksburg, Virginia, Free Lance-Star. "Jim French Tests No. 11 Jinx Today," May 5, 1971.

Gadsden, Alabama, Times. "Gen. Duke Scratched in Derby," May 1, 1957.

gallopoutblogspot.com. "Tim Tam," January 28, 2011.

Gaming Today. "By Any Name But Willie, Bill Hartack Was a Winner," December 4, 2007.

Garymooreracing.com, accessed July 11, 2015.

Georgeff, Phil. *And They're Off! My Years as the Voice of Thoroughbred Racing.* Lanham, MD: Taylor Trade, 2002.

Gettysburg, Pennsylvania, Times. "Mrs. Graham Is Provoked by Hartack," October 23, 1957.

Guilliams, Cliff. "Bill Hartack Excelled at Winning Races, Not Friends." *Evansville, Indiana, Courier & Press,* December 2, 2007.

Hirsch, Joe. "The Front Runner." *Sports Illustrated,* September 15, 1956.

Hollywood Casino at Charles Town Races Media Guide. 2014.

Hong Kong Jockey Club. Email to author, July 13, 2015.

Hong Kong Standard. "Jockey Club Fraudsters Guilty," January 4, 2013.

Horsemen's Journal. "Hartack Revisited," June 1979.

Hunter, Avalyn. *The Kingmaker: How Northern Dancer Founded a Racing Dynasty.* Lexington, KY: Eclipse Press, 2008.

The Independent. "Obituaries: Juan Manuel Fangio," July 18, 1995.

InterMountain.com. "The 1950 Snowstorm Was in a Class by Itself," February 7, 2009.

Johnstown, Pennsylvania, Tribune. "Blacklick Township Senior Class of 1950" (photograph), June 1950.

Johnstown Discovery Network (website). "History of Coal in Cambrian County," accessed August 18, 2015.

Keeneland Association. Email to author, July 20, 2015.

Kelley, Robert F. *Racing in America, 1937–59.* New York: Jockey Club, 1960.

Kentuckyderby.com. "My Old Kentucky Home," accessed March 20, 2015.

Kentucky Derby Media Guides. 1981, 2011, 2012.

Kentucky Derby Souvenir Magazine. "Determine," 1991.

Kingman, Arizona, Daily Herald. "Ex-Jockey Bill Hartack Makes Return as Racing Official," September 9, 1981.

Kriegel, Mark. *Namath: A Biography.* New York: Penguin Books, 2005.

Lakeland, Florida, Ledger. "His Strong Desire to Win…" March 24, 1963.

Legacy.com, accessed September 10, 2008.

Leggett, William. "She Can Handle This Field." *Sports Illustrated,* June 7, 1976.

Lewin, Sam "The Genius," and Frederick C. Klein. *The Education of a Horseplayer.* New York: Hawthorn Books, 1969.

Life. "He Wants to Stay Put," October 5, 1953.

Linn, Ed. "What Makes Willie Hartack Burn?" *Sport,* June 1959.

Los Angeles Herald-Examiner. "Flower Child," May 4, 1969; "The Prince Almost Too Perfect," May 4, 1969.

Los Angeles Times. "Hartack Stays Mad at World," April 21, 1965; "Hard Old Hartack," July 7, 1968; "Hartack's Race Protest Denied," June 24, 1970; "Triple Frown," May 9, 1985; "The Golden Boy," February 24, 1986; "Kentucky Derby Notes," May 1, 1986; "French Horses Are Cutting It Close," November 9, 1987; "The 1968 Kentucky Derby: The Victory That Wasn't," May 1, 1988; "Sad Anniversary: 20 Years

After Making History, Jockey Diane Crump Is Injured in Fall," March 1, 1989; "From Ace Jockey to Fred's 'Baby,'" May 17, 1997; "Eddie Arcaro, 'The Master,' Is Dead at 81," November 15, 1997; "From Claim to Fame," June 2, 1999; "Overlooked Horse Has Nice Timing," June 3, 1999; "It's No Laughing Matter to Funny Cide's Trainer," May 19, 2003; "Anchor and Sportscaster Was Also an Actor," October 1, 2008.

Louisville Courier-Journal. "Hartack Obliges His Fans, But Keeps Press Waiting," May 3, 1964.

Mann, Jack. "Jack Mann." *Washington Star*, October 28, 1968.

_____. "Jack Mann." *Washington Star*, May 1, 1969.

Maryland Jockey Club Media Guide. 2012.

McBride, Mac. Emails to author, May 26, 2015, and June 2, 2015.

Melton, Howard, Jr. Telephone message for author, June 9, 2015.

metrolyrics.com. "*Back in the Saddle Again* lyrics," accessed August 25, 2015.

Miami Herald. "Hartack Gets New Agent," March 30, 1960.

Miami News. "Barbizon Wins Rich Garden State Race," October 27, 1956; "Hartack's Agent Is a Bright Guy," March 31, 1957; "Tumult, Shouting in Flamingo," March 3, 1958; "Gourmets and Gourmands," March 21, 1959; "Will It Happen Again?" May 19, 1959; "Agent Resigns, Lashes Hartack," March 30, 1960; "Hartack's Losing His Riding Touch," May 9, 1960; "Turf Official Gives Hartack Clinical Eye," August 7, 1960; "Hartack Admitted Mistake," March 30, 1961; "Carry Back Outruns Crozier, Wins Muddy Florida Derby," April 2, 1961; "Odd Project Lures Hartack on Vacation," September 21, 1961; "Hartack Suspended," February 22, 1962; "Jolley Stews on Hartack's Ride of Ridan," February 22, 1962; "Ussery Makes Advance Plan for Big Stake," March 14, 1962; "Leroy Jolley Finds Derby Grind Rough," May 3, 1962; "Hartack Makes Unique Plea," May 4, 1962; "Unusual Plea Gave Baeza Derby Chance," May 6, 1963; "Elder Hartack Killed by Shots," June 22, 1963; "Big Pete's Record Still Unblemished," June 23, 1963; "Did The Scoundrel Win After All? Ask Writers," May 3, 1964; "Barbs Delight's Owners Take $10,000 Gamble," May 17, 1967; "The Glitter's Gone," May 23, 1968; "George Lewis Muddles 3-Year-Old Scene," January 22, 1970; "Hartack Heading for Hong Kong," September 26, 1974; "Backtracking with Agent Lenny Goodman," January 17, 1980; "Round-the-Clock Guards Ran Up Tuna Trial Cost," February 8, 1980.

Mid-Atlantic Thoroughbred. "Mountaineer Park on Speed Course with Slots," October 2002.

Milwaukee Journal. "Success Costs Hartack Cash," October 24, 1957; "Top Horse Race Sire, Bull Lea, Dead at 29," October 17, 1964.

Montreal Gazette. "Jockey Rides Seven Firsts at Woodbine," May 17, 1967; "Hartack Reprimanded After Abusing Fan," July 27, 1971.

Moran, Paul. "The Saratoga Season." ESPN.com, September 6, 2000.

Moss, Randy. "The Bill Hartack You Didn't Know." NTRA.com, November 28, 2007.

Munster, Larry. Email to author, July 10, 2015.

Nack, Bill. Email to author, September 17, 2015.

Nagler, Steve. Email to author, July 21, 2015.

National Geographic Atlas of the World. Fourth Edition. Washington, DC: National Geographic Society, 1975.

National Museum of Racing and Hall of Fame.

New York Daily News. "1960 Kentucky Derby Brought Mixture of Sadness and Joy," May 1, 2010.

New Yorker. "The Race Track: Down They Go," July 19, 1958; "A Cup Goes West," November 2, 1968.

New York Racing Association Media Guide. 2013.

New York Times. "Pet Bully Defeats Dutch Lane in Highweight Handicap," September 23, 1954; "Joe Jones Beats Pet Bully by 2 Lengths in Vosburgh Handicap," October 12, 1954; "Pet Bully Takes $24,050 Princeton," October 21, 1954; "Needles Outruns Fabius in Derby," May 6, 1956; "8–1 Shot Triumphs: Iron Liege Gains Nose Victory for Sixth Calumet Derby," May 5, 1957; "Silky Sullivan Runs 4th; Hartack Breaks Leg," April 27, 1958; "Erb Looms as Tim Tam's Rider in Kentucky Derby on Saturday," April 28, 1958; "Valenzuela Will Ride Tim Tam in Trial Today," April 29, 1958; "Texan Replaces Injured Hartack," May 1, 1958; "Hartack Returns After Injury, Finishes in Money in 2 Races," May 29, 1958; "Cavan Captures $114,600 Belmont; Tim Tam, 3–20, Lame After Finishing Second," June 8, 1958; "Hartack (Don't Call Me Willie) Enters Jockeys' Club," September 18, 1958; "Tomy Lee Beaten; Drops from 2d to 3d as 2–1 First Landing Wins Champagne," October 12, 1958; "Calumet Trio Elected Into Turf Hall of Fame," August 16, 1959; "On the Dawn Patrol," May 4, 1961; "A Day of Vindication," May 6, 1962; "Bill Hartack, as Seen by Hartack," May 5, 1964; "Bold Lad, Hartack Up, Takes Derby Trial by 4 Lengths," April 28, 1965; "Dr. Isby Is the Runner-Up in Stepping Stone Purse," April 30, 1967; "Barbs Delight: A Chaser for Dr. Fager," September 2, 1967; "Quicken Tree, Coast Invader, Wins Manhattan," August 10, 1968; "U.S. Charges Hartack Owes $805,250 on Tax Lien on House," October 13, 1968; "The Prince and the Peasant," May 4, 1969; "Persecution Complexes," May 6, 1969; "Majestic Prince Gallops and Walks at Belmont," May 23, 1969; "Arts and Letters and Majestic Prince Show High Speed in Workouts," May 28, 1969; "Arts and Letters Easily Beats Majestic Prince," June 8, 1969; "Was It Won or Lost?" June 8, 1969; "Jockey in a Million," June 9, 1969; "Saturday Night," June 9, 1969; "Saul Silberman, 75, Race Track Owner," February 20, 1971; "Cannonade Takes Giant Derby Step," May 4, 1974; "Horse Becomes Royalty on Kentucky Derby Day," May 4, 1974; "Giants Playing Down Hicks-Gregory Brawl," December 8, 1977; "TV Sports: On Target with Ferdinand," May 5, 1986; "Raymond Guest, 84, Ambassador, Polo Player and Breeder of Horses," January 1, 1992; "Lenny Goodman, Jockeys' Agent, 76," September

26, 1996; "Lord MacLehose, 82, Governor of Hong Kong and Chinese Scholar," June 12, 2000; "From Rock Bottom, Jockey's Unlikely Ride to Top," May 23, 2004; "Tim Tam, 50 Years Later," April 25, 2008; "A Pioneer Woman Jockey Recalls Her Tough Ride to Finish Line," March 21, 2009; "The Doc's Legacy at the Derby," April 30, 2009.

Nichols, Joseph C. "Majestic Prince Scores Easily in Non-Betting Louisville Dash." *New York Times*, April 27, 1969.

NYRA.com. "Hall of Fame Trainer T.J. Kelly Dies at 93," April 19, 2013.

Ocala, Florida, Star-Banner. "Between You 'n' Me," February 1, 1960; "Lucky Debonair Upsets Jacinto," March 7, 1965; "Hartack Enters Hialeah Race," January 31, 1967; "ABC Telecast of Wood Memorial a Disgrace," April 20, 1982; "ABC-TV Set for Eighth Derby Telecast," April 29, 1982; "Local Family, Friends Had Influence on Jockey," May 15, 2004.

Palm Beach Post. "Fabius Wins Derby Trial," May 2, 1956; "Federal Hill Wins Derby Trial," May 1, 1957; "Cavan Wins, Turns Lame," June 29, 1958; "'We Had It, Didn't We?'" May 6, 1962.

Palm Beach Times. "Arcaro to Be Highest-Paid Star in World of Sports," October 10, 1952.

Palmisano, Gary. Email to author, August 20, 2015.

Pedigreequery.com, accessed September 8, 2015.

Perrone, Vinnie. "Recalling Clem Florio's Matchless Gift for Life." *The Maryland Horse*, July 2008.

Philadelphia Inquirer. "Maybe Venetian Way Was On the Wagon?" May 23, 1960.

Pinterest.com. "Northern Dancer," accessed September 14, 2015.

Pittsburgh Post-Gazette. "Wheeling Island Fire Is Raging," February 3, 1936; "Agent Lang Walks Out on Jockey Bill Hartack," March 31, 1960; "Slayer Gets 1 to 5 Years," October 15, 1963; "The Waterford Wizard," April 16, 1973; "Troubled Waters Deep in Life of Torquato Sr.," July 27, 1984; "Art Rooney Sr. Enjoys Kentucky Derby from Up Close," May 9, 1988.

Pittsburgh Press. "Today's Racing at Wheeling Off," June 4, 1941; "By George, He'll Run," May 1, 1970; "Hartack's Night a Nightmare," August 22, 1970.

Post Time USA. "San Juan Capistrano Day Afforded Longden Fond Memories," March 2003.

Prescott, Arizona, Daily Courier. "Chet Forte Dies of Heart Attack," May 19, 1996.

ProPublica.com. "The Long History of Horse Racing's Addiction to Doping," May 2, 2014.

Reading, Pennsylvania, Eagle. "Field of 13 Seen for Coast Derby," April 20, 1967; "Favorite First," April 23, 1967; "Hartack-Longden in Last Place," July 1, 1969.

Riverfront Times. "Hall of Fame Jockey Bill Hartack Found His Final Resting Place in a Small Missouri Town," July 29, 2015.

Rome, Georgia, News-Tribune. "Hartack Joins Elite, Gets 4,000th Win," December 15, 1970.

Rudy, William H. *Racing in America, 1960–1979*. New York: Stinehour Press, 1980.

St. Petersburg, Florida, Evening Independent. "Hard Riding Jockey Wins Many Races," December 16, 1960; "Hartack Owes a Million in Back Taxes," June 21, 1978; "Hartack Hired at Tampa Bay Downs," November 12, 1985.

St. Petersburg, Florida, Times. "Riders Revolt, Organize New Association," July 23, 1966; "Sailstone Withdrawn; George Lewis Looks for Derby Position," April 27, 1970.

Santa Anita Park Media Guide. 2011–2012.

Sarasota, Florida, Herald-Tribune. "Imbros Wins Rich California Stakes; Ties World Mark," June 13, 1954; "Pet Bully Wins Rich Handicap in Record Time," September 7, 1954; "Trainer Vic Sovinski Fires Jockey Hartack," May 21, 1960.

Saturday Evening Post. "New Golden Boy," May 3, 1958.

Schenck, Cathy. Keeneland Association Library, Lexington, Kentucky. Emails to author, March 3, 2015, and May 3, 2015; letter to author, February 26, 2013.

Searcy, Jay. "An Odd Couple at Garden State Park: Jimmie Ward Is a Bug Rider. Bill Hartack Is a Legend. Together, They Win." *Philadelphia Inquirer*, May 1, 1995.

Shoemaker, Bill, and Barney Nagler. *Shoemaker: America's Greatest Jockey*. New York: Doubleday, 1988.

Shoemaker, Willie, and Dan Smith. *The Shoe*. Chicago/New York/San Francisco: Rand McNally, 1976.

Singapore New Straits Times. "Brosnan Bitter Over Scandal," May 28, 1988.

Smith, Dan. Emails to author, May 26–27, 2015.

Smith, Red. "Red Smith's Views of Sports" (syndicated column), May 5, 1957.

Sowers, Richard. *The Kentucky Derby, Preakness and Belmont Stakes: A Comprehensive History*. Jefferson, NC: McFarland, 2014.

Spartansburg, South Carolina, Herald-Journal. "Little Current Runs Away with Preakness," May 19, 1974.

Spirit of Jefferson Farmers Advocate. "Mrs. Brant Will Be Charged with Murder of William Hartack Sr.," June 27, 1963.

Spokane, Washington, Spokesman-Review. "Bill Hartack Sets New Mark as Nadir Wins Richest Race," October 27, 1957.

Sports Illustrated. "Hero at Pimlico," May 28, 1956; "In Chicago: Greek Game Wins Futurity on Foul," September 10, 1956; "With 19 2-Year-Olds Running for $319,210, the Garden State Was Barbizon's Day," November 5, 1956; "Double Trouble," April 8, 1957; "Picking the Derby," May 6, 1957; "The Baby Comes Into His Own," May 13, 1957; "How You, Willie?" May 13, 1957; "$427,000 in Two Minutes," July 22, 1957; "Say Hello to Jimmy Jones," March 17, 1958; "Conversation Piece: Lady Liz of Llangollen," June 9, 1958; "Triumph of Class Over Mud," November 3, 1958; "Big Happy Week for Jim Norris," April 6, 1959; "Two for the Big Money," April 13, 1959; "Heartache and Bally Ache," April 11, 1960; "Venetian Shows the Way," May 16, 1960; "Whatever Happened to Bill Hartack?" June 24, 1963; "The Tyranny of the Little Men," April 27, 1964; "The Dancer Dazzles Old Kentucky," May 11, 1964; "Three for the Triple Crown," May 25, 1964; "One More to Make It Nine," June 1, 1964; "Taken for a Virginia Reel," June 15, 1964; "Roses for the Shoe," May 10, 1965; "A Hard Ride All the Way," March 27, 1967; "My Feuds with Officials and the Press," April 3, 1967; "The Days of the Roses," April 10, 1967; "19th Hole: Foul Claim," May 1, 1967; "Clarion Call: $62.20!" May 15, 1967; "It May Be a Two-Horse Derby," April 7, 1969; "A Royal Neck for Bill's Fifth," May 12, 1969; "The Prince Ducks the Big One," May 26, 1969; "The Man Takes Charge of His Horse," June 2, 1969; "Revenge Was Sweet," June 16, 1969; "Man in the Middle Jewel," May 21, 1973; "Double-Barreled Derby Threat," May 7, 1974; "The Cannon Takes Aim," May 14, 1974; "A Hero Who Has Gone On to Happy Valley," May 23, 1977; "The Days of the Roses," April 20, 1985.

Stevens, Gary. *The Perfect Ride*. New York: Citadel Press Books, 2002.

Sydney Morning Herald. "Bill in Clover," June 16, 1978.

The Telegraph (Great Britain). "Great and Good Celebrate Lewis' 70th," December 22, 2005; "Bill Hartack Was a Fierce Competitor," December 6, 2007.

thehandicappersedge.com. "Sherman Compares California Chrome with Hall of Famer Swaps," accessed September 14, 2015.

Thoroughbred and Harness Racing Action. "The 100 Greatest Horses of the 20th Century," December 22, 1987–January 4, 1988.

Thoroughbred Champions: Top 100 Race Horses of the 20th Century. Lexington, KY: Blood-Horse Publications, 2000.

Thoroughbred Racing Associations Directory & Record Book. 2015.

Thoroughbred Record. "The Remarkable Mr. Hartack," April 15, 1961; "The Belmont," June 10, 1969; "He Comes Up Roses," May 2, 1970; "Post Parade," December 26, 1970.

Thoroughbred Times. "Hartack in Chicago," July 14, 1962; "All But Forgotten—By a Nose," July 13, 2002; "Racing Legend Bill Shoemaker Dies," October 18, 2003; "Unique Talent," December 8, 2007.

Thoroughbred Times Racing Almanac 2009. Lexington, KY: Thoroughbred Times Books, 2008.

Time. "Man on a Horse," May 17, 1948; "Bully & the Beasts," February 10, 1958; "Horse Racing: Looking for a Triple," February 25, 1966; "Women: Hold Fast to Life & Youth," October 28, 1966.

Toby, Milton C. *Dancer's Image: The Forgotten Story of the 1968 Kentucky Derby*. Charleston, SC: History Press, 2011.

Toledo Blade. "Bill Hartack Derby Slight Shocks Vet," May 5, 1961; "Strike Halts Opening at Santa Anita," December 27, 1969.

Toronto Star. "Cauthen's Agent Sets High Goals," May 2, 1977; "Dance Smartly One in a Line of Northern Dancer's Legacies," November 1, 1992; "Hartack Still Rides Hard," July 20, 2007.

True. "Racing's Angriest Man," April 1960.

Turf & Sport Digest. "The Drugstore Derby," June 1960.

Victoria, British Columbia, Advocate. "Hartack Target of Second Guessing," June 9, 1969.

Walker, Bruce. Emails to author, November 30, 2012, and December 1, 2012.

Washington, Pennsylvania, Observer-Reporter. "Hartack Returns to Waterford Park," August 19, 1970.

Washington Post. "Room to Run," May 19, 1967; "Hartack: Happier in a Hong Kong Saddle," February 12, 1977.

Washington Star. "Big Stables Don't Look for Hartack Anymore," May 19, 1963.

Wikihorseworld.com. "Tomy Lee," accessed September 10, 2015.

Wikipedia.org. "List of Belmont Stakes Broadcasters"; "List of Kentucky Derby Broadcasters"; "List of Preakness Broadcasters," accessed September 19, 2015.

Wilmington, Delaware, Sunday Morning Star. "Chick Lang, Star Jockey, Is Dead," June 15, 1947.

Worldweatheronline.com, accessed July 9, 2015.

Young, Dick. "Young Ideas." *New York Daily News*, May 13, 1983.

YouTube. "Majestic Prince—1969 Preakness," accessed January 20, 2013; "Majestic Prince—1969 Kentucky Derby (In Color)," accessed March 20, 2015; "What's My Line?, May 10, 1964," accessed May 6, 2015.

Index

www.ingramcontent.com/pod-product-compliance
Ingram Content Group UK Ltd.
Pitfield, Milton Keynes, MK11 3LW, UK
UKHW060611180726
13836UKWH00012B/2508